Organization–Representation

Organization–Representation

Work and Organization in Popular Culture

edited by

John Hassard and Ruth Holliday

SAGE Publications
London • Thousand Oaks • New Delhi

First published 1998

SAGE Publications Ltd
6 Bonhill Street
London EC2A 4PU

SAGE Publications Inc.
2455 Teller Road
Thousand Oaks, California 91320

SAGE Publications India Pvt Ltd
32, M-Block Market
Greater Kailash – I
New Delhi 110 048

British Library Cataloguing in Publication data

A catalogue record for this book is available
from the British Library

ISBN 0 7619 5391 4
ISBN 0 7619 5392 2 (pbk)

Library of Congress catalog card number 97–069195

Typeset by Mayhew Typesetting, Rhayader, Powys
Printed in Great Britain by The Cromwell Press Ltd,
Trowbridge, Wiltshire

Contents

Illustrations

Contributors

Ian Aitken is senior lecturer in film and media at the University of the West of England. He is also course leader of the university's MA in film studies and European cinema. His publications include *Film and Reform* (1990, 1992) and *The British Documentary Film Movement Reader* (1978), along with a number of articles on British and European cinema and the documentary film movement. He is currently researching British cinema in the inter-war period and writing a book on realism and film theory.

Joanna Brewis is a senior lecturer in organizational behaviour at the University of Portsmouth Business School. She has a BSc (Management Science) and a PhD (Management), both from UMIST. Her PhD thesis used Foucault to explore the implications of the ways in which members of organizations understand the classic modernist dichotomy between sex and work. Her research interests centre on gender, sex and sexuality in organizations, and she has published in the journals *Gender, Work and Organization, Management Learning* and *Human Relations.*

Pippa Carter is senior lecturer in the Department of Management Systems and Sciences at the University of Hull, having previously studied at the University of Lancaster, Manchester School and Aston University. Her research interests are in the field of organization theory, with particular regard to the ontological and epistemological conditions of organization, the function of management and the nature of work. These research interests are informed by the radical critique of organization theory. Her current research is concerned with the potential contribution to organization theory of poststructuralism and the modernist/postmodernist debate.

Robert Cooper is Professor of Social Theory and Organization and Director of the Centre for Social Theory and Technology at Keele University. His research interests lie in the interaction of cybernetics, information theory and technology, and in the relationship between modern art theory and social theory.

J. Martin Corbett is senior lecturer in industrial relations and organizational behaviour at Warwick Business School. He has researched and written extensively on the relationship between technology and organization. Publications include *Technology and Organization: Power,*

Meaning and Design (with Harry Scarbrough, 1992) and *Critical Cases in Organizational Behaviour* (1994).

Christopher Grey is a lecturer in organizational behaviour at Leeds University Business School. He previously worked at the School of Management, UMIST, and has been visiting fellow at Stockholm University. His main current research interests are in organization theory, professional socialization, and critical management education. He co-edited *Rethinking Management Education* (with Robert French, 1996). He coordinated the ESRC Critique and Renewal in Management Education seminar series and is reviews editor of *Management Learning*.

John Hassard is Professor of Organizational Behaviour at Keele University. Previously he taught at the London Business School and Cardiff University. His publications include *Time, Work and Organizations* (1989), *The Theory and Philosophy of Organizations* (1990), *The Sociology of Time* (1990), *Sociology and Organization Theory* (1993), *Postmodernism and Organizations* (1993) and *Towards a New Theory of Organizations* (1994). His research interests lie in organization theory and industrial sociology.

Ruth Holliday teaches social and cultural theory at Staffordshire University. Her early work included a number of papers and a research monograph (from her PhD thesis) on small firms. She is currently working on an ESRC-funded project on sexual identity in and out of work, looking at verbal and visual representations of the 'self'. She is author of *Investigating Small Firms: Nice Work?* (1995).

Norman Jackson is a senior lecturer in the Department of Management Studies at the University of Newcastle upon Tyne. After a number of years in engineering management, he gained an MA in organizational psychology at the University of Lancaster and a PhD from Aston University, having also studied at Manchester Business School. His research contributes to the radical critique of organization theory and he is particularly interested in the possibility of non-surplus repressive organization. He is currently researching the contribution of the modernist/postmodernist debate to this possibility.

Linda McDowell teaches geography at Cambridge University and is a fellow of Newnham College. Her main interests are in the changing nature of employment in contemporary Britain and in feminist theory. She edited *Defining Women* (1992) with Rosemary Pringle and is author of a larger study of gender and merchant banking *Capital Culture: Gender at Work in the City* (1997).

Rolland Munro is Reader in Accountability in the Department of Management at Keele University. He is also a founding member of the Centre for Social Theory and Technology. His doctoral work attempted to reconcile systems theory and semiotics, and was followed by a five-year ethnographic study of a large company. He is editor (with Jan

Mouritsen) of *Accountability: Power, Ethos and the Technologies of Managing* (1996) and (with Kevin Hetherington) of *Ideas of Difference: Social Spaces and the Labour of Division* (1997). He is evolving a particular view of the consumption thesis, with published papers on belonging, identity work and organizational culture and has a long-standing commitment to treating accounting as a control technology.

Maggie O'Neill is a senior lecturer in sociology at Staffordshire University. She specializes in the area of critical theory, prostitution, ethnographic field methods and participatory action research. Maggie has conducted extensive ethnographic action research with women and young people working as prostitutes, including comparative research with colleagues in Spain. Her publications include work on responses to child and juvenile prostitution for the Children's Society, and a feminist analysis of prostitution, *Prostitution and Feminism* (forthcoming). Her research interests and forthcoming publications are on Adorno, feminism and critical theory.

Martin Parker is a lecturer in social and organizational theory in the Centre for Social Theory and Technology at the University of Keele. He previously taught sociology at Staffordshire University. He researches and writes on organizations, culture, social theory, ethics and anything else that takes his fancy.

Warren Smith is a lecturer in organizational theory in the Management Centre, Leicester University. Although holding degrees in management and organization studies, his current interests are the cultural reception of science, the cinematic representation of violence and the ethical consequences of cause-related marketing.

Peter Stead is a senior lecturer in history at the University of Wales, Swansea. His publications include *Film and the Working Class* and biographical studies of *Richard Burton* and *Dennis Potter*. He has been a visiting Fulbright Fellow at Wellesley College, Massachusetts, and Wilmington, North Carolina. He was a founding member of *Llafur, the Society for the Study of Welsh Labour History*. He is on the executive of the Welsh Academy and is a frequent broadcaster. In 1979 he contested his native constituency, Barry, for the Labour Party.

Acknowledgements

We would like to thank Rosemary Nixon, Hans Lock and Pascale Carrington at Sage for their help in the preparation of this manuscript; the BFI for the provision of the film stills included in this volume, especially Mandy Rowson, Martin O'Brian and their colleagues in the stills department. The editors would also like gratefully to acknowledge the use of copyright material in the illustrations from the following people and organizations: Central Office of Information, Columbia Pictures, UGC Lumiere Pinewood, Twentieth Century Fox, Warner Brothers, the BBC for Business (tel. 0181 576 2361), Jez Coulson and Insight, Carlton, the Kobal Collection, Hodder and Stoughton, Design and Artists Copyright Society, and Toni Dove.

Every attempt has been made to obtain permission to reproduce copyright material. If there are any omissions, please contact the editors.

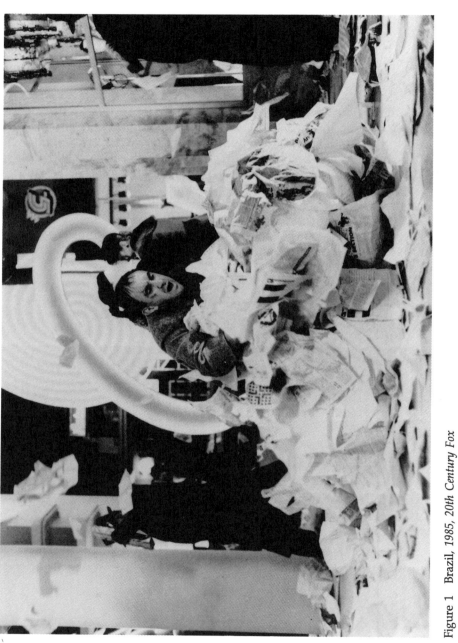

Figure 1 Brazil, 1985, 20th Century Fox

Introduction

John Hassard and Ruth Holliday

This book covers a variety of insights into the way in which organization is represented in the popular media. Drawing on organization theory, this text aims to unpack, decode and interpret messages and ideologies in contemporary representations of organization, whether these are Hollywood movies or ethnographic/documentary films, children's literature or the popular and 'quality' press. The focus of the book is frequently the material largely undiscussed in 'mainstream' organization theory, as popular culture offers more dramatic, more intense and more dynamic representations of organization than management texts. Consequently, where organization studies texts present rationality, organization and monolithic power relations, popular culture plays out sex, violence, emotion, power struggle, the personal consequences of success and failure, and *dis*organization upon its stage. Does popular culture present only an idealized, sensationalized view, then – one irrelevant to the lived experiences of organizational participants? Or are such glimpses and insights perhaps the very focus, the heart of organizational life, too long ignored by mainstream theory? Furthermore, do the ways in which such representations are presented carry with them some deeply rooted ideological persuasions, ensuring that their audiences accept and conform to the values of organizational society? Or are they implicit critiques of modern (and postmodern) capitalist frameworks? Finally, do we, the audience, passively receive such ideologies or do we rather recreate our own meanings in the light of our lived cultures and cultural capital?

It is our intention in bringing together the chapters in this volume to take a critical look at filmic, literary, televisual and journalistic portrayals of organizations, and to explore the ways in which these portrayals both remark on and inform current organization theory and practice. This agenda reflects not only a theoretical imperative to explore the linkages between 'image' and 'reality', 'fact' and 'fiction', but also a pedagogic desire to use commonplace media representations in the classroom as an aid to teaching and learning how organizations work. A cross-disciplinary focus, taking elements from management and organization theory, sociology, geography, media and cultural studies, film theory, and the interface between each, has allowed the authors to consider a diverse set of methodological and epistemological issues. First, however, it is necessary for readers unfamiliar with the debates to cover the key theories surrounding representation.

The Organization of Representation

The debate about realism and representation in popular culture became a political one in the late 1960s after the publication of work on ideology by Althusser and on discourse by Foucault. These approaches problematized the notion of the 'truth' advanced by a text. Since the truth can only be established by reference to the social context in which such truths are produced, then analysis involves reference beyond the text. For realism, this would involve some comparative judgements about the relationship between the text and the reality it claims to represent. However, even if 'reality' is to be represented as it is, without recourse to reconstruction, actors, scripts and so on, certain problems still emerge. In documentary film, for example, what and who should be filmed and how? Should lighting or different kinds of camera technique be used? Should the camera fix its gaze on a person talking or on those responding and reacting? If the film is to be shown on television, for example, how and where should it be edited? Thus realism is shown to be not a 'window on the world', nor a mirror that reflects it, but a set of conventions or constructions deriving from different historical moments. The representation of reality depends on shared recognition by producers and audiences of dominant images and ideas, codes and conventions, rather than any deeper understanding of universal truths. But, despite shared recognition, there may still be little consensus on how to interpret those representations, and there will always be possibilities for alternative readings. Texts that one person may judge realistic another may not, depending largely on life experiences or situated cultures. What is realistic is thus a controversial and subjective concept.

What also becomes apparent is that subjective interpretations of reality are rarely apolitical. For Althusser, the mass media, in all its forms, is simply an ideological tool of the capitalist state. For the Frankfurt School, it is simply a culture industry, mass producing mass culture for a mass audience. It is no more and no less than a deliberate manipulation of the masses. Codes and conventions are therefore far from being simple cinematic ones, an aid to audience understanding, but rather loaded and imbued with politically pacifying meanings and messages. Through interpellation, the media actively hails and constructs capitalist (and other) subjects. The media positions us ideologically in collusion with capitalism, and through curtailing, then satisfying, our curtailed dreams, it prevents radical thought and revolution. While these approaches are now recognized as rather simplistic, Gramsci, writing much earlier than Althusser, presents a rather more sophisticated approach.

For Gramsci, dominant classes do not simply rule but lead society, through moral and intellectual guidance. This explains why the working classes appear to support and subscribe to values that bind them to the dominant power structure. Dominant ideas become naturalized over time, and accepted as being for the common good. Hegemony is not a condition without conflict, but rather conflict is ideologically channelled into 'safe' struggles. In order to achieve and maintain hegemony, the ruling classes must continually make concessions to subordinate classes or groups. Thus, dominant groups negotiate with subordinate ones and culture is marked by processes of resistance (to dominant cultures) and incorporation (into dominant cultures). Organic intellectuals (powerful representatives of the dominant class) organize hegemony through cultural and moral leadership. Thus, hegemony is a process of winning consent, but if consent cannot be won then the repressive apparatus of the state can always be used to implement force.

While the two perspectives that we have addressed so far argue that representation offers a partial or inaccurate picture of reality, for structuralism there is no external, pre-existing reality to refer to. Rather, reality is constructed through language and mediated through signs. Reality is created through discourse. There can be no 'realism' in film or literature because there is no knowable external reality with which to compare it: it is simply an effect, a way of positioning the subject. Reality is only accessible through a series of mutually exclusive discourses or theories and therefore ceases to have any value. A text is therefore only realistic in as much as it conforms to a reader's existing ideology. Instead of the viewer being the judge of the text's realism, he or she is constructed by it. The structures of the text produce the viewer as subject. The subject is thus effect as well as agent. Ideology produces popular culture and popular culture produces ideology. The text is not simply mimetic but performative. This is achieved typically by the expunging of all traces of the text's production, thus cloaking the text's fabricated nature. The meaning then seems to derive 'naturally', from outside the text itself – it is self-evident. This method is used most obviously in documentary film, often accompanied by a 'voice-over', guiding the viewer around secondary and often competing discourses, thus asserting the authority of the metanarrative.

This might be particularly pertinent in discussions of post-structuralism. For Foucault, for example, words and discourses acquire their truth not by reference to any external reality, but from the people who use them. There is thus a 'politics of truth'. The way in which some discourses are privileged as true, others as false, is intrinsically related to the power relations that produce or deny them. Because realist film or literature represents a powerful discourse then the viewer interprets the representation as real because it is produced by an 'expert' – the one who knows the truth. Furthermore, identification with realist characters allows viewers to 'know themselves', thus positioning themselves as subjects of such discourses. In this way, audiences are created and affirmed as subjects.

The Representation of Organization

When we move to less realist genres many of the same questions apply. What kind of representations of organizations are most prevalent and why? Which aspects of these organizations are emphasized or de-emphasized? And what 'truth' about organizations do such depictions attempt to tell us? Up until the 1960s, many television dramas centred on the home, but during the 1970s 'family' (in the sense in which it is most frequently represented) became more problematic. Since all people have some knowledge of home and family life, there were problems in making representations appear realistic, especially when images of the family are overwhelmingly positive and comforting and experience of the family often is not. As Ella Taylor (1989: 110) explains 'more often than not the domestic setting becomes the repository for conflict and fear, not only about the family itself, but also about the ramifications of broader social changes for private life.' Television and film producers therefore had to look around for something to replace this troublesome genre, and thus the workplace substituted for, and came to express, an idealized construction of the family.

> The enclosed, obligatory environment of the workplace offers the same com-bination of intimacy, emotional intensity, and dramatic tension as the family group. But at a time when the family, particularly the middle-class suburban family, is perceived (at least by cultural critics) as increasingly privatized and removed from public life, the workplace opens its characters and invites its viewers to greater participation in the world outside, both organizational and beyond. (Taylor, 1989: 111)

However, the vast majority of people work in jobs that are ultimately boring and have few possibilities for social interaction. This is incom-patible with television's love of glamour and drama. Thus, certain kinds of workplace or profession were chosen in order to maintain this dramatic interest. The added advantages of such policies is that they were seen to appeal to a new generation of professional workers and the much greater number of women entering the workplace, thus adding a touch of 'realism' for these viewers. Probably the most popular of such representations are police and hospital dramas. Britain, for example, produces *The Bill, Prime Suspect, Casualty, Cardiac Arrest*; from the USA we get *NYPD Blue, Homicide, ER, Chicago Hope*, and from Australia and New Zealand a plethora of daytime soaps include *The Young Doctors, The Flying Doctors* and *Shortland Street*.

While a number of writers have focused on such dramas, exposing them as simple morality tales, there are many organizational aspects to such programmes worthy of note. For example, police dramas can be typologized into three phases (Moran, 1995). *Dixon of Dock Green*, for instance, fits with the 'conventional' phase and is characterized by a strict adherence to the letter of the law within a clearly defined hier-archical bureaucracy. *The Sweeney* marks a move to the 'unconventional':

'Management structures and official police procedures have atrophied into mock bureaucracy to which [only] lip service is paid' (Moran, 1995: 1). Police forces are characterized as masculine and ruled by charismatic 'heroic' officers not senior (bureaucratic) managers. Finally, the 'managerialist' phase, exemplified by *Between the Lines, The Chief* and *Prime Suspect*, portrays increasingly dynamic environments and focuses on officers of the highest rank, their connections with other institutions (such as politicians) and possibilities for their corruption. Thus, the modern police drama emphasizes what Moran (1995) calls the need for *glasnost* and accountability, and the move from police force to police service.

A long tradition of British and American police dramas represents maverick officers and their disdain for bureaucracy and hierarchy: Regan from *The Sweeney* was probably one of the first, but *Inspector Morse* and *Cracker* are typical contemporary examples. These themes tend to be now more or less universally recurrent in police drama. *The Bill*, for example, depicts many instances of the paperwork 'getting in the way' of 'real' crime fighting. Detectives are unable to get 'back out there' until mountains of crime sheets have been filled in. *The Bill* is also interesting in terms of hierarchical organization depicting constant tension between the CID and the uniformed officers (plods). The CID are portrayed as maverick, bending or even breaking the rules, using informers and coercive practices which the 'uniforms' wouldn't dream of. There is tension, too, between the new and the old, with the old-guard CID appearing less entrenched by bureaucracy and more inclined to bring justice at any cost. Breaking the rules, however, invariably has its ambiguous consequences, again reminding us that bureaucratic organization is the only real way to bring 'true justice'. This is in marked contrast to the private investigator who is at liberty to use more unorthodox methods. Belonging to the police force is thus a constraint, but it also provides power and protection:

> constraints apply differently depending on the police-officer's position within the institution, and on the depiction of legality and bureaucracy on which the story is premised. When the institution is obstructive or corrupt, the police-officer, usually now a junior officer, can only rightly discharge his or her function for the story (i.e. the duty that the officer owes to a superordinate morality) by stepping outside secular rules. (Sparks, 1992: 133)

The US crime drama *Homicide: Life on the Street* is often less about the street and more about the office. The programme frequently centres on the petty squabbles and banter of the station house. In one episode, for example, much of the programme is given over to Frank Pembleton and Tim Bayliss, partners feuding because Pembleton has omitted to buy Bayliss's lunch on the office sandwich run. Pembleton (a black officer) explains his mistake by commenting that a grilled cheese sandwich is so 'white boy' that he can't be expected to remember it. But the situation is later resolved after days of Bayliss bringing in food for all but his partner when his post tray, briefcase and desk are filled with grilled cheese sandwiches. Such are the everyday squabbles of the office. However, more 'conventionally organizational' issues are also dealt with. When Megan Russert is demoted, a position becomes available as captain. Giadello, whom everyone hopes and expects to replace her, is not given the job. Instead, it is given to Roger Gaffney, an officer who is openly misogynist and racist – calling Frank Pembleton 'boy'. His unsuitability is marked again by his insistence on sticking to rules and punctuality. Similarly, when Kay Howard is promoted to sergeant, the power appears to go to her head, leaving other detectives negotiating their new hierarchical relationship with difficulty.

Interestingly, it is not simply the police but also the 'villains' who can be characterized organizationally. The majority of criminal protagonists are hidden exactly by their outward respectability, coded through their occupational position – businessmen, policemen, politicians. Richard Cross from *Murder One* is a good example. Exterior respectability masks inward sleaze – embroilment in an 'underground' world of sex, drugs, conspiracy and so on. The mirrored structures of legal and criminal organizations are expertly portrayed in *Kiss of Death* (1995, discussed in Chapter 10) and intertwined in *The Firm* (1993) where a legal firm is discovered to be covertly run by the Mafia. However, this is an unusual representation in some senses, as most dramas aim to accentuate the differences between 'rational' law and order and madness in the pursuit of crime. As Sparks (1992: 143) explains:

> The pursuit of wealth and power by criminals is not rational and instrumental: it is obsessive, neurotic. It is connected not only to ruthlessness but also eccentricity. It is encoded in excessive consumption, physical handicap, sexual inadequacy, reclusiveness, often deploying the motif of the opulent home, with its grounds patrolled by private armies of retainers and savage guard dogs.

One might also add, then, that for the villain the public and private are thoroughly merged. The villain's home is also his or her organizational headquarters, unlike the police, who invariably have to manage conflict between work and home life.

Hospital dramas also invariably tackle organizational issues. In the BBC's *Casualty*, for example, there is an emphasis on NHS funding. The issues of waiting lists, lack of resources leading to patients being left to die in corridors, and hospital closures causing patients needing immediate care being driven to far-away hospitals, are all covered. So, too, are the tensions between the new NHS trusts and the 'real' medical staff. The boardroom has become a regular feature in which doctors confront accountants and the battle between patient welfare and budget controls is fought out. Similarly, in *ER*, issues are raised when patients have limited or no health insurance, leaving them ineligible for treatment. Issues concerning the long hours that doctors and junior doctors work, the pressures that they face, and the consequences for patient care are frequently raised. So, too, are the moral issues involved in medical research and the poaching of new equipment from one under-funded department by another. This is a far cry from early shows such as *Doctor Kildare*. Kildare battled not with colleagues but with disease, human folly and ignorance. Hospital administrators were kindly and compassionate. 'They were part of the system and the system functioned on behalf of the people' (Taylor, 1989: 141). Contemporary hospital dramas set up dichotomous relationships: the 'real' medics and the bureaucrats, the good professionals and the bad. This perhaps reflects two concerns of contemporary society. The first is a kind of anti-intellectualism that distrusts professionalism based on technical knowledge and expertise. Witness the contrast in *ER*, for example, between Dr Ross (who saves a drowning boy from a sewer, thus breaking the rules of the emergency services, and subsequently flies the boy to his own hospital, instead of the nearest, to save his life) and another doctor in the hospital whose patients are guinea-pigs for his own medical research. The second concern reflects the creation of a new enemy – the organization itself. The boundaries of power and authority break up and realign organizations, creating new and contrasting meanings of professionalism.

While the stories of such dramas may be simple morality tales, the representations of organization within them are frequently different from conventional understandings of the workplace. Such programmes reject the image of the rational, disembodied, unemotional workplace, replacing it with representations of embodied, personal, emotional and frequently petty settings and interactions. Broader issues of funding, cost centres and bureaucracy are also a target for criticism, although the blatant breaking of rules is sometimes tinged with ambiguity: the cop gets a result but at what personal cost to innocent third parties? A key feature of the television workplace drama is its focus on the small unit of workers (the small firm in *Taxi* or the unit of medics in *M*A*S*H*) who form their most important relationships with each other:

> workplace settings . . . invariably serve as sites for the development of primary relationships of solidarity, authority, and subordination more commonly associated with families than with secondary occupational groupings. In an age when workplaces are typically large, rationalized, streamlined, the television workplace is a haven within a harsh and unprepossessing institutional world – cozy, even ramshackle, but above all lived-in, strewn and cherished personal articles. (Taylor, 1989: 136)

In recent times, Hollywood has produced a plethora of films concerned with the corporation. Films addressing women in work, for example, range from *Working Girl* (1988, a callous career woman's gentle secretary successfully takes her place) and *Baby Boom* (1987, a successful career woman inherits a child and is forced to leave her organization, eventually finding love and entrepreneurial success producing baby food in a small town) to *Disclosure* (1994, a senior woman manager sexually harasses her male subordinate). Such films have been welcomed in the popular media, celebrating women's inclusion in representations of the workplace. However, closer scrutiny reveals that these films frequently draw upon rather crass stereotypes of the 'career bitch' or of the choice between a career or a man (a woman can't have both). In *The Hand that Rocks the Cradle* (1992), for example, a woman nearly loses her husband and children to her nanny, and *Disclosure* presents the hyper-sexualized and obsessive career woman. As Elspeth Probyn (1990) argues, in many cases new traditionalism and post-feminism conspire to return women to the home. For example, witness Hope's tortured deliberations over whether to return to work after having her baby in the yuppie lifestyle drama *Thirtysomething*. Single career women in the show are depicted as having miserable and empty lives, constantly aware of their ticking biological clocks (see Heide, 1995).

Another popular Hollywood genre is the 'entrepreneurial success story'. This category finds its roots in the less rosy *The Man in the White Suit* (1952, an inventor discovers an everlasting fabric that eliminates the need for replacement clothes), a critical British film about the battle between inventor and capital, but might include films such as *Big* (1988, a young boy is magically given a man's body and becomes a major success in a toy company), *The Hudsucker Proxy* (1994, a naïve small town boy battles with a corrupt organization to become its successful director), or *The Secret of my Success* (1987, again a young post boy becomes a successful corporate executive). Such films take organizations as their focus and portray them as boring, unadventurous, mechanical institutions, rife with internal wranglings and powerplays, organized by corrupt managers whose financial motives outstrip ethical concerns for the health of 'the company'. Into these scenarios come oddballs, social misfits, outsiders, who transform the organization and its members through enthusiasm, creativity and entrepreneurialism. These characters' lack of cultural capital and naïveté in the business world is exactly what contributes to their eventual success. But the organization is portrayed as their 'home' – the place where they can best achieve what they have the potential to be. *Big* is interesting in this respect as the character, portrayed by Tom Hanks, eventually returns 'home' to his childhood. Though he displays exceptional talent in the toy company in which he works, success does not ultimately bring happiness. He is not ready yet. He must first complete his childhood – he must grow up in order to appreciate wealth and status. Such films must almost certainly be read as a portrayal of the 'American dream', yet through the extraordinary nature of the characters and creative situations that they activate we must also read these films as a comment on the usual boringness and lack of creativity of the US corporation.

The anti-bureaucracy sentiment, which is a recurrent theme of almost all representations of organization, is most fervently taken up in the British film *Brazil* (1985). In this film, air-conditioning engineers are forced underground into a kind of rebel task force: their mission, to fix air conditioning without having to fill in the excessive paperwork imposed by company regulations. Organization in *Brazil* is portrayed as essentially alienating, focused on petty squabbles and managerial incompetence. One dramatic scene shows a horrified man struggling as bits of paper blow on to his body, sticking to him and eventually killing him. The hero's only escape from such a society is into madness. Other recent blockbusters focusing on the corporation also mingle comment on capitalism with science fiction and fantasy. The Tyrell Corporation in *Blade Runner* (1982) is typical of omnipotent organizations running rife in futuristic societies also presented in *Alien* (1979), *Terminator* (1981) and *Robocop* (1987). In *Alien*, for example, all crew members of the Nostromo work for an organization ('the company') whose sole aim is to return an alien life form to Earth in order to use it in the development of weapons technology. To this end, all human or cyborg crew members are expendable.

> Hence, the latter are victims at once of the corporation's greed and of an incomprehensible, sinister, and overwhelmingly powerful natural creature that in a sense wreaks vengeance for its disturbance by human beings. Indeed, by their transformation of nature into commodity, human beings have become true aliens. (Byers, 1990: 40)

The alien resembles absolutely the 'other superorganism, itself victor in evolutionary struggle: the multinational (soon to be interstellar) organization' (Gould, 1980: 283). Furthermore, the corporation employs technology in the form of Ash, a robot, to assist with its mission. Ash is initially indistinguishable from the others; their lack of emotion matches his. They are motivated by greed; he is programmed by it. Emotion is overruled by procedures, and breaking procedures – letting the crew member with the alien attached to his face out of the airlock – is what gets the crew into trouble in the first place. Crew members die in order of their alignment with organizational goals and values. Ripley is saved, though tormented, because her affinity with values of organizational calculability and indifference is tempered by compassion. This theme is raised once again in *Blade Runner*. The Tyrell Corporation produces replicants – human-style androids. Replicants are to work as slaves; however, in time, replicants begin to develop human emotions. In order to make these emotions more controllable, each replicant is given false human memories and a limited four-year lifespan. Some replicants have come together as rebels, presenting a threat to the Tyrell Corporation which in turn hires assassins (blade runners) to find and kill them. Deckard is the film's hero and is one such blade runner. To perform his job he must be cold and ruthless – organizational – but as replicants become more 'human' his job becomes harder. He meets Rachael. She is a replicant who thinks she is human. Through his relationship with Rachael, Deckard is 'rehumanized'. But is Deckard, in fact, human? Is he a replicant after all? Was his earlier lack of emotion, which enabled his service to Tyrell, produced by Tyrell itself? Byers (1990: 45) summarizes these points extremely well:

Blade Runner, like *Alien*, finally retreats from the implications of its radical critiques into filmic clichés and individualist solutions. Created within . . . Hollywood . . . the films are bound, consciously or not, by formidable constraints . . . Their strongest common element in this regard is their insistence on the dehumanization necessary for human survival in a world dominated by mega-corporations. Human relationships to the robotic villain of *Alien*'s glossy high-tech spaceship, and to the more complex but equally fearsome replicants of *Blade Runner*'s futuristic film noir vision of urban decay, function to raise this issue in powerful terms.

We must also consider the flipside of popular culture representations of organization: that is, the entry of certain forms of organization – or management – into popular culture. Management gurus have become significant media celebrities, fronting TV series, appearing on chat shows, and regularly topping the bestseller lists with their latest ideas, which have significantly proliferated (Watson, 1994). Gurus such as Tom Peters and Robert Waterman and John Harvey Jones command star status (and fees), and have spearheaded a whole new literary genre: replacing the 'airport novel' (trashy, lightweight fantasy to be read on a plane trip, then discarded), we have the 'airport management guide' (of which we could say the same). Their approach – endless use of metaphors, the coining of catchphrases, aphorisms and acronyms – has also impacted on popular culture, with 'management-speak' entering the everyday lexicon. But it is not only these gurus who have impacted on popular culture: the heroes and villains of organizations also have their 15 minutes of fame (at least). Robert Maxwell and his sons Kevin and Ian, Ivan Boesky, and Nick Leeson have all recently found fame (or infamy) as a result of their business practices.

Ultimately, then, what can be said about popular representations of organization? To return to the workplace drama series, such shows focus not on the large corporation but the small firm or unit within them. Institutionalized relationships are coded as instrumental and detached from humanity. Instead, the focus is the personal relationships between co-workers. The television workplace, then, is first and foremost a world of emotionality and community, thus avoiding any attempt at realism in terms of most organizational members' actual experiences of them. 'In a society based on centralized institutional power the television workplace expresses local autonomy. In the midst of the large, anonymous city it creates family and community. Where managerial and technical controls have imposed rigid homogeneity, television celebrates diversity, human initiative and tolerance of individual and group differences' (Taylor, 1989: 148).

The same themes are emphasized in the 'entrepreneurial success' genre. In all the films the hero is in some sense 'out of place' in corporate America – an individual surrounded by the monotony of the homogeneous machine or, even worse, the corrupt and self-interested boardroom. Images of the large conglomerate swallowing up or perhaps callously asset-stripping smaller, more unique, more individual firms abound. Other images portray the stranglehold that the large bureaucracy imposes on creativity and talent. Finally, the futuristic organization is greedy, malevolent and all powerful. Human life is irrelevant, dispensable, insignificant and must be dispensed with if it poses a threat to profit. Corporate heads are self-obsessed, insane, immoral or deviant, and interested only in further gain for its own sake. The future is organization out of control. What all these representations have in common is their disdain for organization and its objectives. Organization is portrayed as dull, evil or simply avoided altogether by a refocus on social relations. Organization has become a metaphor for modernity. The scientific rationality of the corporation embodies our fears for the loss of our humanity, and therefore our anti-modernist tendencies.

Although this brief introduction is far from an exhaustive list of possible 'organizational readings' in popular culture, it begins to suggest possibilities for such a focus of study. Some of the themes raised here are taken up in the following chapters. The book as a whole brings to the forefront a neglected area of study in organization theory, if not in film studies. The ensuing chapters are written by authors from many disciplines, and each sheds light in a different way on the issues discussed. The use of this and similar material in the teaching of organizational concerns should enhance our understanding of how knowledge about organizations is both represented and constructed in both theory and culture.

Organization of the Book

The 'truth' about organizations and how it is created through realist films is taken up in this volume by three authors. In Chapter 1 Ian Aitken looks specifically at the way in which work and occupation are represented in the documentary film movement, and the way in which these films incorporate often contradictory themes about work, craft skills and institutional occupation. He argues that regional and traditional themes, as well as manual and craft skills, are emphasized and celebrated over and above national issues and administrative and institutional structures. The films focus on tradition and continuity; while capitalism and the city are regarded as morally ambiguous, the films display a preoccupation with nature and landscape, and large public organizations.

John Hassard, in Chapter 2, explores how the world of work and organizations is represented in *cinéma vérité*. The chapter charts the evolution of theories and techniques developed explicitly to produce increasingly unmediated film images of work and organizations. Examining films associated with such styles, Hassard considers important questions of artefact in films that claim to represent 'everyday reality'. Through discussion of theory and evidence, the chapter poses the question of whether the key metaphor for the ethnographic organizational documentary should be 'fly on the wall' or 'fly in the soup'.

While John Hassard draws on a number of realist films about organizations, Peter Stead (Chapter 3) argues that the film historian has to look quite hard for either documentary or fictional films that set out to show the basic realities of trade-union organization. It is also ironic that, given the radical talk of many film-makers and critics of the 1940s and 1950s, when films on this subject were eventually made they turned out to be critical of many union practices. The first serious criticism of union power came in the late 1950s when, quite suddenly, incipient suburban mutterings were fuelled by film and television producers. *I'm All Right Jack* was released in 1959; *The Angry Silence* in 1960; and in 1961 the BBC launched a comedy series, *The Rag Trade*, the catchphrase of which was 'everybody out!' Peter Stead re-examines this surprising and unexpected concern with trade-union power along with the political and cultural motives of those who produced them.

Joanna Brewis argues, in Chapter 4, that, while its scenario may promote understanding of the complexities of harassing behaviour in organizations and may also move away from conventional norms of the woman as victim, the film *Disclosure* (1994) at one and the same time consolidates understandings of women as threatening and unnatural in their organizational success. Furthermore, *Disclosure*'s eroticized portrayal of sexual harassment may generate understandings that fail to accept it as unwanted and abusive. While other films, such as *Wall Street* (1987), touch on the issue of sexual harassment (perhaps to add a touch of realism), *Disclosure* is the first major film to deal with this subject centrally since the comedy *Nine to Five* (1980), starring Dolly Parton. Surprisingly, the film casts the woman as harasser, perhaps in an attempt by Hollywood to deflect the realities of harassment.

Ruth Holliday, in Chapter 5, still focusing on sexuality, explores the movie *Philadelphia* (1993) – Hollywood's so-called 'ground-breaking AIDS picture'. While the film may be valuable in exploring organizational dynamics, such as powerplays and homosocial behaviour, and also the way in which AIDS and 'rampant' homosexuality are conflated, the movie is ultimately conservative. In its liberal calling for tolerance towards gay men (and lesbians and bisexuals) in organizations, it implicitly positions its audience as heterosexual, therefore leaving binary divides between homosexual and heterosexual unchallenged.

Maggie O'Neill takes the Western as inspiration in Chapter 6, focusing on the portrayal of the brothel as a workplace. In three films, *Rio Bravo* (1959), *The Wild Bunch* (1969) and *Unforgiven* (1992), she highlights the issues of masculinity and desire and their relationship to death and violence. Such representations are not simply outdated depictions of a bygone age but have real implications for and resonances with prostitutes working in saunas, clubs and bars today.

Christopher Grey explores the children's novel in Chapter 7 and its role in the construction of organizational realities. A number of popular children's stories from the *Jennings, Famous Five* and *Swallows and*

Amazons series are addressed. Children's literature has a very obvious role in social conditioning, such that the lessons learnt from childhood reading have the potential to provide an interpretative framework for later life, much as educational theorists have argued that the 'hidden curriculum' operates to socialize children into hegemonic values and behaviours. The particular texts chosen have been widely read by children over a number of years and especially during the childhoods of those currently in positions of influence in present-day organizations. The chosen texts are criticized for their tendency to replicate a set of 'middle-class' values and, more especially, of sexist, racist and élitist discourses. The specific focus of this chapter is on organization in two senses: first, organization as a *noun* is treated in terms of the kind of organization to be found in the stories; secondly, organization as a *verb* is considered, identifying the ways in which conduct, such as the structuring of activities and the regulation of behaviour, is organized.

Norman Jackson and Pippa Carter look at the construction of management gurus in Chapter 8. The academic use of popular media is nowhere more prevalent than in management and organization studies, where management gurus appear on television, on video and in popular literature communicating their wares. Unlike other academic disciplines, which tend to aim such populist materials at lay audiences, the primary audience for management and organization theorists is practising managers, and the aim is to inform and shape organizational practice. With contemporary figures, the favoured form of media projection has been the video – few have achieved the pinnacle of their own television series as in the case of Sir John Harvey Jones – where the great man or woman conducts a sort of 'master class'. A well-known example of this is Herzberg's *Jumping for the Jelly Beans*. Jackson and Carter focus on Herzberg's creation as management guru. It is an especially interesting case as the video was first recorded in the early 1970s, then reissued as a 'management classic' by the BBC about 15 years later. In the reissued version, however, the BBC significantly edited Herzberg's performance. This chapter examines the implications and insights that this 'classic' raises.

Linda McDowell's contribution (Chapter 9) examines the background to a number of films, plays and novels categorized as 'sexy–greedy'. The US versions may be morality tales (see Denzin's work on *Wall Street*, for example), but the British genre seems to be an unabashed celebration of greed. At the same time, the financial pages of the press increasingly portray money men (and less frequently women) as key players in an exciting drama. The press coverage of Nick Leeson and the 'Barings' scandal' is the most interesting recent example. This chapter compares the characteristics of the 'fictional cast' of the popular media and cinema with the 'real' recruits to the financial world of three banks in the City of London.

Rolland Munro (Chapter 10) looks at 'normal atrocities' through the lens of Barbet Schroeder's film *Kiss of Death*. As Schroeder and Derrida portray them, the car and philosophy are both *vehicles* of masculinity. Schroeder's plot also lets us follow Derrida. In one particular scene, the 'hinge' is when the hero is brought by car, via carlift, to a car park to what the audience expects to be his execution. The car lifts (Derrida's 're-lever') us into a moment when hood and racketeers turn into FBI and police. The forces of good and evil are no mere duality propping each other up. Both racketeers and the police call themselves 'organizations' and are structural equivalents. The organizations are masculine and mad. We find a similar moment in Derrida. Instead of a ritual execution of Foucault by the new radicals, the postmodernists and post-structuralists turn into the forces for ordering and organizing thinking. As Derrida goes masculine to outmaster the master, the madness of his 'massacre' reduces him to a footnote to Foucault. Finally, this is linked to the repertoires of 'macho management', and its 'normal atrocities' of dismissals, redundancies and factory closures, and the proximity of masculinity, madness and reason.

Opening Part IV, on organizational futures, Martin Parker and Robert Cooper (Chapter 11) examine some of the themes raised in films focusing on the 'cyborganization'. Using these films as a starting point, it is possible to describe the general processes by which human actors (bodies as organisms) in organizational and institutional settings supplement their incompleteness by engineering and developing technologies that combine with bodies to create new 'cyborganic' spaces populated by 'cyborganisms'. This form of analysis can then have implications for the study of organizational theory and formulations of human agency and identity.

Warren Smith (Chapter 12) takes the virtual organization as his focus. Virtual reality technologies offer the potential to produce simulated environments that create the impression that we are in spaces other than those we actually inhabit. This simulated environment may be a dark dungeon in a role-playing game, a simulated building design, or a shared space through which we transcend our geographical separation, a 'virtual organization' in which we go about our daily business. For many writers, everything important to the life of individuals will be found for sale in cyberspace. But what does it mean to organize, or be organized, in this 'virtual organization'? We may be persuaded to imbue virtual reality with mystical overtones, portraying it as offering the opportunity to transcend normal visions of reality. It can be a free space in which the unshackled participants can exercise self-expression and self-discovery. It could offer the opportunity to re-enchant the world of science and technology. However, this chapter suggests that virtual reality is actually a supremely ordered representation of our apparently disordered world.

J. Martin Corbett also develops the theme of the futuristic organization (Chapter 13). He examines the relationship between present-day technology and the ways in which this informs representations of science fiction organizations on the cinema screen. Today's preoccupations with technology thus inform futuristic representations. However, science fiction depictions of organizations and technology also influence present-day developments in organizational technologies. Two conventional models are used in such films: first, technology dominates through the creation of new knowledge or, directly, in the form of machines (techno-logical determinism); secondly, malevolent (usually male-dominated) organizational élites shape and control productive and reproductive technologies. Since contemporary organizations also adopt these ways of understanding technological development, then ideological analysis in media and cultural studies can be shown to benefit understandings of 'real' organizations.

References

Byers, T.B. (1990) 'Commodity futures', in A. Kuhn (ed.), *Alien Zone: Cultural Theory and Contemporary Science Fiction Cinema*. London: Verso.

Gould, J. (1980) 'The destruction of the social by the organic in *Alien*', *Science Fiction Studies*, 7: 3.

Heide, M.J. (1995) *Television Culture and Women's Lives*. Pennsylvania: University of Pennsylvania Press.

Moran, P. (1995) 'Prime time suspects: fictional television portrayals of policing in the UK'. Paper presented at the Research, Film and Videotape Conference, Bolton, 2–3 February.

Probyn, E. (1990) 'New traditionalism and post-feminism: TV does the home', *Screen*, 31: 2.

Sparks, R. (1992) *Television and the Drama of Crime*. Buckingham: Open University Press.

Taylor, E. (1989) *Prime Time Families: Television Culture in Post-war America*. Berkeley, CA: University of California Press.

Watson, T. (1994) 'Management "flavours of the month": their role in managers' lives', *The International Journal of Human Resource Management*, 5: 4.

Figure 1.1 Drifters, 1929, Central Office of Information

PART I
REALISM AND REPRESENTATION

1

The Documentary Film Movement
The Post Office Touches all Branches
of Life

Ian Aitken

The films of the British documentary movement continue to be an important resource for historians investigating social and cultural activity during the 1930s. However, few detailed analyses of the ways in which these films represent work and leisure have been undertaken. In this chapter, I will attempt to carry out such an analysis, looking at the films produced between 1929 and 1939, and focusing on five films in particular: *Drifters* (1929), *Night Mail* (1936), *Roadways* (1937), *Job in a Million* (1937) and *The City* (1939). I will attempt to demonstrate that these, and other films made by the documentary movement, convey a number of often contradictory themes relating to issues of work, craft skills and institutional occupation, and that the existence of these complex thematic configurations make the films rewarding objects of study.

The emergence of the documentary film movement can be associated with two critical developments which affected British society during the period: the growth of the state; and the growth of corporate capitalism. These developments stimulated the expansion of the public relations industry, and it was this expansion which ultimately brought the documentary film movement into being. These developments did not, however, take place to any significant extent until 1914, after which the British state adopted a much more interventionist role, and the corporate sector of the economy expanded rapidly. The expansion of the state during the First World War led to a corresponding growth in government publicity, as new propaganda agencies, including the Ministry of Information, were established. The cinema was also involved in this, and a new genre of war films appeared, the most important of which was *The Battle of the Somme* (1916).[1]

After the war, attempts were made to reverse the wartime expansion of the state, and to return to policies of economic liberalism. However, these attempts ultimately failed, and the state continued to expand throughout the inter-war period (Aldcroft, 1983). The period also saw a significant growth in the corporate sector of the economy until, by 1935, the ratio of that sector to the rest of the economy was similar to that of America (Aldcroft, 1983). During this period, therefore, British society changed from one based on free-market structures and a non-interventionist state to one based on corporate capitalism and a strong state.

As part of the general policy of abandoning government controls after 1918, the wartime propaganda system was also reduced in size. However, a considerable expansion took place in the commercial advertising and public relations industries, and national expenditure on advertising and publicity almost doubled between 1920 and 1928 (Crawford, 1931). This expansion mainly took place in the private sector, and in a number of municipal organizations;[2] central government commissioned little, the prevailing view within the civil service and government departments being that the state should not become actively involved in the dissemination of publicity.

The context from which the documentary film movement emerged, then, was characterized by the growth of mass society, corporate capitalism, organized labour and increased state intervention. Inevitably, the various elements within this social configuration turned to the media of mass communication in order to advance their interests, and many turned to the most popular of these media – film.

The EMB Period, 1927–34

In 1924, John Grierson, the founder of the British documentary film movement, was awarded a fellowship to study problems of social integration among immigrant communities in America.[3] At the end of this research, he concluded that the cinema offered the best means of integrating diverse social groups into society, through the production of films that emphasized the interconnection between the individual and the social. However, Grierson believed that the commercial film industry would not make such films in significant numbers, and he turned, instead, to the only other possible source of such films: the state.

While in America he had become aware of debates taking place in Britain concerning the role of post-war state publicity and propaganda. On his return to Britain in 1927 he contacted the Empire Marketing Board (EMB), then the largest government publicity organization in Britain, seeking a position. He was eventually appointed to the post of Films Officer there in 1928 (Swann, 1989). In contrast to Grierson's ambitions, however, the scope for the production of socially purposive films at the EMB was limited. The EMB had initially been established as an inferior substitute for protectionist legislation (Amery, 1953). The EMB's task was to publicize and market Empire products, but the main emphasis was on market research, rather than on proactive publicity.

In theory, these limited terms of reference should have severely jeopardized Grierson's aspiration to create a new social cinema at the EMB, but he was eventually able to realize this objective with the support of sympathetic colleagues. The Secretary to the EMB, (Sir) Steven Tallents, believed that new policies had to be developed in order to create effective Empire publicity. He therefore looked beyond traditional spheres of civil service recruitment and enlisted staff on temporary contracts from industry and the media. Grierson's was one such appointment. Eventually, nearly 70 per cent of the EMB's staff were drawn from outside the civil service, and it was this unusual staffing culture that facilitated the consideration of new ideas, and allowed Grierson to manoeuvre within the narrow limits of the EMB's terms of reference (Lee, 1972).

In terms of subject matter, the films made at the EMB between 1929 and 1933 often failed to conform to the imperative of marketing Empire products for the British market. The first film to be produced, Grierson's *Drifters* (1929), was about deep-sea fishing in Scotland. This was followed by *Conquest* (Grierson, Wright), a re-edited compilation of footage from Hollywood films, and then by a series of short 'poster' films made by Basil Wright and Paul Rotha. These 'poster' films were 30 ft loops of film, shown continuously at exhibitions, and Paul Rotha (1973) recalls that they had titles such as *Scottish Tomatoes, Butter, Australian Wine*, and so on. A number of other single-reel films were also made during 1930: *Lumber, South African Fruit, Canadian Apples* and *Sheep Dipping*. Their authorship is uncertain, although it is likely that they were made by Basil Wright and Paul Rotha.

The films produced in the following year (1931) were more advanced. Basil Wright directed *The Country Comes to Town*, on food and milk supplies brought to London from the country, and *O'er Hill and Dale*, about a sheep farm in the Scottish Borders. Arthur Elton made *The Shadow on the Mountain*, about research into grass-growing techniques in Wales, and *Upstream*, on salmon breeding in Scotland. Edgar Anstey joined an Admiralty expedition to Labrador and made *Uncharted Waters* and *Eskimo Village*. Marian Grierson re-edited the earlier *Lumber* to make *King Log*, on the lumber industry in Canada, and Robert Flaherty filmed *Industrial Britain*. From the spare footage from this film Marian Grierson edited together a silent, single-reel film entitled *The English Potter*.

The primary concern of these films is the representation of aspects of working-class and rural culture, with a particular emphasis on the depiction of craft skills. Work as a physical activity, embedded within the social relations of the small production unit, and the rituals and techniques of skilled labour, emerge as a recurrent theme. In contrast, there are few representations of large-scale industry or mass labour. Where scientific research or technology is touched upon it is frequently set against the natural world and the rural hinterland, suggesting a concern with exploring the relationship between man and nature, rather than that between man and technology. Representations of metropolitan life and culture are also conspicuously absent from these films, and, with few exceptions, the remit of publicising Empire products in the British market is largely ignored.

One of Grierson's principal strategies for circumventing restrictions on film-making within the EMB was to seek commissions from outside organizations, and the final group of films to emerge from the EMB Film Unit was largely commissioned by external organizations. Stuart Legg directed the first of these, *New Generation* (1932), for the Chesterfield Education Authority. Donald Taylor made *Lancashire at Work and Play* (1933) and *Spring Comes to England* (1934) in association with the Ministries of Labour and Advertising. Marian Grierson made *So This is London* (1933) and *For All Eternity* (1934) for the Travel and Industrial Association. Evelyn Spice made a number of short films for schools on the English seasons, and Stuart Legg made two films for the General Post Office (GPO): *The New Operator* (1933) and *Telephone Workers* (1933). Basil Wright made *Cargo from Jamaica* (1933) and *Windmill in Barbados* (1933) for the EMB and the Orient Line, and then went on to make *Song of Ceylon* (1934) for the Ceylon Tea Company. Arthur Elton made the six-reel *Aero Engine* (1933) and *The Voice of the World* (1934) for the HMV company, and Harry Watt made *Six-Thirty Collection* (1934) and *BBC Droitwich* (1934) for the GPO and the BBC respectively.

The commissioning institutions for these films were all either public bodies or commercial corporations and trade associations, and this configuration of sponsorship reflected the growth of such institutions during the inter-war period (Mowat, 1955; Pollard, 1962). It was these organizations that increasingly employed public relations officers and commissioned films for public relations purposes. The type of sponsorship emerging from this context also reflected the increasing importance of industries based on communications technologies. For example, two recently created public corporations, Imperial Airways and the BBC,[4] commissioned several films from the EMB, the best known of which is Arthur Elton's *The Voice of the World*.

In these films, as in the earlier ones, a continuing concern for rural and regional identity and the value of craft skills can be identified, most notably in *Lancashire at Work and Play* and *Spring Comes to England*. There is also a persisting engagement with the identity of indigenous cultures, particularly in Basil Wright's three films: *Cargo from Jamaica*, *Windmill in Barbados* and *Song of Ceylon*. However, a shift of focus is also apparent: alongside the enduring emphasis on the rural, the indigenous and craft labour, an engagement with issues of technology, communication and transport becomes increasingly evident.

Scientific development is often viewed ambivalently in these films: sometimes being seen as progressive and emancipating, and sometimes as a potential threat to traditional mores. Technology is viewed in the same ambivalent way, as both progressive and a threat to traditional labour. This equivocal attitude towards technological development is at its clearest in Basil Wright's films, particularly *Song of Ceylon*, whereas Arthur Elton's *Aero Engine* and *The Voice of the World* represent a more positive stance towards technological and scientific development.

A considerable variety of workers and work are represented in these films, including postal workers, radio operators, scientists, engineers, labourers, fishermen, managers, telephone operators, sailors, lumberjacks, farmers, priests, shepherds, teachers, agriculturalists, explorers, steel workers, potters and factory workers. However, between 1929 and 1934, the focus gradually switches from representations of manual labour to representations of semi-skilled and skilled labour, and a parallel switch also occurs from the representation of lower-class to lower middle-class workers. At the same time, a rhetoric of modernity, associated with the new industries and technologies, also challenges the original concern for the representation of lower-class experience found in the earlier films. This concern originated from Grierson's conviction that the documentary film should probe below the surface of events in order to explore underlying truths. According to Grierson, visual images of the 'gestures which time has worn smooth' (the way in which a fisherman draws in a net or a miner hews coal from the coal face) can express the underlying experience of a community (Grierson, 1933: 214). Such a perspective inevitably privileges traditional subjects, and this means that, in the exploration of contradictions between the traditional and the modern, it was the traditional that was accentuated. This can be seen most clearly in Flaherty and Grierson's *Industrial Britain* and, most importantly, in Grierson's *Drifters*.[5]

Drifters

To a significant extent, *Drifters* (1929) is a film about work and the institutions of work. It contains many sequences displaying the skills and techniques of manual labour, such as stoking a boiler, hauling in nets, gutting fish, fuelling an ocean-going liner, and barrelling fish in the marketplace. *Drifters* also depicts different occupations within the fishing industry, such as deep-sea fishing, fish processing, packaging, buying and selling, and distribution by rail and by sea. Despite its representation of institutions, however, *Drifters* is essentially about a particular kind of working activity, deep-sea fishing, and not about the institutions that sustain that activity.

The representation of technology in films produced by the documentary movement is often equivocal. Technology is sometimes regarded positively, as in *The Voice of the World*; sometimes more ambivalently, as in *Coal Face* or *Song of Ceylon*. The technology depicted in *Drifters*, however, is an integral part of the fishermen's activities. Like the fishermen, the steam winches and engines which the fishing boat relies on are strong and reliable. A comfortable harmony between man and machine is depicted here, exemplified by the scene in which a man stoking the engine's boiler withdraws a spade full of hot coals from the furnace, and casually lights his cigarette from it.

However, if technology and machinery are represented positively in *Drifters*, commerce and commercial institutions are not, and the film makes a number of comments about the way in which the labour of deep-sea fishing is commodified and degraded by market forces. Grierson makes this statement, in one scene, through the device of superimposing an image of fishing at sea over an image of fish being packed into a barrel at the market. This criticism of the way in which human activity is debased within an economic system ruled by utilitarian values is a recurrent motif in Grierson's writings, in *Drifters*, and in other films made by the movement.

Drifters also celebrates the consolations and gratifications of the masculine, professional group. Strength, endurance and dexterity are emphasized, as is the camaraderie of the working environment. The world of work on board ship is a closed masculine world, in which the rituals of communal leisure are emphasized, and in which the continuity of generations is accented, with young, middle-aged and older sailors working collectively. This is an image of work based around a model of traditional labour, in which knowledge is passed on through a combination of peer and kin relationships, and in which the value of the traditional, intimate and organic lower-class working community is foregrounded.

Drifters is primarily concerned with the representation of working-class people and, although the film encompasses the activities of the marketplace, as well as those associated with deep-sea fishing, it contains few representations of management or administration. The focus is on working-class, rather than middle-class or lower middle-class experience, and the scenes set in the marketplace have a quite different atmosphere and signification from those shot on the fishing boat. The latter are marked by reflection and a sense of space, or by the dramatic struggle of man against nature; while the market is presented in terms of bustle, chaotic movement and instrumental activity. The market is an alienating social space, less moral and worthwhile than the communal life of the boat.

Nevertheless, the representation of the market in *Drifters* is not entirely negative. At one level, as already mentioned, the film questions the value of the market, seeing it as morally inferior to the world of craft labour. However, at another level, the film emphasizes the overall unity of manual skills and commerce necessary within modernity, showing deep-

sea fishing as part of a larger system of interconnection, involving production, marketing and international distribution. This dual representation is the product of underlying contradictions within Grierson's
ideological position. On the one hand, he was committed to making
documentary films which communicated a sense of national interconnection, while, on the other hand, he was dedicated to a positive
portrayal of lower-class experience. These two objectives are potentially
incompatible, as the aspiration towards the portrayal of unity sometimes
conflicts with the requirement to portray disadvantaged lower-class
experience affirmatively. This ambivalence results in a number of
tensions, contradictions and uncertainties within *Drifters*.

Drifters was the most important film made by the documentary
movement between 1929 and 1936, and is typical of the themes and
preoccupations of the EMB period. It is essentially concerned with
regional and lower-class communities, and with traditional forms of craft
and skilled labour. The representation of commerce, industry and
technology in *Drifters* is, in contrast, of only secondary concern (Aitken,
1990). This is also the case with the other important film made during the
EMB period, *Industrial Britain* (1931).[6] *Industrial Britain* is atypical of the
films produced by the documentary movement because of the extent of
external intervention in its production. It was filmed by an outsider
(Robert Flaherty), and also suffered from a voice-over commentary which
was imposed upon it by the commercial company which distributed the
film.[7] These extrinsic factors make the film's place within the overall
production of the documentary movement uncertain, and so I do not
propose to examine it closely here.[8]

Nevertheless, and despite these external influences, clear correspon-
dences with *Drifters* and other films made during the EMB period can be
found in *Industrial Britain*. Although the film looks at a number of
industries: the steel, coal-mining, ceramic and glass-making industries,
the focus is entirely on craft skills and techniques, and extensive passages
depicting the operation of a furnace, the making of a ceramic pot and the
hand-blowing of glass into goblets and other containers predominate.

The voice-over commentary accompanying the film constantly extols
these craft skills, but the heroic and jingoistic tone which the commentary adopts is, to a significant extent, an artificial element superimposed over *Industrial Britain's* characteristic EMB period concerns. If
one looks closely at the editing and photography in the film, and
disregards the commentary, one finds the same concern for craft labour
and working-class and regional identities that can be found in *Drifters*.
Both films are pervaded by a form of liberal, humanist sentiment, which
shows workers as individuals possessing integrity, judgement, and a
knowledge drawn from experience. It would be a mistake, therefore, to
believe that these films were guilty of attributing a sort of 'naïve
heroism' to these workers, and it would also be a mistake to believe that
such a naïve level of characterization is to be found in other films made

by the documentary movement. There are no 'heroic' workers in the films of the documentary movement, only workers who deserve respect.

Song of Ceylon

Unlike *Industrial Britain*, Basil Wright's *Song of Ceylon* (1934) was made entirely by the documentary movement, and was not influenced by the sort of external factors which affected the former film. It is, therefore, a more appropriate object of study. The thematic concerns of *Song of Ceylon* are similar to those of *Drifters*, and a consideration of this film helps to illustrate the continuity of these themes within the documentary movement between 1929 and 1934. The original commission for what eventually became *Song of Ceylon* was a request to produce four short films on the tea industry in Ceylon (Rotha, 1973).[9] For various reasons, primarily Grierson's insistence on fully realizing the aesthetic potential of the material that had been filmed, this strategy was abandoned, and a single film emerged, divided into four sections: 'The Buddha', 'The Virgin Island', 'The Voices of Commerce' and 'The Apparel of a God'. The first and last sections are concerned with rural, traditional and religious themes, while the two central sections explore conflicts between the traditional and the modern. The overall focus of the film is on traditional culture, and this is reinforced by the use of a voice-over narration taken from a seventeenth-century traveller's account of the island. The spirit of the film is accurately captured by Graham Greene:

> The last reel, 'The Apparel of a God', returns by way of the gaudy gilded dancers in their devils masks to the huge images on the mountain, to a solitary peasant laying his offerings at Buddha's feet, and closes again with the huge revolving leaves, so that all we have seen of devotion and dance and the bird's flight and the gentle communal life of harvest seems something sealed away from us between the fans of foliage. We are left outside with the bills of lading and the loudspeakers. (Greene, 1934; quoted in Rotha, 1973: 125–6)

Just as *Drifters* elevates the communal world of traditional labour over the commodified world of the market, *Song of Ceylon* elevates traditional culture, with its organic beliefs and values, above the commercial infrastructure of dockyards and warehouses. Traditional themes structure both films, and the persistence of these preoccupations indicates the presence of a dominant paradigm within the documentary film movement. From 1932 onwards, however, that paradigm increasingly came into conflict with the needs of sponsors who required representations of more modern practices, processes and procedures.

The GPO Film Unit, 1934–39

In 1934, following the abolition of the EMB, Grierson and his film-makers took up new appointments as public relations film-makers for the Post Office. The EMB had always had a tenuous existence, and its end came in July 1930, when the May Committee, which had been appointed in order to draw up a programme of national public expenditure cuts, recommended its abolition on the grounds that its continuation was 'unjustified in the existing financial circumstances'.[10] The EMB survived abolition in 1930 because of the political turmoil that broke out around the collapse of the Labour government that year, but it eventually succumbed to the growing consensus that it was an anachronistic institution with little contemporary relevance.

Arguments that the EMB Film Unit was equally anachronistic also began to gain ground after 1930. A Treasury Committee, established in order to scrutinize film-making at the EMB, advised against, arguing that government film production was a 'difficult and speculative enterprise, best left to commercial companies'.[11] When the Film Unit moved to the GPO in 1934, the Treasury sanctioned the transfer for a period of six months only, and this context of institutional and governmental resistance to the establishment of the documentary film movement as a state-funded entity continued throughout the 1930s (Swann, 1989).

Most of the films produced at the GPO between 1934 and 1939 were short two-reel films dealing with aspects of the Post Office and its communication systems. *Cable Ship* (Legg, 1933) dealt with the repair and maintenance of submarine telephone cables. *Weather Forecast* (Spice, 1934) concerned the collection and dissemination of weather information. *Six-Thirty Collection* Anstey, Watt, 1934) dealt with the collection, sorting and dispatch of mail at a major London sorting office. *Under the City* (Elton and Shaw, 1934) dealt with the maintenance of telephone cables, and *Droitwich* (Watt, 1934) with the erection of radio station masts (Rotha, 1973). *We Live in Two Worlds* (Cavalcanti, 1937), *Line to Tschierva Hut* (Cavalcanti, 1937) and *Four Barriers* (Cavalcanti, 1937) all concerned aspects of national and international communications systems, and the most well-known film of the period, *Night Mail* (Wright, Watt and others, 1936), concerned the Royal Mail train delivery service.

In these films, the shift from representations of the regional, the rural and the traditional to representations of the modern and the metropolitan becomes more marked. The shift is particularly apparent in important films like *Night Mail* and *BBC Voice of Britain*, but lesser films, such as *Under the City* and *Droitwich* also indicate an increasing turn away from the underlying concerns of *Drifters*, *Industrial Britain* and *Song of Ceylon*. Cavalcanti's three films also introduce an international dimension around issues of international communications technology which is quite different from the representations of national trade-based technologies in the earlier EMB films.

The documentary movement also made films from outside bodies during the GPO period, and this enabled it to continue both its representation of social issues, and its exploration of film-making techniques. *Granton Trawler* (Grierson, Anstey, Cavalcanti, 1934), although not externally commissioned, was, like the earlier *Drifters*, set in the milieux of deep-sea trawler fishing, and, like *Drifters*, was concerned with the exploration of film technique, most notably in the use of non-synchronized sound. *Fishing on the Banks of Skye* (1934) also dealt with trawler fishing, but employed more conventional editing and narrative strategies.

Two films which represent basic industries, but which also return to the central concerns of films like *Drifters* and *Industrial Britain*, are *Coal Face* (Cavalcanti and others, 1935), and *Spare Time* (Jennings, 1939). *Coal Face* is an account of the coal-mining industry, and the film contains information about the distribution of coal mines and the quantity of coal produced in regional coal fields. However, this technical information is presented in a cursory fashion, and the film dwells in much more detail with working conditions within the mines. One scene, in which two miners break for lunch underground, is presented in a strikingly naturalistic manner. Individual details (dialect, appearance, gestures, small-talk) are focused on, and information concerning the relationship of those details to larger institutional structures is marginalized, just as information about commercial and industrial structures is marginalized in *Drifters*.

Spare Time (Jennings, 1939) is similar to *Coal Face* in that it also concentrates on the cultural background of the workers it portrays, rather than on the world of work and industry. Although the film deals with three industries: textile manufacture, coal mining and steel production, it focuses on the leisure culture that has developed around these industries, and does not examine organizational processes. Both films mark a return to a concern with cultural identity and popular experience that is characteristic of the EMB period.

Another group of films made for a variety of external organizations between 1934 and 1939 examine social and public issues of education, pollution, housing policy, nutrition and unemployment. These include Paul Rotha's *Shipyard* (1934) and *The Face of Britain* (1934–5) for the Central Electricity Board, *Housing Problems* (Elton and Anstey, 1935) for the Gas, Light and Coke Corporation, *Workers and Jobs* (Elton, 1935) for the Ministry of Labour, *Enough to Eat* (Anstey, 1936) for the British Commercial Gas Corporation, *Today We Live* (Rotha, 1937) for the National Council for Social Service and the Land Settlement Association, *Eastern Valley* (Rotha, Alexander, 1937) for a South Wales mining cooperative, *Children at School* (Wright, 1937) and *The Smoke Menace* (Taylor and Grierson, 1937) both for the gas industry, *The Face of Scotland* (Wright, 1938) and *The Children's Story* (Wright, Shaw, 1938) for the Scottish Development Council and *Wealth of a Nation* (Alexander, 1938) for the Scottish Office.

As a group, these films are more sociological and less concerned with formal experimentation than many of the other films made by the documentary movement. In general, they adopt a didactic approach, conveyed through voice-over commentary, and, with the possible exception of *Coal Face*, they are among the most politically outspoken of the films made by the movement, often because they were based on existing social research material.[12] They can therefore be placed midway between films such as *Drifters* and films such as *Droitwich*: although they are concerned with the representation of institutional procedures and structures, they also retain a concern for the representation of lower-class experience.[13]

Night Mail

One of the key documentary films of the period, and one which exemplifies some of the characteristic ways in which the documentary movement represented work and organizations, is *Night Mail* (Wright, Watt, Cavalcanti, Auden and Britten, 1936).[14] *Night Mail* is an account of the operation, over the course of a single day and night, of the Royal Mail train delivery service, showing the various stages and procedures of that operation, and the interactions between employees and managers.

The film begins with a voice-over commentary describing how the mail is collected and made ready for transit. Then, as the train proceeds along the course of its journey, we are shown the various regional railway stations at which it collects and deposits mail. Inside the train, the process of sorting goes on, and we see procedures such as the pick-up of mail bags at high speed. As the train nears Edinburgh, there is a sequence – the best known in the film – in which the poetry of W.H. Auden and the music of Benjamin Britten is superimposed over montage images of the racing train wheels. Finally, an emotive voice-over, narrated by Grierson, emphasizes the importance of the mail to national communication.[15]

In *Night Mail* a tension between the regional and the national can be observed which can also be found in other films made by the documentary film movement. Although the film's narrative architecture is concerned with issues of national communication and distribution, its thematic centre is more concerned with representations of regional accents, forms of behaviour, place names and environments. The railway and the mail service are represented, not as a modern, national communication system, but as constituting a set of institutional practices based within traditional and regional milieux. This elevation of the regional above the national in the film is further reinforced by the depiction of the railway as separate from the metropolitan environment. The only images of the city which appear are those shot in railway stations, and little attempt is made to link the railway and its workers with an external city environment.

A similar tension between the national and institutional, and the regional and cultural, also pervades the representation of work practices in the film. A scene shot within a (supposedly) moving mail carriage shows postal workers sorting mail and provides information on how this process is carried out, but its main function is to emphasize the regional dialects and *badinage* of the sorters. The film concentrates on the interaction between the sorters, and, as in the 'lunch break' scene in *Coal Face*, provides little information on how these interactions are embedded within a more extensive organizational infrastructure. What we see, in effect, is a close, intimate working environment, like the interior of the ship's cabin in *Drifters*.

In contrast to the sensitivity with which the working-class sorters are represented, managers are represented far more distantly. The train supervisor appears inconsequential, as he wanders through the sorting carriages, and the film seems to imply the existence of distinct though subdued tension and distance between sorters and managers. The representation of management in the film is, in general, either equivocal or missing altogether and, in this respect, *Night Mail* is typical of many other films made by the documentary movement.

Night Mail also appears implicitly to emphasize the repetitive and uncomfortable nature of postal work. The collection and delivery of mail takes place at night, in dimly lit regional stations which appear cold and unwelcoming. Although the postal workers appear absorbed in their work, few, if any, scenes show that work as fulfilling, and the relaxed sociability that is evident in other scenes is missing from the shots of agitated activity as mail is loaded and unloaded from the trains. Although *Night Mail* contains no explicit representation of postal work as oppressive or unpleasant, the visual style adopted in some scenes is dark and equivocal, indicating the presence of a critical attitude towards the austere nature of working conditions.

Night Mail also channels representations of mass technology, speed, power and volume of mail away from an account of the industry and organization of postal delivery, and into an imagistic study of the train as a powerful image of technology, in its natural element speeding freely into the countryside, away from the dark, noisy, and unfriendly city stations. The emphasis here, as in *Drifters* and *Industrial Britain*, appears to be on the relationship between technology and natural forces, rather than on that between technology and the commercial. *Night Mail* mobilizes a metaphor of the speeding train, disseminating communication, and uniting the regional and the national, the technological and the rural. However, the imperative of describing mundane postal services fits uneasily with this more abstract project, and the film's ostensible mission is further undermined by its partisan inclination towards one side of the opposition between the regional/rural/cultural and the national/industrial/organizational.

This emphasis on the rural and the regional recurs in many of the films made by the documentary movement in the late 1930s. *The Horsey Mail* (Jackson, 1938) is set in Winterton, a coastal village in Norfolk. *The Islanders* (Holmes, 1937) is set on Eriksay, Guernsey and Inner Farn islands. *Spare Time* (Cavalcanti, Jennings, 1939) is set in Wales, the Midlands and Lancashire. *Granton Trawler* (Grierson and others, 1934), *The Saving of Bill Blewitt* (Cavalcanti, Watt, 1937) and *North Sea* (Cavalcanti,

Watt, 1938) are all set in Scottish fishing communities. *A Midsummer Day's Work* (1939, no cited director) is set in Amersham.

Where films are set in cities they tend to concentrate on the representation of working-class people, as in *Job in a Million* (Spice, 1937) about the training of a young Post Office messenger boy; *Mony a Pickle* (Cavalcanti, 1938) about a young couple saving up to buy a house; and *Nine for Six* (no credits, 1939) about the Post Office telegraphy service. Films set in the city which do not concentrate on working-class subject matter are relatively rare. They include *The Fairy of the Phone* (Cavalcanti, Wright, Coldstream, 1936), a comedy with musical sequences about the telephone directory; *N or NW* (Cavalcanti, Lye, 1937), a comedy – set in Islington – about the need to use correct postal codes, *Roadways* (Cavalcanti, Legg, Coldstream, 1937) and *The City* (Cavalcanti, Elton, 1939) about road transport and road congestion, respectively. These last two films merit particular attention here because of the ways in which they represent organizations and labour within the city.

Roadways

Roadways (Cavalcanti, Legg, 1937) is almost unique among the films made by the documentary movement in that it charts the growth of a commercial profession: that of road haulage and carriage.[16] The film begins with an introduction covering the growth of commercial road traffic. This is followed by shots of motorway service stations, new link roads, and the service sector industries that have developed alongside them. After this section, with its emphasis on technological and commercial development, the film changes direction to focus on the social benefits brought by the car, particularly its role in enabling people to travel outside the cities, and into the country. Finally, towards the end of this opening sequence, a brief historical account of the growth of road transport is given, in which we are told how the industry grew rapidly after the end of the First World War, when groups of demobilized servicemen combined in order to operate as lorry and coach operators.

These opening sections of the film are ambitious, covering the historical development of the commercial road transport industry, the sociological and cultural impact of the motor car, and the building of new roads and services to meet the needs of commercial and private traffic. What is particularly interesting is that the development of the new road transport industry is explained by alluding to the creation of a skilled workforce, trained in operating and maintaining motor vehicles during the First World War. This location of the origins of the industry in the social dislocation of demobilization is curiously rendered: the war is presented almost as a source of renewal and development.[17]

Up to this point in the film the growth of the road network and the new commercial carriage and haulage industries are represented as positive developments. However, after explaining the origins of the industry in post-war demobilization, the tone of the film becomes more negative as we are shown how the growth of monopoly and the expansion of coach and lorry fleets is putting the driver cooperatives created by the war out of work. What was brought precariously into being by war and demobilization is now jeopardized by big business and, although the film does not explicitly make the point, it would seem that those who became self-employed drivers, a transient, partly itinerant workforce, were a group particularly prone, for one reason or another, to dislocation through economic and social change.[18]

The tone of *Roadways* becomes even more pessimistic when the dangers of over-competition and declining safety and environmental standards within the industry are considered. A dramatized reconstruction shows a driver falling asleep at the wheel, then causing an accident; while lorry transport is shown lowering the quality of life for those living in congested streets. The mood of the film has now changed considerably from its initial discourse, which unambiguously promoted the benefits of road transport.

Roadways then goes on to explain how this context of accelerating deterioration was partly resolved by the implementation of government legislation to raise standards and reduce environmental damage. We are told that the 'era of control has begun'. There then follows a clear endorsement of the need for government regulation. The counter-argument, that government should not intervene in the affairs of a private industry such as road transport, does not appear. Nevertheless, the film finally concludes on a pessimistic note concerning the ability of government regulation to force the industry to act in a socially responsible manner: 'We hold our British roads in trust for the future, what will the future inherit from us?'

In *Roadways*, a distinction is made between the public infrastructure of roads and the private commercial exploitation of those roads by a potentially socially irresponsible industry. The new road-building schemes are, throughout, seen as progressive embodiments of modernity, epitomized by that symbol of motorized modernity – the roundabout. The new haulage industries, on the other hand, are seen as pre-modern, untrustworthy and reckless. However, a clear opposition is established between the private companies which ignore safety standards, and the drivers whom those companies employ. *Roadways* does not suggest that individual drivers are to blame – only the private companies that employ them and force them to disregard public regulations.

A clear opposition between public regulation and private commercial enterprise is suggested in *Roadways*, and, although the film does not call for the nationalization of the road freight industry (that would have been far too controversial), it does emphasize the superiority of publicly regulated road transport. One scene in the film illustrates this by showing how thoroughly Post Office drivers are trained. We are shown a young trainee driver receiving driving instructions from an older driver.

The instruction is given in a kind, careful and paternal manner, and this is clearly linked to a more general characterization of the Post Office as a conscientious and socially responsible institution.

Roadways also exhibits that typical preoccupation of the documentary film movement, a preoccupation that runs from *Drifters* (1929) to *Listen to Britain* (1941), and which finds its expression in scenes of intimate, lower-class social interaction. In *Roadways* we are shown scenes set in a motorway transport café, where drivers relax and discuss the problems of the day. Regional accents prevail in an atmosphere characterized by friendliness and accessibility. One driver leaves the café area to go upstairs to the dormitory. The room is spartan, with a number of beds laid out close to each other, some of them already occupied. As the driver prepares for bed, he wakes up another, but there is no tension between them, only an understanding of each other's situation. The shared understanding of a requirement to cope with the rigours of work is shown to surmount the inevitable tensions generated by the austere and demanding conditions associated with that work.

The function of this scene is to reinforce one of the underlying ideologies of *Roadways*: that public regulation and management are required, not only in order to improve social conditions in general, but also, and perhaps most importantly, to improve the working conditions of this transient and overburdened workforce. This sequence returns us in spirit to the curiously rendered beginning of the film, when we learnt how demobilized men were reluctantly precipitated into an unpredictable and precarious industry. We now see these men in close up and this adds (literally) 'flesh' to the film's reformist imperatives, which otherwise could only be delivered at an abstract, didactic level.

Roadways clearly displays its message that public regulation and government intervention are necessary in order to manage the excesses of private enterprise, and that the Post Office, as a public organization, has an important social role to play. Such an overt and, in terms of private industry, antagonistic statement must have been problematic for the Post Office, then under criticism from the private sector for its monopoly over the British postal system. There were also many within the Post Office who resented the liberal image projected by the documentary movement, and who campaigned against the movement. These civil servants were uncomfortable with films such as *Roadways*, films that were supposed to advertise Post Office services, and not make general political claims about the social irresponsibility of private industry and the intrinsic superiority of the public sector.[19]

However, there were also others within the Post Office who defended the movement: public relations men who had joined the Post Office from the EMB, the BBC and other public service organizations, and who agreed with Grierson that the Post Office had an important social role to fill.[20] One can see a film such as *Roadways* as emerging rather audaciously from this, admittedly tenuous but committed context of support.

Job in a Million

Another film which covers issues of institutional occupation in some
detail is Evelyn Spice's *Job in a Million* (Spice, 1937), a film about the
training of a young GPO messenger boy.[21] The film portrays the progress of the boy from the time that he is taken on as a trainee, through
his first experiences of work, to the point where he successfully
completes the examination for employment within the Post Office.[22]

Like *Roadways*, *Job in a Million* makes the point that the status of the
Post Office as a nationalized institution makes it superior to organizations within the private sector; and, as in *Roadways*, *Job in a Million*
also emphasizes the Post Office's commitment to the social welfare of its
employees. This position is evident from the very beginning of the film,
when the voice-over commentary provides information on the Post
Office's role in addressing the problems faced by young school leavers.
The commentary argues that a distinction should be made between
'dead-end jobs' and the pensioned employment available within the Post
Office, and also claims that the Post Office is actively seeking to recruit in
underprivileged sections of the community.

Job in a Million also emphasizes relationships between the Post Office,
municipal authorities and vocational guidance organizations. A benevolent social coalition is depicted, in which social workers, local authorities
and nationalized institutions like the Post Office work together to
improve the condition of the underprivileged young. The young Post
Office trainee is represented as nurtured by a supportive network which
leads, eventually, to secure, pensioned employment. This supportive
network is portrayed very positively in *Job in a Million*, but its paternalistic, middle-class character is also evident in the attitudes adopted by
social workers and employers towards the young, working-class, aspir-
ant trainees. Here, in *Job in a Million*, as in so many other films made by
the documentary movement, the sheer magnitude of the class divide in
1930s England is revealed in considerable, if unintentional, detail.

Job in a Million also displays a concern with rational and scientific
planning which was widespread among reformers in the 1930s. The
reorientation of political liberalism after 1931 led to the emergence of a
number of groups, such as the Next Ten Years Group and Political and
Economic Planning, which advocated the adoption of long-term social-
planning strategies (Aitken, 1990). These ideas also had a strong
influence on the documentary film movement, and films such as *Housing
Problems*, *Roadways*, *The City* and *Job in a Million* all exhibit a belief in the
virtues and necessity of 'planning'.

The concern with planning appears at a number of points in *Job in a
Million*, and one of the most interesting of these concerns the psychological testing of school children. The commentary discusses the problems involved in ensuring that children find appropriate jobs, and claims
that 'vocational selection' at an early age is the answer. 'Psychologists

believe that children should be specially selected to fill the needs of modern industry . . . [but] . . . vocational selection of children in this country is still at an experimental stage.'

This proposition, with its connotations of intensive streaming, and the concomitant notion that children should be 'selected' in order to fill the needs of industry, rather than receive an education that would fulfil their overall potential, is not questioned in *Job in a Million*. The lack of a critical stance on this issue within the film can be viewed as symptomatic of the occasional tendency of the documentary movement to associate itself with the priorities of bureaucrats and 'uplifters' (rather than the interests of working-class people) and of the widespread, and often naïve, belief that planning would solve social problems.[23]

The Post Office's role as an equitable and unprejudiced recruiter is strongly emphasized in *Job in a Million*. Two boys, both studying to pass their Post Office entrance examinations, are seen in their own home environments. The first boy, from a middle-class background, lies reading on a pleasant, spacious lawn, while the second boy, from a working-class background, perches precariously next to a rubbish bin, book in hand, in a squalid stairwell. The voice-over commentary accompanying these sequences states that, while some of the Post Office's aspiring trainees are more privileged than others, boys from under-privileged backgrounds have a good chance of obtaining employment with the Post Office: 'Look here, we take boys in from all types of homes. For some boys it is not so easy to study at home, others are more fortunate, but in the Post Office each boy is given an equal chance.' Although *Job in a Million* makes a distinction between two different environments here, it does not specify that distinction in terms of class and social position. However, we can assume that entry into the Post Office at this level was largely confined to boys from working-class and lower middle-class backgrounds, and that it is boys from these back-grounds who are represented in the film.

Job in a Million also emphasizes the quality of training within the Post Office. This 'training' includes job experience and study, but it also includes social training. We are shown the wide range of leisure facilities available at the Post Office, including physical activities such as boxing, swimming and cricket, and more erudite activities such as singing and playing chess. Two main themes emerge here. The first concerns the training of boys to become appropriate adults through a socialization process that includes cultural, as well as occupational, experience. The second concerns representations of physical culture. These scenes, which are similar to those found in fascist and communist films of the period, emphasize the healthy pursuit of collective outdoor activity as an essential part of the cultural bonding experience.[24]

A dialectic between hierarchy and equality also appears to structure *Job in a Million*. The Post Office is frequently represented in the film as an institution where, regardless of background, every individual has the opportunity to develop. However, this egalitarian discourse tends to be carried by the voice-over commentary, while the visual documentary footage and the language used by individuals in the film convey a discourse that is far from egalitarian. Hierarchical relations appear frequently in *Job in a Million*, indicating that the Post Office is a distinctly class-differentiated institution, where authority relations prevail and are enforced.

One scene in *Job in a Million* that illustrates the often simultaneous presence of these two discourses of hierarchy and egalitarianism is the final scene, set in an assembly hall, in which those boys who have successfully passed their examinations wait to receive their certificates. While the voice-over stresses the open and liberal ethos of the Post Office, the boys sit stiffly and regimented, strictly conforming to the rules of the institutional ceremony. There are similarities here with the rows of regimented clerks in *The City*, and the total conformity which the boys express towards their institutional positioning is striking.

Another opposition within *Job in a Million* which appears in the scene mentioned above is that between those whose primary concern is to 'care' for the young recruits and those whose role is to enforce discipline and authority. During the awards ceremony we are shown images of those carers who have successfully brought their charges through, and the film appears to establish them, and the values that they hold and practise, as more important than those individuals who are associated with the enforcement of hierarchy and authority.

If *Job in a Million* mobilizes discourses of welfare and authority, it appears that sometimes the discourse of welfare is the dominant one and sometimes it is the discourse of authority. However, both discourses become fully integrated in the final sequence of the film, in which elegiac metaphors of organic unity are drawn upon to characterize the Post Office. We are told that each boy is a crucial element in the organization, and that each is personally responsible for the overall success of the Post Office. 'On your faithful performance of a public service will depend the future greatness of the Post Office. The Post Office touches all branches of life. . . .' This grand oratory, with its vocabulary of 'faithful per-formance', the 'greatness' of the Post Office and the relation of the Post Office to 'all branches of life', evokes an image of the corporation as a unified organic entity which provides its employees with a vital role within the system, and places public service before all else. The often incompatible discourses of welfare, equality, hierarchy and authority found in *Job in a Million* become fused here into a metaphor of the Post Office as a living system that binds social life together.

The City

The City (Cavalcanti, Elton, 1939) looks at the difficulties caused by traffic congestion in London.[25] Its narrative structure is complex and comprehensive, covering the history and growth of London, the problems of the inner cities, and the inconveniences experienced by suburban commuters. *The City* also employs the metaphor of 'traffic' in order to conduct an impressionistic study of the ways in which social and cultural behaviour are fashioned by the car.

The City begins with a voice-over commentary in local idiom which invokes a symbolism of community and integration through a characterization of London as the commentator's 'local village'. The film then examines the issue of commuting through a depiction of scenes from suburban commuter life, and through a discursive account of the growth of suburbia. After this we are shown examples of inner-city deprivation, and, finally, the affluence and privilege of the Royal Borough of Westminster. These radically different social environments are presented as constituting a diverse but interconnected society containing areas of disadvantage. Although social inequality is not explicitly represented as an issue, but rather as a 'fact of life', the film does, indirectly, stress the need to respond positively in order to help the disadvantaged working classes in the inner city.

This opening section is followed by two parallel sequences depicting work routines in organizations associated with different social class positions. In the first sequence, we are shown a number of scenes portraying the lower middle-class white-collar workforce which was expanding rapidly during the 1930s. In a large office building in the city, young female clerks are shown sitting in rows, processing commercial and official correspondence. The overall impression is of an over-regulated environment in which work is repetitive and monotonous. However, this impression is contradicted by the appearance and disposition of the clerks, who appear smart, poised and assured. *The City*'s representation of this metropolitan clerical labour is, therefore, ambivalent – it is depicted as both oppressive and, in some way, fulfilling.

This sequence is followed by its counterpart, a scene shot in the sorting room of a major London post office. Here, there is a similar emphasis on large numbers working within an extensive open space, and dealing with repetitive work. Like the lower middle-class female clerical workers, these male working-class postal workers seem self-possessed and, although they do not display the composed assurance of the clerical workers, they exhibit an energetic vigour which indicates that their working environment is less constrained. There is less ambiguity, and a more positive representation of this type of organizational work in *The City* than is the case in earlier representations of clerical work, and this partisan bias towards manual as opposed to administrative or managerial work is also characteristic of the documentary movement as a whole.

These two sequences suggest that the repetitive clerical work generated within a modern society affects workers irrespective of divisions of social class. However, there is a marked difference between these two sequences and the earlier ones which contrasted the different social environments of the suburbs, inner cities and affluent boroughs. In these earlier sequences the problems of inner-city deprivation are depicted as more substantial than those associated with suburban commuting; while, in the latter two sequences, the constraints upon working-class labourers are depicted as *less* substantial than those affecting lower middle or middle-class workers.

The only manifestation of discontent over work in *The City* occurs when a secretary at the Ministry of Defence directs a resentful glance at the administrator who has re-filled her in-tray. So, while the film makes abstract points about the need to advantage the working class, the only substantial (even though limited) example of characterization within these sequences is associated with a lower middle-class, as opposed to working-class, workforce. Narrative processes of characterization and identification are centred on the middle rather than the working class here. These narrative processes do, admittedly, signify at an ironic, as well as at an empathetic, level: we are encouraged to feel superior to, as well as to identify with, the secretary. The issue of gender also arises here: it is women, rather than men, who appear fractious and discontented. Nevertheless, despite the presence of these implicitly ironic elements, it is clear that, when faced with the possibility of centring characterization in the working class, *The City* is unable to do so.

Conclusion

A number of characteristic themes involving the representation of occupations in the films of the documentary movement emerge from this study. The earlier films are primarily concerned with regional and traditional themes, while issues relating to a national context are covered superficially and schematically. These films also emphasize the importance of manual and craft skills, and find more merit in these areas than in organizational or administrative activity. A considerable amount of consideration is given to descriptions of techniques and processes of work in these films, while administrative routines and institutional structures are depicted indifferently and ambivalently. Commerce and, by implication, capitalism are also regarded ambivalently, sometimes as an instrumental area operating outside fields of moral discourse, and sometimes as a threat to traditional practices. This opposition between modernity and tradition also leads to a lack of representation of the city, and of metropolitan culture, in the films.

The romantic evocation of tradition and continuity in these films also influences their depiction of nature. Nature is represented as an entity against which traditional communities pit themselves and acquire knowledge of their own condition, rather than as a utilitarian resource for modern corporations. This 'pantheistic' theme was influenced by a number of factors, including Grierson's preoccupation with the Scottish landscape, his appropriation of classical German philosophy (Ellis, 1968,

1973; Aitken, 1989, 1990) and the influence of Soviet films such as Alexander Dovshenko's *Earth* (1930) and Victor Turin's *Turksib* (1929).[26]

As the documentary film movement developed during the 1930s a shift in direction becomes apparent in the films being made, as films dealing with technical, metropolitan and commercial subjects become more prevalent. Nevertheless, despite this shift in emphasis, the central concern of the later films remained the same as the earlier ones. Given this, one can argue that the films of the documentary movement as a whole must be seen as more concerned with the study of popular cultural experience than with the development of a public relations film genre that would promote the objectives of institutional organizations. Of course, this study of popular culture was severely constrained by the limitations conferred by sponsorship, but, nevertheless, it constantly re-emerges as a recurrent theme in the films produced by the movement between 1929 and 1939.

A number of other characteristic themes can be identified within this body of films, from *Drifters* in 1929 to *Spare Time* in 1939. There is an emphasis on the value of large public organizations, as opposed to unregulated competitive business. There is a concern for promoting social reform, and an associated concern for representing lower-class experience, which surfaces in nearly all the films. There is a concern with rational and scientific planning, and the social benefits such planning brings. Oppositions between authority and equality, discipline and freedom, and work and leisure can also be identified as characteristic themes within these films.

The films of the documentary movement contain a complex, often contradictory, body of representations, and this degree of contradiction is also detectable in the films' depiction of occupational labour. Work is depicted sometimes positively, as in the case of the traditional knowledge possessed by intimate working groups, and sometimes more ambivalently, as in the case of the repetitive and over-regulated labour endured by administrative and clerical workers. Similarly, occupational organizations are depicted sometimes negatively, as operating outside the sphere of public interest and contributing towards the degradation of craft skills, and sometimes as valuable in their size, comprehensiveness and public role: 'the Post Office touches all branches of life.' Although these oppositions appear frequently in the films, they do not, in the end, add up to a consistent or systematic ideology. This, however, is hardly surprising, given the contradictions within Grierson's ideology, and the difficult context of sponsorship within which the documentary film movement had to work.

Notes

1 *Britain Prepared* (1915) was the first major film produced. This was followed in 1916–17 by the production of 26 short films, and five longer films, the most important of which

was *The Battle of the Somme* (1916). The period is covered in Aitken (1990), and more extensively in Low (1948), Taylor and Saunders (1982) and Reeves (1986).

2 A genre of publicity and promotional films also emerged from this context. Most of these films were made by Labour and Liberal local authorities, although some government departments and charitable associations also produced some. They include the National Association for the Prevention of Tuberculosis's *Air and Sun* (1924), Bermondsey Council's *The Ivory Castle* (1926) on nutrition, the Ministry of Agriculture and Fisheries' *The Rat Menace* (1925) and the London County Council's *Housing Bonds* (1926).

3 Grierson was awarded a Laura Spellman Rockefeller Foundation Fellowship to undertake social research in the United States in 1924. His task was to study 'immigration and its effects upon the social problems of the United States' (see Hardy, 1979; Aitken, 1990).

4 Public corporations established after the First World War were the Forestry Commission (1919), Imperial Airways (1924), the General Electricity Board (1926) and the British Broadcasting Corporation (1926).

5 *Drifters* (1929): directed by John Grierson; photography by John Grierson and Basil Emmott; edited by John Grierson and Margaret Taylor; produced by New Era Films for the EMB; distributed by Associated British Film Distributors. First exhibited at the thirty-third meeting of the Film Society at the Tivoli Palace on the Strand on 10 November 1929, sharing the bill with Sergei Eisenstein's *Battleship Potemkin* (1925). First commercial screening at the Stoll Picture House, London, on 9 December 1929.

6 *Industrial Britain* (1931): direction and photography by Robert Flaherty; production and editing by John Grierson; editing by Edgar Anstey; distributed by Gaumont British Distributors; commentary by Donald Calthorp.

7 Gaumont British Distributors distributed six EMB films during 1933: *Industrial Britain, The Country Comes to Town, O'er Hill and Dale, Upstream, The Shadow on the Mountain* and *King Log*.

8 Others do not take this view of *Industrial Britain*. For example, Brian Winston (1995) argues that the film is central, and indicative of the documentary movement in general. I disagree. While the film does contain many of the characteristic themes of the documentary movement, its production circumstances rule it out from consideration as a central, or typical, documentary movement film.

9 *Song of Ceylon* (1934): directed by Basil Wright; produced by John Grierson and Alberto Cavalcanti; photography by Basil Wright and John Taylor; music and sound track by Walter Leigh; narration by Lionel Wendt. Winner of the Prix du Gouvernement Belge at the Brussels Film Festival of 1935.

10 Report from the Committee on National Expenditure (May Committee), July 1930 (British Library, Official Publications Library, Session 1930–1931, Vol. 16, p. 1, Cmd 3920, Treasury). The Committee was appointed on 17 March 1930; its terms of reference: 'to make recommendations for effecting forthwith all practicable and legitimate reductions in the national expenditure'. The case of the EMB is dealt with on p. 132.

11 First and Second Reports from the Select Committee on Estimates, April and July 1928 (British Library, Official Publications Library, Reports Committee 2, VI, 181).

12 *Enough to Eat* was based on Sir John Boyd Orr's report entitled *Homes, Food and Income*, while *The Smoke Menace* drew on the study of pollution by Professor J.P.S. Haldane, and *The Face of Britain* drew on J.B. Priestley's social study of England, *English Journey* (1934).

13 These films are among the least well-known films made by the documentary movement. Because they were largely made outside the EMB and GPO, they have not been included on the Post Office's collection of video cassettes: *The GPO Film Unit Presents: Volumes 1–7*. However, these films are extremely interesting, and deserve greater attention than they have received to date.

14 *Night Mail* (1936): directed by Harry Watt; edited by Basil Wright and Albert Cavalcanti; produced by John Grierson, with contributions from Stuart Legg, W.H. Auden (poetry) and Benjamin Britten (music); distributed by Associated British Film Producers.

15 In *Documentary Diary*, Paul Rotha (1973) is critical of Grierson's intervention here, describing his narration as 'sob-throated' and 'sentimental'.

16 *Roadways* (1937, 14.5 mins): directed by Stuart Legg and William Coldstream; produced by Alberto Cavalcanti; edited by R. Stocks; assistant director Ralph Elton; music by E.H. Meyer; photography by J. Jones and H. Fowle.

17 No mention is made of the growth and development of this profession in any of the general histories of the period, such as Mowat (1955), Taylor (1965), Branson and Heinemann (1973) and Stevenson (1984). A social study of it might well be rewarding, however, illustrating how these groups of workers adapted to the social dislocations of the time by making use of new technologies, working routines, and means of communication.

18 Of course, the First World War has often been portrayed in terms of renewal and development by artists and historians. One thinks immediately of Arthur Marwick's two historical studies, *The Deluge: British Society and the First World War* (1965) and *Britain in the Century of Total War: War, Peace and Social Change, 1900–1967* (1968). Both books look at the way in which war created the conditions for social change and development. However, these works, and others which examine the impact of the war, also comment on the negative and destructive impact of the war. There is no sense of this in *Roadways*.

19 When Stephen Tallents left his post as public relations adviser in 1935 in order to take up a position at the BBC, the Film Unit found itself subject to tighter administrative control. Although Tallents's successor, Ernest Crutchley, was generally supportive of the Film Unit, he also laid down procedures for making it conform more closely to standard civil service practices. Crutchley, and others in the Post Office, felt that the film-makers should restrict themselves more to making films publicizing Post Office services, rather than films tackling general social and cultural themes. It was also feared that the Film Unit's activities might turn the Treasury, the Conservative Party and the commercial film trade against the Post Office. The Post Office had a rather poor image at the time, and some officials were concerned that the wrong type of publicity, in films that could be deemed 'leftist', might make the situation worse.

20 The chief supporter was Sir Stephen Tallents, but others included William Crawford, who had worked with Tallents at the EMB, and, to a lesser extent, Ernest Crutchley, Tallents's successor. In addition, the Post Office Film Unit Committee and Public Relations Committee were, in general, supportive of Grierson and the film-makers, repeatedly defending the Film Unit against Treasury attempts to limit the scope of its operations. Despite this level of support, however, pressure from outside the Post Office continued to be applied on the Film Unit throughout the period.

21 *Job in a Million* (1937, 11.5 mins): directed by Evelyn Spice; produced by Albert Cavalcanti; edited by Norman McLaren; music by Brian Easton. Filmed in London.

22 One interesting aspect of the boy's background is that he appears to come from a single-parent family. No information is given to explain the absence of a father, and it is unclear how audiences at the time would have interpreted this. Nor do we receive any information concerning the economic circumstances of the family, or whether the mother was in receipt of benefits. This ambivalence is typical of the film, which is very vague about the social circumstances of the individuals it portrays.

23 This naïve attitude to the benefits of planning appears strikingly in *Housing Problems*, where new council estates are presented as the solution to the problem of poor housing. The various difficulties associated with the building of these estates, such as the displacement and relocation of inner-city communities away from the working environment, is not dealt with. Above all, viewers today are aware that these same council estates are now perceived as deeply problematic. The estate featured most prominently in *Housing Problems*, the Quarry Bank Estate in Leeds, no longer exists.

24 These types of representations can be found in films of the Nazi period, such as Leni Riefenstahl's *Olympia* (1936), but they can also be found in Dudow and Brecht's *Khule Wampe* (1932), which features extensive footage of Communist Party sporting events.

25 *The City* (1939, 19.5 mins): directed by Ralph Elton; produced by Alberto Cavalcanti;

edited by R.C. McNaughton and J. Chambers; photography by H. Fowle; filmed in London. Features a talk by Sir Charles Bressey, urban planner, on the history and growth of London.

26 Apart from Eisenstein's *Battleship Potemkin* (1925), the three Russian films that had the biggest impact on Grierson were *Turksib* (Victor Turin, 1929), *Storm over Asia* (Vsevolod Pudovkin, 1928) and *Earth* (Alexander Dovshenko, 1930). Grierson (1930) described *Earth* as 'one of the greatest films ever made', and *Turksib* as possessing 'astonishingly skilful editing . . . [and] . . . sheer brilliance of technique'.

References

Aitken, I. (1989) 'John Grierson, idealism and the inter-war period', *Historical Journal of Film, Radio and Television*, 9 (3): 247–58.

Aitken, I. (1990) *Film and Reform: John Grierson and the Documentary Film Movement*. London: Routledge.

Aldcroft, D.H. (1983) *The British Economy between the Wars*. Oxford: Philip Allen.

Amery, L. (1953) *My Political Life*. London: Hutchinson.

Branson, N. and Heinemann, M. (1973) *Britain in the 1930s*. London: Panther.

Crawford, W.S. (1931) *How to Succeed in Advertising*. London: World's Press News.

Ellis, J. (1968) 'The young Grierson in America', *Cinema Journal*, 17: 28–38.

Ellis, J. (1973) 'Grierson at university', *Cinema Journal*, 41: 28–38.

Grierson, J. (1930) 'Cinema', *Artwork*, Winter.

Grierson, J. (1933) 'Flaherty, naturalism and the problem of the English cinema', *Artwork*, Autumn.

Hardy, F. (1979) *John Grierson: a Documentary Biography*. London: Faber and Faber.

Lee, J.M. (1972) 'The dissolution of the EMB', *Journal of Imperial and Commonwealth History*, 1 (1): 49–59.

Low, R. (1948) *The History of the British Film, 1914–1918*. London: Allen and Unwin.

Marwick, A. (1965) *The Deluge: British Society and the First World War*. Oxford: Bodley Head.

Marwick, A. (1968) *Britain in the Century of Total War: War, Peace and Social Change, 1900–1967*. Oxford: Bodley Head.

Mowat, C.L. (1955) *Britain between the Wars*. London: Methuen.

Pollard, S. (1962) *The Development of the British Economy*. London: Edward Arnold.

Priestley, J.B. (1934) *English Journey*. London: Heinemann.

Reeves, N. (1986) *Official British Film Propaganda during the First World War*. London: Croom Helm.

Rotha, P. (1973) *Documentary Diary: An Informal History of the British Documentary Film, 1928–1939*. New York: Hill and Wang.

Stevenson, J. (1984) *British Society 1914–1945*. London: Penguin.

Swann, P. (1989) *The British Documentary Film Movement, 1926–1946*. Cambridge: Cambridge University Press.

Taylor, A.J.P. (1965) *English History 1914–1945*. London and Oxford: Clarendon.

Taylor, Philip and Saunders, Martin (1982) *British Propaganda during World War One*. London: Macmillan.

Winston, B. (1995) *Reclaiming the Real*. London: British Film Institute.

2

Representing Reality: *Cinéma Vérité*

John Hassard

The important film makers of the future will be amateurs.
Attributed to Robert Flaherty, c. 1925, by Jean Rouch (1992)

This chapter examines the history of the ethnographic documentary, and notably how, in the British tradition, it has been used to represent the 'real world' of work and institutions. The dynamic of this history is one of attempts to gain ever more direct and unmediated images of people and events. We are talking about 'fly-on-the-wall' documentaries, or that style of film-making commonly referred to as *cinéma vérité* – film truth.

The chapter adopts the following structure. The first section forms an introduction to the *cinéma vérité* approach and prepares the way for a historical review of ethnographic studies of work and institutions in the following section. This review reveals how such ethnographies have been a central concern of *cinéma vérité* film-making, especially in Britain. Studies developed under five main styles – the world-of-labour film, the 'free cinema' movement, the modern television documentary, the hyper-realist documentary and video diaries – and each style is explored. This review is complemented with a sociological discussion of the representational nature of *cinéma vérité* in which the extent to which the genre achieves its claim to offer privileged access to everyday 'reality' is examined. The relationship between the ethnographic documentary and its textual perspective is found to be a specific one: our experience of reality is therefore one of being 'represented' rather than 'reproduced'.

Film and Truth: a Partial History

I hate the word 'documentary', it smells of dust and boredom. I think 'Realist' films much the best.
Alberto Cavalcanti, quoted in Sussex (1976)

In *The Cinema and Social Science*, de Heusch (1962: 13) writes, 'When Lumière definitely established a technique and sent his cameramen all over the world, the ethnographic and sociological cinema was born.' Elsewhere, Morin (1956: 14) notes how the precursors of the cinema intended to develop the cinematograph as a 'research' instrument in order to study the 'phenomena of nature'. While the ingenuity of Lumière's techniques made it likely that the cinematograph could,

RELEASED BY CINEGATE. **JUVENILE COURT** DIRECTED BY FREDERICK WISEMAN

Figure 2.1 Juvenile Court, 1973, *NBC*

potentially, become an 'objective' instrument with which to capture social behaviour, Morin (1956: 15–16) notes, however, that it was not long before the 'illusionists' had taken this new type of 'microscope' away from the 'scientists' and transformed it into a 'toy', thereby reviving the 'tradition of the magic lantern and the shadow play'.

It is against this historical development, in which, as Morin suggests, the cinematograph becomes 'snatched away' from science, that we find 'cinema truth' – for Morin, one of the basic aims of early film-making – being *re*introduced into the film-maker's art. Throughout the century, documentary film-makers, in particular, have addressed the problem of how to make their films more 'real' and 'truthful'. The history of documentary film-making has seen a range of styles emerge in this quest. For the most part, these have been subsumed under one generic title: *cinéma vérité*.

What *is* Cinéma Vérité?

According to its proponents, the aim of *cinéma vérité* is simply to present the 'truth'. In *French Cinema since 1946*, Roy Armes (1966), for example, argues that *cinéma vérité* offers a 'rejection of the whole aesthetic in which the art of the cinema is based. An interesting visual style and striking beautiful effects are rejected as a hindrance to the portrayal of the vital truth' (1966: 125).[1]

Over the years, however, critics have pointed to confusion about the basic aims of *cinéma vérité*, and suggested that under its banner all kinds of films have been made, many of which are unrelated to the original philosophy. Debate over the value and purpose of *cinéma vérité* was particularly heated in the early 1960s (notably around the time of the famous 1963 Lyon Conference on *cinéma vérité*, organized by *Radio Télévision Française* and attended by such notables as Jean Rouch, Edgar Morin, Robert Drew, Richard Leacock, Mario Ruspoli, Albert and David Maysles and Michel Brault). While proponents, such as Armes, heralded *cinéma vérité* as the 'true' art of cinema, critics branded it as 'anti-art'. Among the critics, James Lipscombe (1964: 62), for example, argued that the term '*cinéma vérité*' had become used so loosely that most of the films produced in its name 'have absolutely nothing in common except celluloid'. In a similar vein, Charles Ford claimed that *cinéma vérité* was the 'biggest hoax of the century', and that 'nothing is more fabricated, more prepared, more licked into shape, than the so-called improvisation of *cinéma vérité*' (Natta, 1963; quoted in Issari and Paul, 1979: 12). Such diversity of views has made *cinéma vérité* one of the most controversial subjects in film studies, with this controversy enduring to the present day.[2]

The philosophy and method of *cinéma vérité* ostensibly began with Vertov's work on the concept of 'kino-eye' in 1919, but it was during the 1960s that the style became widely adopted and discussed in film-making circles. The term '*cinéma vérité* was first used in a stylistic sense, as a tribute to Vertov's work, to describe *Chronique d'un Été* (1962), a film collaboration between the anthropologist Jean Rouch and the sociologist Edgar Morin.[3] According to Issari and Paul (1979: 6), such was the impact of *Chronique d'un Été* that the term 'spread like wildfire' (Issari and Paul, 1979: 6), one result being a proliferation of definitions in which *cinéma vérité*:

> acquired different names from its founders, practitioners and critics in accordance with their understanding of the style. To Jean Rouch and Edgar Morin it was *cinéma vérité*; Richard Leacock called it 'living camera'; Mario Ruspoli, the Maysles brothers, and Louis Marcorelles were amongst those who favoured 'direct cinema'. William Bleum designated the style as 'mobile camera', but William Jersey selected the term 'realistic cinema'. Italians named it 'film inquiry'. To Armondo Plebe it became 'synchronous cinema'; to Colin Young, 'cinema of common sense'; to Jean Claude Bringuier, 'cinema of behaviour'; to Norman Swallow, 'personal documentary' or 'tele-vérité'. Others dubbed it 'film journalism', 'truth film', 'direct shooting' and 'free cinema'.
> (Issari and Paul, 1979: 7)

Of all the terms coined, however, two have proved the most enduring: *cinéma vérité* and 'direct cinema'. Although they come from largely similar historical roots, and while their associated films have many similarities, their proponents often testify to separate philosophies, the main difference residing in the function of the film-maker. While the practitioner of *cinéma vérité* (in the Rouch and Morin style) deliberately intervenes, hoping that greater 'spontaneity' and 'truth' will be stimulated by the participation of the film-maker in the event filmed, the 'direct' film-maker claims to take an 'objective' stance, merely standing by in the hope that a situation, already tense, will resolve itself in a dramatic crisis (see Barnouw, 1975).[4]

In terms of stylistic influence, it is 'direct cinema' that has become the exemplar for the 'film truth' movement generally. In this style, the film-maker tries above all to avoid 'judgement' and 'subjectivity'. The object is to convey the phenomenology of a social situation; to film people as they live their everyday lives. The philosophy states that the film-maker's role is to reveal the most essential parts of this reality, not to create a new one (Issari and Paul, 1979).[5] The 'direct' film-maker should dispense with those elements of method that serve to distort 'truth'; that is, with the 'professional camouflage' of conventional film-making, such as scripts, scenes, studies, actors and so forth. Films are to be made of 'ordinary' people in 'real' situations, the only acceptable aids being lightweight cameras and portable sound equipment. As the film-maker is only interested in events as they naturally unfold, no direction is permitted. In the more 'pure' forms, there is no plot, no preconceived dialogue, and no questions are either posed or answered. The philosophy states that, in shooting a film, the crew's task should be confined to following subjects and filming their moments of personal drama. Decisions concerning action should rest with the subject: the film-maker merely decides whether or not to film a particular piece of action.[6]

Landmark Contributions

The development of the range of approaches that were subsumed under the general heading of *cinéma vérité* can be followed first, by discussing the ideas and works of two of its founders, Dziga Vertov and Robert Flaherty, and, secondly, by describing how *cinéma vérité* has been shaped in what we will call the French, American and British schools of documentary. Each of these schools offers a distinctive approach to ethnographic film-making and, especially in the British tradition, with regard to work and institutions.[7]

Dziga Vertov and Kino-pravda

It was in the hands of the Russian film-maker Dziga Vertov (1896–1954, real name Denis Arkadievitch Kaufman) that a documentary style based on 'film truth', or *kino-pravda*, was first developed in theory and practice (Petric, 1978). Vertov is associated with what has been termed the 'extremist theory' of the sociological film, the view that the cinema should rid itself, as Sadoul says, 'of everything which has not been taken from life' (1940: 172).[8]

In line with the prevailing philosophy of 'socialist realism' in early Soviet film-making, Vertov argued that *kino-pravda* required the non-participation of the film-maker as a fundamental condition of attaining sociological authenticity.[9] If the movie camera was to be an effective tool in influencing the masses, it was necessary to present 'realistic' images of their everyday lives. Instead of staged sets, real locations would be used, in which peasants played peasants and workers played workers. If film-making was to become a truly proletarian art, Vertov believed its function was to portray the life of the people in all its intense and intimate detail (Lawson, 1964: 73).[10]

Given the technology available to him, however, Vertov was perhaps somewhat over-ambitious in his claims to be providing a *kino-pravda* approach for anything more than short sequences of film. In order to achieve 'truthful' images with cumbersome technology, his early films saw the use of hide-aways and telephoto lenses, as in his famous filming of a family weeping at a grave. Written in the early 1920s, a time when film-making technology was in its infancy, his original ideas on the sociological film reflect prophecy more than practice.[11] Vertov, however, remains the father figure of *cinéma vérité* in that his philosophies reflect the core ideas of the movement.

Robert Flaherty's Nanook of the North

The other founding father of the *cinéma vérité* documentary was the American trapper-prospector Robert Flaherty, who, during 1920–21, spent 15 months making a publicity film in Hudson Bay for the French fur company Revillon, a film screened in 1922 as *Nanook of the North*. In its original version, *Nanook* is a silent 38-minute portrait of the world of the eskimo (in 1925 Flaherty re-edited a slightly longer version with soundtrack; see Flaherty, 1972). The story develops through scenes which alternate between descriptions of the everyday struggle for existence and the tenderness of family life. Through documenting Nanook's interminable wanderings in search of subsistence, Flaherty's subject becomes not just the hero of an ethnographic film, but a symbol of all civilization. The first American film in the *cinéma vérité* style, *Nanook* remains highly acclaimed and widely screened.

The high quality of *Nanook*, however, is often attributed to the large amount of preparatory work undertaken by Flaherty (as also with his masterpiece *Man of Aran*, 1934; see Calder-Marshall, 1963). Contrary to 'purist' forms of direct observation, where subjects receive a minimum of briefing, Flaherty studied Nanook and his family in detail before filming. As de Heusch (1962: 35) notes, 'Flaherty does not follow Nanook about in order to take pictures: he enters into conversation with him, he asks him to cooperate closely in the sociological portrait.'

Because of the elaborate manner in which the scenes are reconstructed, the extent to which *Nanook* represents 'film truth' is obviously questionable. The well-known scene where Nanook and his family wake up in an igloo, for example, is achieved by Flaherty removing the roof in order to have enough space and light to shoot! (Winston, 1979). In Flaherty's hands the documentary becomes 'a work of art imbued with rationality and truth' (de Heusch, 1962: 35–6). *Nanook* is constructed like a fictional film in which the main character acts the part of himself within the framework of a prepared story. The story is conveyed in accordance with the demands of the director.[12]

The French School: Rouch and Morin's Chronique d'un Été

Historians of *cinéma vérité* commonly claim that the development of increasingly unobtrusive film-making technologies brought the notion of the 'cinema eye' closer to reality (see Barnouw, 1975; Issari and Paul, 1979). It is claimed, for example, that a classic example of such technological progress was witnessed in the development of the 16mm camera with portable sound equipment, notably in the work of the French anthropologist turned film-maker, Jean Rouch. Rouch is often considered the founder of ethnographic cinema because he was seen to overcome a number of traditional film-making handicaps simply by using lighter technology. Synonymous with the so-called 'French School' of the documentary film, Rouch is the figure most readily associated with the term *'cinéma vérité'*.

It was as an anthropology student at the Sorbonne that Rouch first proposed the camera as a medium for recording ethnographic data. This was put to the test in his early fieldwork in Africa, when in 1946 he took a 16mm Bell and Howell on expedition to the Niger River to research hippopotamus hunting (*Chasse à Hippopotame*, 1948). During this expedition, Rouch took the unusual step of abandoning his tripod in order to achieve greater freedom in shooting. Although the end result was reams of unstable footage, Rouch had suggested an approach whereby the camera moved directly into the main scenes of action. In so doing, Rouch's work became unique among anthropological films of the time (see Cameron and Shivas, 1963).

Rouch's next film-making innovation came through his experiments with early portable tape recorders. In a series of films made in Africa during the early 1950s, he recorded the sights and *sounds* of native life using a direct-filming approach. The 'authenticity' of these films is attributed to Rouch's ability to record subjects too involved in events or rituals to be affected by the presence of the camera (Cameron and Shivas, 1963). His most successful film in this respect was *Les Maîtres Fous* ('The Manic Priests', 1954), which portrays the failure of detribalized groups in Ghana to adapt to white culture. Rouch's apparent success in recording anthropological data gave rise to the description of him (attributed to Edgar Morin) as a 'diver' film-maker because of his ability to dive-down into 'real' situations (Cameron and Shivas, 1963).

Rouch, however, is best known for a film made in collaboration with Morin and the French-Canadian film-maker Michel Brault on the lives of Parisians, *Chronique d'un Été* (Chronicle of a Summer, 1961). According to Rouch, *Chronique d'un Été* was an attempt to combine Vertov's theory and Flaherty's method (see Armes, 1966). Initially 21 hours long, but later cut to 1 hour 45 minutes, the film begins by showing the reactions of passers-by to the question 'Are you happy?' It continues by interviewing them in detail about, for example, their likes, dislikes, hopes and anxieties. In the final scenes, we find the participants viewing the film in a screening room: the footage describes their reactions to the interview process.

Although technically *Chronique d'un Été* benefits from the development of real-time (rather than post-synchronization) sound recording, it appears to suffer methodologically from the fact that most of its subjects appear uneasy in front of the camera. When questioned, the majority of the subjects appear paralysed or dumbfounded, and fail to say anything. More than any other landmark documentary, *Chronique d'un Été* highlights the issue of whether the camera should be used to record action or to stimulate it. In the hands of Rouch and Morin, the *cinéma vérité* film becomes not so much a recording of what would happen if the camera was not there, as what happens because the camera *is* there. As a result, the style of *Chronique d'un Été* appears to be not so much 'fly on the wall' as 'fly in the soup'!

The American School: Drew Associates' Primary

In contrast, the American tradition, based on the 'direct-cinema' approach, adopts a more Cartesian orientation. The exemplar of this is found in the collaborative work of Robert Drew, Richard Leacock and colleagues (including film-makers Albert Maysles, Donn Pennebaker and Gregory Shuker) – or Drew Associates – and their classic documentary in the 'living-camera' style, *Primary* (1960).

Providing funds to develop sufficiently mobile 16mm equipment, *Time-Life* commissioned the living-camera 'project' for which Drew Associates were to make a news film equivalent of the magazine's well-known news-spreads. To this end, Drew and Leacock negotiated an agreement with Senators John Kennedy and Hubert Humphrey to record their political campaigns in the 1960 Wisconsin primary election. The plan was to follow the candidates and film their activities without 'intruding'. No lighting was to be used; the crew would film only what was in front of them; they would go into situations 'cold'.[13] By employing this method, Drew felt that not only would the 'facts' of a situation be revealed, but also the 'essence' or 'feeling'. The 'living' camera would report the 'emotional' as well as the 'intellectual' truth. 'Internal forces' would be revealed by studying 'external forces' (Leacock, 1992). Like Vertov, Drew Associates presumed that the essence of a situation would be captured when subjects were too tired, relaxed or involved to protect themselves from the scrutiny of observers.[14]

The film is commonly considered a 'breakthrough' in that, with relatively small, quiet and portable technology (a modified 16mm Auricon and a Nagra tape recorder synchronized by a Bulova electronic watch system), the camera operator could now 'walk in and out of buildings, up and down stairs, film in a taxi or limousine', and all the time 'get sound and pictures as events occurred' (Leacock, 1992). Two teams, each comprising only a camera operator and sound technician, were able to follow the candidates and their entourage and 'record their actions without undue interference' (Leacock, 1992). Frequently screened, the result was a film with a strong Vertovian flavour, in which the subject matter was treated in a largely 'disinterested' fashion, the action following no plot other than the train of events that led to Kennedy winning the election (Leacock, 1992).

Work and Institutions in the British Documentary

> We couldn't afford what they have in feature films – that is a rocker set . . . all we could afford to do was to move by hand, out of picture, certain things like balls of string hanging down, make them sway regularly to give the impression of the train moving, and get the chaps to sway a bit.
>
> Harry Watt on the making of *Night Mail*, quoted in Winston (1979: 3)

From the 1930s to the present, and especially since the advent of television, large audiences have been found in Britain for films which centre upon the relationship between individuals and their workplaces. These films developed under the five main styles shown in Table 1.

Table 1 *The five main styles of British documentary*

Style	Period	Films	Maker
World-of-labour	1930s–40s	*Drifters* *Night Mail*	Grierson Watt
Free cinema	1950s–60s	*Everyday except Christmas* *Momma Don't Allow*	Anderson Reisz
Modern TV documentary	c. 1965	*Police* *The Ark*	Graef Dineen
Hyper-realist documentary	c. 1985	*Fire* *DEA*	Oxley Hamann
Video diaries	c. 1990	*Low Paid Work* *Video Diaries*	Ray General public

World-of-labour Films

The origins of work-related *cinéma vérité* in Britain lie in the early world-of-labour films of producer-theorist John Grierson (see Manvell, 1946; Barnouw, 1975; Beveridge, 1979; Forsyth, 1979; Aitken, 1990, and Chapter 1, this volume). In his 1929 silent film on the herring fishing industry, *Drifters*, Grierson effectively screened the first European documentary. *Drifters* was revolutionary in European film-making in that for the first time the focus for large-screen entertainment was nothing more exotic than the work of labourers.

In important respects, Grierson's work reflects the influence of both Vertov and Flaherty. While the Soviet style is evident in Grierson's concern for social problems, Flaherty's style underpins the quest to record the 'heroic' nature of 'ordinary' existence (Aitken, 1990).[15] Holder of a doctorate in social sciences from Glasgow University, Grierson's work is driven by a concern for the ethical and sociological purpose of the documentary film. As Agel (1953: 45) notes, Grierson's aim is 'to exalt human toil and civic virtues' and above all 'to magnify the unconscious beauty of the physical effort involved in labour'.[16]

Grierson's work subsequently influenced the social and industrial documentaries of Paul Rotha, whose work represents an early attempt to demystify the structure of British industrial society, especially the role of the state. Among Rotha's best-known films are *Shipyard* (1935), concerning the construction of a ship and the reactions of the community in which the shipyard is based, and *Rising Tide* (1935, later retitled *Great Cargoes*), which deals with extensions to the Southampton docks and the interdependence of various commercial activities (see Rotha, 1967; Aitken, 1990).

In his theoretical treatise, *Documentary Film Art*, Rotha (1936) explains his approach to the sociological film through praising Flaherty's technique and commitment, but criticizes his over-romantic and idyllic

conception of a primitive struggle with nature, an image far removed
from, and with little to say about, the alienating realities of the modern
industrial world. Rotha's view was that serious documentary film-
makers should focus on the social realism of industrial civilization; they
should concentrate on ethnographic issues that confront large masses of
the world's population (Rotha, 1967). For Rotha, the idyllic documentary
largely avoids any conscious social analysis.[17]

Although none of the works of the early British documentary school
achieved the prominence of, say, Flaherty's works, many were still of
high quality. One such mini-classic is Basil Wright's *Song of Ceylon*
(1934). Sponsored by the Empire Marketing Board, the film highlights, in
striking contrast, the co-existence of a pre-industrial civilization and
Western civilization. Developed in three parts, *Song of Ceylon* celebrates
the island's Buddhist rites and craft occupations, before contrasting such
serene rituals with the bustle of modern commercial activity. Ethno-
graphically, the film is important in that it represents one of the first
attempts to show the co-existence of two cultures (see Barnouw, 1975;
Aitken, 1990).

Other quality documentaries of the early British school generally find
Grierson and Wright acting in collaboration with Alberto Cavalcanti or
Harry Watt in industrial or other work-related settings. For example, it
was Grierson who produced Cavalcanti's *Coal Face* (1936), a study of
mines and the lives of miners, while Cavalcanti in turn produced Watt's
North Sea (1938), a further study of seafarers based on a reconstruction of
incidents that occurred during the great storm of 1937. The latter film
departs, however, from the early requirements laid down by Grierson in
that it employs actors and tells a scripted story.

This was also the case with Watt, Grierson and Wright's classic of the
period, *Night Mail* (1936), which tells the story of the night run by the
postal train between London and Glasgow, and centrally the work of
postal workers receiving, sorting and dispatching mail during the run.
Produced by the esteemed Film Unit of the General Post Office, the
scenes of *Night Mail* were created by the real situation being observed
separately from the film-making. The film-makers (notably Basil Wright)
would observe the subject matter, make notes on appropriate actions and
phrases, and then develop this information into a script from which
actors could reconstruct the reality. Despite its *cinéma vérité* feel, the
interior scenes of *Nigh Mail* were actually filmed on a sound stage at
Blackheath studios (BBC, *Arena – The GPO*, 1983).

Watt's style of utilizing the resources of fictional film-making was
particularly influential in the 1940s, especially for depicting the lives and
work of personnel in military and auxiliary occupations. His account of a
bombing raid on Germany, *Target for Tonight* (1941), for example, plays
extensively on the theme of intense human undercurrents in wartime life.
Also similar in style, but more celebrated, was Humphrey Jennings's
description of the work of the Auxiliary Fire Service, *Fires Were Started*

(1943). In this film, Jennings reconstructed a routine situation – the work of a fire station in the period before an air raid – and developed this towards a dramatic climax, in this case a fire in which one of the fire-fighters is killed. In this and other work, Jennings operates at the inter-face between the documentary and the fictional film. In the Flaherty tradition, he makes use of the drama inherent in everyday life, a collective drama in which the heroes are anonymous, like ourselves (see Jennings, 1982).

Free Cinema

After the Second World War, the British documentary film escaped from its role of creating a propagandist view of British society through what came to be known as the 'free cinema' movement. The aim of 'free cinema' was to return to a more direct approach to the ethnographic, especially working-class, documentary.

The origins of free cinema lie in the pages of the short-lived Oxford University magazine *Sequence* (1949–52: 14 issues). The editors of *Sequence*, Lindsay Anderson and Gavin Lambert (and later Karel Reisz), severely criticized British film-making for presenting a view of the nation from the perspective of the pre-1914 bourgeoisie. It was Anderson's view, in particular, that British film-making was devoid of critical analysis, especially regarding the class system. According to Robinson (1973: 292), the *Sequence* view was that British film-makers had characterized 'the function of the working class [as] to provide "comic relief" to the sufferings of their social superiors'.

The term 'free cinema' was first coined in February 1956 as the head-line for a National Film Theatre programme of short films. The notes for the programme explain how the movement's films are 'free in the sense that their statements are entirely personal. Though their moods and subjects differ, the concern of each of them is with some aspect of life as it is lived in this country today.' The attitude is one of 'a belief in freedom, in the importance of people and in the significance of the everyday' (quoted in Robinson, 1973: 294). The *Sequence* philosophy was to show the way 'ordinary people' enact their 'everyday lives'. The objective was for these films to possess a 'feeling of freshness' in docu-menting the 'real environment in which people work and play' (Robinson, 1973: 294).[18]

The classic of the free cinema movement is undoubtedly Anderson and Reisz's *Everyday except Christmas* (1957), a film about night work at London's Covent Garden market. The film begins with the image of a shed somewhere far out of London, in which a lorry is being loaded with food and flowers at the very moment that the BBC announcer is saying 'goodnight' to listeners. From every corner of the country similar lorries are speeding towards the capital and Covent Garden market. While the lorries are unloaded, dealers prepare their stands: boxes are opened, apples are polished, workers pause for tea and a chat. A large, well-dressed man gives orders, the major retailers arrive and bargain, and a small trader loads a hand cart. Housewives and itinerant merchants buy after the retailers have gone, an old women sells flowers, tramps pick up any damaged fruit. Finally, the lorries are loaded with empty packing cases and depart for the four corners of Britain.

In recording these scenes, the camera carefully studies the faces of traders and customers and catches their subtle yet commonplace gestures.[19] In so doing, *Everyday except Christmas* achieves an ethnographic montage in which each face contributes to the effect. As in much of Anderson and Reisz's work, the class structure of Britain is reflected in scenes which document the ebb and flow of work and rest. The philosophy leans upon Vertov's theories in that the goal is to show the audience elements of the 'real world' in which it lives.

The Modern Television Documentary

From the 1960s onwards, television replaced the short or feature length film as the main medium for disseminating *cinéma vérité* in Britain. Indeed, since the series *The Family* (1974) made famous the Wilkins family of Reading,[20] British television audiences have been bombarded with *cinéma vérité* productions.

The advent of television, however, did not alter the trend of British *cinéma vérité* film-makers to be preoccupied with understanding the nature of work and institutions. If anything, the trend has been accentuated, as witnessed by the list of television series screened during the early and mid-1990s, which include *Flying Squad* (police officers, BBC, 1990), *The Duty Men* (customs officers, BBC, 1991), *Fire* (firefighters, Thames, 1991), *DEA* (drug enforcement officers, BBC, 1992) *Town Hall* (town councillors, BBC, 1992), *The Ark* (zoo keepers, BBC, 1993), *The Adventurers* (venture capitalists, BBC, 1993), *Turning the Screws* (prison officers, Channel 4, 1993), *Skipper* (trawlermen, BBC, 1993), *Coal* (coal-miners, BBC, 1994), *The Factory* (factory workers/managers, Channel 4, 1995), and *When Rover Met BMW* (car workers/managers, BBC, 1996). In recent years, there has also been a wealth of one-off documentaries on work and institutions, notably in the *Cutting Edge* (Channel 4), *40 Minutes* (BBC), *Nice Work* (BBC), and *Undercover* (Channel 4) television series.

British television-based *cinéma vérité* has been influenced considerably by the work of the American film-maker Frederick Wiseman, who, from the mid-1960s, made a series of investigations for US television into the relationships between individuals and institutions. As much as John Grierson or Lindsay Anderson, it has been Wiseman's technique of using documentary film for observing social relationships that has influenced a generation of young British *cinéma vérité* film-makers, including Roger Graef, Nick Broomfield, Diane Tammes, Chris Oxley and Molly Dineen.

An early expression of this influence was found in Graef's series *The Space between Words* (BBC, 1972), which looked at 'communication' in five institutional settings: the family, school, work, diplomacy and politics. The series was innovatory for British television in that it focused on 'ordinary situations' and presented the images with the minimum of introduction. Graef's idea was to 'let viewers develop their own theories of communication'. In filming the series, Graef's policy was 'never to use lights, or staged scenes, to keep the equipment out of sight, and to have the minimum of people in the room'. To minimize the effect of his presence, Graef even had a rule of 'never looking any of the subjects being filmed in the eye'! Graef has noted, ironically, how the response of the media to this radical venture was to interview academics and critics in order to obtain 'professional' expectations of the issues raised by the films, a practice completely anathema to the project (Graef, 1992).

Graef is better known, however, for documentaries that examine the relationship between organizational practices and institutional politics. Examples here are his films on investment in new technology at British Steel, and the allocation of spare beds in the National Health Service, both filmed during the 1970s. His most well-known work in this style, however, was a later series documenting the lives and work of members of the Thames Valley Police Force (*Police*, 1982, with Charles Stewart). In this series, Graef succeeded in combining the apparent objectivity of direct cinema with contemporary social issues, which, in the case of one episode, 'A Complaint of Rape', led to widespread public debate. The *Police* series laid new ground for British *cinéma vérité* in that it opened up issues that the subjects themselves were not aware of, thus instigating a self-discovery process. In his more recent work, Graef has remained true to this direct-cinema style, notably in his account of the work of prison officers, *Turning the Screws* (Channel 4, 1993).

The institutional documentaries of Diane Tammes also reflect a direct-cinema style. In her documentary *Casualty* (Channel 4, 1991), for example, an institution is described with relatively few edits or guiding commentaries. The film reflects that variant of the direct-cinema philosophy associated with the British National Film School, which suggests that the longer a sequence is allowed to run the more 'truthful' the images are likely to be. Tammes, however, has admitted to becoming 'less strict' with herself over the years (Tammes, 1992). While her early work was 'purist' in that 'the camera was there simply to see how people interacted', if the situation demands, she now engages in dialogue with subjects from behind the camera. 'Truth', she suggests, 'is about what people actually come away with at the end of the film.' The problem is that 'everyone who makes a film is just putting their own truth on the screen' (Tammes, 1992).

This style of partial intervention is evident in the work of Molly Dineen, and in particular her series on zoo keepers, *The Ark* (BBC, 1993). Originally aiming to make 'a film about a zoo', Dineen ended up telling a story about 'a British institution undergoing radical change'. For example, as financial problems loomed large, Dineen explains, it became a case of 'suits versus beards'. In other words, 'the management men and the financiers against the scientists and academics' (Guardian, 1993a: 53). As the crisis at the zoo came to a head, problems of 'human resource' management began to take priority over 'animal' management. Consequently, her style of film-making became increasingly investigative, with Dineen, from behind the camera, probing to uncover the layers of political intrigue underlying the decisions on redundancy and restructuring.[21]

A style of film-making that actually makes overt the construction of the *cinéma vérité* film was developed in Britain from the mid-1980s onwards in the work of Nick Broomfield. When in 1990, for example, Broomfield (with Joan Churchill) made a follow-up (*Juvenile Liaison II*) for Channel 4 of his earlier institutional film *Juvenile Liaison* (1975), he brought to the fore his own problems as a film-maker, especially of tracing the original participants and gaining their renewed consent.

This style of focusing on what goes on *behind* the scenes was used by Broomfield to great effect in his later film *The Leader, the Driver and the Driver's Wife* (Channel 4, 1991). Exploiting the off-screen drama, Broomfield documented his difficulties in trying to secure an interview with the South African right-wing politician Eugene Terreblanche, the result being a black comedy of trial and tribulation. This style of film-making could not be further removed from Broomfield's earlier work: here the camera is anything but anonymous. Broomfield has remarked that, as his film-making style matured, he felt increasingly hide-bound by having to keep to a 'pure' *cinéma vérité* approach, for in the film-making process 'things don't happen when they are supposed to happen.' Broomfield argues that the associations you make throughout a film are often much richer than simply documenting what happened. For Broomfield, therefore, the notion of 'objectivity' is no longer tenable in documentary film-making. By keeping the 'pretence' of objectivity, and thus failing to share personal experiences, he feels the audience is less able to evaluate the final product (Broomfield, 1992).

The Hyper-realist Documentary

A further move away from the traditional philosophies of *cinéma vérité* has been signalled by the prevalence of a story-telling function in television-based work. Increasingly, documentary film-makers seem preoccupied with finding in 'real life' the kind of heightened drama most usually contained in scripted work.

An example of this style, now commonly referred to as 'hyper-realist' documentary, was *DEA* (BBC, 1992), a series on the United States Drug Enforcement Agency. *DEA* was very much in the style of American TV fiction, using music, voice-over and cutting to heighten the sense of tension and pace. The first episode of *DEA*, for example, sets up the undercover cop, Eddie, as a charismatic character who might be played otherwise by Robert Di Niro or Gene Hackman. The film is shot in a dramatic way, with the images being coupled with the classic narrative as to whether Eddie will or will not apprehend the villain, the film then working towards this end.

DEA is thus shaped very much like a Hollywood film, and exemplifies the way that hyper-realist documentaries seek 'strong' situations, characters and narrative. Like the fictional film, the hyper-realist style of *cinéma vérité* (which is occasionally, and inappropriately, referred to as 'reality TV') seeks to entertain the audience by taking it into 'another world'. As with Frederick Wiseman's influence on British direct cinema during the 1970s, this is a style which stems largely from contemporary American documentary film-making.

Among British film-makers, the hyper-realist style was evident in Chris Oxley's series on the work of the Fire Service, *Fire* (Thames, 1991). In filming firefighters, Oxley faced the problem of entertaining a television audience, yet accurately representing an occupation in which, for long periods, relatively little appears to happen. Oxley (1992) has described how he 'deliberated long and hard' over the issue of 'accuracy'. Indeed, to give a 'true' picture of the work of firefighters he even considered 'producing an episode in which little happened'; that is, where people were involved only in maintenance, inspection and cleaning work. As a contract film-maker, however, Oxley was forced to face 'the crucial fact that this was a programme that was going to go out on ITV, and ITV want high ratings.' Subsequently, the decision was made that 'watching little happening was just not very exciting.' The main issue facing contemporary documentary-makers, Oxley argues, is 'trying to capture reality, but also facing the problem of packaging that reality'. As Oxley notes, one of the current challenges to television *cinéma vérité* film-makers is that people want 'not only realism transferred to the screen . . . [but for] . . . something to be done with that realism to make it entertaining' (Oxley, 1992).[22]

Video Diaries

In recent years, one of the most popular forms of television *cinéma vérité* has seen members of the public use 8mm video camera technology to record personal 'diaries', a development which resonates strongly with Flaherty's statement, made in the 1920s, that the important film-makers of the future would be amateurs. An example of this is the BBC series *Video Diaries* in which members of the public are given 'video 8' equipment and asked to record events in their everyday lives. It could be argued that these personal documentaries reflect many of the qualities that the *cinéma vérité* pioneers sought in terms of 'directness' and 'authenticity'.[23]

In work settings, the use of video 8 in diary form has been employed in the Channel 4 series *Cutting Edge*. Frequently, films in this series take the form of covert ethnographies broadcast under the title *Undercover*. One programme employing this method that aroused considerable media attention was *Low Paid Work* (1993), in which former BBC film-maker Sima Ray spent three months undertaking covert observation in shops, factories, restaurants and nursing homes throughout Lancashire. Concealing a camcorder in a shoulder-bag, Ray filmed the situations she encountered as a young Asian woman in search of employment and accommodation. During the period of observation, all the jobs she managed to secure were remunerated at very low rates. One of the lowest paid jobs Ray obtained was, in fact, obtained through the local *Job Centre*, a state-run agency.

Through covert observation of the relationship between employers and employees, Ray's film portrayed vividly the feelings of hopelessness and depression experienced by low-paid workers, in this case during a period of high unemployment. The film drew a sharp contrast between the low-paid worker's struggle for existence and the luxurious lifestyles enjoyed by many employers. These contrasting images were silhouetted against a background in which the state frequently failed to prosecute employers who broke the law, and where the government was concerned to veto European Community legislation on minimum wages.[24]

Reading *Cinéma Vérité* as a Signifying System

> It has become more difficult to think of ethnographic films as definitive representations of events, independent of the process that produced them, and ethnographic film-makers have begun to look upon their work as more tentative forays into cultural complexity . . . [and as] . . . parts of a continuing enquiry.
>
> MacDougal, 'Ethnographic Film', (1978), p. 415

> *Cinéma vérité* film-makers claimed to be as unobtrusive as possible, to become like flies on the wall . . . Received wisdom has it not that *cinéma vérité* film-makers achieved such invisibility, but that all the evidence of their inevitable obtrusiveness wound up on the cutting room floor.
>
> Hall, 'Realism as a style', (1991), p. 28

In contrast to the philosophies of Vertov and Grierson, a key argument of recent theoretical writing on *cinéma vérité* is to regard the truth claims of the genre as in some way 'fictional'. In contrast to the early 'purist' assumptions of direct cinema (which rest upon the Cartesian belief that reality enjoys an independent existence), current sociological assessments of the fly-on-the-wall documentary suggest that its products are in many ways as fictional as those of popular cinema.

It is argued, for example, that through editing and associated processes both genres come to contain similar elements of plot, character, situation and event (see Renov, 1986; Hall, 1991; Nicholls, 1991). As such, both offer cultural images that present the viewer with challenges or dilemmas, build heightened tensions and dramatic conflicts, and ultimately terminate with resolution and closure. In sum, it is claimed that *cinéma vérité* documentaries operate with reference to a 'reality' that is socially constructed, one which is, above all, the product of signifying systems.[25]

On pursuing these arguments about the constructed nature of *cinéma vérité*, we find the signification process, as for other fictional accounts, being subject to scrutiny over its role in (re)producing hegemony. The claim of *cinéma vérité* to be accessing some privileged reality 'out there' becomes treated itself as an ideological effect (Nicholls, 1991). Acknowledging the constructed basis of *cinéma vérité* serves to undermine, for example, the claims to 'moral' superiority of, for example, Vertov, Flaherty, the British world-of-labour film-makers and the proponents of direct cinema.[26] It serves also to suggest that *cinéma vérité* offers assess to *a* world rather than to *the* world. While *cinéma vérité* films appear to direct us towards *the* world, they remain constructed 'texts'; they offer representations rather than replications. Such representations reflect truth claims not only of what we discover in the social world, but also of what interpretations, meanings and explanations can be assigned. The social world is made manifest through agencies of external authority, through representatives. We experience a historical world made available through picture-windows in which social practices are telescoped, dramatized and reconstructed.

One of the main hegemonic products of this process is our impression of encountering the *cinéma vérité* world as if it were being presented for the first time. The world made available to us is one we perceive as Newtonian and Cartesian: a world comprised of reason, realism and common-sense; a world waiting to be discovered through technology. We discover what we take to be the *only* thing we *can* discover. We are presented with a universe that fits within the framework of its representations.

In this representational process, elements of style, structure, and perspective freely mix. When the filmic argument takes shape we move beyond the factual world to that of the construction of meaning through a system of significations. In so doing, we never experience a pure correspondence between evidence and perspective, for facts become fashioned by arguments that in turn rely on strategies and conventions for their accomplishment (Shotter, 1993).

The so-called 'objectivity' of the *cinéma vérité* film can, therefore, be read as an ideological representation which operates in the guise of 'common-sense'. Barthes (1974) calls this institutionally enforced nature of representation the 'zero-degree style', for it adopts a posture of innocence and neutrality in the face of systems that provide the foundations upon which institutional perspectives represent themselves.[27] The direct-cinema documentaries of, for example, Wiseman and Graef are never as neutral as they appear, for they embody a distinctive view of institutions like hospitals and prisons in a way that reflects strategies of resistance over a mechanistic, bureaucratic logic. The 'third dimension' (Lukes, 1974) of this hegemonic process is that which is accomplished without overt commentary. In *cinéma vérité* we tend to perceive only the particular arrangements of sound and image. 'Objectivity' is constrained by decisions of what should, and should not, merit being 'commented' upon.

In sum, these representational and ideological arguments suggest that *cinéma vérité* documentaries always present *a* truth rather than *the* truth. *Cinéma vérité* films contain authorial 'voice' and, as such, what we experience is less the world 'reproduced' as 'represented'. This is so 'even if the evidence they recruit bears the authenticating trace of the historical world itself' (Nicholls, 1991: 118).

Conclusion

> I think this objective–subjective stuff is a lot of bullshit. I don't see how a film can be anything but subjective.
>
> Frederick Wiseman, quoted in Levin (1971: 321)

This chapter has offered technical and modal descriptions of a range of documentary film-making styles established under the generic title *cinéma vérité*. In the main, these styles followed the early philosophies of Dziga Vertov and John Grierson in advocating a progressively 'direct' and 'natural' approach to film-making in which everyday events are recorded without the traditional, cinema-based props of scripts, staging, lighting and so on. Proponents explain their development by recourse to a 'determinist' theory in which technological innovations (for example, mobile 16mm technology with synchronized sound in the early 1960s, and 8mm video technology in the mid-1980s) allow the capture of increasingly 'unobtrusive' images through the eyes of a metaphoric 'fly on the wall'.[28]

The chapter has addressed this technical and stylistic history at two main levels, methodology and critique. For the former, as a social scientist, the author found the promise of *cinéma vérité* to reduce levels of obtrusiveness and reactivity in observation fascinating. Methodologically, *cinéma vérité* seemed to offer a textual layer additional to, yet different from, those employed in traditional sociological research. It appeared that a film record could add to the diversity of data collected on, for example, work and institutions. There seemed the potential for *cinéma vérité* to contribute to a spirit of triangulation through providing more 'immediate' images than could be obtained by other research methods.

In seeking such 'authentic' and 'authoritative' images, *cinéma vérité* used technologies of method similar to those found in traditional social research. In particular, *cinéma vérité* seemed to offer parallel forms of observation to those employed in sociological fieldwork, namely *overt* and *covert*. Of these, the *overt* approach predominated in terms of frequency of use. In the landmark film deploying this approach, Drew Associates's *Primary*, the aim was to take a 'living' camera 'openly' into the scenes of action in order to record the 'emotional' as well as 'intellectual' truth. Assuming low levels of reactivity, proponents of 'direct cinema' claimed that their approach would see technology used to 'reveal' rather than 'create' reality. It was argued that when subjects became familiar with the film-making process, the camera could gather forms of data that the interview, for example, could not.[29]

In contrast, the method of *covert* observation was practised historically far less by *cinéma vérité* film-makers, the reason for this again being related to technology. Although Vertov used a covert approach to obtain 'authentic' images, his observations were restricted by the technology available to him. To obtain the famous footage of a family weeping at a grave, for example, he was forced to operate a heavy, static camera with a telephoto lens from a hide-out some distance from the scene.

During the 1980s, however, developments in 'micro' technology promoted greater interest in the use of covert observation. In Sima Ray's documentary, *Low Paid Work*, extremely strong work-related images were obtained using a camcorder hidden in a shoulder-bag. Methodologically, Ray's work signals that many of the traditional problems associated with *cinéma vérité* (notably those of negotiating access and obtaining non-reactive data) may be overcome through using compact, mobile and, above all, hidden equipment. Technologically, if not stylistically, this seems to represent a stage close to that of 'camera pen', where a story is recorded as directly on film as it is on paper.[30]

As well as a methodological review, this chapter has undertaken a *critical* analysis of the relationship between 'realism and representation', indicating the significant shortcomings in the technological determinist argument that underpins much of the methodological explanation of *cinéma vérité*. Initially from the standpoint of method, but increasingly from that of deconstruction, it is apparent that an equally appropriate metaphor for *cinéma vérité* could be the 'fly in the soup', rather than the 'fly on the wall'.

Initially, we demonstrated the potential for *artefact* in *cinéma vérité*. Nowhere was artefact found to be more apparent than, ironically, in the film that was credited with giving the genre its name, Rouch and Morin's *Chronique d'un Été*. In this film the technology intervenes purposefully to stimulate action. In so doing, the camera serves to intimidate those whose 'natural' behaviour it (seemingly) wishes to record. As a result, what is produced is not so much a recording of what would happen if the camera were not there, but what happens because the camera *is* there.

The fly-in-the-soup metaphor received further support when stylistic criticisms made of the world-of-labour films reached their logical conclusion in the views of young British documentary film-makers, such as Nick Broomfield, Diane Tammes and Chris Oxley. Unlike Grierson and Cavalcanti, who emphasized the potential for revealing 'truth' through documentary, the professional training of contemporary film-makers requires them to acknowledge that notions of 'objectivity' are 'no longer tenable' in *cinéma vérité* (Broomfield, 1992).

Subsequently, critical reviews of the documentary film movement, together with work on 'authority' and 'knowledge', proved influential in directing us towards an appreciation of the ideologically enforced nature of representation. In the process, earlier methodological concerns with overcoming unobtrusiveness became defused by discussions of the relativity of authorial presence and the ideology of 'common-sense'. Awareness of the ideological effects of *cinéma vérité* helped to deconstruct many of the methodological assumptions upon which 'purist' approaches were founded. It was argued, accordingly, that *cinéma vérité* documentaries operate with reference to a 'reality' that is the product of 'signifying systems'. What we discover in *cinéma vérité* is a 'historical' world in which reality is telescoped, dramatized and reconstructed. Claims to be accessing 'objective' reality are reduced to the status of ideological effects. The objectivity of *cinéma vérité* film becomes nothing more than an ideology operating in the guise of 'common-sense'.

Notes

1 One of the chief proponents, Jean Rouch, remarks, '*Cinéma vérité* means that we have wanted to eliminate fiction and get closer to real life. We know that we must only pose the problem of truth to arouse questions in the spectator' (Natta, 1963; quoted in Issari and Paul, 1979: 12), and also that 'The only thing I want to say about *cinéma vérité* is that it would be better to call it cinema-sincerity, if you like. That is, that you ask the audience to have confidence in the evidence, to say to the audience, "This is what I saw. I didn't fake it, this is what happened . . . I didn't change anyone's behaviour. I looked at what happened with my subjective eye and this is what I believe took place"' (quoted in Levin, 1971: 135).

2 See, for example, Eaton (1979), Issari and Paul (1979) and Barsam (1992) for reviews of the *cinéma vérité* debates of the 1960s.

3 The term '*cinéma vérité*' does in fact appear once in Vertov's notebooks (see Sadoul, 1940).

4 Direct cinema is 'direct' in the sense that technical professionalism is considered secondary to the effort to record the 'feel' of a situation. The basic philosophy is that the film-maker should work without preconceived ideas and find what is inherently dramatic in a situation, rather than impose structure on it (see Barnouw, 1975; Barsam, 1992, and n. 6 below for further details on method).

5 'In the lexicon of *cinéma vérité*', writes James Blue, 'creation as the artist's duty has been replaced by authenticity, beauty by honesty, and preconception, in the making of the film, by attentive submission to the subject.' As such, the classic documentary film-maker is 'drummed out' for having 'used' life for the dissemination of a 'selfish point of view' (1965: 23).

6 Because the camera operator is deemed the most important person in the crew, in *cinéma vérité* it is common for the film-maker to adopt this role. Indeed, *cinéma vérité* practitioners often avoid terms such as 'director', 'editor', 'recordist' and 'camera operator' (or cameraman, cinematographer) and instead substitute the general term 'film-maker'. As the documentary record largely results from the ability of the camera operator to keep pace

with events, the concept is that editing should be a logical progression from filming. In practice, however, it is common for the camera operator to select the sequence of images and then, through the editing process, decide which points in the sequence are the most meaningful and revealing. To remain faithful to the philosophy and the situation, the film-maker must be convinced that the editing process reflects the character, atmosphere and unfolding of events. The situation must be allowed to develop in a natural way, rather than be forced into a particular shape or pattern. Viewers must think that they are experiencing what the camera operator experienced when the situation was filmed. (This is, of course, the moot point from the perspective of the epistemology of the ethnographic film, and one that we discuss at length below.

To explain this practical technology further, one of the most common techniques used in *cinéma vérité* film-making is that of shooting a series of long, continuous shots rather than many short ones. The argument is not only that this is the way life is lived, but also that it allows the viewer to digest sufficient footage to be able to feel the 'rhythm' of conversation or action that leads up to a particularly charged or insightful moment. For editing purposes, this often means cutting sequences close to the way they were actually shot. Again, the principle is that the editing process must, as far as possible, be 'true to life', rather than footage being manipulated by the editor to create a 'new' and essentially 'different' reality, again a contentious issue epistemologically. *Cinéma vérité* films can thus often be expensive undertakings, because a camera operator may have to shoot thousands of feet of film so that, in editing, a viable choice is available for selecting the material considered most appropriate for unfolding the progression of events.

Another important principle of the more 'pure' forms of *cinéma vérité* is that there should be no explanatory narration. As the aim is to develop an 'accurate' portrayal of an event as it happened, narration can only detract from the 'reality' presented. As already stressed, the purpose of *cinéma vérité* is to treat the viewer as an observer who is witnessing an event as if for the first time. To place a narrative 'intermediary' between the event and the viewer is thus considered counter to the basic philosophy. Occasionally, however, film-makers are tempted, or forced, to use narration in order to give a film a basic structure or to form a bridge between gaps in the story caused by lack of footage; that is, to substitute for situations the film-maker missed with the camera. In its pure form, however, *cinéma vérité* stands alone, without any explanatory narration.

7 See Aitken (Chapter 1) for a detailed analysis of a major school of ethnographic documentary in Britain, that influenced by John Grierson.

8 Vertov was by training a musician who, after the October Revolution of 1917, worked as a caption editor for the Soviet newsreel *Kino-Nedelia* (Film Weekly). Subsequently becoming a newsreel cameraman, in 1919 he issued his first theoretical treatise, 'Kinoks-Revolution', in which he condemned the story-film as alien to the needs of Soviet audiences, calling instead for a new style of reporting based on 'real life' documentary. In 1922, this manifesto appeared in extended form in the magazine *Lef*, with Vertov presenting in detail his theory of the 'cine-eye'. It was in the same year that he organized *Kino-Pravda* (cinema truth or *cinéma vérité*) as a film supplement to the official Soviet state newspaper, *Pravda*. Vertov went on to produce 23 editions of the magazine (see de Heusch, 1962; Levin, 1971; Issari and Paul, 1979; Barsam, 1992).

9 Vertov advocated a radical and systematic doctrine of cinematographic realism in which the camera was merely an eye, with every aspect of staging – lighting, actors, make up, studios, etc. – being rejected. The film-maker was to have no 'creative' task prior to editing (see Petric, 1978, on this point).

10 Vertov developed a concept of 'catching people unaware' as the key to film truth; that is, 'getting them with the camera-eye at a moment when they are not acting and letting the camera strip their thoughts bare'. To know what people are really like, Vertov argued, the film-maker must be able to 'peer behind the mask they assume before others' (Vertov, 1963: 20; quoted in Issari and Paul, 1979: 25).

11 Although Vertov was able to record newsreel events in a seemingly genuine manner (ceremonies, meetings, sports, etc.), when he wanted to study 'feelings' he found it

necessary to use a covert 'candid camera' approach – one that restricted many of his takes to relatively short and discrete pieces of action. Vertov subsequently argued that it was 'not enough to show bits of truth on the screen, separate frames of truth'. He argued, instead, that 'these frames must be thematically organized so that the whole is also the truth' (Vertov, 1963: 55; quoted in Issari and Paul, 1979: 28). To this end, Vertov's work sees the progressive use of montage as a technique for aiding the 'struggle to reveal truth'. Influenced by his work as a newsreel editor, the cine-eye became not just a recording instrument, but one which could be 'organized' through an editing process. As such, Vertov's work is given increasingly to cross-cutting, slow motion, split screen, still photography, and so on. The increasingly artificial feel of his documentaries is nowhere more evident than in his best known work, *Man with a Movie Camera* (1929), a documentary of summer life in Leningrad, in which much of the action is produced by the use of staged scenes with extremely obtrusive camera work. Whereas Vertov claimed that his films were 'objective' documents about Soviet life, as Lawson (1964: 86) observes, 'There were contradictions in Soviet life far beyond the vision of Vertov's camera-eye. What he captured was an emotion much simpler than the reality.' See also Levin (1971) for a critique of Vertov's later work.

  12 Calder-Marshall (1963) suggests that, despite the amount of staging in *Nanook*, ethnographers have generally supported the 'authenticity' of the account. He suggests that the 'truthfulness' of the film is commonly attributed to the reciprocal sense of feeling and understanding developed between observer and observed. Through spending considerable time in securing Nanook's cooperation, Flaherty was able to film a subject, Calder-Marshall suggests, who subsequently appeared 'natural' in the presence of alien technology. (See Barsam, 1992, for an alternative view of the 'authenticity' of Flaherty's accounts.) In rejecting methodologically Vertov's notion of the pure camera-eye, Flaherty's subjects appear to 'act out' their own condition. With the active participation of the subject, the filming process becomes one of both description and communication. There is no pretence at capturing 'pure' reality: instead, issues of authenticity rest with the film-maker. In a methodological sense, the approach is one of 'participant' rather than 'scientific' observation: the film-maker as sociologist takes part in the situation, but also attempts to stimulate the situation.

  13 The origins of both *Primary* and the 'living-camera' style lie in Robert Drew's theory that, in being almost exclusively verbal (i.e. based on interviews) American TV journalism of the 1950s was 'cinematically dead' (Leacock, 1992). A photographer-reporter for *Time-Life*, Drew had been impressed by a television actuality documentary by Leacock, and subsequently contacted him with a view to a collaborative news-based project in which the camera would act as a 'neutral bystander', only reporting events as they were 'actually revealed'. The goal was to develop a living camera whose function was not to dramatize an event, but to describe it without seeking to judge (Leacock, 1992).

  14 Unlike Rouch's later work, where the presence of the camera modifies the action, for Drew and Leacock people should not be affected if the situation is sufficiently intense or relaxed. According to Leacock (1992), in the living-camera style the film-maker neither asks subjects questions, nor gives them directions. The object is to present evidence on the basis of which viewers can make up their own minds. The method depends upon a code of conduct that asserts that the purpose of filming is to capture a natural situation, albeit one that must come to an unavoidable conclusion.

  15 In this respect, consider also Flaherty's own world-of-labour documentary *Industrial Britain* (1933).

  16 Agel (1953: 45) also notes, however, that as a result of this objective, early British industrial documentaries tended to be 'somewhat drab'!

  17 For Rotha, this is a particular problem in Flaherty's *Man of Aran* (1934), where the system of large land-owner estates, under which the peasants suffer, is ignored.

  18 The National Film Theatre programme included two *Sequence* films: *O Dreamland* by Lindsay Anderson, and *Momma Don't Allow* by Karel Reisz and Tony Richardson. In *O Dreamland*, Anderson (using 16mm technology provided through a subsidy from the Experimental Fund of the British Film Institute) describes, in a rather mordant way,

the forms of entertainment available at the Dreamland amusement park, Margate. In a similar vein, Reisz and Richardson's experiment with 16mm, *Momma Don't Allow*, portrays an evening at a London dance hall. Although the film favours a simple reportage style, there are nevertheless threads of a plot as the film follows three main characters (a butcher, a hairdresser and a cleaner) who meet their partners for an evening of frenetic dancing.

19 The film's success owes much to the celebrated camera work of Walter Lassaly, whose name often appears in the credits of Reisz's films.

20 Some of the most memorable scenes of British television-based *cinéma vérité* indeed took place in the series *The Family*, made by Paul Watson in 1974. Watson's style contrasted markedly with that of his film-making peers in that, from the beginning, both the camera and the producer were actively involved in the film. While *The Family* is often classified as a fly-on-the-wall documentary, Watson's film is, in fact, extremely interventionist. Watson's 'presence' in *The Family* is nowhere more noticeable than in the memorable, if rather preconceived, scene where the future bride and groom argue over whether the camera should be present at the wedding, a scene in which Watson intervenes personally to defend its use. It must also be remembered that each episode of *The Family* was filmed only days before being transmitted to a national television audience. As a result, responses from the public were fed back to the family almost immediately through the media. The fact that this process influenced the Wilkins's behaviour is nowhere more evident than in the post-wedding scenes, where the impact of newspaper coverage seems to take the participants out of the realm of the ordinary family and into that of the 'superstar'. As with Rouch's *Chronique d'un Été*, the result is that *The Family* ends up being, once again, less fly on the wall, more fly in the soup.

21 Dineen's series offers a very clear and direct perspective on the relations between senior management and workforce at the zoo. The construction of the film leaves us in no doubt as to which side we should support in the conflict. We are presented, for example, with a very sympathetic view of the keepers as decent, hard-working folk, who will have to go through the ignominy of re-applying for their jobs. While the keepers are portrayed positively, the senior managers are portrayed extremely negatively. Notable here is the zoo's director, a 'Thatcherite' who apparently wishes to dispose of a large proportion of the workforce and reorganize those remaining into 'mini business centres'. The film signals, however, that there is still one 'acceptable' face among the existing management team, in the form of the senior curator, the proverbial knight on a white charger. As the political turmoil comes to a head, the zoo's 'watchdog' committee, the Zoo Reform Group, gains influence and, aided by some keepers, rises successfully against the director. The resolution of the series sees the departure of the director and his replacement by the senior curator.

22 A further example of television-based *cinéma vérité* which offers a form of hyper-realism was the BBC series *From Wimps to Warriors* (1992). In this series, personal feelings were explored in an almost existential way. In the 'Bermondsey Boy' episode, for example, the slow, late-night car ride through London revealed the central character's personal construction of reality, as he discloses the nature, purpose and relationships of the forms of street-life that are fleetingly encountered.

23 An episode of *Video Diaries* that received particularly positive reviews was the football-related film, *On the March with Bobby's Army* (1991 series). Based on the experiences of an England supporter abroad, the film reflected the dissonance of someone adopting, simultaneously, the roles of 'reveller' and 'recruit'. A video diary approach was also used with graphic effect in the episode 'Away the Lads' of the BBC series *40 Minutes* (1993). In John Alexander's film, a group of nine 'lager-loving lads' from the North-East of England recorded their exploits when on holiday in Benidorm, the result being, as the *Guardian* (1993b: 22) suggested 'an orgy of beer, beach and bird-watching'.

24 In the BBC's *Video Nation* (1994) series, the video diary method was employed to survey (qualitatively and subjectively) British social attitudes through a series of short, personal films shown on weekday nights prior to the programme *Newsnight*.

25 See Carroll (1983), Renov (1986) and Hall (1991) for critical analyses of mediation in *cinéma vérité*. Renov, in particular, offers an analytical framework that claims that meaning

is signified, 'from history to viewer', through four distinct 'stages' of mediation: the historical real, the pro-filmic, the text, and the spectator.

26 Nicholls (1991: 192) argues that it was claims to this moral high-ground that facilitated the sponsorship of major national film production bodies such as the GPO and Empire Marketing Board in Britain and, later, the US Information Service and National Film Board of Canada. Here, the dominant ideology was founded on the assumption that while the fictional film had 'deceived and distracted' through favouring 'fantasy and illusion' the *cinéma vérité* film would avoid the 'illusory world' through offering a 'realistic and humanitarian' alternative.

27 Barthes (1977: 17) argues that the truth claims of the photographic image emanate from the co-existence of two forms of message, 'a *denoted* message, with is *analogon* itself, and a *connoted* message, which is the manner in which the society to a certain extent communicates what it thinks of it'. In this process, each photographic image transmits an image of some literal reality. At the most basic level, during transmission obvious alterations occur, whether in colour, proportion, size, etc. However, these changes do not amount at any point to a transformation of the image. It is not necessary to devise a separate *code* to relay the message, for the image is the perfect analogue of the image it represents. Barthes suggests that the photographic image is thus a 'message without a code'. However, images are frequently presented with supplementary images – ones that are separate from their analogical content. Such messages are presented by the style of the reproduction, which is as a result of a particular 'treatment' of the image. This treatment is a coded message which offers a meaning, not always contained in the analogous image itself, whose acceptability is dependent upon cultural norms and values. For Barthes, it is the co-existence of denotative and connotative messages that represents a paradox upon which photographic claims to truth are founded. The first is absolutely analogical, the second simply coded rhetoric. As Barthes suggests, the photograph possesses exceptional power in being able to pass off as a denoted message one which is, in effect, heavily connoted.

28 A similarly determinist argument is found in the social research methods literature. It is suggested that although ethnographic film-making has been largely ignored in social research, enormous potential exists for its use (see, for example, Nachmias and Nachmias, 1989; Judd et al., 1991). As a method of data collection, it is claimed that 8mm technology, in particular, presents an opportunity to accrue images as valid and reliable as those produced by surveys, interviews or more traditional forms of observation.

29 In Britain, recent examples of overt observation include Molly Dineen's exploration of employee relations at London Zoo, *The Ark*, and Roger Graef's study of prison officers, *Turning the Screws*. Although both adopt the overt approach, these series differ methodologically in that Dineen employs a largely 'participative' form, while Graef's is 'non-participative'. In the traditional 'non-participative' (or direct-cinema) style, Graef attempts to divorce himself from the subjects' interactions and to film without direction or discussion. Dineen, on the other hand, frequently 'participates' through probing for clarification or information on particular issues.

30 The ethical basis of covert observation is an issue frequently discussed in research methods texts. Often, covert observation is criticized on the grounds that it invades personal privacy, fails to provide informed consent, and can potentially do harm (Bulmer, 1982; see also Shils, 1959). Those who champion the method, however, argue that problems stemming from researcher deception are a price worth paying for relatively unmediated and uncontaminated data sets. It is argued that the true flow of social events can only be documented through concealing a researcher's identity (see Rollins, 1985, on this point).

References

Agel, H. (1953) 'Esthétique du cinéma', *Positif*, 7: 45–52.
Aitken, I. (1990) *Film and Reform: John Grierson and the Documentary Film Movement*. London: Routledge.

Armes, R. (1966) *French Cinema since 1946. Vol. II: The Personal Style*. Amsterdam: Ellerman Harms.

Barnouw, F. (1975) *Documentary: A History of the Non-fiction Film*. New York: Oxford University Press.

Barsam, R. (1992) *The Non-fiction Film*. Bloomington, IN: Indiana University Press.

Barthes, R. (1974) *S/Z*. New York: Hill and Wang.

Barthes, R. (1977) *Image–Music–Text*. London: Fontana.

Beveridge, J. (1979) *John Grierson: Film Maker*. London: Macmillan.

Blue, J. (1965) 'Thoughts on *cinéma vérité* and a discussion with the Maysles Brothers', *Film Comment*, 2 (4): 15–21.

Broomfield, N. (1992) Interview on *The Late Show*, BBC Television, March.

Bulmer, M. (ed.) (1982) *Social Research Ethics*. London: Macmillan.

Calder-Marshall, A. (1963) *The Innocent Eye: The Life of Robert J Flaherty*. London: W.H. Allen.

Cameron, I. and Shivas, M. (1963) 'Interviews', *Movie*, 8: 15–22.

Carroll, N. (1983) 'From real to reel: entangled in nonfiction film', *Philosophical Exchange*, 14: 5–45.

Eaton, M. (ed.) (1979) *Anthropology–Reality Cinema: The Films of Jean Rouch*. London: British Film Institute.

Flaherty, F. (1972) *The Odyssey of a Film Maker*. New York: Arno Press.

Forsyth, H. (1979) *John Grierson: A Documentary Biography*. London: Faber and Faber.

Graef, R. (1992) Interview on *The Late Show*, BBC Television, March.

Guardian (1993a) '*The Ark* in the storm', 17 January.

Guardian (1993b) 'Watching brief: *40 Minutes – Away the Lads*', 2 March.

Hall, J. (1991) 'Realism as a style in *cinéma vérité*: critical analysis of *Primary*', *Cinema Journal*, 30 (4): 24–46.

de Heusch, L. (1962) *The Cinema and Social Science*. Paris: UNESCO.

Issari, M. and Paul, D. (1979) *What is Cinéma Vérité?* Methuen, NJ: Scarecrow Press.

Jennings, M. (1982) *Humphrey Jennings: Film-maker, Painter, Poet*. London: British Film Institute.

Judd, C., Smith, E. and Kidder, L. (1991) *Research Methods in Social Relations*. Fort Worth, TX: Holt, Rinehart and Winston.

Lawson, J. (1964) *Film: The Creative Process*. New York: Hill and Wang.

Leacock, R. (1992) Interview on *The Late Show*, BBC Television, March.

Levin, R. (1971) *Documentary Explorations*. New York: Doubleday.

Lipscombe, J. (1964) 'Correspondence and controversy', *Film Quarterly*, 18 (2): 60–8.

Lukes, S. (1974) *Power: A Radical View*. London: Macmillan.

MacDougal, D. (1978) 'Ethnographic film: failure and promise', *Annual Review of Anthropology*, 7: 402–25.

Manvell, R. (1946) *Film*. London: Macmillan.

Morin, E. (1956) *Le cinéma ou l'homme imaginaire*. Paris: Flammarion.

Nachmias, D. and Nachmias, C. (1989) *Research Methods in the Social Sciences*. New York: St Martin's Press.

Natta, E. (1963) 'Pro e control il cinéma-vérité', *Rivista del Cinematografo*, November: 415–20.

Nicholls, B. (1991) *Representing Reality: Issues and Concepts in Documentary*. Bloomington, IN: Indiana University Press.

Oxley, C. (1992) Interview on *The Late Show*, BBC Television, March.

Petric, V. (1978) 'Dziga Vertov as theorist', *Cinema Journal*, 1: 41–2.

Renov, M. (1986) 'Rethinking documentary: towards a taxonomy of mediation', *Wide Angle* 8 (3/4): 71–7.

Robinson, D. (1973) *The History of World Cinema*. New York: Doubleday.

Rollins, J. (1985) *Between Women: Domestics and their Employers*. Philadelphia: Temple University Press.

Rotha, P. (1936) *Documentary Film Art*. London: Faber and Faber.

Rotha, P. (1967) *The Film Till Now: A Survey of World Cinema*. London: Spring Books.

Rouch, J. (1992) Interview on *The Late Show*, BBC Television, March.

Sadoul, G. (1940) *Histoire d'un art: le cinéma*. Paris: Flammarion.

Shils, E. (1959) 'Social enquiry and the autonomy of the individual', in D. Learner (ed.), *The Human Meaning of the Social Sciences*. New York: World Publishing.

Shotter, J. (1993) *Cultural Politics of Everyday Life*. Buckingham: Open University Press.

Sussex, E. (1976) *The Rise and Fall of the British Documentary*. Los Angeles: University of California Press.

Tammes, D. (1992) Interview on *The Late Show*, BBC Television, March.

Vertov, D. (1963) 'Fragments', *Artsept*, 2: 20–1.

Winston, B. (1979) 'Documentary: I think we are in trouble', *Sight and Sound: International Film Quarterly*, 48 (1): 2–7.

3

The Cultural Representation of Trade Unions

Peter Stead

In the Swansea of 1960, as in other British towns, the pattern of film promotion and exhibition was very much what it had been for decades. Box office was declining and there were relatively fewer cinemas, but there were still literally hundreds of films to be seen during the course of the year. These films were advertised in the press in small black announcements, sometimes accompanied by a basic sketch or brief slogan. They were succinctly reviewed by national and local critics, but then largely publicized by word of mouth in such a way that ensured that those who missed a film downtown could catch it later in the suburbs. It was rare, indeed, for this routine to be punctured by controversy, and only occasional complaints from ministers of religion necessitated a particular film being mentioned in news columns. There were complaints of a different sort, however, in the spring of 1960 following the release of a new British film, *The Angry Silence*. In Swansea, readers of the evening paper found the news columns carrying a passionate debate on the film even before it had opened in the town. Clearly this was a most unusual film.

Agency reports had suggested that the South Wales Area of the National Union of Mineworkers were calling for *The Angry Silence* to be banned. In Swansea, the editor of *The South Wales Evening Post* decided to send a reporter to investigate and in particular to interview Will Whitehead, Area President of the NUM. Whitehead explained that his Union was specifically contacting the so-called welfare cinemas in South Wales valley towns, which were run by locally elected committees and which traditionally had been closely linked with the miners, to ask them 'to consider the advisability of showing this film because it sets out to denigrate and deride the trade union movement at the local level'. He conceded that he had no evidence as to how many of his members had seen the film prior to their discussions on it but went on to stress that his main concern at that time was 'to build up a core of men who will administer the union at local level in the best traditions of the trade union movement'. His fear was that 'if you are going to have people making this sort of film, then it is going to bring us into bad odour with

Figure 3.1   The Angry Silence, *1960, Carlton*

the public.' Warming to his subject, Whitehead ended with a plea: 'Why don't they make a film which shows the excellent work done by the trade union movement especially at branch level and give some encouragement to these lads who are doing a very difficult job under what I would describe as sometimes very difficult circumstances?' (*South Wales Evening Post*, 14 April 1960).

The *Evening Post* did not leave it there and clearly needed to consider both sides of this promising story. They went straight to the top, to David Kingsley, managing director of British Lion who were distributing the film. Kingsley much regretted the possibility of organizations banning a film because of disapproval of its content and agreed that 'people should be able to see the film and make their own decision'. He particularly regretted the NUM approach to welfare cinemas for often they were the only picture-house in certain communities, and consequently his South Wales area manager would be contacting cinemas to persuade them 'that the film is "good entertainment"'. His line was that 'the trade union side of *The Angry Silence* is a very minor part of this film and certainly there is not any attack on trade union leaders or leadership.' He emphasized that 'where there is criticism it is at the apathy of the rank and file' (*South Wales Evening Post*, 14 April 1960).

The editor of Swansea's paper knew that he was on to a good thing. London critics had already stressed the merits of the new film, and there was every indication that there would be considerable local interest in any twist he could put on the story. In an unprecedented and rather surprising way, cinema and politics seemed to be coming together. Only the year before, the South Wales miners had been upset by what they had taken to be an anti-trade union film, *I'm All Right Jack* (1959). At that stage the *Evening Post* had only referred to the film as a comedy featuring a familiar cast and had not felt tempted to relate the satire to the pattern of local industrial disputes. Things were rather different now. Politics pervaded the air. It was only six months since the Conservatives under Macmillan had won a stunning electoral victory, and yet there was no sign of union militancy abating, especially at the local level. One glimpse at the columns of the *Evening Post* makes clear why the editor should be interested in a row over a new anti-union film. British Lion still had two 1959 films on show in Swansea: out in the suburbs they were still catching up on Peter Sellers as the shop steward in *I'm All Right Jack*, as well as reliving the atmosphere of an election in the gentle but often amusing by-election tale *Left, Right and Centre*. Meanwhile, readers could catch up on the latest details of local strikes by lorry drivers, engineers and miners. There was a major dispute at the local 3Ms plant over union recognition for 470 hourly-paid workers: the American manager wanted a secret ballot, whereas the unions argued that the level of support rendered a ballot unnecessary. The NUM was always in the news, especially as it was calling for another ban, this time of the South African cricketers.

Eventually, *The Angry Silence* came to town. In the Albert Hall's advertisement it was announced as 'The frankest, most daring film ever made in Britain'! The local critic was quite prepared to match this hyperbole as he made his contributions to a debate that he obviously wanted to sustain. 'Reactions in this part of the world to *The Angry Silence*', he reflected, 'have not been golden' but, while trade unionists were 'loud in their condemnation of its content', he wanted it known that 'moviegoers have voiced with equal power their praise of its content!' His summing up was ingenious: 'It is not the purpose of this critic to suggest that the truth hurts: only to recommend it as a brilliant and intelligent picture that should not be missed' (*South Wales Evening Post*, 30 April 1960).

With the film now showing in the town, it was time for an *Evening Post* editorial. In a leader entitled 'The Angry Noise', the editor confessed that 'we haven't seen it yet', but suspected that he had that in common with the local executive of the miners. The point that the *Post* wanted to reiterate was that 'no good can come of this secondhand censorship': the union 'should surely be willing to trust its members and their families to make up their own minds' for 'to suppress ideas is always a dangerous activity and one which boomerangs on the suppressor' (*South Wales Evening Post*, 2 May 1960). Almost certainly, the writer had more than the debate on *The Angry Silence* in mind. A couple of days earlier, the South Wales miners in conference at Porthcawl had debated a motion critical of 'the capitalist press', although they had not called for any ban. He would also have been aware that his readers might possibly be inconvenienced by a token bus strike likely to be called for the following Saturday. This was no bad time to be focusing on the unions. As for 'the angry noise' occasioned by the film, he thought 'this sudden bashfulness is surprising': 'trade union leaders have never before been renowned as a class for their susceptibility to criticism' (*South Wales Evening Post*, 2 May 1960).

Obviously this was a moment to cherish. The South Wales miners had foolishly overstepped the mark and the *Post* was enjoying rapping their knuckles. Over and above that, though, *The Angry Silence*, whether seen or unseen, had given the opportunity for those who were increasingly concerned about union militancy to begin a new phase in which, to a degree not seen since the 1920s, the tactics and operations of the unions could be, if not questioned, at least commented on. The Conservative election victory of 1959 might well have given union critics greater confidence, although there had been very little direct anti-union talk during the election campaign and, even in 1960, telling points were made disingenuously or in oblique quips. What is so fascinating about looking at the promotion and reception of *I'm All Right Jack* and *The Angry Silence* is that we catch glimpses of a relatively unique example of how mainstream British popular culture was reflecting the great sea-change in public attitude. Insiders, and those in businesses connected to the

Conservatives, knew what was happening but caution still had to be their watchword. The Boulting brothers could with some justice argue that they had been responsible for a number of films which satirized every aspect of British society and that in *I'm All Right Jack* 'the old shower were back' in a film that was meant to attack both sides in industry as well as the way in which television reported disputes. Certainly, they could never have predicted that Peter Sellers would so cherish and develop the part of the shop steward Kite. Nevertheless, it seems that John Boulting, the director and co-writer of the film, had modelled Kite on an ETU shop steward who had caused him great difficulty at the studio (Walker, 1981: 108; Richards and Aldgate, 1983: 115). There were many strands in the film, but what everyone remembers is Kite and the early sequences of trade-union satire both of which had been given an edge by a production team which knew well what they were depicting.

The Boulting brothers were part of the group that controlled British Lion and, in that capacity, played a part in the saga that eventually led to the release of *The Angry Silence*. This film was very much the baby of an independent production company, Beaver Films, which had to live up to that name to get any backing. British Lion at first thought the project uncommercial, and when they eventually agreed to back it they did so on the basis of minimal support. There is no evidence that the Boultings, who had on several occasions in the past been associated with political films, such as *Fame is the Spur* (1947) and *High Treason* (1951), were on the look-out for an anti-union film. When *The Angry Silence* saw the light of day two aspects of its reception stood out. British Lion promoted the film as 'the most daring ever made' – clearly they wanted all the commercial advantage and kudos that would accrue from having released a political film – and yet, at the same time, they had to deny that it was an anti-union film. They arranged a special showing for the miners and other union leaders, and this strategy had seemed to work as the union delegates were able to report back that 'abuses of power were what was under attack not articles of faith' (Walker, 1974: 98). But it was the other aspect of the film's reception that was more important than this special showing for, quite crucially, the critics loved the film: British Lion and Beaver could relax a little, their project would not be a disaster, there might even be a profit. Bryan Forbes, co-producer and writer, enjoyed the 'sustained applause' at the opening and then a few hours later the 'wildly extravagant' praise in the first editions (Forbes, 1974: 280). For the *Daily Express* it was 'a topical, controversial, vitriolic masterpiece'; for *The Times*, 'a film of rare quality and impressive realism'; and for the *Daily Mail* 'vastly entertaining as well as thought provoking'![1]

The quality of the film most approved by the critics was its 'honesty', the implication being that the time was ripe for a story that highlighted trade-union abuses. 'Something that really needed saying' was the message running through most reviews: a point that was to be reiterated in American notices later in the year. Writing in the *New Republic*, Stanley Kauffman recalled that Dickens had dealt with the theme of a trade unionist 'sent to Coventry' in *Hard Times*. For Kauffman, *The Angry Silence* dealt with a situation that Dickens would have easily recognized. It was a 'well-made and disturbing film' and its success was a reminder that 'American film-makers have not touched this toweringly important subject.' What Kauffman explained was that the film's message was effectively delivered because 'technically the picture is above reproach': the dialogue was 'pungent' and 'well-characterized'; the photography was 'a ruthless album of the ugliness of factory and factory workers' life'; and supporting actors were all authentic – whether they were management or workers, they 'seem never to have done anything but those jobs'. His chief praise he reserved for the leading players, Richard Attenborough and Pier Angeli. Their performances 'are representative because they are not consciously typical . . . they are human beings first and therefore can state a case for their group.' Quite remarkably, Kauffman added a judgement that might have raised the eyebrows of many British critics, for this playing of 'little people' in a way that was 'not consciously typical' was a quality he found lacking in most American films (Kauffman, 1966: 192). This, of course, had been an age-old complaint about British cinema, but now both British and American critics were stressing the unique quality of *The Angry Silence*. A serious film had been made that still genuinely entertained: above all, as the *Daily Mail* summed it up, 'matter and manner are for once wholly in harmony.'

More than anything else, the successful outcome of *The Angry Silence* project was a personal triumph for Richard Attenborough. He was the star of the film, he was co-producer and, as his colleague Bryan Forbes has explained, it was 'Bunty' (Attenborough) whose persistence and ingenuity eventually allowed a deal to be worked out with British Lion. There were many contributions to the shaping of the film. Nanette Newman spotted the original press story about a worker being 'sent to Coventry', Michael Craig and his brother wrote a synopsis, Bryan Forbes developed the script, and Guy Green directed. Nevertheless, it bears all the hallmarks of an Attenborough venture. Nobody was in a better position to appreciate the need for 'matter and manner' to come together in British cinema. From the outset of his career, he had been brought face to face with issues of realism, class and seriousness. He had made his debut, aged 19, playing a frightened stoker in Noël Coward's *In Which We Serve* (1942), and he first achieved fame in the part of the young gang leader Pinkie Brown in John Boulting's 1948 version of Graham Greene's *Brighton Rock*. There followed a period in which he became all too aware of how British producers were yearning for some of the success that the Americans were having with social-problem films: he became rather typecast as a young troublemaker while juvenile delinquency became almost the theme of the decade. He was longing for better parts in better films and was to be very grateful when his close friend, John Boulting, gave him new opportunities in his satirical comedies, including *I'm All Right Jack*. It was his desire for more control over his work that led him into production and into setting up Beaver Films with Bryan Forbes: 'I am really an actor-manager' he was later to tell David Robinson (Hacker and Price, 1991: 72; Robinson, 1992). Clearly, he spotted the potential in the part of Tom Curtis, the worker who suffers because of his refusal to join a strike. He invested enormously in *The Angry Silence*, both financially and emotionally, and his gamble paid off. If was, says Robinson, 'a natural Attenborough subject', an ordinary guy, utterly honourable and decent, whose main passions in life are football and his wife, who becomes a hero and a martyr when he stands out against what he takes to be the stupidity of the crowd. Attenborough saw the potential for drama and he milked it to the full. His performance doesn't start well: at the outset he is too chatty and self-conscious – a middle-class Englishman trying to impersonate a worker – but later in key scenes with the shop steward he generates real power and brings the character alive.

The Angry Silence had come about largely because a leading British actor-producer had wanted a good part and found it in the plight of a worker opposing a wildcat strike. The film represented a straightforward piece of opportunism by one man and his production team. Their timing had been perfect, although they could not have predicted at the outset that by 1960 criticism of wildcat strikes would be more general and the Conservative mood of the country even more pronounced. What they could have expected was that there would still be critics calling for a more socially realistic British cinema. Their film had been made on location in Ipswich as a direct response to that critical debate; but, of course, they had responded to the challenge in their own individual way. In fact, they had stolen the thunder of the critical left: they had beaten them at their own game. The critic and film-maker Lindsay Anderson had hated the politics of the 1954 American film *On the Waterfront*, but in the years that followed it was exactly the power and passion of that kind of film that he wanted British directors to emulate. Location shootings, industrial settings and more realistic acting were now being prescribed for British producers (see Anderson, 1955: 127; 1957). 'For years and years', argued the *Spectator's* Isabel Quigley in 1959, 'we have known that the British film picture of ourselves was phoney: everyone in the country knew it, it was one of the big national lies that everyone concurred in' (*Spectator*, 26 June 1959, quoted in Hewison, 1981: 155). In his own eyes and in those of Fleet Street, Attenborough had started to tell the truth, but it was not the truth that many wanted to be told.

Attenborough was clearly annoyed by the threatened trade-union boycott of his film which he described as being 'fascist behaviour' much along the lines he had depicted (*Sunday Dispatch*, 17 April 1960, quoted in Hill, 1986). He would have been angered more by the intellectual criticism that followed. The film's genesis in one actor's desire for a good role is all too obvious throughout the telling of the story. It may well have been the case that most wild-cat strikes were called on flimsy pretexts but that was no excuse for the film not to attempt any explanations of either individual or mass motivation. The broad but unexplained hints of communist influence are merely irritating, and at regular intervals the story lapses into melodrama. Perhaps Attenborough felt that he had to rely on juvenile delinquents at key points just for old times' sake, and perhaps it was loyalty to the original author, Michael Craig, that explains his particularly unsatisfactory part in the film. He, more than most, was clearly slumming it in Ipswich, conscientiously dropping his aitches as he tried to develop his archetypal unthinking weak striker. When he eventually comes to the point of confession and admits to 'feeling dirty', it is almost as if he were apologizing for the film as a whole (see Stead, 1989). According to Bryan Forbes, Craig's story had come to Beaver Films at a time when they were considering making an anti-apartheid film. They had been saved from that venture by a trade-union story. But why was it not a story sympathetic to the unions? Why wasn't it the kind of film that both Lindsay Anderson and Will Whitehead were longing to see?

In Britain, film production was a subculture and one largely cut off from other strands of life. It had always been shaped by the constraints of the market, of censorship and by a sense of total inferiority in the face of American dominance. It had its own career structure, which people entered at an early age, and it tended to live off its own resources and ingenuity without feeling the need to broaden its frame of reference. In his 1946 novel *Prater Violet*, Christopher Isherwood had depicted the workings of a London film studio in the 1930s (Isherwood, 1946). Drawing on his own experience, he described a situation in which nobody at the studio, and least of all the intellectual narrator, could write authentic dialogue for 'common people'. Two decades on that challenge remained, and some sense of it was reflected in Bryan Forbes's boast that in his script he had 'got closer to colloquial working-class people than some of my contemporaries writing directly for the cinema'. In the novel it was made clear to the intellectual that what film needed was technicians, for 'the movies aren't drama, they aren't literature: they're pure mathematics.' And that is why it was a small group of professional actors like Newman, Craig, Forbes and Attenborough who came up first with a union story rather than any left-wing intellectual. Isherwood had a technician make it quite clear to the intellectual why he was out of place in the studio: 'All you workers have such bloody romantic attitudes. You think you're too good for the movies. Don't you believe it. The movies are too good for you.' The movies were a world apart. For decades, intellectuals in Britain had despised them. Then in the 1930s and 1940s, inspired by foreign example and suddenly made aware of the importance of popular culture, they began to wonder whether the domestic product could be improved, but well-established routines and old habits were difficult to change.

The trade unions, too, were a world apart, another subculture with its own logic and career structure: another business in which technicians had been needed rather than romantics and intellectuals. And, like the film industry, it too had found itself in a situation in which it didn't have to worry too much about intellectuals and romantics, largely because during the previous 70 years it had won two major political battles. We have to remind ourselves just how small had been the Victorian trade-union movement: it had formed just one strand in a wider and complex social structure. Then, at the end of the century, price increases and improved education allowed the movement to double in size. It was precisely at that point that the Webbs came along to persuade middle-class intellectuals to accept the logic and value of the union phenomenon. The Webbs argued that 'the history of Trade unionism is the history of a State within our State and one so jealously democratic that to know it well is to know the English working-man as no reader of middle-class histories can know him' (Webb and Webb, 1920: ix). A new generation of politicians and political thinkers and journalists came to see trade unions as an essential buttress of democracy, an essential part of the process whereby workers became citizens. As the Hammonds explained, institutions like the unions were a 'pronounced' and 'positive' aspect of 'artisan civilisation' for 'the man who spends his life "making the twenty-fourth part of a pin" needs some sphere for his imagination' (Hammond and Hammond, 1932: 247).

Of course, the story of the unions had been a struggle, and the Webbs had confirmed that by describing the trial and sentencing of the Tolpuddle Martyrs in Dorchester in 1834 as 'monstrous' and 'scandalous'. The unions loved that story and incorporated it into many of their banners. But, as Professor Phelps Brown (1960) reminds us, the 1890s were not the 1830s. Many employers still felt inclined to challenge the unions but in many cases union leaders were pushing at half-open doors: the country was institutionalizing collective bargaining. By 1906, there was a trade unionist in the Cabinet, almost 50 trade unionists in the Commons and, as Phelps Brown (1960: 123) explains, the country's system of individual relations was 'the most mature in the world', although only one-sixth of wage-earners were union members. Further pressure on wages was to lead to another doubling of membership in the 1910–13 period but, of course, it was the First World War that ensured the unions their position at the top table of the political system, to make them what Phelps Brown and others have described as an 'estate of the realm'.

There was never any need for the unions to fight a battle across the culture and, of course, that was true of the labour movement as a whole. Recognition and, indeed, encouragement of the unions and a fuller working-class franchise had come within a society in which there were highly developed educational and recreational outlets. In a sense, all that was needed was pressure-group politics. That early period in which working-class readers had rediscovered socialism, and which was best represented by Robert Blatchford's *Clarion* and by Robert Tressel's novel *The Ragged Trousered Philanthropist*, gave way to a more Masonic sense of brotherhood. Both Ross McKibbin (1974) and Gordon Phillips (1992) have emphasized the degree to which labour 'organised for organisation's sake', and Phillips further argues that labour, unlike the Chartist and liberal movements of the previous century, never became a 'popular crusade' with large denominations and an effective press and failed to emulate the German socialists in forming 'cultural offshoots' (McKibbin, 1974, Phillips, 1992: 33). In these ways, labour remained highly sectarian and consequently its much-valued independence was bought at a price. Labour, of course, only became the largest party in the House of Commons in 1929, and it did not achieve an overall majority until 1945. Sectarianism had deterred many supporters, not least, as Peter Clarke has so effectively shown, the intellectual leaders of the liberal cause. As late as 1923 there were 159 Liberal MPs, and in 1929 five million voters still supported the liberal cause (Clarke, 1978: 235). There were many Liberals who shared L.T. Hobhouse's fears that 'Trade Unionism can be protective in spirit and oppressive in action' and that 'the oppressive capacities of a trade union could never be left out of account' (Hobhouse, 1911: 38). There were many non-political intellectuals who felt that too. In the Victorian period, there had been great middle-class novelists very much in sympathy with working men or women, but since those days things had changed. The working class had now organized and, what is more, middle-class workers had taken a closer look at working-class culture and decided that it was not for them. The time had come, as John Carey (1992) explained, for workers to dissociate themselves from the masses and their material concerns. The age of Mrs Gaskell and Dickens had given way to that of Gissing and Lawrence; and Lawrence it was who best summed up the new literary ethos. His argument was that all the workers' concern for 'industrialism, only wages and money and machinery' and nothing else meant that 'they understood mentally so horribly'. He thought it inevitable that politics would be 'a reduction to the lowest terms' and 'that is why we are bound to get something like Guild-Socialism in the long run' (Lawrence, 1950: 93, 94). The arts in general abandoned the labour movement and indeed the experiences of common people. Meanwhile, the country developed a film industry in which nobody ever thought to make films out of Lawrence's novels, stories or plays. The technicians knew best.

Gordon Phillips (1992) has related how Labour 'tried but failed' to develop a range of cultural institutions: that trying was most in evidence in the 1930s. Stephen Jones, in particular, has shown how active trade unionists and socialists developed independent cinema, theatre and sport in Glasgow, Newcastle, South Wales, the East End and especially in

Manchester and Salford in that decade (Jones, 1986, 1987). In those areas, too, there were local proletarian writers whose work helped to sustain the cause (Snee, 1982: 171). But all these efforts were essentially local and sectional and had to take their place in a culture that was still effectively controlled by London and Hollywood. What was more important was that, under a more professional leadership, trade unionism was recovering its numerical strength and its bargaining position. Quite crucially, the appreciable differences between middle-class and working-class incomes allowed the unions to achieve a position of strength in the new industries developing in the Midlands and South of England. It was that recovery that allowed the unions to win their second great political battle. In 1939 the country went to war again, and in 1940 Mr Churchill sent for Mr Bevin of the Transport Workers. The unions were now clearly seen to be an 'estate of the realm'. If Mr Churchill appreciated that point, so too did another generation of intellectuals who were now recruited to run Whitehall. As Addison (1975) and Skidelsky (1975, 1993) have shown, from 1940 on it was the intellectuals who 'created the dynamic for reconstruction'. Given a new function in the war machine, it was, says Skidelsky, 'the cleverest people' who 'defined the agenda of politics for the post-war period' and that included working with the unions (Addison, 1975). Quite rightly, Ken Coates (1982: 171) highlights the TUC Conference at Blackpool in 1945 as the moment of triumph which signified that the unions 'had arrived'.

Not that the country perceived it in quite that way. People still thought in strictly parliamentary terms and that meant emphasizing personality. Mr Churchill had given way to Mr Attlee who was helped by Mr Morrison and Mr Dalton: meanwhile, Mr Bevin was now running the world. The symbolic significance of Bevin was milked to the full: everyone knew that the Foreign Secretary had left school when he was 10 to work on a Somersetshire farm at 3/6d a week. Little was said, however, about the power structure that had made his career possible and the relationship between it and parliament. Indeed, as Henry Pelling was later to argue, this emphasis on the power and influence of Bevin might well have served to create the impression that the unions had entered a new phase of responsibility. That there was another side to trade-union activity had been shown in the number of wartime strikes but, as Pelling (1986) and Andrew Roberts (1995) have noted, very little was made of them not least because of wartime censorship. The unions had every reason to be happy with the fact that they had won political power in spite of having a low profile in the culture and in the press. With so many friends in high places, there was no need to worry about image or cultural representation. There was no possible reason to ask why feature films or novels so rarely dealt with unions even when the working classes were the subject matter or to question why playwrights so ignored the drama of industrial relations. Of course, open criticism of the unions became increasingly general in the press of the mid-1950s but even then complacency had not been punctured. 'For many years after 1945', Jean Seaton (1982: 272) argued, 'the trade unions accepted their media image fatalistically as routine misinterpretation: it did not seem to affect their influence over Government which developed dramatically' (Hopkins, 1963: 123).

All of this background explains why the film-maker Lindsay Anderson and the trade-unionist Will Whitehead were to feel so frustrated at the end of the 1950s. The great irony, however, was that their frustration was being expressed at a time when British culture was changing more dramatically than at any time since the Victorian period and it was becoming far more democratic. These changes, though, were just a little too late for the British film industry which thereby once again illustrated just how cut off it was from the most creative energies in the country. The changes were a little late, too, for the trade unions. In Britain at that time there were two at first quite distinct strands. All over the country there were young people who wanted to express themselves in novels, plays and music that reflected their own rather than metropolitan standards and themes. If there was inspiration to hand it was largely American, and it was necessary therefore that their depictions and means of fulfilment involved individual success and a degree of mobility. It was this sense of cultural release that was described as 'Anger' and which opened up popular culture as never before. The second development came in the universities where influential dons were smashing the restraint of their disciplines and redefining the whole meaning of culture. Most influential were the historian E.P. Thompson, who showed how workers could be 'rescued from the anonymity', and the literary critics Richard Hoggart and Raymond Williams, who fully illustrated the extent to which nationally a culture had been hijacked by élites.

It was to take some time before these strands of anger and criticism came together and even then their victories were won within the sectional activity of education and the arts rather than nationally. What was interesting, too, was that neither strand was organically linked with the unions. Writers and musicians 'did their own thing', while even socialist intellectuals expressed their reservations with regard to union activity. Hoggart rather dismissed unionists as belonging 'to the earnest minority', while Raymond Williams, who had very briefly praised the unions for their collective democracy in *Culture and Society*, went on in *The Long Revolution* of three years later to talk of 'sectional self-interest' and to confess that it was 'not surprising that many people never see in the trade union movement merely a set of men playing in the market in very much the terms of the employers they oppose' (Williams, 1958: 314; 1961: 328). Williams was fully aware that strikes were part of the 'British way of life' and in his novels he set out to identify their place in his set of values. Nobody was less interested in cinema than Williams, and in his novels the drama is more in the ideas than in the action, but it is still interesting that nobody even thought to film his *Second Generation* (1964) in which 'the daft old trade unions' and a labour dispute are at the core of a family's debate on its values (Williams, 1964: 100, 129).[2] As influential as he was in general terms, Williams stood alone in realizing the ways in which political values needed to be argued out and established precisely at that point where the public, the personal, the economic and the cultural coincide.

Of course, the world of trade union democracy that the Webbs and Hammonds had applauded was still in existence for those who cared to look. One writer who did look was the American Clancy Sigal. His career had taken him from the radical Chicago of the 1930s into union work and eventually to Hollywood where he became all too aware of how history can be suppressed as new mythologies are created. He fled to Europe to write his 1961 classic autobiographical novel *Going Away* in which he provides an alternative social history of America by celebrating trade-union memories of victories and more often defeats: 'other men may have their Yorktowns and Little Big Horns and Gettysburgs. For me and my family to rank with Haymarket and Lawrence there was always Coeur d'Arlene where the pioneer dream was killed' (Sigal, 1961: 115). As he was writing his book, Sigal recharged his radical batteries by visiting the South Yorkshire coalfield and reporting his findings in another documentary novel, *Weekend in Dinlock*. Here we find an American writer discovering that in the pit village 'a genuine public' still exists and operates in a 'unique and strong way', for 'as many villagers express opinions as receive them': through 'the union branch there is an opportunity to immediately and effectively answer back'. The visitor notes that 'opinion finds ready outlets in actions – and authoritative institutions have not (yet) destroyed the autonomy of the village (Sigal, 1970): 58; Laing, 1986). What clearly fascinated Sigal was the relationship between the rank and file and their elected leader, a subject which then, and for a quarter of a century thereafter, cried out to be filmed.

Clancy Sigal had gone north to check his radicalism just as most English writers were heading south. Eventually, Lindsay Anderson was to make a film with David Storey, the most important of these writers, and although *This Sporting Life* (1963) was a film that showed what might have been in terms of realism, by 1963 it had long been clear that theatre rather than film was to be the cutting edge in the new cultural dispensation. It was too late for British film to celebrate the unions, and cinema audiences were left with the clear images of that infuriating shop steward Kite and of the mass stupidity which had led to Richard Attenborough's discomfort (Stead, 1996).

Now it was the age of television, a medium that was deeply influenced by the Thompson, Hoggart, Williams way of thinking and which from the 1960s encouraged new writing. But it was also a news medium that made very apparent and familiar the frequency of strikes and the power of industrial union leaders. Television viewers were also fed a regular diet of sit-coms, one of the most popular of which in the early 1960s was *The Rag Trade*, a show in which the shop steward Paddy (played by Miriam Karlin) would regularly blow her whistle and bellow 'Everybody out!' The culture had moved on but not by that much.

Notes

1 The London critics reviewed the film in the week beginning 6 March 1960. See the British Film Institute file and also Hill (1986: 199).

2 For Williams's fiction, see Smith (1993), ch. 10: 'Border Loyalties'.

References

Addison, Paul (1975) *The Road to 1945*. London: Jonathan Cape.

Anderson, Lindsay (1955) 'The last scene of *On the Waterfront*', *Sight and Sound*, 24 (3): 127.

Anderson, Lindsay (1957) 'Get out and push', in Tom Maschler (ed.), *Declaration*. London: MacGibbon and Kee.

Carey, John (1992) *The Intellectuals and the Masses*. London: Faber and Faber.

Clarke, Peter (1978) *Liberals and Social Democrats*. Cambridge: Cambridge University Press.

Coates, Ken (1982) 'The vagaries of participation, 1945–1960', in Ben Pimlott and Chris Cook (eds), *Trade Unions in British Politics*. London: Longman.

Forbes, Bryan (1974) *Notes for a Life*. London: Collins.

Hacker, Jonathan and Price, David (1991) *Take 10, Contemporary British Film Directors*. Oxford: Clarendon.

Hammond, J.L. and Hammond, Barbara (1932) *The Town Labourer, 1760–1832*. London: Longman (first published in 1917).

Hewison, Robert (1981) *In Anger*. London: Weidenfeld and Nicolson.

Hill, John (1986) *Sex, Class and Realism*. London:

Hobhouse, L.T. (1911) *Liberalism*. London: Williams and Norgate.

Hopkins, Harry (1963) *The New Look*. London: Secker and Warburg.

Isherwood, Christopher (1946) *Prater Violet*. London: Methuen.

Jones, Stephen G. (1986) *Workers at Play*. London: Routledge.

Jones, Stephen G. (1987) *The British Labour Movement and Film*. London: Routledge.

Kauffman, Stanley (1966) *A World on Film*. New York: Harper and Row.

Laing, Stuart (1986) *Representation of Working-class Life, 1957–1964*. London: Macmillan.

Lawrence, D.H. (1950) *Selected Letters*. London: Penguin.

McKibbin, Ross (1974) *The Evolution of the Labour Party*. Oxford: Oxford University Press.

Pelling, Henry (1986) 'The impact of the war on the Labour Party', in Harold L. Smith (ed.), *War and Social Change: British Society in the Second World War*. Manchester: Manchester University Press. pp. 129–48.

Phelps Brown, E.H. (1960) *The Growth of British Industrial Relations*. London: Macmillan.

Phillips, Gordon (1992) *The Rise of the Labour Party*. London: Routledge.

Richards, Jeffrey and Aldgate, Anthony (1983) *Best of British*. Oxford: Blackwell.

Roberts, Andrew (1995) 'We didn't pull together', *Spectator*, 6 May, p. 14.

Robinson, David (1992) *Richard Attenborough*. London: National Film Theatre.

Seaton, Jean (1982) 'Trade unions and the media', in B. Pimlott and C. Cook (eds), *Trade Unions in British Politics*. London: Longman. p. 272.

Sigal, Clancy (1961) *Going Away*. New York: Ian Dell.

Sigal, Clancy (1970) *Weekend in Dinlock*. Boston: Bard.

Skidelsky, Robert (1975) 'Review of Paul Addison's *The Road to 1945*', *Spectator*, 25 October.

Skidelsky, Robert (1993) *Interests and Obsessions*. London: Macmillan.

Smith, Dai (1993) *Aneurin Bevan and the World of South Wales*. Cardiff: University of Wales Press.

Snee, Carol (1982) 'Working class literature or proletarian writing', in Jan Clark et al. (eds), *Culture and Crisis in Britain in the Thirties*. London: Lawrence and Wishart. pp. 165–91.

Stead, Peter (1989) *Film and the Working Class*. London: Routledge.

Stead, Peter (1996) '*I'm All Right Jack*: film in context', *History Today*, 46 (1), January.

Walker, Alexander (1974) *Hollywood England*. London: Michael Joseph.

Walker, Alexander (1981) *Peter Sellers*. London: Weidenfeld and Nicolson.

Webb, Sidney and Webb, Beatrice (1920) *The History of Trade Unionism*, 1660–1920. London (first published 1894).

Williams, Raymond (1958) *Culture and Society, 1780–1950*. London: Chatto and Windus.

Williams, Raymond (1961) *The Long Revolution*. London: Chatto and Windus.

Williams, Raymond (1964) *Second Generation*. London: Chatto and Windus.

Figure 4.1 Disclosure, 1994, *Warner Brothers*

PART II
SEX AND VIOLENCE

4

What is Wrong with this Picture? Sex and Gender Relations in *Disclosure*

Joanna Brewis

This chapter takes as its primary focus the Warner Brothers' film *Disclosure* (1994), starring Michael Douglas and Demi Moore.[1] *Disclosure* is the first major English language feature film to take as its main subject the controversial issue of workplace sexual harassment. Other films have, of course, dealt with sexual harassment in the organization; for example, *The Secret of My Success* (1987) and *Wall Street* (1987). However, in many of these films, the episodes of harassment exist as subsidiary developments in the plot, included, one might suggest, for the sake of capturing a 'real' organizational atmosphere. The possible exception is *Nine to Five* (1980), which could be seen to focus more specifically on harassment, but to a large extent arguably emerges as a commentary on the nature of female friendship and the possibilities of fighting back against male oppression that such friendship provides.

Disclosure narrates the tribulations of Tom Sanders (Michael Douglas). Sanders is expecting a promotion to become Vice-President of Advanced Operations and Planning at the Seattle site of the information technology company DigiCom. DigiCom is in the process of merging with publishing company Conley–White, a move which will net DigiCom's Chief Executive Officer, Bob Garvin, some hundred million dollars. A central component in the merger is DigiCom's Arcamax CD-ROM, a ground-breaking product. Sanders, as the current Head of the Manufacturing Division within the Advanced Products Group (APG), oversees the production of Arcamax, a process beset with problems that are significantly affecting product integrity. The merger with Conley–White is also to involve the spin-off of the APG, making it public. This will mean substantial profits for everyone who works in the division, given that they will have the opportunity to purchase shares cheaply before the stock is sold publicly. Despite Sanders's expectations, however, an ex-lover of his (Meredith Johnson, played by Demi Moore) is appointed over his head. Sanders is shocked, upset and resentful at this turn of events. Despite his chagrin, however, Sanders agrees to attend a late meeting with Johnson that evening. During this meeting, Johnson makes very explicit sexual advances towards Sanders, to which he nearly succumbs. However, in the end, Sanders rejects Johnson's enticements, making her extremely angry. When he arrives at work the following day, Sanders is informed by Philip Blackburn, the DigiCom lawyer, that Johnson has complained of his sexually harassing her at their meeting. In his turn, Sanders consults lawyer Catherine Alvarez, an expert in the field of workplace harassment, who advises him to do the same. The result is a DigiCom internal mediation at which a rather improbable *deus ex machina* intervenes. Sanders realizes that the entire interaction between him and Johnson would have been recorded on a friend's answering machine because when she had made her advances to him he had been speaking to the machine on his mobile phone and had failed to hang up. Sanders obtains the tape and proves Johnson to be a liar. DigiCom promise Sanders one hundred thousand dollars in compensation for his 'pain and suffering' and also guarantee that Johnson will only remain *in situ* during the merger, after which an excuse will be made about her having to leave because of a medical emergency. Sanders and Alvarez are triumphant. However, when Sanders returns to work that evening, an e-mail warning from an anonymous colleague makes him suspicious that all is still not well. Indeed, by another lucky chance, Sanders happens to overhear a conversation between Blackburn and Johnson which reveals that, at the following morning's merger announcement, Johnson is to ask Sanders questions about the Arcamax CD-ROM that will show him to be responsible for the problems in the production line – and thus discredit him. By means of complicated electronic trickery, which features strongly throughout the film, Sanders gathers evidence to show that Johnson herself has ordered changes to the production line specifications in order to blame him for these problems. At the merger announcement, Sanders mounts a counter-offensive, revealing Johnson's activities by means of video tape of her visit to the Kuala Lumpur plant where Arcamax is manufactured and memos that prove that she has asked for the changes to be made. As a result, Johnson is replaced by Stephanie Kaplan, who is subsequently revealed to be Sanders's anonymous e-mail correspondent.

Having briefly summarized the plot of *Disclosure*, the chapter now moves on to establish the theoretical commitments which underpin the analysis of the film here.

Theoretical Commitments

This chapter employs a Foucauldian reading of *Disclosure* as a piece of knowledge about organizations, as an interpretation of working life in the modern social. The discussion makes particular use of the connection that Foucault (1977, 1979, 1980, 1982) draws between power, knowledge and subjectivity – his idea that we come to know ourselves *solely* through the powerful operations of knowledge, that we are subject to power such that all that we know of ourselves consists of its effects. For Foucault, there is no such thing as human nature, nothing so 'solid' within humans as to constitute any kind of essence or enduring truth. He suggests that: 'there is no sovereign, founding subject, a universal form of subject to be found everywhere. I am very sceptical of this view and very hostile to it. I believe, on the contrary, that the subject is constituted through practices of subjection' (Foucault, 1988: 50).

Foucault argues that we are subject to and made subject by the power/knowledge regimes that exist within modernity (in other words, the age which we currently inhabit), that we define ourselves through the multiplicity of knowledges that are available to us. According to Foucault, power does not operate over us; rather, we subjugate ourselves to its operations. We come to 'know' 'ourselves' through a process of subjection, of subjectification. Power for Foucault is therefore much less repressive than it is productive – of all that we 'know' of 'self':

> The individual is not be to conceived of as a sort of elementary nucleus, a primitive atom, a multiple and inert material on which power comes to fasten or against which it happens to strike, and in so doing subdues or crushes individuals . . . it is already one of the prime effects of power that certain bodies, certain gestures, certain desires, certain discourses, come to be identified and constituted as individuals . . . the individual is an effect of power. . . . (Foucault, 1980: 98)

What concerns Foucault, however, is that our preoccupation with the truth of ourselves, with finding out 'who' we 'are', blinds us to this process of subjectification – and means that we are trapped within a particular kind of subjectivity, that we are unable to experiment with ways to be other than those we define as true. The key to intellectual analysis, for Foucault, therefore lies in making the operations of power visible, in discussing what it means for us to relate to self in particular ways – so that we may be able to take up a more active and engaged process of self-fashioning (Foucault, 1985, 1986, 1988, 1990).

In line with Foucault's epistemology, it is suggested in this chapter that *Disclosure* may have generated significant subjectifying effects, given the huge success of the film. It is the concern of this analysis to identify the possible consequences of this powerfulness: what might it mean for individuals to come to define themselves through the piece of knowledge about organizations that is *Disclosure*? The overall remit of the chapter, then, is to ask: 'What are the consequences for individuals and/or the community if they embrace this text?' (Nothstine et al., 1994: 5).

Further to this argument that *Disclosure* constitutes a piece of knowledge with potential subjectifying effects, Denzin (1995: 24) argues that contemporary society is undergoing a process of 'cinematization', that the social is 'a culture which came to know itself, collectively and individually, through the images and stories that Hollywood produced'. Elsewhere, Denzin suggests that the only kind of human subject that currently exists is a 'postmodern version of the self that stands [inside] the structures of meaning produced by the contemporary consciousness industries . . . the postmodern mediated self . . . finds its moral solidarity in those narrative tales that circulate in the cinematic culture' (Denzin, 1995: 215).

In other words, contemporary human subjects come in large part to know themselves through the meanings and images presented to them in cinema. For Denzin, this marks a transition from modernity to post-modernity. It is possible to suggest, then, that the kind of analysis undertaken in this chapter, of *Disclosure* as a subjectifying power/knowledge regime, allows insights into how (post)modern individuals come to know themselves. In sum, this analysis proposes that *Disclosure* is both rhetoric and poetic (Medhurst and Benson, 1984: xv). That is to say, *Disclosure* is seen here to constitute a *persuasive* cultural artefact, not simply a piece of art. Furthermore, the focus here is much less on what those who made the film intended than on the effects that it might be seen to generate. *Disclosure* is analysed as a text in its own right, as something that operates quite independently of the agenda of those who created it (Foucault, 1986; Bordo, 1992; Blair et al., 1994; Denzin, 1995).

The discussion of *Disclosure* presented here will deal with two main issues:

1 *Disclosure* has been lauded for its position on the issue of workplace sexual harassment: the reversal of roles in which a woman becomes harasser and a man her victim. However, it is argued here that it is rather too glib to praise the film for this reason, given the way in which the female harasser is portrayed. This representation is argued to constitute and consolidate understandings of working women as threatening and, moreover, unnatural in their organizational success.
2 It is suggested that the highly eroticized portrayal of sexual harass-ment in *Disclosure* may constitute subjects who fail to accept that harassment by definition is unwanted and abusive, subjects who rather see the victim of harassment as 'asking for it' or at least enjoying 'it' in some way.

Men, Women and Work in *Disclosure*

Perhaps the element of *Disclosure* that has achieved the most notoriety is its depiction of sexual harassment deriving from a woman and directed at a man. Indeed, reviewers have praised *Disclosure* for 'putting a spin' on the issue of sexual harassment. Certainly, this representation of sexual harassment is entirely at odds with that offered by liberal feminist literature on harassment, which presents harassment as a set of behaviours utilized by men in organizations to debase and degrade their female colleagues (MacKinnon, 1979; Benson and Thomson, 1982; Hoffman, 1986; Fain and Anderton, 1987; Ehrenreich, 1990; Stringer et al., 1990, among others). Indeed, some of the commentators in this area suggest that it is not possible for a woman genuinely to harass a male colleague, to make unwanted and intimidating sexual advances to him in the same way as men do towards women, because of the societal power differentials between men and women. The fact that it is Johnson who harasses Sanders in *Disclosure* therefore goes against the grain of the depiction of harassment in the literature which has emerged around it. It is salient to quote Barry Levinson here, producer-director of the film, cited in *Disclosure*'s production notes (n.d.: 3):

> The film allows us to approach the idea of sexual harassment with fresh eyes. Because the roles are reversed, it allows women to say to men 'feel what it's like to be in our shoes.' The flip-flop of roles illuminates some behaviors which we might not otherwise be sensitive to, by forcing us out of our polarized views.

It is the case that Sanders's experience of harassment in *Disclosure* is, in some respects, true to what harassment literature identifies as characteristic of the experience of being harassed. For example, in making a complaint, Sanders endangers his own position in the company. Bob Garvin is extremely angry when it is revealed that Sanders has consulted a lawyer and means to complain to the State Human Rights Commission if Johnson is not sacked. Indeed, he tells Blackburn to call DigiCom security and have Sanders 'thrown out on the sidewalk'. Sanders also jeopardizes his marriage: initially concerned that his wife Susan should not find out about the incident in Johnson's office, he does not tell her what has transpired. Susan only inadvertently finds out through Sanders's colleague, Mark Lewyn. She is horrified, firstly, that Sanders has not told her that he and Johnson had been previously involved and, secondly, that he has not told her about what had happened at their meeting. Furthermore, while Susan agrees to attend the internal mediation for Sanders's sake, she finds the proceedings extremely upsetting, especially when it is revealed that Johnson has performed fellatio on Sanders during the meeting between them. Susan harangues Sanders afterwards for claiming that he and Johnson had not 'had sex' (for example, she refers sarcastically to 'this non-sex sex thing'). Susan also tells Catherine Alvarez that the fellatio will be extremely hard for her to forget. These risks to one's organizational position and one's personal relationships as potential consequences of making a complaint of sexual harassment are also writ large in the literature on harassment.

None the less, it seems too simplistic to argue that men watching *Disclosure* may come to define themselves as possible victims of harassment and therefore become a good deal more sensitive towards their female colleagues, as Barry Levinson implies is the case. This is because the depiction of the relationship between men and women in organizations in the film is much less than subversive in another way. In fact, *Disclosure* could be seen to represent what Gitlin (cited in Dow, 1994: 111) refers to as a 'recombinant' packaging of an already well-established understanding. In *Disclosure*'s presentation of Meredith Johnson in particular, it is possible to argue that the film as a piece of knowledge is 'caught up in a system of references to other bodies, other texts, other sentences' (Foucault, cited in Blair et al., 1994: 373).

This 'recombinant' character of *Disclosure* can be seen in the way in which the film presents working women and their sexuality as a threat to their male colleagues. Other 'corporate' films which feature successful working women are characterized by the same theme – *Working Girl* (1988), *Baby Boom* (1987) and *Presumed Innocent* (1990), for example. These films present women who achieve organizational success as overly competitive, overly aggressive, as willing to go to any lengths to secure their organizational future. Returning to *Disclosure*, Johnson is, in the first instance, a surprise appointment. Johnson has gained her DigiCom experience at another location within the empire – the Silicon Valley home offices – and has been re-located to Seattle. Furthermore, she is appointed to head up the APG when she reputedly has little technical expertise or, indeed, experience. In fact, Sanders protests to the other APG division heads, Mark Lewyn, Don Cherry and Mary Anne Hunter, that 'This is a technical division. [Johnson] doesn't know the difference between software and a cashmere sweater.'

From the point where Johnson enters the film, then, it is implied that she has much less right to the position she has achieved than does Sanders, who has ten years' experience in the technical division. Indeed, Sanders actually claims at one point that he 'built this place'. There is some speculation among the APG division heads as to how Johnson has secured the position, much of it centring on her relationship with Bob Garvin:

Lewyn: [to Sanders] Hey, let me guess, [Johnson's] attractive? . . . Great rack, nipples like pencil erasers?
Sanders: She's attractive, yeah, she's very attractive.
Lewyn: You think she's sleeping with Garvin?
Cherry: Ah, that's why he bought the Nordic track . . .
Lewyn: You know, it's a curse to be me. Life holds no surprises.

The following conversation, which takes place later in the same scene, is also significant:

Hunter: [to Sanders] Well, now you can sleep your way to a better job.
Cherry: [sarcastically] Yeah, right!
Hunter: Wait a minute, why? Why her [Johnson] and not Tom? He's not attractive?
Cherry: Because men and women are different.

In this second exchange, Cherry implies that men would not use the tactic of 'sleeping their way to the top' – but that women do.

Here, a particular representation of Johnson begins to emerge. It is implied that she has gained her organizational advantage by illegitimate means – by using her sexuality. In a different vein, it is suggested elsewhere in the film that Johnson enjoys a father–daughter relationship with Bob Garvin, specifically when he formally introduces Johnson to the APG team:

> I've always wanted to be able to give you the most advanced, the most original leadership that I could . . . [but] there's always been so much opposition from the nay-sayers and the poo-pooers to any break with tradition. I mean, every time I've wanted to promote a woman, to break the glass ceiling, it's always been the same story – 'but Bob', 'but Bob'. I've thought about it often since my daughter's death that, in today's climate, had she lived, it would be extremely rare that she ever got to run a company. So it has a special meaning for me when I tell you that this Friday when we announce the merger we will also announce that the new Vice President for Advanced Operations and Planning here in Seattle will be Meredith Johnson.

Here, Garvin almost goes as far as to suggest that Johnson is a proxy for his daughter. In this scene, it is again possible to identify the theme that Johnson's promotion has had little to do with her own abilities – rather, she is a 'pet' of the (male) boss.

In *Disclosure*, then, Johnson is represented in one instance as having traded on her sexuality to achieve organizational success and, in another, it is implied that Garvin especially favours her because she reminds him of his dead daughter. Indeed, aside from Garvin's accolades to her (he tells Saunders, for example, that Johnson has rescued the Conley–White merger by suggesting the APG spin-off), Johnson's actual abilities are either dismissed as inadequate or simply not discussed.

It is interesting to note that *Disclosure*, in this denigration of its female lead, is redolent of another piece of knowledge about men and women in organizations, the 1970s situation comedy *The Mary Tyler Moore Show* (Dow, 1994). This long-running series was heralded at the time as path-breaking in its depiction of lead character Mary Richards as a successful working woman. However, as Dow points out, the series actually presents Richards as heavily dependent on boss Lou Grant; he is very paternal towards her and storyline after storyline proves that she relies on his guidance, that she 'cannot really "make it on her own"' (Dow, 1994: 107). Furthermore, as *Disclosure* unfolds, Johnson grows steadily more dislikeable. Indeed, so unpleasant does she become that she takes on Cruella De Vil-like proportions, becoming a virtual caricature. After the incident with Sanders in her office, for example, Johnson is the spurned and vindictive woman. As Sanders retreats, she screams at him: 'You son of a bitch! You get back here and finish what you started, do you hear me? Get back here and finish what you started or you're fucking dead. Do you hear me? You are fucking dead.' The next day,

Johnson dupes Sanders into being late for an important meeting (with the Conley–White team) and at the same meeting manages to raise doubts about his trustworthiness. So she is conniving and manipulative.

Other episodes in the film consolidate this image of Johnson. During the mediation process, Alvarez discovers that 10 of Johnson's male DigiCom subordinates have suddenly left the company or requested transfers. The clear implication at this stage of the film is that she is a serial harasser who is notorious across DigiCom for her sexual exploits. Johnson also lies her way coolly through the mediation itself. She tells those assembled that Sanders attacked her physically, pulling her hair and forcing her to her knees, whereupon he put his penis into her mouth. She says that she feels extremely uncomfortable having to recount the story, accepts a glass of water and produces a very convincing tremble as she drinks it. She continues by telling of how Sanders tore off her underwear and threw her down on a piece of scaffolding, and of how she was only able to fight him off by kneeing him in the groin. As Johnson 'breaks down', Philip Blackburn concludes her story by telling the mediation that Johnson didn't want to press formal charges because she didn't want to destroy Sanders's career or his marriage, but that she cannot continue to work with him. This is because, as Johnson herself claims, 'I would be too frightened. I'm frightened just sitting here.' As the mediation progresses, the audience is left in little doubt as to exactly how far Johnson will go to protect her own position. Johnson is also extremely ungracious in defeat, telling Alvarez at the close of the mediation that:

> You wanna put me on trial? Let's at least be honest about what it's for. I am a sexually aggressive woman and I like it. Tom knew it and you can't handle it. It is the same damn thing since the beginning of time. Veil it, hide it, lock it up and throw away the key. We expect a woman to do a man's job, make a man's money and then walk around with a parasol and lie down for a man to fuck her like it was still a hundred years ago – well, no thank you!

The disapproving faces of the mediation personnel reveal their distaste at Johnson's outburst – it seems that she has finally revealed her 'true colours'. Furthermore, in the closing stages of the film, and as if to reinforce how manipulative Johnson is, Sanders also discovers that she has deliberately introduced low-grade materials into the Arcamax manufacturing process so as to discredit him.

In sum, the steady and relentless way in which Johnson's character, integrity and abilities are undermined during *Disclosure* means that at no point are the audience encouraged to identify with her. It is Sanders who wins audience loyalty, not Johnson: 'the "grammar" of the story places the . . . spectator with the hero' (Mulvey, 1989: 32). In the film, Sanders is the helpless, hapless hero, battling against the powerful corporate machine. Johnson, on the other hand, is presented as corrupt, dangerous and disturbed, as a 'Single Working Woman' who represents 'calamity and destruction' (Denzin, 1995: 121), who threatens 'law and organiza-tion'. Johnson is depicted, then, not only as undeserving of her position, but, furthermore, as conniving, ruthless and exploitative. Successful woman in a man's world she undoubtedly is, but her success is identified in the film as the product of manipulation and megalomania on her part. Her closing remarks to Sanders make her arrogance and burning ambition very clear: 'I've had calls from ten head-hunters with job offers in the last hour. Don't be surprised if I'm back in ten years to buy this place.' Overall then, *Disclosure* implies that 'women's power is always achieved illegitimately and at the expense of men, and sometimes at the expense of women' (Smith, 1989: 34).[2]

Not only is Johnson an organizational usurper, she is also presented as no kind of role model for the working woman. Sanders regularly appears (a) in the company of his conventionally nuclear family, often in the well-appointed but comfortable family home; (b) coming from the family home; or (c) going to the family home – the Seattle ferry is a recurrent motif in his life. Johnson, on the other hand, never appears outside the DigiCom building – she exists as workplace creature only. Other clues to Johnson's one-dimensional existence include her revelation during her attempted seduction of Sanders. She tells him that she has only an orange and 'a couple of' bottles of champagne in her refrigerator at home. In the same conversation, she mocks marriage:

Johnson: I guess it can be a bit inhibiting.
Sanders: What's that?
Johnson: Domesticity.
Sanders: Ah, you'd be surprised.
Johnson: Well, I don't imagine you can jump her from behind because all of a sudden you get excited by the way she bends down to pick up the soap. You remember that, don't you [referring to their past relationship]?
Sanders: Yeah, I remember that.
Johnson: And you miss it.
Sanders: I have my compensations.
Johnson: Oh, course you do. Life's a series of trade-offs. Isn't that what you tell yourself?

Here Johnson makes it clear that she despises marriage and domesticity – again coding herself as a corporate being through and through. Later in the film, Johnson is shown using the gym at work, then returning to her office immediately after her work-out. Her life revolves around work and she appears to have little or no private life; indeed, she even conducts her sex life at work, with male colleagues. Consequently, to borrow a term from Gherardi (1995: 135), there is some 'ratification' of Johnson's organizational achievements – she is presented as an individual who has had to give up all vestiges of a private life in order to attain the position that she has. Johnson is not a 'real' woman with a home, a partner or a family; nor is she a 'superwoman' because she cannot manage a successful domestic life as well as a successful career.[3]

Disclosure, then, seems much less than disruptive in its portrayal of women in organizations. Not only is it strongly reminiscent of other films and television programmes in a similar genre, but many organizational analysts emphasize that men in organizations are already suspicious of the women with whom they work (see, for example, Sheppard, 1989; Lurie, 1992; McDowell and Court, 1994; Brewis et al., 1997). This hostility is seen to manifest itself, in particular, in a derogation of the woman who successfully competes with her male colleagues. This woman is often accused of being exactly the kind of character that Johnson represents in *Disclosure* – overly aggressive, overly competitive, threateningly sexual and so on. Such a derogation can be seen, argue these researchers, not only to punish the successful female, but also to serve as a warning to other working women not to get 'above themselves'. As Sheppard (1989) points out, women managers in organizations have, as a result, to deploy certain kinds of strategies to avoid being punished or ostracized for their success:

> While a number of women respondents see themselves as successful and confident, they also acknowledge the continued existence of discrimination and double standards applied to women. They have developed strategies which allow them to maintain personal distance from such problems, saying that solutions lie with individuals rather than with the organizational structure, that sexism is a 'fact of life' and that women need to 'laugh off' sexual politics . . . strategies which are more assertive or insistent raise gender (which is to say, femaleness) to a level of awareness that is challenging or threatening to the (male) status quo. Insistence on gender equity involves taking less individual blame for what is understood as a structural phenomenon . . . such an analysis lays the blame outside oneself, but also fosters feelings of powerlessness and alienation. (Sheppard, 1989: 156)

Given the above, it seems that *Disclosure* may serve only to consolidate subject positions that already exist; that the representation of Meredith Johnson in this film is likely to confirm the understanding on the part of working men that their female colleagues are a threat, that they have no legitimate claim to organizational success and that they must be punished should they be seen to have achieved that success. However, there is an important facet of *Disclosure* other than the 'cartoonish' depiction of its main female character that marks the film as dangerous in particular ways. The next section of this chapter assesses the possible effects of the way in which sexual harassment is represented in the film.

Sexual 'Harassment' in *Disclosure*

Those involved in *Disclosure*, like executive producer Peter Giuliano, insist that: '"Disclosure" is a story about power and wielding power . . . Whether you control people sexually or through fear for their life or loss of their work and social reputation, it's really just manipulation' (Giuliano, cited in *Disclosure* production notes, n.d.: 3). Indeed, the 'tag line' of the film is 'Sex is power'. This phrase is very much in keeping with an understanding of sexual harassment as being a set of sexualized behaviours that are unwelcome or unwanted, a set of sexualized behaviours that are underpinned by more or less explicit coercion.

However, it is argued here that *Disclosure* may actually be seen to generate a very different understanding of sexual harassment; that is to say, an understanding of harassment that casts the recipient as not entirely unreceptive to the behaviour. In the first instance, it is important to note that the audience knows that Sanders and Johnson have been involved before; that is to say, the audience knows that he has desired her in the past. It is also the case that Johnson is portrayed in a highly eroticized way throughout the film. Indeed, the first time that the audience sees Johnson, all that is actually visible of her are her legs, clad in sheer tights and high heels. She is ascending a staircase while Sanders watches – needless to say, appreciatively – from the bottom. The second shot of Johnson is very similar. Here she is sitting in Garvin's office, her skirt high on her thigh; the only difference here is that this time the camera eventually pans up to her face.

Aside from the obviously sexualized clues of the tights and the high heels, Johnson also dresses in a particular way. She is 'the embodiment of a particular kind of male fantasy, wearing tight business suits which accentuate her attractive figure' (Smith, 1989: 23).[4] Apart from being tight, Johnson's suit jackets are also usually buttoned low, emphasizing her breasts. Further, she has a penchant for sleeveless blouses and short skirts. There is also talk of Johnson's appearance among the other characters in the film. After Garvin has introduced her to the team, Sanders and his APG colleagues Mark Lewyn and Don Cherry joke about how sexy Johnson is:

Lewyn: [to Sanders] Now, [Johnson] doesn't give you a boner? Because, you know, I definitely have lift-off. [To Cherry] What about you, Frisky, got a little wood in your life?
Cherry: She's very nice.
Lewyn: Yeah.
Sanders: [to Lewyn, laughing] I'll call you tonight, tell you what the company line is [on Arcamax].
Lewyn: Oh, don't give me that! Come on, you have a sexual urge every 20 minutes. It's a physiological certainty. You know, it's hard-wired into your limbic brain. You can't fight it – why would you want to fight it? Live a little! I mean, ten years from now you're going to need a fork-lift to get a hard-on, pal.

These constant visual and verbal references to Johnson's sex appeal mean that, by the time the so-called harassment scene unfolds, Johnson is firmly coded as an object of desire (Denzin, 1995). Furthermore, this scene makes it explicit that Sanders is sexually attracted to Johnson. It is true that, when Johnson makes her intentions clear – entwining herself around his neck while he is making a 'phone call and saying: 'Let's get down to business' – Sanders initially struggles, repeating 'no' and 'wait'. Johnson does not listen to his entreaties, pushing him on to a chair, straddling him and unbuttoning her blouse. She places his hands on her breasts and subsequently on her buttocks. Johnson then unbuttons Sanders's shirt and begins to fondle his groin, telling him: 'Why don't you just lie back and let me take you? I could have had anybody and I picked you. Now you've got all the power.'

None the less, while Sanders has protested throughout this series of events, he is also clearly aroused, given his constant grunting and sighing. When Johnson begins to fellate him, he seems to give in to his desire for her and, indeed, at this point takes control of the encounter. Sanders pushes Johnson on to her back, asking her: 'so you wanna get fucked, huh?'[5] He pins her beneath him, takes off his jacket, rips off her blouse and then begins to kiss her breasts. Then Sanders tears off Johnson's underwear, grins at her triumphantly and digitally penetrates her. He scrambles on top of her, seemingly to achieve penile penetration. She is urging him on. Their sprawl across a piece of scaffolding in the ante-room of Johnson's office, the discomfort involved, seemingly underline the powerful nature of their passion. Ironically, however, it is this position that brings Sanders 'to his senses'. He catches sight of himself and Johnson in a glass screen, says 'oh God, look at us' and, while she is exhorting him to 'put it in', tells her 'No, no, no, no, I can't do this . . . I'm not gonna do this . . . I'm not gonna do it, no.' Eventually, he pushes her away and she falls on to the floor.

In this crucial scene, then, Sanders is reluctant only in the first instance, and even then not entirely reluctant – he is clearly fighting his desire for Johnson. Subsequently, he becomes a willing (not to say proactive) participant in the proceedings. His 'realization' at the scene's dramatic climax, the way he backs off saying 'I'm not gonna do this', is a clear indication that Johnson, Cleopatra-like, has had him, albeit temporarily, in her sexual thrall. Highly charged as their brief erotic interaction is, it seems that Sanders is tempted much more than he is coerced. So *Disclosure* offers a representation of sexual harassment in which the recipient succumbs to the sexual advances before deciding that, in fact, he has made a mistake; this is a representation in which it is difficult to ignore the desire of the so-called victim for the so-called harasser.

Importantly, accounts of sexual harassment in the literature bear little resemblance to the office scene in *Disclosure*. The following is typical:

> Anne felt uncomfortable with the way Kent stared at her each time she walked into his office. His eyes would move from her head to her toes but his gaze would always end at her chest. Anne felt he was undressing her . . . he started to touch her . . . He expressed his wish to go on business trips alone with her . . . However hard she tried to ignore what was happening, she felt she was suffering. She felt victimized; she 'felt raped'. There was a sense of injustice as she had not done anything wrong. She lost her appetite and her weight dropped. She came down with colds more often and no longer looked forward to work. (Wilson, 1995: 260–61)

Anne's description of being harassed by her manager indicates quite clearly her distress and unhappiness at being treated in this way. Sanders, on the other hand, seems concerned only that he should not be unfaithful to his wife, or at least that she should not discover his brief infidelity. He tells Johnson that 'This never happened' as he makes his hasty exit from her office. Furthermore, as already discussed, Sanders is so concerned about Susan's possible reaction that he fails to tell her the whole truth about the incident even when she becomes aware of what has taken place.

The argument here is not so much that the representation of sexual harassment in *Disclosure* is somehow false or inauthentic but, rather, that this representation of harassment could be seen to generate understandings that attribute at least some blame to the recipient of harassment. Sanders complains *only because Johnson accuses him of sexual harassment and also begins to make his working life difficult in other ways.* Previous to his consulting Alvarez, events in the film imply that Sanders has taken the decision not to refer to the incident again, rather to try to continue in a much more professional and formal relationship with Johnson. In the mediation, for example, he tells of how he did not initially complain about her behaviour because he thought the incident was best forgotten. So it is only when Sanders attends the Conley–White meeting where she wrongfoots him, and hears of Johnson's suit against him, that he approaches Catherine Alvarez. This chain of events seems to imply that Sanders himself recognizes his own complicity in what has taken place between him and Johnson.

Significantly, the literature around sexual harassment indicates that complaints of harassment are very often attributed to some behaviour on the part of the recipient. An interesting example is the claim of Clarence Thomas's team, made during the US Senate hearing held to determine whether he had sexually harassed former employee Anita Hill, that Hill was an erotomaniac. It was suggested by Thomas's team that Hill craved male sexual attention to the extent that she was often forced to imagine it. The implication was that Hill had incited, if not actively invited and welcomed, any sexualized behaviour from Thomas, and, furthermore, that she had probably invented the allegations in their entirety in any case. Evidence presented to support these allegations included the so-called 'pube affidavit'. This document, signed by a former student of Hill's, claimed that, on receiving a graded assignment from her, he found that she had inserted pubic hairs between the pages (Phelps and Winternitz, 1992). Ludicrous though these accusations may be seen to be, the fact that Thomas's team were able to make them in a formal Senate hearing may be seen to reflect the stereotype that recipients of harassment ask for, or at least welcome, the sexual attention that they receive.

It is also important to note evidence that recipients of harassment may fail to complain altogether because *they understand themselves* to have encouraged their harasser in some way. Writers including Renick (1980) and Grauerholz (1989) claim that women frequently understand themselves as little more than objects for men's sexual relief. Bremer et al. (1991) similarly suggest that younger women especially may be unsure whether their unhappiness at being harassed is actually warranted – that they fear that they have somehow provoked, incited or welcomed this behaviour. Case studies of harassment bear this out. Julie, interviewed for the BBC TV series *Making Advances* (1993), assumed that her supervisor's harassing behaviour was her fault because it was directed at her alone. This behaviour included her supervisor dropping a coin down the front of Julie's blouse and then attempting to retrieve it, him asking her to hold his penis when he went to the toilet, and beginning to unbutton his trousers in front of her.

Here, then, it can be argued that *Disclosure* does much to reinforce the damaging stereotype that the recipient of harassment has some role to play in the harassing behaviour: that they in some way have invited it or at least failed to indicate that they do not welcome the advances. The film's portrayal of Sanders struggling with his desire for Johnson, and only eventually rejecting her, does little to suggest that sexual harassment is by definition a set of behaviours that the recipient does not welcome. Indeed, it does precisely the reverse. Given that the understanding that victims of harassment 'ask for it' seems already to be well embedded in the modern social, *Disclosure* can be argued to constitute or, perhaps more accurately, consolidate subjects who understand sexual dynamics in the organization in potentially problematic ways.

Conclusion

It is important to return, finally, to Foucault, and to acknowledge his emphasis on resistance to the subjectifying effects of knowledge. For Foucault (1980, 1982), knowledge is never all-powerful, it is never totalizing, because it is we humans who settle ourselves among particular subject positions and therefore we are always able to resist particular definitions offered to us. The very fact that modern power/knowledge regimes can only be sustained by the activities of human subjects means that these regimes are always open to 'rearticulation' (Knights and Vurdubakis, 1994). As Foucault himself argues, 'power is only exercised over free subjects and only insofar as they are free . . .' (Foucault, 1982: 221). Foucault (1979, 1980, 1982) also emphasizes that power is always fragmented. As he says, power is 'in reality an open, more-or-less coordinated (in the event, no doubt ill coordinated) cluster of relations' (Foucault, 1980: 199).

The variety of knowledges currently in existence means that the particular way in which an individual will define him/herself is not predictable. Additionally, Foucault suggests that it is precisely the process of subjection, of subjectification, that makes us able to resist – that it is the power effects of knowledge that mean that we come to define ourselves as thinking, active subjects, and therefore as able to refuse what we are told is true about ourselves. As Foucault (1979: 143, emphasis added) points out, 'It is not that life has been totally integrated into techniques that govern and administer it; *it constantly escapes them.*'

An instance of resistance that is particularly relevant to this chapter is that of the Queer Nation campaign against the film *Basic Instinct* (1992). Burke (1995) describes in detail how the radical gay rights group strove, on discovering that the main female character in *Basic Instinct* was a homicidal bisexual, to make their objections known as strongly as possible. Burke recounts how the group continually picketed the San Francisco film set; how they used mirrors, glitter and horns to affect the filming itself; how billboards all over the country were scrawled with the words 'Catherine did it!' so as to reveal the film's denouement; and how she herself met the writer Joe Esterhazy and star Michael Douglas (him again!) to try to persuade them to re-write the plot so that it was less derogatory to the gay/bisexual community. It is true that the collective efforts of Queer Nation were perhaps less than successful; *Basic Instinct* was released with little of the original substance of the plot changed. However, this does not detract from the main argument here: that individual subjects are capable of resisting particular definitions of themselves in a way that reveals that they are not entirely subject to the powerful effects of particular knowledges. Consequently, it would be misguided to suggest that *Disclosure* is 'all-powerful' with regard to those who view it – rather, it seems that individual subjects may well choose to resist the definitions that it offers.

This chapter has argued that *Disclosure* represents a piece of knowledge about organizations and, more specifically, about the ways in which men and women interact at work. It is suggested that this piece of knowledge may have generated certain subjectifying effects among those who were exposed to it. Far from breaking with already well-established stereotypes of successful working women as threatening, highly sexualized, greedy and so on, the film simply reaffirms this view. However, as subjects, we are constituted through a multiplicity of knowledges of which cinematic narrative is only one. This multiplicity may limit the power of *Disclosure* as a piece of knowledge. *Disclosure* cannot be assumed to be totalizing in its effects over and through its audiences.

Acknowledgements

I gratefully acknowledge the invaluable assistance of John Sinclair and Trudy Mercer, and the editors of this volume.

Notes

1 All quotes from *Disclosure* cited in this chapter are taken from the Australian home video version of this film (Warner Brothers/Warner Home Video, 1995).

2 Indeed, it becomes clear at the end of the film that Johnson's success has, in fact, involved the marginalization of other women – Stephanie Kaplan, who is eventually promoted into the position that Johnson leaves, being a case in point. Indeed, immediately after Johnson's promotion is announced, Sanders and Kaplan commiserate with each other because neither of them received the promotion.

3 Given this argument – that Johnson is depicted in *Disclosure* as having had to pay for her organizational success by giving up much of her private life – it is salient to reproduce a somewhat lengthy quote from Michael Douglas (who plays Tom Sanders in the film). Here Douglas is talking about *Fatal Attraction* (1987), in which film he also starred and which attracted no small amount of censure for its portrayal of a single woman driven mad by a one-night stand with a colleague: 'Look, the film isn't putting down single girls who have it all but want more, it just says that nasty things can happen. If you want to know, I'm really tired of feminists, sick of them. They've really dug themselves into their own grave. Any man would be a fool who didn't agree with equal rights and pay but some women, juggling with career, lover, children, wifehood, have spread themselves too thin and are very unhappy. It's time they looked at *themselves* and stopped attacking men. Guys are going through a terrible crisis right now because of women's unreasonable demands. In my case I made *Fatal Attraction* and the next thing is the feminists are ripping me apart and have interpreted it as a metaphor for all single women. My mind boggles at their arrogance' (cited in Smith, 1989: 25). In the light of both *Fatal Attraction* and *Disclosure*, it is interesting to note Douglas's argument that working women cannot expect to have 'it' – a home, a happy marriage, children and organizational success – 'all'.

4 Here Smith is actually talking about another ill-fated fictional career woman, lawyer Teddy Barnes in the film *Jagged Edge* (1985).

5 It is perhaps significant that Sanders does assert his sexual prerogative – that Johnson is not permitted to play the sexual aggressor throughout their encounter.

References

Benson, D.J. and Thomson, G.E. (1982) 'Sexual harassment on campus: the congruence of authority relations, sexual interest and gender stratification', *Social Problems*, 2 (9): 236–51.

Blair, C., Jeppeson, M.S. and Pucci, E., Jr (1994) 'Public memorializing in postmodernity: the Vietnam veterans memorial as prototype', in W.L. Nothstine, C. Blair and G.A. Copeland (eds), *Critical Questions: Intervention, Creativity and the Criticism of Discourse and Media*. New York: St Martin's Press. pp. 350–82.

Bordo, S. (1992) 'Postmodern subjects, postmodern bodies: review essay', *Feminist Studies*, 18 (1): 159–75.

Bremer, B.A., Moore, C.T. and Bildersee, E.F. (1991) 'Do you have to call it "sexual harassment" to feel harassed?', *College Student Journal*, 25 (3): 789–801.

Brewis, J., Hampton, M. and Linstead, S. (1997) 'Unpacking Priscilla: subjectivity and identity in the organization of gendered appearance', *Human Relations*, 50 (10): 1275–304.

Burke, P. (1995) *Family Values: A Lesbian Mother's Fight for her Son*. London: Abacus.

Crichton, M. (1994) *Disclosure*. London: Arrow.

Denzin, N.K. (1995) *The Cinematic Society*. London: Sage.

Disclosure (1995) Warner Brothers/Warner Home Video (Australia).

Dow, B.J. (1994) 'Hegemony, feminist criticism and *The Mary Tyler Moore Show*', in W.L. Nothstine, C. Blair and G.A. Copeland (eds), *Critical Questions: Invention, Creativity and the Criticism of Discourse and Media*. New York: St Martin's Press. pp. 102–17.

Ehrenreich, N. (1990) 'Pluralist myths and powerless men: the ideology of reasonableness in sexual harassment law', *Yale Law Journal*, 99 (6): 1177–234.

Fain, T.C. and Anderton, D.L. (1987) 'Sexual harassment: organizational context and diffuse status', *Sex Roles*, 17 (5–6): 291–311.

Foucault, M. (1977) *Discipline and Punish: The Birth of the Prison*. London: Allen Lane.

Foucault, M. (1979) *The History of Sexuality, Vol. I: An Introduction*. London: Allen Lane.

Foucault, M. (1980) *Power/Knowledge: Selected Interviews and other Writings 1972–1977*, ed. C. Gordon. Brighton: Harvester Press.

Foucault, M. (1982) 'The subject and power', in H.L. Dreyfus and P. Rabinow (eds), *Michel Foucault: Beyond Structuralism and Hermeneutics*. Brighton: Harvester. pp. 202–26.

Foucault, M. (1985) *The History of Sexuality, Vol. II: The Use of Pleasure*. Harmondsworth: Penguin.

Foucault, M. (1986) *The Foucault Reader*, ed. P. Rabinow. Harmondsworth: Penguin.

Foucault, M. (1988) *Politics, Philosophy, Culture: Interviews and other Writings, 1977–1984*, ed. L.D. Kritzman. New York: Routledge.

Foucault, M. (1990) *The History of Sexuality, Vol. III: The Care of the Self*. Harmondsworth: Penguin.

Gherardi, S. (1995) *Gender, Symbolism and Organizational Cultures*. London: Sage.

Grauerholz, E. (1989) 'Sexual harassment of female professors by students: exploring the dynamics of power, authority and gender in a university setting', *Sex Roles*, 21 (11): 789–801.

Hoffman, F. (1986) 'Sexual harassment in academia: feminist theory and institutional practice', *Harvard Educational Review*, 56 (2): 105–21.

Knights, D. and Vurdubakis, T. (1994) 'Foucault, power, resistance and all that', in J.M. Jermier, D. Knights and W.R. Nord (eds), *Resistance and Power in Organizations*. London: Routledge. pp. 167–98.

Lurie, A. (1992) *The Language of Clothes*. London: Bloomsbury.

McDowell, L. and Court, G. (1994) 'Performing work: bodily representations in merchant banks', *Environment Planning D: Society and Space*, 12: 727–50.

MacKinnon, C. (1979) *Sexual Harassment of Working Women: A Case of Sex Discrimination*. New Haven, CT: Yale University Press.

Medhurst, M.J. and Benson, T.W. (1984) 'Introduction: rhetorical studies in a media age', in M.J. Medhurst and T.W. Benson (eds), *Rhetorical Dimensions in Media: A Critical Casebook*. Dubuque, IA: Kendall Hunt. pp. ix–xxiii.

Mulvey, L. (1989) *Visual and other Pleasures*. Basingstoke: Macmillan.

Nothstine, W.L., Blair, C. and Copeland, G.A. (1994) 'Invention in media and rhetorical criticism: a general orientation', in W.L. Nothstine, C. Blair and G.A. Copeland (eds), *Critical Questions: Invention, Creativity and the Criticism of Discourse and Media*. New York: St Martin's Press. pp. 3–14.

Phelps, T.M. and Winternitz, H. (1992) *Capital Games: Clarence Thomas, Anita Hill and the Story of a Supreme Court Nomination*. New York: Hyperion.

Renick, J.C. (1980) 'Sexual harassment at work: why it happens and what to do about it', *Personnel Journal*, 59 (8): 658–62.

Sheppard, D.L. (1989) 'Organizations, power and sexuality: the image and self-image of women managers', in J. Hearn, D.L. Sheppard, P. Tancred-Sheriff and G. Burrell (eds), *The Sexuality of Organization*. London: Sage. pp. 139–57.

Smith, J. (1989) *Misogynies*. London: Faber and Faber.

Stringer, D.M., Remick, H., Salisbury, J. and Ginorio, A.B. (1990) 'The power and reasons behind sexual harassment: an employers' guide to solutions', *Public Personnel Management*, 19 (1): 43–52.

Wilson, F.M. (1995) *Organizational Behaviour and Gender*. London: McGraw-Hill.

Figure 5.1 Philadelphia, 1993, *Columbia Pictures*

5

Philadelphia: AIDS, Organization, Representation

Ruth Holliday

Reading mainstream organization studies textbooks one could be forgiven for thinking that sexuality is not an issue relevant to the workplace. However, wandering to the margins of the discipline, one discovers a small but growing body of work that is beginning to address these issues. For example, Burrell and Hearn (1989) have explained the absence of discourses of sexuality from organizations and organization studies in two ways. First, since sex is treated as something that is not supposed to happen at work, it has been assumed to be relevant only to the private spaces that people inhabit outside working hours. The second explanation is historical in that it assumes that sexuality has been eradicated from organizations at some time in the past ('like scurvy', as Burrell and Hearn put it) and that, consequently, when sexuality does become apparent, it can be instantly dealt with.

Against these assumptions, gender studies are beginning to provide detailed accounts of how men resist sex equality in organizations (Cockburn, 1991) and the way in which men's (hetero)sexuality and capitalism conspire to create barriers to women's advancement (Collinson and Collinson, 1989). However, in many ways, workplace policies have moved faster than the textbooks in this area. The introduction of equal opportunities policies (Cockburn, 1991), then specific policies around sexual harassment (Gutek, 1989) and HIV/AIDS (Goss, 1994; Goss and Adam-Smith, 1995), have forced organizations to consider sexuality at least in passing. In particular, looking at sexual harassment has forced managers to consider non-harassing behaviour (or 'mutual sexuality') as well as harassment. In doing so, the plethora of sexual behaviours at work has become visible, and therefore public.

Starting from work on harassment, Barbara Gutek (1989) has brought the issue into the academic arena. She has focused on the difference in definitions of sexual behaviour, and in so doing has identified clear gender disparities in perceptions of it. She suggests that since in many different cultures characteristics associated with femaleness are also those perceived as being sexual, and that similarly definitions of maleness focus around those associated with organizations, then women will always be seen as sexual and men as organizational. In her study, for example, a man who entered the secretaries' office in his organization playing with the zip of his trousers was not seen as behaving sexually, whereas a woman who offered to get a coffee for a male colleague was. In the public sphere of work, then, women's sexuality will always be seen as problematic as well as omnipresent. In the same way, homosexuality and bisexuality will always be seen as problematic in heteronormative organizations. Thus, while straight men may be attributed organizational identities at work, others will be identified solely by their problematized gender or sexuality.

This line of argument goes some way to explaining the absence of sexuality from heteronormative organizational discourses, both academic and work-based (although some resurgence has been witnessed around the issues of sexual harassment and AIDS). But if such discourses are missing in these spaces, they are certainly not missing from popular culture or from our experiences. How many films about work use the office affair as their central theme? Given that popular culture both informs and reflects experience, perhaps it is here that we need to look for insight.

The central theme of this chapter is a critique, based on both organization studies and film studies, of the film *Philadelphia* (1993), tracing the linkages between AIDS, homosexuality and heterosexism in both organization and representation. I will also discuss the issues of illness and death which AIDS inevitably brings into the workplace. Finally, I will examine some of the limitations of the film as a product of the (heteronormative) organization which produced it – Hollywood. Despite its storyline, the narrative structure of *Philadelphia* promotes heterosexual identification, as I will later show. I will also be looking at possibilities for queer readings, given that even a film made about a gay man with AIDS is targeted at a heterosexual audience.

Philadelphia, directed by Jonathan Demme, is a film about Andrew Beckett (played by Tom Hanks), an extremely talented lawyer and a gay man with AIDS, who is sacked from Wyant, Wheeler, Hellerman, Tetlow, and Brown, the law firm where he works, allegedly for incompetence. He hires a black attorney, Joe Miller (Denzel Washington), to take on his case.[1] Miller is renowned for taking the cases that no one else will take on, although his own homophobia initially leads him to refuse to help Andrew. The largest part of the film centres on a courtroom drama in which Andrew and Joe try publicly to uncover the prejudice and discrimination that has led to Andrew's dismissal. The trial is a long one. As Andrew's health deteriorates, Joe's homophobia diminishes. First, however, I will focus on the portrayal in the film of corporate America, its cultures and its prejudices; and, in doing so, I will draw on organization theory in order to read the film from this perspective.

Philadelphia and Organization

I will start by looking at the organizational culture through two significant pieces of evidence given at the trial. The first scene involves Anthea Burton, a black woman (played by Anna Deavere Smith). She is a paralegal who is training at night school to become a lawyer and who we know from an earlier scene has achieved 98 per cent in her latest exam. Generally, associates do not socialize with paralegals but we also know that she and Andrew spend time together in and out of work, and have a good relationship. Joe Miller begins his questioning of Burton:

> *Joe*: Have you ever felt discriminated against at Wyant, Wheeler?
> *Anthea*: . . . well, yes.
> *Joe*: In what way?
> *Anthea*: Well . . . Mr Wheeler's secretary, Lydia, said that Mr Wheeler had a problem with my earrings . . . apparently Mr Wheeler felt that they were too . . . 'ethnic' is the word she used. She told me that he said that he would like it if I wore something a little less garish, a little smaller, and more 'American'.
> *Joe*: What did you say?
> *Anthea*: That my earrings are American . . . they're *African*-American.

Law firms such as Wyant, Wheeler are very interesting culturally. They are defined in terms of strict hierarchies running from the most senior partners (those in the name of the firm) to associates, to paralegals, to the support staff at the bottom. There is often very little socializing between layers (Davis, 1993). Such firms tend to be paternalistically managed, with star associates being occasionally nurtured for a place as a senior partner if their performance is outstanding. This, of course, is what happened to Andrew Beckett when he achieved sponsorship from Charles Wheeler (Jason Robards). Named partners help to enforce the paternalistic culture and also personify the organization in a more literal sense than in other kinds of organizations. Thus Wheeler is the 'cultural champion' of his firm. For Wheeler to have made such a comment about Anthea's earrings represents – and in reality reinforces – a culture where openly expressed prejudice is acceptable. Based on this interchange we can therefore assume that such values underpin the culture at Wyant, Wheeler.

A second example of the discriminatory culture at Wyant, Wheeler is shown while Andrew is in the dock. As he discusses life in the firm, the scene shifts to the Racket Club. Andrew and the partners are sitting in a steam room, towels draped loosely over their laps:

> *Seidman*: What do you call a woman who has PMS and ESP at the same time?
> *Wheeler*: I don't know, Robert what – do you call her?
> *Seidman*: A bitch who knows everything!
> *Kenton*: Sounds like someone I know.
> *Wheeler*: Hey Walter, how does a faggot fake an orgasm?
> *Kenton*: He throws a quart of hot yoghurt on *your* back!
> [Andrew does not object, he merely holds his head back, gritting his teeth.]

Interestingly, this joke positions 'you' getting yoghurt on 'your' back. In order to get the joke, 'you' (assumed to be heterosexual) have to be there. Homophobia, though it attempts to rigorously police the binary opposites of heterosexual and homosexual, in the very act of doing so fails to maintain the categories upon which it draws.

Humour is often used in organizations (as elsewhere) to reinforce cultural norms. It can also be oppressive, as Wendy Parkin (1993: 186) explains:

> A woman may hear a sexist joke which men think is funny but may cause the woman to feel anger. Accusations of 'losing one's sense of humour', 'being unable to take a joke', 'over-reacting' are commonplace. Depending on her place in the organization a woman may challenge, show anger, ridicule or politely smile and hide her feelings. All of these are emotional costs of sexism and sexual harassment.

In the same way, Andrew bears the emotional cost of homophobia. This is tinged with relief in this particular instance at not having already told Charles Wheeler that he is gay (something that he had earlier intended to do). Interestingly, this very concealment is later turned back on Andrew for 'pretending to be somebody he wasn't. Thus a prejudicial and discriminatory culture at Wyant, Wheeler is clearly revealed, while Andrew's ambivalence towards being out at work chimes with the experiences of countless lesbians, gay men, bisexual and transgender people in organizations (Stewart, 1991). By effectively 'outing' Andrew in the course of the court case, his employers also 'out' themselves as homophobic since, by firing him because of his sexuality, they transform him, in Helena Flam's words, from 'internal dissenter [with]in an organization into [the organization's] public critic' (1993: 73).

(Homo)Social Spaces

Wyant, Wheeler's culture is overwhelmingly shaped by heterosexual masculinity. To examine this further I will return to the Racket Club and other work-related social spaces depicted in the film. Although *Philadelphia* centres on the courtroom, the workplace and Andrew's apartment, other spaces prove to have key importance in the portrayal of Wyant, Wheeler, the organization. These spaces are social ones: the places where key members of organizations meet outside the workplace (which Stacy and Davis, 1983, call 'intermediate zones' straddling the public and the private). Again, there are key issues about work organizations that can be addressed through analysis of such spaces and behaviour deemed appropriate therein.

The spaces in question are represented in *Philadelphia* by an executive box at a basketball game and by the Racket Club. Paradoxically, a further intermediate zone is Wheeler's office, where Beckett is summoned after hours to be made a partner of the firm during the early part of the film. The first thing to note is that these spaces are exclusively male. Although the office includes a female secretary during the day (seen when Andrew is fired), at night it becomes a men's drinking place. The men are relaxed and sociable, and there is plenty of homosocial physical contact in terms of hand-shaking and back-patting. The air of satisfaction, the glasses of scotch and the almost familial male bonding are reminiscent of the dining room after the women have 'withdrawn'.

The Racket Club is the most blatantly exclusive – it is a men-only club. Furthermore, the physical interaction between the men in this setting would exclude women, as, to return to an earlier point, a woman's behaviour in this context would always be seen as sexual (because of the problematization of women's sexuality) while the men's behaviour is perceived as strictly social. This distinction is made all the more bizarre when we look at examples of such male behaviour. For example, Jeff Hearn explains: 'Horseplay between men . . . consists of intense physical contact, in the form of "high-jinks", such as grabbing of men's genitals from behind, poking fingers up bottoms, rubbing chests, attacking with brooms . . . or simply hearty behaviour with hugging or firm hand contact' (Hearn, 1985: 124).

This is classic homosocial behaviour – the socially acceptable form of male–male intimacy (Sedgwick, 1985). It is sexual behaviour but always laced with denial. As Hearn (1993: 158) has written: 'Men's organizational relations with other men are often charged with desire . . . This usually blatant desire by men for the company of other men exists in tension with the "male sexual narrative" and dominant heterosexuality of most organizations.' Horseplay is often accompanied by derogatory jokes about women, marriage and homosexuality. Conducted by heterosexual males, it is 'just good fun'. Thus, homosocial activity is engaged in while heterosexual performance is continuously and repetitively performed (see Butler, 1990). Given that (hetero)masculinity is also contingent on denigrating women, the fragility and tenuousness of heterosexuality is exposed exactly at the moment of this performance. However, were a gay man to be identified within the group, the dynamics would instantly change, since 'innocent' horseplay then becomes overtly (homo)sexually charged; the performance is exposed *as performance*, and heterosexuality is undermined. This is exactly the scenario enacted at Wyant, Wheeler when Andrew's sexuality is exposed. Thus, Joe addresses this question to Charles Wheeler:

> *Joe*: Isn't it true that when you realized that Andrew Beckett, your golden boy, your future senior partner, was gay and had AIDS it drove a stake of fear through your heterosexual heart – remembering all the hugs, the hand-shakes, the intimate moments in the sauna, the friendly pats on the backside that you and Andrew exchanged like guys exchange sometimes . . . it made you say 'My God, what does this say about me?'
> *Wheeler*: Mr Miller, you may tap dance around me all you wish with your innuendoes and locker-room fantasies. The truth still remains that your client worked when he wanted to work, telling us what he thought we

needed to know about who he really was. Andy insisted on bending the rules, and his work suffered tremendously in the long run as a result of that.
Joe: Will you explain this to me like I'm a six-year-old, Mr Wheeler, 'cos I just don't get it. Why makes these rules that you're talking about, huh? You?
Wheeler: Read your Bible, Mr Miller, Old and the New Testament. Pretty valuable rules in there.

Joe clearly alludes to homosocial behaviour and how the realization of a gay participant shifts it into the homosexual or homoerotic domain; social behaviour becomes sexual or erotic because of the problematization of gay men's sexuality in organizational space.

The other important point to be raised in relation to this dialogue concerns Wheeler's response. Wheeler complains that Andrew did not tell him 'who he really was' (that he was gay) and that he 'bent the rules' (of heterosexual behaviour). What is interesting is why this should matter in a workplace when such issues are supposed to be essentially 'private' (Stewart, 1991). Marny Hall (1989: 126) discusses this in respect to lesbians in organizations:

> the person known to be homosexual must do nothing in particular in order to be perceived in terms of excessive eroticism ... [Further,] unlike the heterosexual, whose entrance into the organization marks his or her exit from familial roles, the homosexual, definitionally conscripted for the social/sexual projections of the dominant culture, cannot exit from affectivity any more than s/he can avoid the sentence of never-ending eroticism.

Like the lesbians in Hall's study, Andrew Beckett becomes 'definitionally conscripted' as a gay man, and therefore as hypersexualized, pathologically predatory and promiscuous. And in the current era of 'panic sex' (Kroker et al., 1989), these characteristics are compounded by the perceived threat of AIDS.

Because the discourses of AIDS are collapsed with those of homosexuality, then homosexuality itself becomes invested with the 'threat' of contagion. This is illustrated in another scene from *Philadelphia*. Andrew and Joe are sitting together with the intention of rehearsing the day's questions. Andrew is connected to a drip and his concentration is waning. At this point the emphasis of the soundtrack switches from the questions to the background music. It is the aria 'La Mamma Morta' from *André Chenier*, sung by Maria Callas. Andrew becomes engrossed in the music, translating each line for Joe as it plays, finally miming along. The music reduces him to tears and Joe escapes from the room, nearly (but not quite) turning back to comfort Andrew. The disturbing effect that this scene has on Joe is illustrated by the continuing music while he hugs his wife and child when he returns home. The scene is explained by Taubin (1994: 28) thus:

> Had he been alone and doing this performance for himself, he might have acted with more abandon. But he is not alone, as the reverse angle cutting of the scene emphasises. He is trying to communicate something about himself as Andrew while taking into consideration Joe's limitations ... Even so, the

boldness of the emotion terrifies Joe, who makes a fast retreat . . . In a more sentimental film, Joe would have hugged Andrew and homophobia would be eradicated forever. Instead, Demme lets us understand that what Joe has seen in Andrew and has been moved and shaken by, and even envious of, is everything Joe has repressed in order to be a [heterosexual] man.

Thus, Joe cannot show emotion, even less comfort a gay man, because this would put at risk his masculinity, his heterosexuality. Emotion, caring, empathy, the argument goes, are alien to heterosexual men whose masculine identity is so fragile. Instead, the straight man must comfort himself by engaging in firm hand-shakes and slaps on the back with his contemporaries. However, there may also be a homophobic assumption in Taubin's explanation – that gay men are necessarily more sensitive and emotional than straight men. We must be wary of such an assumption.

In the following section, I shall focus on the impact of AIDS in organizations, revealing through a reading of key scenes from *Philadelphia* how the logic of organizations is ruptured by what David Goss (1994) calls the 'disorganization' of AIDS.

AIDS Panic and Death

There are still many unknowns in the prognosis of HIV and AIDS. The relatively recent discovery of AIDS means that knowledge is still limited, while the complex of infections, diseases and conditions which comprise acquired immuno-deficiency syndrome inhibit the progress of 'AIDS science'. However, government campaigns quickly responded to the issue. What can only be described as 'gruesome' advertising campaigns were launched in the UK and US, presumably in order to scare people out of having sex. This reaction, as Tamsin Wilton and Peter Aggleton (1991) points out, must be interpreted as the product of the culture which created it. Thus, in a homophobic and erotophobic culture, advice such as AIDS activist Cindy Patton's ('Don't get semen in your anus or vagina') gets transformed into something rather vague about exchanging bodily fluids. The message – 'Don't have penetrative sex' – is unthinkable since anything else is simply perverse, and thus 'Don't have sex' becomes the inevitable message in a Judeo-Christian society, and what better threat with which to enforce it than the threat of death?

Such responses have led to a (perhaps unjustified) conflation of HIV and AIDS with death. Susan Sontag (1988), writing on the 'fatalism' of AIDS, especially as a 'stages syndrome' – from HIV infection to ARC (AIDS related complex) to so-called 'full-blown' AIDS – explains how this gives it the language of a 'death sentence'. This is, of course, linked, as I will show later, to the way in which AIDS is often constructed as a punishment for immorality (homosexuality, promiscuity and injecting drug use, for example) and this is contrasted with the plight of 'innocent victims' (recipients of infected blood products, for example). The issue of death structures the whole narrative logic of *Philadelphia*, leading us inevitably to Andrew's death. We know at the outset that there is no hope of recovery, even reprieve, and that victory in court will be overshadowed by the loss of Andrew's life.

Fear of AIDS is further tinged by its reintroduction of a clear link between sex and death, something that Susan Sontag suggests displaces 'rational' thinking (about the improbability of transmission) with a pure panic that sees danger everywhere: 'Infectious diseases to which sexual fault is attached always inspire fears of easy contagion and bizarre fantasies of transmission by nonvenereal means in public places' (Sontag, 1988: 27). This is explored in the film when Joe shakes hands with Andrew. Later, on discovering Andrew's illness, Joe asks for an HIV test, unable to believe that he could not possibly have contracted AIDS this way.

The issue of transmission in public places is particularly relevant to the workplace. Discrimination against people with AIDS is built on panic – about contagion, about death – as is discussed later. In addition, death and illness are conceived as being out of place in organizations (despite the fact that work is a major contributor to health problems, and that organizations do have to deal regularly with the death of employees still in service; see Kearl, 1989). As Wendy Parkin (1993: 177) suggests, organizations try to keep issues of death (as well as issues of sexuality) firmly in the private sphere: 'This denial of death in the public realm has parallels with the denial of sexuality so that the emotions of grief and mourning are assumed to belong to the private realm, as is sexuality.'

To deal with illness, death and mourning, formal workplace procedures have evolved, governing the ways in which an organization responds: how much sick leave or compassionate leave is allowed for whom, who can attend funerals, how and when an employee is replaced, and so on. Peter Marris (1986: 91) writes that 'death creates no crisis in corporate life.' While this is true in one sense, in another death represents a profound crisis, a crisis which has to be 'managed', since organizations must be healthy, and very much alive.

AIDS and Moral Panic

Just as AIDS is commonly linked with inevitable death, it is important to make clear the conflation of AIDS and (male) homosexuality, a conflation that remains dominant within organizational contexts (as elsewhere). AIDS has reframed attitudes towards homosexuality, and become a powerful legitimizing force in homophobic discourse and practice. As Hugh Robertson (1988: 142) points out:

> In recent years there has been a rising tide of homophobia within the workplace as the spread of AIDS has been closely identified with gay men . . .

[I]n every workplace where there are lesbians and gay men who are open about their sexuality, there is increased prejudice against them under the guise of fear of AIDS.

At Wyant, Wheeler, this conflation is evident time and again: Andrew Beckett's sexuality is seen as contagious (Taubin, 1994). In the novelization of *Philadelphia*, for instance, extra dialogue, in a scene where the firm's partners discuss the summons Wheeler has just been handed by Miller at the basketball game, shows how Andrew's illness and his sexuality are seen as equally threatening. In one instant, Wheeler says 'Andy brought AIDS into our offices, into our men's rooms, he brought it into our annual goddamn family picnic!', while in the next, when partner Bob Seidman suggests being compassionate, he yells: 'Compassion! Beckett sucks cock, Bob. He takes it up the ass. He's a goddamned pervert!' (Davis, 1993: 109–10).

The link between AIDS and homosexuality is cleverly exposed in the courtroom by Joe in the following interchange. Joe is questioning Jamey Collins about his involvement in the mysterious disappearance of Andrew's file (which was the reason given for sacking Andrew). Suddenly he turns to Jamey and says:

Joe: Are you a homosexual?
Jamey: What? [with panic in his voice]
Joe: Are you a homosexual, answer the question. Are you a homo, are you a faggot, you know, a punk, a queen, a pillow biter, a Mary, a rump roaster . . . ARE YOU *GAY*?

The courtroom erupts as people from all sides voice their objections.

Conine: Objection! [Jumping from her seat]
Judge: Order!
Conine: Where did this come from? Suddenly counsel's attacking his own witness. Mr Collins's sexual orientation has nothing to do with this case.
Judge: Please have a seat Ms Conine. Would you approach the bench Mr Miller. [Whispers] Would you kindly share with me exactly what's going on inside your head because at this moment I don't have a clue.
Joe: Your honour, everybody in this courtroom is thinking about sexual orientation – you know, sexual preference, whatever you want to call it. Who does what to whom and how they do it. I mean they're looking at Andrew Beckett and they're thinking about it. They're looking at Mr Wheeler, Ms Conine, even you your honour, they're wondering about it. Trust me, I know that they are looking at me and thinking about it. So let's just get it out in the open, let's get it out of the closet. Because this case is not just about AIDS is it? So let's talk about what this case is really all about – the general public's hatred, our loathing, our fear of homosexuals, and how that climate of hatred and fear translated into the firing of this particular homosexual, my client, Andrew Beckett.
Judge: Please have a seat, Mr Miller. In this courtroom, Mr Miller, justice is blind to matters of race, creed, colour, religion, and sexual orientation.
Joe: With all due respect, your honour, we don't live in this courtroom, though, do we?

What does this mean for organizations within a homophobic society? Within the discourses of formally rational modernist bureaucracy, AIDS is not a problem. Disease can be treated by science just as the science of management can formulate policies for its control within the workplace. 'Rationally' there is extremely low risk of contracting HIV occupationally. So why does AIDS present such a threat? Obviously, AIDS itself does not; but rather its discourse does. As David Goss and Derek Adam-Smith (1994: 9) write, 'the early characterization of AIDS as a "gay plague" has meant that it carries with it a constant reference of homosexuality . . . such that where the formally desexualized discourses of organization encounter AIDS this threatens a resexualization.' Furthermore, its conflation with death again threatens organizations: it is a reminder to the reification discourses associated with systems theory (organizations as living organisms) of the inevitability of organizational death. It also throws the private once again into the public in the form of the emotions surrounding death.

Therefore, AIDS threatens organization in two ways. First, it resexualizes the workplace and therefore undermines both the formally rational, sexless organizational discourse and the accepted pattern of male homosocial behaviour, which, in turn, threatens the very power base upon which organizations are built – white, masculine heterosexuality. Secondly, AIDS threatens modernist discourse as it cannot be cured by science, thus destroying modern society's unconditional faith in science to provide panaceas (Yingling, 1991). The science of management cannot be used to control AIDS in the workplace because of homophobia – irrational fear – which also undermines the modernist 'rational' discourse of human capital theory. It similarly threatens systems theory, which reifies organizations and represents them as living, thriving, growing organisms. AIDS, therefore, is seen as a 'cancer' eating away at organizational well-being.

Philadelphia as Film

The message of *Philadelphia*, however, is finally about tolerance.[2] This is highly significant since in this very message the film interpellates its viewers *as heterosexual*. Thus, a film which appears to centre on the plight of a gay man with AIDS is ultimately addressed to a straight audience. This, of course, explains many of the more bizarre aspects of the film, such as the lack of any attempt at realism in the portrayal of Andy and Miguel's relationship.

The ideology of the film can be unpacked in a number of ways, but I will focus on examples already described. I have used these initially in an organizational analysis to provide liberal understandings of the ways in which homophobia operates and is revealed in the film. I will now take these to a deeper level of criticism to expose the contradictions of the film's message and its ideological structure.

The first contradiction I will discuss is the film's attempt to portray Andy as contrary to popular gay stereotypes. For example, Tom Hanks emphasized in one interview that there was no need for Andy to 'put on a feather boa and lipsync to Judy Garland records' to prove he's gay to the audience (Mueller, 1994: 79) – yet this is ultimately what happens, only it is Maria Callas. So, *Philadelphia* apparently counters the heterosexual myth that you can tell, simply by looking, who is gay and who is not. This is echoed in Joe's cross-examination of the witnesses, asking them whether or not they are 'homosexual', and through an incident in which a young black law student comes on to Joe – to Joe's disgust. Joe asks the young man 'Do I look gay to you?' to which the student responds 'Do *I* look gay to you?' Yet the whole story of the film is of the partners at Wyant, Wheeler 'discovering' Andy's homosexuality and firing him; it is discovered through the marker of a Karposi's sarcoma lesion on Andy's neck. Andy's exposure of the lesions on his body at the trial becomes synonymous with the exposure of the truth itself – that the partners had recognized Andy's AIDS and thus his homosexuality. Thus, the lesion is the signifier of homosexuality; the fantasy that homosexuality is after all visible is restored. As Allen (1995: 625) explains, 'This . . . is an example of what Edelman [1994] has called homographesis, the hetero-sexual fantasy of the inevitable visibility of homosexuality that serves, finally, to assert the radical distinctiveness of the heterosexual and the homosexual.'

Through the transposing of sexual orientation on to the surface of the body, Allen argues, this also affirms the fantasy of 'definitionally con-scripted' sexual identity marked externally by the *absence or presence* of a sign. Thus, the body can only be one of two things – either straight or gay. However, through the textualization of such markers (their recog-nition as signs), 'homographesis' – the recognizability of the homosexual – becomes semiotic not essential. This then calls into question the very idea of heterosexuality itself. In order to escape this recognition, the film employs a further manoeuvre, by projecting a highly fractured and unstable identity on to the homosexual (Andy's not being 'out' and thus presenting another version of himself at work, for example, or his desire for both monogamy and casual sex) so that the heterosexual can stand in contrast as internally coherent.

Heterosexuality is produced in two ways. First, a pedagogical narrative refers heterosexuality to its origins in 'nature' (reproduction). Hetero-sexuality, the argument goes, is necessary for the continuation of the human race, and thus is both natural and inevitable. Thus, heterosex is disconnected from desire and located in procreation. The heteronarrative is therefore the inevitable progression from love, to married monogamy, to children. However, once made explicit, this ideology collapses: what about celibates, infertile couples and post-menopausal women – are they heterosexual? Thus, heterosexuality also employs a performative narrative – a personal narrative of desire for the 'opposite sex'.

In *Philadelphia's* crucial 'opera scene', both these narratives are employed to reinforce Joe's heterosexuality, while Andy's homosexual self is simultaneously splintered. The scene, which I have already described, pictures Andy translating and then miming to 'La Mamma Morta'. Andy is thus presented as taking the roles of both Madelena (the opera character) and Maria Callas (the opera singer). Homosexuality is shown as a 'blurring of the demarcations of self and other, of genders and cultures' (Allen, 1995: 625). In contrast, Joe returns home, first hugging his baby daughter Louise (pedagogical narrative), then snuggling up to his wife (performative narrative). The fact that the music stops and then, as Andy resets his CD player, becomes part of the objective soundtrack of the film does less to suggest Joe's heterosexuality is disturbed than Taubin (1994, cited earlier) implies. The only words Joe says in this scene are 'I love you little Louise' (to his daughter). Andy translates 'I am divine', 'I am love'. Thus, Joe's 'I' is radically different from Andy's 'I', as Allen (1995: 626) explains:

> If Andy's 'I' is an indeterminate locus of shifting identifications, Joe's 'I' is intersubjective, predicated on a distinction from 'you', seen as exterior to the self, [the other] whose very exteriority affirms the unity of the self. In contrast to the instability of identity projected onto Andy, then, Joe's 'I' thus works to deny any possible gaps and fissures in heterosexual identity.

Thus, despite its liberal message of tolerance, *Philadelphia* is ultimately a film that reinforces the immutability of heterosexuality through its interpellation of the audience as heterosexual, its insistence on the homographic fantasy of the radical distinction between hetero- and homosexuality, and through its projection of an unstable identity on to the homosexual.

However, just as the lesion on Andy's neck (signifying homosexuality) can be seen through semiotics as 'only a sign' – a historically and culturally located, ideologically loaded symbol – then so can *Philadelphia* be analysed. If all popular cultural texts, such as *Philadelphia*, are recognized as not only mimetic (reflective of culture) but also as performative (formative of culture) then *Philadelphia* becomes simply another performance in the reproduction of heterosexuality. Thus, the real fragility and precariousness of heterosexuality (in that it must be continuously and repetitively performed in order to maintain its hegemony) is exposed.

Philadelphia as Product

A final interesting point for consideration is that of *Philadelphia* the film as a product of Hollywood, an archetypal 'heteronormative' organization. The movie-press reportage of the film's making and the studio TriStar's promotion reveal an ambivalent stance by the studio, the director and leading players. Demme, for instance, is repeatedly quoted as saying that the film is about *much more* than AIDS, *much more* than homophobia. Given the negative attention Demme received from gay activists for his 1991 film *Silence of the Lambs* (Green, 1994), his continued ambivalence is difficult to reconcile with the grand claims made for *Philadelphia* as Hollywood's ground-breaking AIDS picture.

TriStar's publicity centred on the legal drama, with posters featuring Denzel Washington and a very healthy-looking Tom Hanks either side of a gavel. The by-line was 'No one would take on his case until one man was willing to take on the system.' There was little mention of AIDS in any promotional material and yet Hollywood was congratulating itself on a brave movie and awarding itself Oscars for the same reason.

The cutting of a scene showing a kiss on the mouth between Beckett and his partner Miguel (Antonio Banderas) keeps the practice of Beckett's homosexuality out of sight for much of the film: '*Philadelphia* stops short of confronting straight viewers (to whom it is primarily addressed) with the kind of images that might trigger their homophobia' (Taubin, 1994: 24). Justifying such editing on the grounds of not wanting to alienate an audience characterized as 'unconverted' (Mueller, 1994) resonates with other writing on Hollywood homophobia. Further, while Demme is always careful in discussing his role as a heterosexual man in directing *Philadelphia*, Hanks couldn't do enough in interviews to remind everyone that he's married, that he's Hollywood's 'heterosexual poster boy' (Green, 1994), although, of course, he tells Matt Mueller (1994: 79) that 'some of my best friends are homosexuals'.

TriStar's ambivalence towards *Philadelphia*'s core themes is in fact symptomatic of Hollywood. As Vito Russo pointed out in his pioneering study *The Celluloid Closet* (1981), there is a paradoxical history of the film industry's reluctance to deal with issues of sexuality – paradoxical given the number of (often closeted) lesbians, gay men and bisexuals working within it. The nexus of Hollywood, Washington and the religious right collude to keep representations of all 'alternative lifestyles' (into which catch-all they characterize homosexuality) off the silver screen. They argue, on the one hand, that the 'pink dollar' isn't worth chasing while so much of the potential audience would be turned away by gay-themed movies, and, on the other, that elections – even presidencies (Walker, 1992) – are won and lost over such issues as the 'cultural tone' of the nation (something to which a powerful organization like Hollywood directly contributes). Thus, while Hollywood continues simply to represent America's current value-set for fear of disgusting the moral majority, it neglects its potential role as critic. Far from pushing back boundaries, Hollywood operates firmly within them. As Michelangelo Signorile (1993) shows, Hollywood's self-censoring continues, while popularist attacks on gay film-makers, such as Michael Medved's (1992) diatribe *Hollywood vs. America*, target producers, directors and actors as corruptors of US moral fibre.

Although Hollywood has been showy with AIDS charities, Signorile (1993: 255) still concludes: 'when it comes down to the bottom line, the most ardent Hollywood liberal can behave like the most orthodox right-winger. Money is *always* conservative.' Like the other organizational mainstays of America – Washington and Wall Street – Hollywood maintains homophobia as 'sound business sense'. Interestingly, Signorile looks at recent 'outing' campaigns of Hollywood stars (Jodie Foster and John Travolta being among the most notable), showing how little the attendant rumour-mongering and negative press scrutiny damaged their careers. He suggests that Hollywood's homophobia is becoming more measured. It no longer makes 'business sense' to be too openly anti-gay: better to try to make little of the subject, as in the case of *Philadelphia* (even better to avoid it altogether).

There are those who therefore believe that there is a fundamental incompatibility between homosexuality and this kind of narrative – that because of those involved in the creation of Hollywood films and the assumptions that they make about the audience, there is no space for homosexuality (Miller, 1992). However, despite the attempt to create heterosexual hegemony through the ideology of cultural texts, it must be acknowledged that the eventual construction of the text lies not with its creators but with its audience. *Philadelphia* can be decoded from many reading positions, and its meanings are therefore created differently by different viewers in different situated cultures. Queer readings can thus construct the narrative as queer (they can also construct it as homophobic). Furthermore, consumption of the film narrative itself serves to undermine the very ideology present in the heteronarrative. Through multiple identifications with an array of characters, the viewer experiences multiple desires, thus actually undermining any of the (sexed) identity categories produced or resisted.

Notes

1   *Philadelphia* is the first mainstream Hollywood movie to use a black man to personify 'America'. It is directed by Jonathan Demme, director of *Silence of the Lambs* (1991) and recipient of much criticism over his portrayal of Jame Gumb, the film's anti-hero serial killer, as an effeminate transvestite and therefore, to much of its audience, as gay (Green, 1994). In some ways, then, this film might be seen as Demme's attempt to 'make it up' to the gay community.

2   This section draws heavily on the excellent work of Allen (1995).

References

Allen, D.W. (1995) 'Homosexuality and narrative', *Modern Fictions Studies*, 41 (3–4): 609–34.
Burrell, G. Gibson and Hearn, J. (1989) 'The sexuality of organization', in J. Hearn, D. Sheppard, P. Tancred-Sheriff and G. Burrell (eds), *The Sexuality of Organization*. London: Sage. pp. 1–28.

Butler, J. (1990) *Gender Trouble: Feminism and the Subversion of Identity*. London: Routledge.

Cockburn, C. (1991) *In the Way of Women: Men's Resistance to Sex Equality in Organizations*. Basingstoke: Macmillan.

Collinson, D.L. and Collinson, M. (1989) 'Sexuality in the workplace: the domination of men's sexuality', in J. Hearn, D. Sheppard, P. Tancred-Sheriff and G. Burrell (eds), *The Sexuality of Organization*. London: Sage. pp. 91–109.

Davis, C. (1993) *Philadelphia*. London: Penguin.

Edelman, L. (1994) *Homographesis: Essays in Gay Literary and Cultural Theory*. New York: Routledge.

Flam, H. (1993) 'Fear, loyalty and greedy organizations', in S. Fineman (ed.), *Emotion in Organizations*. London: Sage. pp. 58–75.

Goss, D. (1994) 'Writing about AIDS: framing policy', *Scandinavian Journal of Management*, 12 (1): 57–68.

Goss, D. and Adam-Smith, D. (1994) 'Framing difference: sexuality, AIDS and organization'. Paper presented at the British Sociological Association Annual Conference, Preston.

Goss, D. and Adam-Smith, D. (1995) *Organizing AIDS: Workplace and Organizational Responses to the HIV/AIDS Epidemic*. Bristol: Taylor and Francis.

Green, J. (1994) 'The *Philadelphia* story', *Premiere*, March, pp. 42–7.

Gutek, B. (1989) 'Sexuality in the workplace: key issues in social research and organizational practice', in J. Hearn, D. Sheppard, P. Tancred-Sheriff and G. Burrell (eds), *The Sexuality of Organization*. London: Sage. pp. 56–70.

Hall, M. (1989) 'Private experiences in the public domain: lesbians in organizations', in J. Hearn, D. Sheppard, P. Tancred-Sheriff and G. Burrell (eds), *The Sexuality of Organization*. London: Sage. pp. 125–38.

Hearn, J. (1985) 'Men's sexuality at work', in A. Metcalfe and M. Humphries (eds), *The Sexuality of Men*. London: Pluto. pp. 110–23.

Hearn, J. (1993) 'Emotive subjects: organizational men, organizational masculinities and the deconstruction of "emotions"', in S. Fineman (ed.), *Emotion in Organizations*. London: Sage. pp. 142–66.

Kearl, M. (1989) *Endings: A Sociology of Death and Dying*. New York: Oxford University Press.

Kroker, A., Kroker, M.L. and Cook, D. (1989) *Panic Encyclopedia: The Definitive Guide to the Postmodern Scene*. Basingstoke: Macmillan.

Marris, P. (1986) *Loss and Change*. London: Routledge and Kegan Paul.

Medved, M. (1992) *Hollywood vs. America: Popular Culture and the War on Traditional Values*. New York: HarperCollins.

Miller, D.A. (1992) *Bringing out Roland Barthes*. Berkeley, CA: University of California Press.

Mueller, M. (1994) 'The *Philadelphia* story', *Empire*, March, pp. 74–9.

Parkin, W. (1993) 'The public and the private: gender, sexuality and emotion', in S. Fineman (ed.), *Emotion in Organizations*. London: Sage. pp. 167–89.

Robertson, H. (1988) 'AIDS – a trade union issue', in P. Aggleton and H. Homans (eds), *Social Aspects of AIDS*. London: Falmer Press. pp. 139–53.

Russo, V. (1981) *The Celluloid Closet*. New York: Harper Row.

Sedgwick, E.K. (1985) *Between Men: English Literature and Male Homosocial Desire*. New York: Columbia University Press.

Signorile, M. (1993) *Queer in America: Sex, the Media and the Closets of Power*. London: Abacus.

Sontag, S. (1988) *AIDS and its Metaphors*. London: Allen Lane.

Stacy, M. and Davis, C. (1983) *Division of Labour in Child Health Care: Report to the SSRC, 1983* (December). Coventry: University of Warwick.

Stewart, T. (1991) 'Gay in corporate America', *Fortune*, 16 December, pp. 30–5.

Taubin, A. (1994) 'The odd couple', *Sight and Sound*, March, pp. 24–5.

Walker, M. (1992) 'All the President's gays', *Guardian* (Media Section), 15 October, pp. 2–3.

Wilton, T. and Aggleton, P. (1991) 'Condoms, coercion and control: heterosexuality and the limits to HIV/AIDS education', in P. Aggleton, G. Hart and P. Davies (eds), *AIDS: Responses, Interventions and Care*. London: Falmer Press. pp. 149–57.

Yingling, T. (1991) 'AIDS in America: postmodern governance, identity, and experience', in D. Fuss (ed.), *Inside/Out: Lesbian Theories, Gay Theories*. New York: Routledge. pp. 291–308.

6

Saloon Girls: Death and Desire in the American West

Maggie O'Neill

This chapter critically explores the portrayal of the saloon/brothel as a workplace organization in three films representing images of the American West: *Rio Bravo* (Howard Hawks, 1959), *The Wild Bunch* (Sam Peckinpah, 1969) and *Unforgiven* (Clint Eastwood, 1992). Through these films, it seeks to unravel representations of women and work, focusing on saloon girls and on the structure and organization of the saloon as a workplace. This has resonances for women working as prostitutes in saunas, clubs and bars today. My aim is to triangulate this reading of the fictive texts used here – the three Westerns – with both historical and contemporary documentary material, adding a methodological concern to situate this critical reading within the landscapes of the (Wild) West. My work is thus situated at the crossroads of ethnography, critical theory and feminist thought, and illuminates the complexity and contradictions indicative of gendered relations, the experiences of prostitutes, and the phenomenon of prostitution.

Fictive Texts

My approach follows Helmut Kuzmics' (1994) use of fictional sources, as well as Gayle Ormiston and Raphael Sassower's (1989) use of fictional visions of science and technology which delineates the labyrinthine nature of reality, history and truth. The importance of their work is twofold. First, in trying to reach an understanding and appreciation of the landscape of the West as the 'natural' world that the frontiersfolk peopled, organized, structured and inhabited, it is necessary to look not only at the available historical literature but also at fictive texts, in this case films. Such texts, alongside detailed historical work, allow the possibility of immersing oneself in the social and psychic processes that the frontierspeople would have experienced, inhabited, produced and reproduced: fictive texts such as film and literature can speak to us as 'feeling forms',[1] as examples of the sedimented 'stuff of society'.

Secondly, utilising film to help 'get at' the social organization of prostitution as work in the West, through the image and representation

Figure 6.1   Rio Bravo, *1959, Warner Brothers*

of the saloon as workplace and of the saloon girl as prostitute, necessitates an examination of the inter-relationship between the real and the fictional. The inter-relation between historical and fictive texts provides a kind of triangulation in the research process that enables a better understanding and critique. Our everyday lives are marked by the intermingling of the fictive and the real. And the phenomenon of prostitution as a cultural practice (both in the public imagination and as a lived experience for sex workers, clients, pimps and the representatives of various social agencies involved with prostitutes) is, of course, both 'real' and 'fictive' – a phantasmagoric world where the boundaries between reality and fantasy are often blurred.

A close reading of these (Wild) Western experiences compared with the current lived experiences of women working in saunas and bars in England makes for interesting reading. Interpreting across time and space is a creative endeavour and may throw up some useful similarities and differences in the experiences of prostitutes, helping us to understand better the development of the social organization of prostitution.

Gendered Relations, Death and Desire

Women working as prostitutes were 'outlaws' in the fledgling social organizations of the Wild West. Men, of course, were also 'outlaws', wrongdoers, criminals, bad guys. It is interesting to examine the development of the Western and the shifts in attitude and sentiment towards 'outlaws', particularly prostitutes, within an evolving genre and an evolving society. Film as 'feeling form', representing dominant cultural attitudes, value and feelings towards 'outlaws', can be read not only to 'unmask the images, the *sign* of women [as prostitute], to see how the meanings that underlie the codes function' (Hirschman and Stern, 1994: 576), but also to uncover transgressive possibilities for pleasure in certain moments, fragments and spaces, and to find sites of resistance to sexual and social inequalities.

The three films examined here all represent the prostitute as 'outlaw' to varying degrees. In *Rio Bravo* (1959), the prostitute and gambler's widow, Feathers, provides a discordant presence when she enters the town, the hotel, the room opposite Sheriff John T. Chance. Her entrance is marked by a sexual *frisson* – she offers up her body to the male gaze, with her stance and speech provocative, teasing. Dude is the alcoholic deputy whose life has been ruined by a woman.[2] Stumpy works in the jail, guarding prisoners, making meals and pouring whiskey. A lame old man, he tends to John T. and Dude as a mother would. Women have to be controlled in this environment, and so Stumpy is controlled with orders and recriminations. This oedipal triangle is disturbed by Feathers. She is controlled by her desire for the good and brave John T. (whose extra sexual prowess is marked by the rifle he always carries and his guns slung low around his hips, thus emphasizing his height and girth).

The sexual *frisson* – the temptation of the Sheriff by Feathers – is marked by his resistance to her charms. When he does 'submit' to her embrace it is after she has won him by her actions of selflessness: sleeping outside his room with a rifle to guard him from the dangers of the Burdett gang, thus allowing him necessary sleep; helping to save his life by diverting attention from him with a flower pot through a window; and showing him she wants his approval (as well as what he represents) rather than her old life of gambling and dancing and singing in saloons. John T. walks into Feathers's room after his successful showdown with the Burdetts. She is getting ready to entertain the guests, wearing a black corset, tights and high laced boots.

> you don't like them? Is it because they show so much of me? You like what you see but you decided what kind of girl I was. I wore these before I met you. I wanted you to know what you're getting. I wanted you to get that funny look on your face and tell me not to wear them.

When he does forbid her to go outside the room wearing this garb, she tells him: 'I waited so long for you to say that. I thought you were never gonna say it . . . Tell me something – why don't you want me to wear them? He replies 'Because I don't want anyone but me to see you.'

The saloon as workplace is evident in three key cameos in *Rio Bravo* First, in the opening scenes, the camera scans the saloon. Single women of Latin American origin are seated at tables full of men, talking pleasantly and smiling. There is no real evidence of sexual danger or excitement. The hotel doubles as a bar and place of entertainment, but the only women we meet are Feathers, Consuella (the manageress and wife of Carlos the manager), and the Latin American bartender in the saloon, a woman of middle years with no part in the action. We almost have to read between the lines to access the relationship between Feathers and the saloon girls/prostitutes. The 'action' takes place in hotels and saloons – there is no *real* evidence of prostitution. What is clear is that women as 'other' represent negation of the norm which has then to be resolved in order to maintain that norm. Feathers undergoes the symbolic death of her old lawless life, and is reborn in the light shone by Sheriff John T.'s aura of masculine order, law and regulation.

The Wild Bunch (1969) was thought to have marked a shift in the representation of the Western: the lyrical Western was replaced by realism, so brutal at times that it is almost painful to watch. The 'Wild Bunch' are outlaws being pursued by an ex-outlaw, Thornton, who has been commissioned to find and return them by a railroad owner sick of losing money to the outlaws. Thornton's reward is to stay out of prison. The closing scene has Thornton joining one of the original group and riding off with the Bunch after the violent deaths of most of the original Bunch. There are no clear good or bad guys at the centre of this film.

The scenes of Western life are grimly realistic, even though they are clearly staged within the context of the movie. The opening scene incorporates children watching a scorpion being eaten by ants; this observation of children at the scene of death is resonant throughout the film, echoed in the scenes of the bank robbery (where children play in the square and run to hide behind walls, watching as shooting breaks out), in the scene following the bungled bank robbery (where children set fire to the ants and scorpion, giggling), and in the Mexican village where Mapache's car, pulling along a half-dead Angel (one of the Wild Bunch) is followed almost ritualistically by children, laughing as though at a carnival. Children represent both innocence and forces of destruction. There is no romantic portrayal of the innocence of childhood, no clear demarcation between childhood and adulthood.

The relationship between men and their guns is paramount. In an early scene, Thornton's men are on a rooftop, watching and waiting for the Wild Bunch. A cowboy kisses his gun and the camera focuses upon his face – desire, excitement, intense emotions play there, a heartbeat plays loud and strong, then . . . shooting breaks out. Blood spurts, faces are shot off, women fall, men fall, the square looks like a scene from Dante's inferno, while desire plays out in the faces and actions of those armed with guns.

What is clear in this film is the role and representation of women as other, and the ambivalence of heterosexual gender relations. Women who transgress are doomed. Tereza, Angel's sweetheart, left the village and became General Mapache's whore. The Wild Bunch enter Mapache's village. Angel sees Tereza, dressed in silk, her gestures and looks wanton and overtly sexualized – she is licking the inside of the General's ear. Incensed, Angel raises his gun and shoots her. The General laughs when he realizes Angel intended to shoot Tereza and not him. He invites the Bunch to have a drink. The men are welcomed into the village and women are provided for their pleasure. The focus is upon the women as objects for the satisfaction of men's desire – 'take a look at them beauties' – the emphasis upon the women's breasts: 'Come on, sweetheart, let me see your titties.' It is fragments of bodies that the camera focuses upon – legs and breasts (one frame focuses upon Mapache looking at a woman dancing on a table, her skirt hitched up with wine running down her legs).

The representation of the brothel in *The Wild Bunch* is not as a singular structure or building – women are everywhere for men's pleasure. In one scene, Pike, the leader of the Bunch, is dressing on the edge of a bed. A woman whose breasts are half covered by a white cotton and lace chemise sponges her skin. Pike drinks from a long-necked bottle as she continues to sponge herself. In the same room are two of the Bunch, both with women; the men are quibbling over payment. Pike throws gold on to the table and the men leave. A baby cries in the background.

The brothel and the women are not defined in zones or particular places: they are everywhere for male pleasure and, when necessary, can be used for male protection. In the final scene of carnage, Pike grabs a girl – one of the women from the previous night – as a shield. Another girl from the same room shoots at him and he turns and cries 'You bitch!' as he shoots her. Pyke is finally shot by a child.

The relationship between death and desire is at its most extreme in the celebration of masculinities and violence in *The Wild Bunch*. But it is also central to the ambivalence created around the dichotomy between good and bad, order and disorder. In *The Wild Bunch* there is no real resolution following feminine death – only temporarily, when Tereza's death re-establishes order momentarily lost. At the heart of the film is the centrality of masculine order, a masculine order marked by order and disorder, two parts of the same whole. Women and femininity are simply fragments of male desire, fragments of dystopian possibilities.

Unforgiven (1992) revolves around the ways in which women seek and wreak revenge upon men. The tables are turned: they are not just whores but, through their use and payment of men, they take revenge. The law is unsupportive as they are only whores. The reality of violence in the lives of women working in the brothel and the reality of their relationship to law and order are clearly defined. The film is also thought to have marked a further shift in the Western genre.

The picture opens with a scene from Big Whiskey, Wyoming, 1880. A billiards sign, as seen through torrential rain, opens out to a scene where a man and woman are screwing, she with her stockings on, their rhythm disturbed by screams from the next-door room. There a woman (Delilah) throws water over a man, he holds her down and cuts her face over and over again with a knife. A man (whom we come to know as Skinny, the brothel owner) arrives and holds a gun to the attacker's head: 'Get off her, cowboy.' The Sheriff is called; women tend the girl who is now lying in bed. The Sheriff asks if she is 'gonna die', and is told, 'She gonna live', and that 'She giggled at his teensy pecker.' The Sheriff sends someone to the office for his bullwhip. Alice (one of the saloon girls portrayed as lay leader of the 'girls') asks if that is all he is going to get – a whipping. Skinny waves his contract for the whore: 'No one's gonna pay good money for a cut-up whore.' The Sheriff tells the cowboy who cut her that he must deliver five ponies to Skinny in the spring, and the second cowboy who was at the scene must deliver two ponies to Skinny. Alice protests: 'For what they've done, Skinny gets some ponies and that's it. It ain't fair.' Alice is ordered by Skinny to get back to Delilah.

The next scene has the women organizing revenge. They have $85 in total and need to raise a lot more to pay a contract killer to dispose of the men. Alice says 'Just because those smelly fools ride us like horses don't mean to say we let them brand us like horses. We are whores but we ain't horses.' The following spring the women are hanging out washing at the side of the saloon. The men deliver the ponies and there is a gift for Delilah, an extra pony. The women throw mud at the cowboys. Alice shouts 'She ain't got no face left and you gonna give her a mangy pony.'

The gaze of the camera rests on their angry faces, but the face of Delilah is scarred, soft and expressionless. A hired killer, William Munny, is brought out of retirement. He takes the job because he needs the money; he is now a single parent of two young children, and a farmer whose pigs are dying through disease. Munny is portrayed as having been saved from a life of killing, drinking and gambling by a woman – a good woman. Munny is also horrified at the thought of a woman scarred on the face. For Munny, the perpetrator deserves to die.

Woman as 'Other'

The stereotype of whores in the three films are resonant of 'soiled doves' (Myers, 1982). Feathers has been rescued from her fate by the death of her husband, her own strong character, but more centrally by her desire for the Sheriff. Tereza is a good girl turned bad, a soiled dove killed by the gun of Angel, the childhood sweetheart who cannot bear to see her whoring around Mapache the General. The Madonna turned whore, she betrayed him and he kills her. This leads ultimately to his death. In *Unforgiven*, it is the women who triumph and men who are killed after Delilah's assault. The image of women in the Western is transgressed to a degree in this film. Women are there for male pleasure – they hump every cowboy in town. But, at one and the same time, they resist the stereotype of being used and abused as commodities – they are not horses. The violence meted out to Delilah follows her giggling at her client's little 'pecker'. This is the ultimate sin in the Western, where men's 'peckers' are symbolized by the guns they wear and use. John T. carries a rifle as well as wearing guns, and his is bigger than most. Pike and his followers take hold of a machine gun and try to raze the village to rubble, the scenes of death and carnage revolving around their use of this huge gun. Death and desire are thus ultimately and intimately connected.

Historical Sources

> [T]he stereotype of the Other is used to control the ambivalent and to create boundaries. Stereotypes are a way of dealing with the instabilities arising from the division between self and non-self by preserving an illusion of control and order.
>
> Bronfen, *Over her Dead Body*, 1992: 182

The historian Anne Butler (1985) has examined the lives of prostitutes in the period of the American Wild West through available literature, census lists, police dockets, jail registers, military correspondence, trial testimony, inquests, courts martial, newspapers, post returns and cemetery records, and in doing so elucidates 'some of the patterns of frontier society' (Butler, 1985: 150). Prostitutes participated in the development of (Wild)

Western society, but this has usually been defined in terms of sin/ mockery and morality. The social agencies of the church, the legal system and the media combined to reproduce the dichotomy of prostitutes as moral outlaws and figures of mockery as well as outrage: 'Shrouded in their own grey world, hidden by false names and make believe pasts, and alienated from the main body of society, frontier prostitutes succeeded in blurring their historical identity' (Butler, 1985: xvii).

Frontier prostitutes worked in brothels, saloons and dance halls, as crib women or as streetwalkers. Working in a brothel held the highest status and working on the street the lowest. Crib women were one step up from the street walker, although they were found along dirt tracks on the side of the street. Cribs were small shacks, sometimes little more than tents, clustered together in alleys or along roadways.[3] For Butler, all these women 'made unmistakable contributions to the development of frontier institutions' (1985: xvii). What is of central interest and concern to Butler is how the profession – prostitution – already structured through history and tradition, adapted and functioned in the dislocated frontier societies where major social institutions were transposed and struggled to survive. For Butler, prostitutes deserve a more central place in the story of frontier history.

Two major themes emerge from the work of both Butler (1985) and Myers (1982). First, prostitutes helped to define and underpin the social institutions and order of the American West. The creation of stability and order required politically weak, marginalized populations to show that all people were citizens and would be dealt with 'fairly'; that all were included in the development of social order and social control; and that the legal system would deal with those who transgressed (supported by the Church and the media).

Secondly, prostitution as work revolved around the needs of the men who were at the forefront of developing and stabilizing the frontier lands. In *Unforgiven*, Skinny, the brothel manager, tells the Sheriff 'Oh, them whores are humping all the cowboys coming into town.' Through access to their bodies and through emotional labour, frontier prostitutes provided respite, care, physical and emotional pleasure. For Butler, the men using prostitutes were the men on the margins of 'stable' frontier society. The men she writes about brought further disorder, chaos and instability into the lives of the women working as prostitutes.[4]

These two points have resonances in the representations of relationships between men and prostitutes in the three films discussed here. In *Rio Bravo* it is the Sheriff, John T., who serves as example to and saviour of Feathers from a life of gambling and saloon entertaining. Her attachment to him initially brings chaotic emotions – desire and pain – resolved through his approval and love. Feathers thus fits the 'good-unpunished' archetype of the prostitute in Hollywood films outlined by Hirschman and Stern (1994). In *The Wild Bunch* Tereza exemplifies the 'good-punished' archetype. The man she becomes involved with,

Mapache the General, leads her into a life of sin and depravity and ultimately to her death. In *Unforgiven* the women oscillate between 'good-punished' and 'good-unpunished'. The men in their lives also oscillate between avengers, men who betray, and men who bring violence as the other side of desire. This instability is compounded by the low status and social stigma accorded to prostitutes within the context of fragile communities struggling to develop and maintain social organization, social order and social control. What is clear from the fictive texts used, as well as the historical literature, is that prostitutes both as pariahs and as givers of emotional and physical labour through sexual services were very important to building and sustaining that social order.

Violence dominated the lives of prostitutes, as it does still (see O'Neill, 1995a). Violence from male clients was endemic. It would appear that prostitutes accepted themselves as lesser people in society but showed themselves to be 'pragmatic about the conditions of their lives' (Butler, 1985: 154). These women came from the poorest groups, entering the profession 'with few skills and only rudimentary education. A few exceptions aside, whether in urban or rural frontier settings, [they] came from the ranks of the young and poor' (1985: 151). Indeed, as citizens, they did receive protection from the law but, at one and the same time, this was reduced by virtue of the fact that they were prostitutes.

> For example, at least mild disapproval greeted the murder of a prostitute, and in most cases the law attempted to arrest and try the guilty party. Seldom did community outrage accompany the episode, and so the outcome of the trial and the imposition of punishment could not be depended upon, even in cases where no question lingered about the identity of the killer. (Butler, 1985: 110)

In her research, Butler uncovered only two newspaper reports about raped prostitutes. One of these reported sympathy for the woman until it came to light that she was a prostitute; then the tables were turned completely and the release of the two defendants was demanded. The second case was of a man convicted for rape and subsequently pardoned by a Governor on the recommendation of the warden of the penitentiary, the advice of the prosecuting attorney and the recommendation of numerous citizens. Little Bill, the Sheriff in *Unforgiven*, voices sentiments that are represented in these documents, and still exist in current times, when he champions the right of the cowboy who slashed a whore's face to ribbons with a knife because, it is claimed, she laughed at the size of his 'pecker': 'The hell it ain't like they were tramps, loafers or bad men. They're hardworking boys not given over to wickedness in a regular way.'

Such sentiments remain today. In October 1992 a series of reports on two rape cases against women working as prostitutes made local news in the East Midlands, UK. Consider the following:

> A prostitute broke down in tears as she described how she was allegedly raped at knifepoint by a client . . . She said: 'I asked him for money and he

said "of course". That's when he went to his pocket. I bent down to get my handbag to put the money in and the next minute he had a knife at my throat . . . The knife was at my throat. I was frightened. (O'Neill, 1995a: 134)

The man had carried out a similar attack on a 14-year-old living in local authority care some months earlier, but that case was dropped because of lack of corroboration. The man's defence counsel claimed: 'Two prostitutes with a grudge against a man over money invented stories that he had raped them at knifepoint . . . He should have known he was playing with fire – he should have known that prostitutes can be as hard as nails and as greedy as you like for money' (O'Neill, 1995a: 134).

Involved in the daily experiences of courts and justice, prostitutes reveal(ed) the importance of the institutions representing social order. Through the combined efforts of the press as well as the courts, the need for law and order and the influence and importance of law enforcement was (and still is) brought to the general population. Thus prostitutes in part helped to stabilize the major social institutions while receiving patchy and fragmented responses from these agencies to their own needs and plight.

According to Myers (1982), prostitution was for some a lucrative business, but for most it brought only poverty, disillusionment, illness and death. Saloons, gambling halls and billiard parlours were seen and experienced as major causes of social disorder in the writings of many women in Meyers's survey. Fights, shootings, stabbings, lynchings and outlawry were common in some communities. Vigilante groups were seen and experienced as temporary measures until permanent forms of social control could be established. The people involved were anxious to develop stable forms of social organization, bringing security and peace to their lives and in their attempts they pressured for anti-saloon bills and taxes on gambling halls (Myers, 1982).

The prostitute was central to this saloon, gambling and dance-hall culture. Western prostitutes, Myers writes, are often portrayed as 'nice girls gone wrong'. But the reality from Myers's women's accounts is that:

> some girls entered the profession in order to advance themselves economically or to escape dull and dreary lives on isolated farms and ranches. Many were attracted by the bright lights and excitement of the mining camps and cattle towns and hoped to earn a little nest egg, meet a cowboy rancher, and eventually settle down to a respectable life. Others hoped to become economically independent and viewed prostitution as one of the few professions where women had some chance of financial success. (Myers, 1982: 255)

Prostitutes came from the poorest groups of people. 'They were daughters of cultures where servitude had taken a toll' (Myers, 1982: 151): black women, Chinese women, Mexican women, white women (some of whom were Irish immigrants) and Native American women. Four of the five prostitute groups 'drew directly from cultures where the pre-industrial experience produced women generally accustomed to hard work, few comforts, and life from birth to death that remained exactly the same . . . They brought with them the baggage of the past and became part of the frontier sexual marketplace' (Butler, 1985: 11). For black women, specifically, came the transformation from slave to prostitute which 'flowed from the debilitating social and economic effects of bondage' (1985: 13). The Irish group fitted 'perfectly into the schema of sexual/economic experiences of pre-industrial personalities thrown into the frontier industrial complex' (1985: 14). With a history of dire poverty, dominion by English landlords, and the experiences of the famine, generations of social malaise conditioned them. Similarly, the Native American women were caught up in the transformation of their old society, marked by the arrival of the Spanish in the 1500s and the Anglos in the 1800s, which effectively denied them autonomy both culturally and socially and led them into dependence upon US government and into warfare and sociocultural destruction. For Butler, the involvement of Native American women in prostitution reflects the destruction of Native American social order. The Chinese women initially involved in prostitution had been transported specifically for this purpose. 'These women simply moved from one controlling hierarchy to another without a transformation in their societal roles. Brought from a pre-industrial society and closeted in a minority subculture, Oriental prostitutes had little opportunity to develop changed self-concepts in their new environment' (Butler, 1985: 13).

The commonalities between saloon girls and women working in bars, massage parlours and saunas today are many. Economic need remains the bottom line for women's entry into prostitution as work. As workers, women manage and 'make out' in prostitution. They help clients live out their sexual fantasies, they 'strut their stuff' in the theatre of the brothel, sauna or club. Their relationships with partners and pimps are sometimes violent, often abusive. Their relationships with each other are built upon shaky foundations – they are, after all, in competition with each other for the paying clients who walk through the door. Many of these clients become regulars which brings a little bit of continuity and security of earnings. Prostitutes, it seems, are the end stop in discourses and representations of good and honest women in contemporary society (see Clark, 1980). Indeed, the very category 'prostitute':

> is based more upon symbolic and legal representations of the bad woman or 'whore' than upon an actual set of characteristics . . . Don't be bad like 'Those Women' or you too will be punished . . . You'll never be as good as 'Those Women' unless you're bad and then you're no good. Meanwhile, 'Those Women' are legally stripped of human status. (Pheterson, 1989: 8)

Conclusion

For Helmet Kuzmics (1994) fiction is a prime source in understanding social phenomena, and the study of emotions and psychic processes occupies a central place in his work. What I call a 'politics of feeling' incorporates emotions and psychic and social processes through an examination of 'feeling forms' – literature, art, life stories – and seeks to develop better knowledge and understanding of the human condition through interpretation and translation. In doing so, we move towards praxis, towards purposeful knowledge.[5] Stories are powerful learning tools. The significance of the life journeys of women working as prostitutes is what they reveal about the psychological connections between harsh life experiences, the management of self and self-identity, the embodied experience of selling men access to their organic bodies, and societal expectations. A fragment of a *story* about a life can tell us so much more than one hundred pages of *information* about a life.

In the context of this chapter, fictive texts can show and tell us plenty about the representation of women as prostitutes and about the place of the saloon/brothel as a workplace organization in the development of the American West. Further, exploring fictive texts alongside historical and documentary literature will inevitably throw up material that will have meaning and resonances for women working as prostitutes in bars and clubs and saunas today in the Western world. Consider the following two extracts in relation to the stories of Feathers, Tereza and Delilah told in the films discussed in the chapter.

Annie, described as 'a beautiful Madam with two gold teeth, a battered puss, and the form of a lopsided watermelon' (Myers, 1982: 348) had this to say:

> I've laid it in all of 'em, Borger, Kilgore . . . I threw my fannie 21 times a night, 5 bucks a throw and time old red-eye come up I was eatin' breakfast drunker'n an Indian . . . Some girls get mad at her pa 'cause he won't let her stay out nights . . . so she pulls out. She hits for the lights and tries to save money by staying in the flops. I can pick one out just by lookin' at 'em . . . they're so hungry, and wishing to hell they was back home and afraid to go. Some 'lady' ease up to her . . . and feed her a square . . . and give her a bed . . . Get her in bed once and she's with you from then on. Can't go back then and wouldn't if she could. (Myers, 1982: 255)

The following is an excerpt from a taped discussion with a group of women (Jane, Sam, Moira, Susan and Mary) with whom I was conducting life-story narratives (30 September 1992):

> it becomes such a closed circuit . . . because it is not a job you can go out and admit to the world . . . you have the friends you work with . . . and they become the friends you go out with . . . so in the end you stay within the one circuit. Society looks down on prostitutes morally like it's wrong and it's not wrong . . . Well, it is exciting at first . . . seeing all that money . . . it is unbelievable . . . especially at fifteen and you have things you want to spend it on and you have this man that takes you out once in a blue moon and makes you feel like a million dollars . . . and at fifteen all you're looking for is that knight in the white shining armour to take you away and make you feel loved . . . and then after a while you begin to see what prostitution is really about . . . but imagine a fifteen year old having that kind of money. (O'Neill, 1995b: 130)

What we clearly do not get access to in the classic Hollywood Western is women's voices, narratives, feelings and fears. *Unforgiven* shifts the genre a little towards accommodating women as central characters, around whom the action revolves, and towards an issue that is very women-centred: women as whores and violence against women. Historical material has documented a better picture, a better context in which to examine the social organization of prostitution in (Wild) Western society. What is very clear is triangulating historical material with fictive texts (film) and women's narratives is that the saloon/ brothel as a workplace organization and saloon girls/prostitutes pro- vided sexual and emotional services (care-giving services) for men who in (Wild) Western society were involved in building frontier societies, developing major institutions such as churches, schools, law and order. The saloon/brothel, and saloon girls in particular, provided frontier societies with a marginalized and politically weak population against which fledgling law and order and social control could be measured. The prostitute was and still is the end stop in discourses on good and bad women. It is against the prostitute that we measure relative goodness, purity, and morality.

The saloon/brothel as a workplace organization can be understood as a frontier space: it is located at the juncture between savagery and civilization; it resonates with both desire and danger, with fiction/ fantasy and reality. Working in saloons/brothels is almost theatrical; it is about facilitating imaginings, involving oneself in role play. Whores 'strut their stuff' and clients, who have the money, pay whores to help them escape from the real into the imaginary, into fantasy. But, the fictive texts used here to 'get at' a better understanding of the saloon/ brothel as a workplace organization do, in fact, tell us stories about masculinities and desire.

We can learn so much about gendered relations, and the interconnec- tions between desire and death/violence resonant of masculinities, through exploring and critically examining fictive texts within the con- text of historical and ethnographic material. Of course, to gain a better, fuller understanding of gendered relations we need to see more main- stream films made by women directors.

Notes

1 For a further discussion of 'feeling forms' see O'Neill (forthcoming), and Witkin (1974).

2 The image of woman as destroyer, bringing ruination, draining the energies and life out of her men, is resonant of nineteenth-century writings on the power of 'bad' women (Corbin, 1990; John, 1994) and is also present in the work of Klauss Theweleit (1987, 1989) in his incredible study of masculinities, the emotional core of fascism and the flight from the feminine.

3 See *McCabe and Mrs Miller* (1971) with Julie Christie and Warren Beatty. Their image of scruffy prostitutes working out of canvas tents amidst great snowdrifts struck me as

markedly different from the usual beautifully costumed dance girls of other films' (Butler, 1985: xi).

4 Of course, there are methodological questions one needs to ask of Butler's work. Given the absence of documentary evidence relating to the feeling worlds of women working as prostitutes, it is difficult simply to accept that all men in the women's lives brought chaos and disorder and, given the complexity of their lives and our understanding of gendered relations in the context of their time, this point is likely to be 'true' but certainly not the only 'truth'. Piecing together a story from the documentary evidence available – police dockets, census lists etc. – is a mammoth and painstaking task, but without material speaking of women's and men's feeling worlds we cannot construct a full enough picture on which to then base generalizations.

5 By purposeful knowledge, by praxis, I mean the use to which we put information gathered from primary and secondary research. For example, the inter-relation between a better understanding of a social issue and subsequent social action to promote social change. Purposeful knowledge as praxis is centred upon the mediation between knowledge, power and action.

References

Bronfen, E. (1992) *Over her Dead Body: Death, Femininity and the Aesthetic*. Manchester: Manchester University Press.

Butler, A.M. (1985) *Daughters of Joy, Sisters of Misery: Prostitutes in the American West*. Illinois: University of Illinois Press.

Clark, T.J. (1980) 'Preliminaries to a possible treatment of Olympia in 1865', *Screen*, 2 (1): 18–41.

Corbin, A. (1990) *Women for Hire: Prostitution and Sexuality in France after 1850*. Cambridge, MA: Harvard University Press.

Hirschman, E.C. and Stern, B.B. (1994) 'Women as commodities: prostitution depicted in *The Blue Angel*, *Pretty Baby*, and *Pretty Woman*', *Advances in Consumer Research*, 21: 576–81.

John, N. (ed.) (1994) *Violetta and her Sisters: The Lady of the Camellias' Responses to the Myth*. London: Faber and Faber.

Kuzmics, H. (1994) 'Power and work: the development of work as a civilizing process in examples of fictional literature', *Sociological Perspectives*, 37 (1): 119–54.

Myers, Sandra L. (1982) *Westering Women and the Frontier Experience 1800–1915*. Albuquerque, NM: University of New Mexico Press.

O'Neill, M. (1995a) 'Prostitution and violence: towards a feminist praxis', in M. Hester, L. Kelly and J. Radford (eds), *Women, Violence and Male Power: Feminist Activism, Research and Practice*. Milton Keynes: Open University Press. pp. 130–47.

O'Neill, M. (1995b) 'Prostitution, feminism and critical praxis: transformative possibilities involved in conducting feminist participatory action research with female prostitutes'. PhD thesis, Staffordshire University.

O'Neill, M. (forthcoming) *Prostitution and Feminism: Towards a Politics of Feeling*. Cambridge: Polity Press.

Ormiston, G. and Sassower, R. (1989) *Narrative Experiments: The Discursive Authority of Science and Technology*. Minneapolis, MN: University of Minnesota Press.

Pheterson, G. (1989) *The Whore Stigma: Female Dishonor and Male Unworthiness*. Amsterdam: Dutch Ministry of Social Affairs and Employment.

Theweleit, K. (1987) *Male Fantasies, Vol. 1. Women, Floods, Bodies, History*. Minneapolis, MN: University of Minnesota Press.

Theweleit, K. (1989) *Male Fantasies, Vol. 2. Male Bodies: Psychoanalyzing the White Terror*. Minneapolis, MN: University of Minnesota Press.

Witkin, R. (1974) *The Intelligence of Feeling*. London: Heineman.

PART III
MEN AND SUPERMEN

7

Child's Play: Representations of Organization in Children's Literature

Christopher Grey

Recently, there has been an upsurge of interest in fictional representations as a resource for studying organizations and management (Phillips, 1995). In particular, the novel has been identified as a key area for investigation (Czarniawska-Joerges and Guillet de Monthoux, 1994; Czarniawska-Joerges, 1995; Grey 1996). Novels are held to be a rich source of knowledge for researchers, while also offering an accessible medium for the development of innovative pedagogies (Cohen, 1995; Knights and Willmott, 1995; Thompson and McGivern, 1996).

The use of novels is held to be theoretically innovative because it breaks away from the scientistic pretensions of conventional organizational studies, wherein knowledge is only legitimate in so far as it derives from the deployment of positivistic or quasi-positivistic methodologies, or from fieldwork conducted according to various kinds of interpretative methodologies. Yet, innovative as the engagement with fiction may be, it embodies a residual and problematic realism, in that novels are seen as a point of access into the 'realities' of organizational life. In reading fictional representations, it is suggested, we acquire an insight into organizational realities.

What such an approach ignores, however, is the role of fictional representations in the *construction* of organizational realities. While it has become commonplace in organizational theory, most famously in Morgan's (1986) work on metaphors, to recognize that representations of organization can have such a constitutive effect, this insight has yet to be applied in the developing field of 'fictional' organization studies. This chapter aims to address that gap.

The vehicle through which this issue will be explored is a consideration of a number of popular children's stories. Specifically, consideration will be given to three series of books: Anthony Buckeridge's *Jennings*

Figure 7.1   Swallows and Amazons, 1974, *UGC Lumiere, Pinewood*

series, Enid Blyton's *Famous Five* stories, and Arthur Ransome's *Swallows and Amazons* adventures (a total of around 50 books).[1] The rationale for this approach is that children's literature has a very obvious role in social conditioning, such that the lessons learnt from childhood reading have the potential to provide an interpretative framework for later life, much as educational theorists have argued that the 'hidden curriculum' operates to socialize children into hegemonic values and behaviours.

The role of children's literature in promoting and enhancing particular values is one that has often been recognized: 'As with discourse in general, the discourses of children's fiction are pervaded by ideological presuppositions, sometimes obtrusively and sometimes invisibly' (Stephens, 1992: 2). The question of what values children may consciously or unconsciously be imbibing in their reading is one that has fuelled many controversies over the 'suitability' of particular texts. Attempts to substitute 'improving' novels for 'penny dreadfuls' in the nineteenth century have their counterpart in contemporary debates about the 'political correctness' of children's books, debates which have often centred, in fact, on the work of Enid Blyton (Ray, 1982), one of the authors to be discussed in this chapter. The argument is that if children are exposed to racist, sexist and élitist stereotypes in their early reading this will tend to lead them to espouse such stereotypes in adult life.

While issues of stereotyping have some relevance to the present analysis, the primary focus of this chapter is on representations of organization found within the works discussed. The particular texts chosen have been very widely read by children in many countries over a number of years and especially during the childhoods of many of those currently in positions of influence in present-day organizations (all of the books discussed were originally published between 1930 and 1968). Following the 'conditioning' argument, it might be speculated that such individuals carry with them understandings of organization developed in early childhood. It is not, however, necessary to this chapter to sustain that claim empirically, and no attempt is made to do so. Rather, there is an implicit speculative argument that literature such as that discussed has the capacity to inform the worldviews of those who have read it. More generally, it might be assumed that this argument does not apply uniquely to children's literature: while children may be more 'plastic' and also more spontaneous in their responses as readers of fiction, others too have their conceptions of organization constituted in part through their reading of fiction.

The chapter in no sense provides a comprehensive analysis either of the stories under consideration or of the representations of organization found within them. Space precludes anything other than the raising of some indicative themes for further consideration: that is to say, the aim is to show how children's literature can be analysed to show its ideological content with respect to the representation of organization. In particular, following a general overview of the books under discussion, the chapter will focus primarily on one theme from each of the series. The *Jennings* stories will be considered in terms of their representation of paternalistic bureaucracy, the *Famous Five* for the representation of patriarchal groups, and *Swallows and Amazons* for the representation of the moral meaning of work. It is intended that this partial analysis of very different books will yield some sense of the rich patina of representations of organization to be found in children's stories, and reflection upon the consequences of such representations for the reproduction of organizational life.

Overviews of the Texts

In order to facilitate the more detailed analysis that forms the bulk of this chapter, it will be useful to outline as briefly as possible the main themes, characters and concerns of the three sets of stories to be discussed. The *Famous Five* adventures, published between 1942 and 1968, feature four children – Julian, Dick and Anne, who are siblings, and their cousin George (short for Georgina) – and George's dog, Timmy. Each adventure takes place in the school holidays, often, although not always, in the summer. The children are usually spending the holidays away from their parents, or with George's parents (the bad-tempered scientist, Uncle Quentin, and his long-suffering wife, Aunt Fanny), and adult involvement in the adventures is generally minimal. The adventures themselves typically involve the children gradually uncovering acts of illegality, identifying the criminals, capturing them and turning them over to the police. This is interspersed with more normal holiday activities such as camping, swimming and picnicking.

Despite their popularity, these stories suffer from limited vocabulary and implausible plots. Characterization is also fairly weak and there is no development of character in the stories. The lack of character development is related to the atemporality of the series: the summer holidays come and go, but the children do not age. Each child has a certain set of characteristics that help to structure the story and provide interludes in the plot (occasionally even driving the plot). Thus Julian, the eldest child, is a mature and sensible leader, often patronizing and alarmingly pompous for a boy of around 12 years old. Dick, his younger brother, is also sensible, but is rarely required to take responsibility unless Julian is elsewhere and Dick, naturally, has to take care of 'the girls'. If Dick has a characteristic it is 'pluck': he can usually be relied upon to volunteer for some dangerous or unpleasant task. Anne is easily frightened, dislikes adventures, is passive, enjoys domestic chores and rarely takes any initiative. In short, she is a gender stereotype of the grossest sort. George's main characteristic is that she wants to be a boy, and she tends (whether coincidentally, causally or consequently is unclear) to be bad tempered and impetuous. Finally, Timmy the dog is treated anthropomorphically, and, indeed, so weak are the characterizations of the children that it might almost be said that he is as recognizably human as they are.

The second series of stories to be discussed are the *Jennings* books, which started life in 1948 as radio plays. The main protagonists are Jennings and Darbishire, two schoolboys at a boarding preparatory school. As with the *Famous Five*, the characters never age, remaining in a permanent pre-pubescent limbo. The stories are in a sense adventures, although more accurately consist of a series of incidents, loosely welded together, bounded structurally by the beginning and end of term. These incidents are rarely adventures in the *Five* mould – they rarely involve catching criminals or finding treasure. More often, the incidents are relatively mundane and become noteworthy because of the misunderstandings and complications that derive from Jennings's and Darbishire's foolishness and misconceived logic. In essence, the stories are humorous (unlike the *Famous Five* where there is almost no humour) and the humour is both situational and linguistic (there are some labyrinthine metaphors and surprisingly sophisticated puns).

Jennings as a character is presented as good-natured, thoughtless and active: he dominates Darbishire who is absent-minded, timid and reflective. Other boys, such as Venables, Atkinson and Temple, while featuring in most of the stories, rarely emerge as characters in their own right. Apart from the boys, the main characters are the schoolmasters, and especially Mr Carter and Mr Wilkins. Mr Carter is humorous, tolerant, calm and perceptive, while Mr Wilkins, although essentially good-natured, is inclined to bad temper (or 'bates' to use the schoolboy slang that permeates the stories). Much of the action is driven by the misunderstandings that arise between the boys and their masters, and especially between Mr Wilkins's brusque impatience and Jennings's faulty logic. The only woman appearing regularly in the stories is 'Matron' (we never learn her name), who is loosely described as young, friendly and competent.

In literary terms, these books, then, are fairly weak on plot and characterization, but use a much more extensive vocabulary than the *Famous Five* stories. They are very strong on humour, and, partly for this reason, are much more endearing to the adult reader than the *Famous Five*. They are also endearing for their essential gentleness, and the affection one senses the author has for the characters. While they could undoubtedly be criticized for their middle-class bias and some degree of stereotyping, there is neither the vicious moralizing nor the gross elaboration of gender, race and class prejudices to be found in Enid Blyton's work.

The *Swallows and Amazons* stories are different again from the series already introduced. In a literary sense, they are several streets ahead, and should be regarded as 'serious' literature for children. Ransome exhibits an artistic and moral sensibility that is not matched in any way by Blyton or Buckeridge.[2] Yet in a curious sense they form the archetype from which the *Famous Five* stories derive, since the 12 books in the series, published between 1930 and 1948, have been regarded as instigating the 'holiday adventure' as a genre in children's literature.

The cast of characters shifts much more than in the other series discussed. The main characters are the children of the Walker family – John, Susan, Titty and Roger – and the Blackett family – Nancy (christened Ruth) and Peggy. These families are respectively the Swallows and the Amazons. The stories are set most famously in the Lake District but also on the Norfolk Broads. The children create for themselves a series of fantasy worlds (as sailors, explorers, prospectors, pirates and so on) which are played out seriously, although always accompanied by the characters' awareness of their fantastic nature. The plots are highly structured, although in many cases the action is minimal, consisting primarily of the performance of outdoor skills (camping, sailing, climbing and so on) rather than adventurous activities in the dramatic sense.

Characterization is much stronger than in the other series. Briefly, John is mature, serious, rather humourless and intensely moral; Susan is responsible, domestic and 'cares' for the other children; Titty (unfortunately named for the modern reader) is dreamy, literary, almost mystical; Roger is very much a junior member, adventurous within limits, dependent on others, occasionally humorous. As regards the Amazons, Nancy is plainly the leader, active, somewhat irresponsible and ultimately, within the ethical universe of the stories, immoral.[3] Peggy is more passive, and tends to be less well drawn than the other characters. There are several other children with important roles in the stories, as well as some adult characters, especially the Swallows' parents and the Amazons' mother. Perhaps the most important adult character is Captain Flint, the Amazons' uncle, a traveller, adventurer and writer based, it seems, upon Ransome himself. The stories do not, however, focus upon the character of the adults. Equally, there are a whole series of background characters (farmers, boatbuilders, charcoal burners) who, while not developed as characters, do have some significance in terms of the analysis to be developed in this chapter.

In considering the representations of organization to be found in the three series under discussion, it is necessary to attend to several interrelated issues. These include the ways in which the children organize their activities, or have their activities organized for them, the kind of normative controls that operate, the roles they undertake, the types of power and authority relationships within the stories and so on. It is also relevant to consider how work and occupations in relation to the adults in the stories are represented.

Jennings: the Paternalistic Bureaucracy

These kinds of issue are most easily analysed in the *Jennings* books because here, unlike stories set in holidays, the action is entirely located within a readily definable organization – the school. Indeed, given that it is a boarding school, it might be regarded as a 'total institution' in Goffman's sense; these schools are, in fact, included within his enumeration of such institutions (Goffman, 1961/1968: 16). School stories must be considered to be a major and enduring genre in children's literature, from *Tom Brown's Schooldays* onwards. Boarding schools seem to have been particularly popular, although many, if not most, readers of such stories are unlikely to have attended this type of school.

Jennings attends Linbury Court School, situated near the fictional market town of Dunhambury in Sussex. The school is a clearly defined pyramid of authority relations extending from the Headmaster, 'M.W.B. Pemberton-Oakes Esq. M.A. (Oxon.)', through Mr Carter, to Mr Wilkins, right down to Binns and Blotwell, the most junior boys in the school. Among the boys there is a hierarchy based upon age and experience. The hierarchical authority structure is combined with a system of rules, both formal and informal, which gives the school something of the character of a bureaucracy.

These issues of authority and rules are very well illustrated by Jennings's and Darbishire's early experience of school life. In *Jennings Goes to School* (1953), Jennings makes the mistake on his first day of calling a more senior boy, Temple, by his nickname, Bod: '"You mustn't call him Bod," said Venables, shocked, "New chaps aren't allowed to call fairly senior chaps by their nicknames until their second term"' (*JGTS*: 19). Jennings unwittingly continues to flout school conventions in the dormitory on his first night. Confronting Temple over their respective rights to the washbasin, Temple soaks Jennings's pyjamas with water, causing him to scream. Mr Carter enters the room asking: 'Who was responsible for that screaming noise?' (*JGTS*: 35). When Jennings admits that it was him and tells Mr Carter of Temple's attack, he is rebuked by Mr Carter, who points out that the phraseology of his question was designed to allow the perpetrator to own up without the victim 'telling tales'. Thus, while there is a system of informal rules ordering school life, these are in fact bound in with, and supported and sustained by, the formal authority structure. Nevertheless, this order is negotiable, as the development of the confrontation between Temple and Jennings shows. After Mr Carter's departure, Temple, encouraged by other boys in the dormitory, threatens Jennings: 'You ruinous little sneak, Jennings. You wait! I'll bash you up tomorrow' (*JGTS*: 36).

Darbishire, too, is threatened with a similar fate should he 'get uppish' (he does not). Yet Jennings manages to assert his position when he and Darbishire go, strictly against school rules, to a nearby village the next day, bringing back some sweets as proof of their daring. The outcome of this is that Temple is forced to recognize Jennings's superiority, symbolized by the fact that the former cleans the washbasin and allows Jennings to use his nickname.[4]

Although the rules of the school and the structure of hierarchy are shown here to be negotiable, there are many more cases where rules are shown to be absolutely inflexible, in ways sometimes suggestive of the bureaucratic dysfunctionalism literature. In a story reminiscent of goal displacement (Merton, 1968), again in the early sections of *Jennings Goes to School*, all of the boys are required to write a postcard to their parents informing them of their safe arrival at school. Darbishire points out to Mr Wilkins that his parents are well aware of that fact, having themselves taken him down to school that afternoon. Mr Wilkins responds: 'Can't help that . . . School rules say "write post-card home". All right then, write post-card home. Won't do any harm, will it?' (*JGTS*: 23). The boys therefore write their cards, although the value of them is unclear. Darbishire runs out of space, having written 'I hope you are quite.', but reasons that his parents will understand that he means 'well' and not 'ill', while the full stop will reassure them that he was not 'called away unexpectedly in the middle, or anything'. Jennings makes seven attempts to produce a card acceptable to Mr Wilkins, but even so 'the post-card's message remained for ever a mystery' to his parents (*JGTS*: 23–6).

Although rules are applied inflexibly, as this example shows, it is an important feature of the stories that they be applied humanely, and that exercises of power are legitimate rather than arbitrary. A good example of this occurs later in *Jennings Goes to School* when Mr Wilkins attempts to instil discipline by telling the boys that he has cancelled a football match to punish them for misbehaviour when, in fact, the game has been cancelled because of an outbreak of German measles at the opposing school. On hearing of this plan: 'Mr Carter was shocked. "You can't do that!" he protested. "It's making out that you've got the authority to do things which you can't do"' (*JGTS*: 177). Despite this, Mr Wilkins goes ahead with his plan, but his duplicity is discovered by Jennings, much to Mr Wilkins's embarrassment. The moral of the story is that there are rules of conduct governing how those in authority may behave, and flouting those rules is inadvisable, regardless of one's position in the authority structure. In this sense, the representation of organization can be seen to suggest a rational–legal basis for authority which entails a specific bureaucratic ethic placing limits upon abitrary acts of domination (du Gay, 1994).

The ethical, rather than the repressive, aspects of bureaucracy emerge from the theme of the desirability of rule-governed conduct that permeates the *Jennings* stories. The boys 'were all very happy at Linbury; they all liked the masters, and they knew that the rules of the school were made for their own good and for their own enjoyment' (*JGTS*: 28). It is this stable and benevolent backdrop that forms the setting for most of the action in the stories. In *The Trouble with Jennings* (1960), we learn that the trouble with Jennings is that 'his habit of jumping to wild conclusions sometimes reduced the smooth-running routine of the school to a state of turmoil and chaos' (*TTWJ*: 11).

The plot of all the stories revolves around these wild conclusions (that a spider is poisonous; that Mr Wilkins is retiring; that the school is being burgled, and so on) being acted upon and finally resolved. They are *always* misunderstandings, and they are *always* resolved, which is an important feature in the stories. Jennings in no sense challenges the status quo of the rule-governed school: most of his mischief is unintentional, and causes no more than a passing impact on the school. And why should it be otherwise? The stories are light humour, not textbooks for would-be revolutionaries. But if we reflect on what these stories communicate to their readers, we might reasonably conclude that they contain a series of powerful messages. The most obvious is that organizations (in this case, schools) are sites of authority-based rule structures that are not only immutable but beneficial for all parties. Schooled in school stories, the Jennings's reader of, say, 1960 is now in her (but most probably his) late forties. Of course, she (but most probably he) has had many experiences other than reading Jennings, yet, encountering (or, perhaps, experiencing the loss of) paternalistic bureaucracies in adult life, the former Jennings reader may find some echo of her (his) childhood reading.

Famous Five: the Patriarchal Group

If the *Jennings* stories are suggestive of paternalistic bureaucratic organizations, the *Famous Five* adventures have the character of a patriarchal group. Unlike Jennings, the children are always depicted on holiday, never in school. Moreover, they undertake holidays which are largely unsupervised. We might wonder at the variety of misfortunes that prevent the children's parents from taking a holiday – illness, trees demolishing houses, even kidnapping – but the result is that the children are left predominantly to their own resources. In these circumstances, they undergo a process of group formation that strongly resembles that staple of organizational behaviour courses, Tuckman's (1965) model of 'forming, storming, norming, performing'.[5] In *Five on a Treasure Island* (1942), the first of the stories, the children are formed into a group when their parents force the cousins to spend summer together. The 'storming' occurs principally because of conflicts between George and her cousins. As George puts it, 'I didn't want any of you to come anyway. Interfering in my life here! I'm quite happy on my own. Now I've got to put up with a silly girl who likes frocks and dolls, and two stupid boy-cousins!' (*FOATI*: 20). Anne tells her brothers 'She won't answer if you call her Georgina . . . She's awfully queer, I think' (*FOATI*: 20), and a situation of hostility exists for some time, with 'norming' being achieved through shared interests in Timmy the dog, ice creams and a treasure island. Having resolved their differences, 'performing' takes the form of engaging in adventures. Although differences between George and her cousins sometimes surface in future stories, the Famous Five are formed as a group from then on.

One of the key issues in the initial conflict within the group, which is a recurring theme in the stories, is that of George's gender. She tells Anne that: 'I hate being a girl. I won't be. I like doing the things that boys do. I can climb better than any boy, and swim faster too. I can sail a boat as well as any fisherboy on this coast' (*FOATI*: 19). The contrast between Anne, a stereotypical girl, and George is frequently made. The exchange in *Five Go to Mystery Moor* (1954) is typical: 'The boys don't want us girls round them all the time. We couldn't do the things they do', said Anne. George thought differently. 'I can do *anything* that Dick and Julian do,' she said. 'I can climb, and bike for miles, can walk as far as they can, I can swim – I can beat a whole lot of boys at most things' (*FGTMM*: 10).

George's desire to be a boy, then, is conceptualized in terms of claims of competence in a series of supposedly boy-ish activities. This is bolstered by the use of the name 'George' instead of Georgina, the fact that George has short curly hair, and wears shorts rather than a skirt. George is described as being 11 years old in the first adventure, and the children do not age, so the presumption is that she has not experienced any secondary sexual development. Certainly, she is often mistaken for a boy by adults.

How do the other children react to George? Anne simply reinforces her own stereotyped role by being almost completely subservient to George. While she may question George's status as a real boy, she accepts that, as a quasi-boy, George is of superior status. Julian and Dick accept George in a slightly condescending way, as shown in *Five Go Adventuring Again* (1943):

> 'I believe George felt left-out!' said Julian with a grin. 'Funny old Georgina!'
> '*Don't* call me Georgina' said the little girl, fiercely. The boys laughed.
> 'Ah, it's the same fierce old George, all right,' said Dick, and he gave the girl a friendly slap on the shoulder. (*FGAA*: 18)

In general, George is accorded a type of 'associate membership' of maleness. In this sense, while she might be regarded as a non-stereotyped character, George's character in no sense constitutes a challenge to conventional gender roles: she merely aspires, with a degree of success, to assume a masculine role. This situation might be regarded as analogous to that of the organizational impacts of liberal feminist-inspired moves for equal opportunities at work. It is commonplace that women achieving success in work organizations are often able to do so only in so far as they ape the behaviour of their male colleagues, and that, even then, they are only grudgingly accepted. Acceptance on these terms does nothing to challenge the underlying patriarchy of organizational power relations.

Similarly, although the question of George's role is central to the formation of the group, it does not disrupt its patriarchal functioning.

Within that context, Julian is plainly the patriarch. The possibility of the children having holidays without adult involvement is routinely justified by reference to Julian's responsibility and leadership qualities. As Uncle Quentin says in *Five Get into Trouble* (1949), 'I'd bank on Julian any time to keep the others in order and see they were all safe and sound' (*FGIT*: 12). In all the adventures Julian takes precisely this role. He keeps discipline in the group, to a large extent makes plans and gives orders, and he frequently acts as an educator to the other children. He also seeks to protect the others from potential danger (especially when dealing with criminals), and it is notable that on these occasions George's pretensions to masculinity receive short shrift.

Throughout each of the stories, Julian's authority operates unchecked: there is never any challenge from the other children, who apparently accept it as the natural order of things that the eldest male should be dominant. Yet Julian's patriarchal authority is contextualized by the invocation of wider power structures in the stories. This is important because it conveys to the reader some sense that the functioning of the group is but a part of a wider patterning of social order. Indeed, it is only because of this wider patterning that the patriarchal group structure can be sustained. The most important way in which these issues are played out is the role of the police in the children's adventures. In almost all the books, the story ends when the children hand over the villains and their booty to a policeman (often a 'burly' policeman). The appearance of the police in the story occasions a degree of obsequiousness form Julian, who always addresses the officer as 'Sir'. Thus Julian's authority is clearly delineated by the arrival of a superior male. The issue is not simply that Julian must obey the policeman, but that Julian's authority is revealed to be part of a wider system of power relations. More subtly, the arrival of the police, and the understandings of authority thereby revealed, are part of a wider representation of power and status. For, while Julian is deferential to the police, this deference is tinged with patronage and is mediated by the unstated implication of Julian's social superiority as a member of the middle-classes addressing a working-class functionary, albeit a state functionary.

These issues of status permeate the stories. The children's attitude to the people they come into contact with is entirely determined by status. When dealing with such figures as shopkeepers or fishermen, the children are polite but patronizing. But it is in the treatment of 'outsiders' that status issues become glaring. In many of the adventures, the children meet another child who, for that story only, shares their adventure. These 'extras' are almost always gypsy or circus children, and they are depicted as being barely human. This lowly status is epitomized by the names given to such children, for example 'Sniffer' (a gypsy boy in *Five Go to Mystery Moor*). A typical initial encounter can be found in *Five Get into a Fix* (1958). Here the outsider is Welsh:

At last the child came near to them, as watchful as a hare, ready to run at a moment's notice. The boys sat still and patient, and soon the girl was near enough to snatch a biscuit and retreat again . . .

'What's your name?' asked Dick, not moving from his place, afraid that the child would leap off like a frightened goat. The girl didn't seem to understand. Dick repeated his question, speaking slowly.

'What – is – your – name? What – are – you – called?'

. . .

'Me – Aily,' she said. (*FGIAF*: 52)

The depiction of Aily is in essence the depiction of an animal that has to be lured with food and spoken to with extreme simplicity (in fact, Timmy the dog is accorded greater respect and credited with greater powers of understanding). The comparisons with a hare and a goat underline this. True, Aily – like the other outsiders – develops somewhat as the story progresses, but it is plain that, to the extent to which this occurs, it is to be understood as a consequence of contact with the Five.

The significance of outsiders in the stories goes beyond the introduction of occasional characters. The structure of the stories is bound up with the encounter between 'respectable' society – the children, backed by the police – and others – burglars, smugglers, foreigners, spies and gypsies. The sociological significance of this is considerable, and accounts in part for the controversy of Enid Blyton's work, encompassing issues broader than those of organization. Yet the messages conveyed about organization are striking. The identification of the children with the forces of law and order (and thereby of decency and moral virtue) inevitably has the effect of legitimating the ways in which they organize themselves. This – it is implied – is how decent people conduct themselves. This is how decent people work together. Either you are part of the moral universe, which prizes hierarchy, conformity, knowing-your-place, or you are an outsider, a person beyond the moral pale, perhaps not even fully human. And, since the criminals are always caught, to be such an outsider is not only morally untenable but also impractical. Good is not just right, it is also more effective.

The *Famous Five* stories therefore represent organizations in both the particular and the general sense. In the particular, they validate a model of the patriarchal group that structures many of the practices of work organizations, particularly the operation of teamwork: 'For some women, teamwork is a sustained exposure to systematic discrimination – their ideas are dismissed, their comments overruled, their contributions relegated to clerical or secretarial tasks' (Sinclair, 1995: 305). Plainly there is much that could be said both about the nature of gender discrimination in teams and the socialization processes behind such discrimination. For present purposes, the point is that those boys and girls who read the *Famous Five* in their childhood will have been provided with a template for the roles they will be expected to play later in work groups.

At the general level, readers of the stories will have learned the desirability of conformity, or, to put it negatively, will not have learned any resources through which orthodoxy might be challenged. Again, the importance of conformity in the reproduction of organizations is a topic which could be discussed at length. For example, consider the recent vogue in organizations for culture management programmes in which, under the guise of autonomy, employees are required to subscribe to a unitary set of values defined hierarchically (Willmott, 1993). As in the *Famous Five* stories, within such organizations one is either a conformist to dominant values or an outsider – morally and practically doomed.

Swallows and Amazons: the Meaning of Work

In some respects, the children in *Swallows and Amazons* are as much of a patriarchal group as the Famous Five. The Swallows organize themselves as the crew of a boat in which John is the captain, although the group is more suggestive of a proto-family. John shares responsibility with Susan for the well-being of the group, in which they take paternal and maternal roles. If anything, however, Susan's maternal role is the more dominant in that she acts maternally towards John, even though he is both older and the captain of the boat. Certainly, in times of real crisis it is she who takes the lead, and it is she whom the adults trust to ensure that the practical needs of the children are satisfied. Moreover, when with the Amazons, it is by no means clear that John enjoys greater status than their Captain, Nancy. An illustration of the complexities of the authority relations in the stories can be found in *Swallowdale* (1931). At one point, Titty and Roger are missing on the moors in a thick fog, a potentially life-threatening circumstance. John, Susan and Nancy go to Mary Swainson's farm to check that the others have not sheltered there:

> Mother [would be] so sure that everything was as it should be. And she, Susan, who should have been taking care of the others, did not even know where they were . . . The others looked at her gravely.
> 'What's ado?' said Mary . . .
> 'They're lost . . .' sobbed Susan . . .
> 'It was in the fog,' said John.
> Susan made up her mind.
> 'We must go and tell mother at once . . .'
> 'Susan's right,' said Nancy . . .
> Mary Swainson agreed with Nancy . . . (*SD*: 402–3)

It is plain here that John has no authority in this exchange at all. It is Susan who knows that it is she who is trusted by their mother. It is Susan who decides what to do, and Nancy and Mary who confirm this course of action. John's sole contribution is descriptive, and it is a contribution which is redundant since everyone knows about the fog. Revealingly, as the children set off to tell their mother the news, John unthinkingly continues to play their normal childish game of hiding from 'natives' (adults). The others have forgotten such fantasies, and this suggests that John is, on occasions, more of a child than Susan or Nancy.

In short, the issues of hierarchy, authority and responsibility are much more involved than in either the *Jennings* or the *Famous Five* stories. In fact, the issue of responsibility in *Swallows and Amazons* is a key one, and it would subvert the moral code of the stories if the exercise of responsibility was arrogated to or by one or other individual. All have responsibility to obey a moral code. The moral code is a code of honour and it permeates the books. Thus in *Swallows and Amazons* (1930) much of the story revolves around the relations between the children and Captain Flint, relations initially rendered problematic by the fact that Captain Flint wrongly accuses John of vandalism and will not listen to his explanations. This affront to his honour greatly upsets John, just as, in *Swallowdale*, it is a matter of honour to John that he raises the Swallow from the lake-bed after sinking her. Likewise, in *Secret Water* (1939), Nancy's failure to embrace the moral task of mapping the Broads is symbolic of the development of a rift between the Swallows and the Amazons. Much of the code of honour derives from the family and, in particular, the children's father (for example, it is he who sets the children the map-making task in *Secret Water*). John constantly invokes dicta learned from his father as a guide to action ('one hand for yourself and one for the ship'; 'never be ashamed to reef a small boat in the dark'). Indeed, permission to embark on their first adventure comes in a terse telegram from the Swallows' father: 'BETTER DROWNED THAN DUFFERS IF NOT DUFFERS WON'T DROWN.'

This telegram is important because it establishes the moral significance of *competence*. It is better to die than to be incompetent. To be alive is to be skilful. The whole series is minutely concerned with the deployment and development of skills. Most obviously, there are sailing skills, with which all the children are familiar, and which are described in considerable detail. No less important are camping skills: pitching tents, lighting fires, cooking food. Then there are fishing and swimming and, less frequently, map-making, gold prospecting, fire-fighting, mountaineering and so on. These are not simply incidental activities within some other plot: typically, the exercise of skills *constitutes* the plot. Nor is the exercise of skills simply a matter of 'having fun' or 'playing'. To exercise skills is to become part of a world of dignity and worth. It is notable that when the characters Dick and Dorothea Callum are first introduced in *Winter Holiday* (1933) they are treated with condescension, even contempt, by the others because of their ignorance of sailing and outdoor matters generally, as shown by their inability to light a fire without using newspaper.

Subsequently, Dick manages to acquire status through his mastery of certain skills, and in *Pigeon Post* (1936) he plays a crucial role because his knowledge of chemistry is required to identify and smelt gold (albeit that it turns out to be copper). Indeed, the adventure of prospecting in the high moors is only possible because Dick's knowledge of electricity enables him to construct a device to ring a bell when carrier pigeons arrive at the Amazons' mother's house, this innovation persuading her to give the children permission to camp away from the house.

In the most dramatic of the *Swallows and Amazons* stories, *We Didn't Mean to Go to Sea* (1937) the role of skill is again crucial because the Swallows find themselves accidentally sailing alone, in a strange boat, on the open seas, in a storm at night. Their ability to survive and to sail the ship to harbour in Holland is solely the result of their knowledge of sailing and, in particular, the lessons they learn in the first third of the book from the owner of the ship in which they have their (mis)adventure. It is not simply that the possession of skills enables survival. In Holland, the children meet up with their father, who joins them for a more orderly return trip to England. John, in particular, basks in the approval his father rather obliquely shows for his competence. It is as if the crossing of the sea has been a *rite de passage*, in which the Swallows have finally proved that they are not duffers.

The notion that skills confer moral status upon their practitioners is not one that is simply confined to the children in the stories. One of the most significant motifs of the stories is the way in which the children are integrated into the natural environment and the activities of other inhabitants of that environment. For it is not just the children who inhabit a moral universe predicated on skill. So too do the farmers, fishermen, boatbuilders, charcoal burners and so on. It is as if there is a fabric of existence defined through traditional, practical and rural work which is both the background to the stories and their moral bedrock. These characters are never patronized, either by Ransome or the children, but are depicted as being in harmony with nature and exuding 'natural' good. Even in the 1930s this must have been a very romantic view of the countryside, and its traditionalism may be regarded as problematic in other ways. But, for all that, it is an endearing vision in that it depicts a world ordered not by hierarchy but by morality. As such, it forms a contrast both to the *Jennings* stories, where hierarchy is strongly defined and moral worth comes from a system of rules, and the *Famous Five* stories, where status and hierarchy are viciously imposed and moral worth comes from social status.

Conclusion

The ways in which organization is effected, and the ways in which people operate in organizations, are not fixed and immutable. Rather, they are constructed and accomplished by the collective actions, imaginations and beliefs of human beings. Of course, there are many forces and influences that condition organization, as the discipline of organizational analysis testifies. Yet it is not unreasonable to claim that an understanding of organization needs to include the subjective and inter-subjective processes through which the meanings of organization (as a generality and a particularity) are reproduced. It may be that the most obvious of such processes are the organizational encounters that structure our lives from an early date (the hospital, the nursery and the school), as well as primary socialization experiences.

It is the contention of this chapter that one important mechanism in this context may be the encounter with representations of organization to be found in children's literature. Plainly a similar case could be made for other representational media, such as film, cartoons, or computer games. The examples of children's literature discussed here demonstrate how quite subtle messages about organization are woven into stories, and some of the implications of this have been suggested. Thus, to read *Jennings* is potentially to learn how rule-based organizations operate; to read the *Famous Five* is potentially to learn how teams operate; to read *Swallows and Amazons* is potentially to learn that skilled work invests one with moral worth. The transmission of such messages, and the messages themselves, are much more subtle than is suggested by writing them in this bland and stark form, however. The minutiae of the way in which the relations between, say, the Swallows and the Amazons is played out has the potential to inform readers of a myriad of ambiguities and complexities in social relations.

The three series of texts discussed in this chapter differ considerably, both in their ability to effect a subtle account of social relations and the type of account offered. Equally, the representations of organization offered are rather different. Yet in certain respects there is a similar vision at work, and, speculatively, this might be true of children's literature – at least traditionally – in general. For all of the books depict a world that is orderly and orderable. All of the books suggest a system of meaning inhabited by the characters and available to readers. One way of reading this is to see all of the books as reproducing middle-class values, but this is overly facile. Even from the limited analysis presented in this chapter it is possible to see significant differences in the representation of class and the values associated with it. Another way of reading the orderliness of the stories would be to see it as a way in which adult writers protect youthful readers from the insecurities of reality, and perhaps that is why all of these books have been so popular. However it is conceptualized, what remains clear is that, if, as claimed at the outset of this chapter, children's literature is 'pervaded by ideological presuppositions', one of the core ideological elements present in traditional popular children's literature is the assumption of the centrality of organization to human existence.[6]

Notes

1 The books in the three series under discussion have each been published in a confusing array of editors, impressions and imprints. In the text, the books are referred to

by title, with the year of original publication in brackets afterwards. Where there is a direct quotation, this is followed by an abbreviation of the title (in all cases this abbreviation refers to the last fully named title) and a page number which refers to the following editions: for Anthony Buckeridge's *Jennings* series, London: Collins; for Enid Blyton's *Famous Five* series, London: Hodder and Stoughton, for Arthur Ransome's *Swallows and Amazons* series, London: Jonathan Cape.

2 That is not to say that the Blyton and Buckeridge stories lack some degree of moral concern.

3 Sadly, space precludes giving any extensive analysis of the many interesting themes in the Ransome books, and especially the moral concerns of the author. There is a fairly extensive secondary literature on the stories; see, particularly, Hunt (1991) and parts of Inglis (1981).

4 These early encounters between the boys have some degree of realism in relation to boarding school life in the period. It is notable that, subsequently, Buckeridge rarely gestures towards the implicit violence (albeit humorously presented) of these first scenes.

5 The invocation of Tuckman's (1965) model as an analogy at this point does not imply an acceptance of this model, the universalistic underpinnings of which are problematic.

6 Since preparing this chapter I have become aware of a similar analysis by Ingersoll and Adams (1992), which considers US children's literature with particular attention to motivation, problem-solving, roles and leadership.

References

Cohen, C. (1995) 'What can the study of literature teach the managers of tomorrow?' Paper presented at the New Perspectives on Management Education Conference, Leeds University, January.

Czarniawska-Joerges, B. (1995) 'Narration or science? Collapsing the division in organization studies', *Organization*, 2 (1): 11–33.

Czarniawska-Joerges, B. and Guillet de Monthoux P. (eds) (1994) *Good Novels, Better Management: Reading Organizational Realities in Fiction*, Chur, Switzerland: Harwood Academic Press.

du Gay, P. (1994) 'Making up managers: bureaucracy, enterprise and the liberal art of separation', *British Journal of Sociology*, 45 (4): 655–74.

Goffman, E. (1961/1968) *Asylums: Essays on the Social Situation of Mental Patients and other Inmates*. London: Penguin.

Grey, C. (1996) 'C.P. Snow's fictional sociology of management and organizations', *Organization*, 3 (1): 61–83.

Hunt, P. (1991) *Approaching Arthur Ransome*. London: Jonathan Cape.

Ingersoll, V. and Adams, G. (1992) 'The child is "father" to the manager: images of organization in US children's literature', *Organization Studies*, 13 (4): 479–519.

Inglis, F. (1981) *The Promise of Happiness: Value and Meaning in Children's Literature*. Cambridge: Cambridge University Press.

Knights, D. and Willmott, H. (1995) 'Management as lived reality, management as text'. Paper presented at the New Perspectives on Management Education Conference, Leeds University, January.

Merton, R. (1968) *Social Theory and Social Structure*, rev. edn. New York: Collier Macmillan.

Morgan, G. (1986) *Images of Organization*. London: Sage.

Phillips, N. (1995) 'Telling organizational tales: on the role of narrative fiction in the study of organizations', *Organization Studies*, 16 (4): 625–49.

Ray, S. (1982) *The Blyton Phenomenon*. London: Andre Deutsch.

Sinclair, A. (1995) 'Sex and the MBA', *Organization*, 2 (2): 295–317.

Stephens, J. (1992) *Language and Ideology in Children's Fiction*. London: Longman.

Thompson, J. and McGivern, J. (1996) 'Parody, process and practice: perspectives for management education?' *Management Learning*, 27 (1): 21–36.

Tuckman, B. (1965) 'Development sequence in small groups', *Psychological Bulletin*, 63: 384–99.

Willmott, H. (1993) 'Strength is ignorance, freedom is slavery: managing culture in modern organizations', *Journal of Management Studies*, 30 (4): 515–52.

8

Management Gurus: What are We to Make of Them?

Norman Jackson and Pippa Carter

This chapter examines the constitution of management gurus through textual and visual representations. The concept of a 'guru', in management as elsewhere, is associated with benign and diffuse betterment, but the chapter argues that this association is itself part of the image management that veils the ideologically determined content of gurus' knowledge claims.

Contextualizing the activity of management gurus in terms of a particular vision of the culture of work, it is argued that the reinforcement of this work culture required by its significance in the system of governance is particularly well served by the representations of gurus, especially through their access to, and participation in, what Derrida (1994) calls 'techno-mediatic power'. Reference to a number of examples, particularly in the visual media, illustrates the argument that management gurus can be seen as part of a powerful cultural process for reinforcing the desideratum of organized work.

Joy in Work

There is an enduring desire on the part of those who govern society, and organizations, that we, the governed, should work – or, at least, that those who have a job should work – as hard as possible, as 'efficiently', as possible. While it may, these days, be politically incorrect to speak of *the* working class, we can still speak of *a* working class (see, for example, Derrida, 1994), those who are employed (usually by others rather than self-employed) and who thus include many who would once have been seen as middle class, such as professionals and, particularly, managers. Although managers may not usually be included in the working class, the title of 'manager' is so ubiquitous that it is now attached to many roles that would once have been seen as the province of 'workers'; in addition, managers, of whatever type, have, just like workers, been subjected to substantial labour intensification (see Carchedi, 1980).

This belief in the intrinsic desirability of hard work can easily be traced back, at least to the development of the factory, and has been subject to

Figure 8.1 Jumping for the Jelly Beans, *BBC for Business, 1973*

various explanations, such as the Protestant work ethic, class interest, capitalist greed, the psychology of oppression, and so on. Historically, the harnessing and control of labour power was justified as necessary to feed and clothe a burgeoning industrial proletariat (though this was a self-fulfilling argument), to facilitate colonial aspirations (again, a self-fulfilling argument, see Arendt, 1958), to maintain society and, especially, social order. But today we seem to have reached a point in civil development when these validations are no longer appropriate, yet the desire for more worker effort still increases (Gorz, 1989). It is now easily possible to overfeed the domestic population, Europe no longer has empires, and the claim that work has value as a socializing force has been abandoned (we are told, for example, that there is no link between unemployment and crime, notwithstanding evidence to the contrary), which thus denies any relationship between work and socialization to citizenship.

In economic terms, the response to the over-supply of labour over the past century has been a gradual reduction in 'necessary' working time for individuals, without adverse effect on the 'necessary' levels of production. (Indeed, empirical evidence produced as early as the second decade of the twentieth century demonstrated precisely the opposite; see Rose, 1978 on the so-called Myers School.) Yet, at a time when there is, apparently, a decrease in the absolute demand for labour, we are also seeing sustained effort to intensify labour, in terms of both duration and content, for those with work (Gorz, 1989). At what may be the first point in the development of human-kind that we can produce more than we can consume, how strange that we cannot reap such benefits through an easing of the burden of work.

The reason for this apparent paradox is, in part, attributable to that strange beast, management knowledge. Management knowledge, in the sense used here, constitutes a relatively homogeneous canon that claims to be able to improve organizational efficiency (and, thereby, profit, though the link is rarely demonstrable), in particular through the adoption of specific techniques for the use of labour. The general objective of these techniques is to enable units of labour to be more productive – that is, to work harder. (Although some would say that the aim is for labour to work more efficiently, rather than harder or longer, 'harder' is usually an apparently irreducible requirement of efficiency, as recognized by a recent telecommunications advertisement which exhorted us to 'work smarter, not just harder'!) That such intensification leads inevitably to the emiseration of workers through overwork generally, and specifically causes impoverished health, breakdown of social relations, increased stress, even death, seems to be regarded as not the responsibility of management knowledge. Indeed, a substantial strand of such knowledge argues that such effects are caused by individual weakness, not weakness in the system. Management theorists of this ilk are so convinced of the rightness of increased labour efficiency (though as a normative concept, this is hardly a proper concern for a scientific functionalism), as

indeed are those who control labour, that to argue for labour extensi-
fication is regarded as a heresy. There is no place in this canon, nor could
there be, for the common-sense view that, for physical, social, psychological and economic reasons, necessary labour should be spread equit-
ably among those available to do it. Thus wage labour continues to be a
punishment for those who do it, as does unemployment for those who
do not.

There can be few bodies of knowledge, and few professions, that
contribute so assiduously to the general debilitation of those who are
their object of interest. Yet, in the marketplace of management knowledge, the one criterion by which knowledge claims are judged, approved
and adopted is precisely their ability to intensify labour, even though this
is rarely explicit (it would, after all, sound rather illiberal!). If, however
tortuous the route, management knowledge cannot give the bottom-line
promise of increased labour utilization, its acceptability to managers will
be compromised. In this sense, management knowledge is unusual as
knowledge, because the outcome is specified *a priori*, and the attempt to
justify this outcome in economic terms, such as the need to succeed in the
global economy, cannot be detached from the belief system which
assumes that *this* is the way to, and the necessary price of, such success – a
belief system which, as Derrida (1994: 57) notes in his discussion of
Fukuyama, sees the *telos* of history and of progress as the alliance
of liberal democracy and the free market. As has been widely argued,
management knowledge is an ideologically based canon, biased in favour
of an essentially capitalist interest. It functions as part of the techno-
mediatic hegemony that sustains this dominant discourse (Derrida, 1994).

The conviction that labour intensification is appropriate and necessary
implies a specific belief that labour is not yet producing, in the Taylorist
sense, a fair day's work for a fair day's pay. Since it is also the received
wisdom that modern technology is reducing the direct labour component
of production, it follows that organizations are over-manned. The project
of management knowledge, on behalf of its ideological interest, is thus
twofold: get rid of surplus labour and ensure that necessary labour is
fully productive. Hence recent therapies, such as downsizing, delayering
and business process re-engineering, have appeared in the marketplace
of ideas, alongside other strategies that also tend towards intensification
but claim to do it humanely. But the claim that the absolute demand for
work is declining, and that, therefore, we need fewer workers, seems at
odds with experience. If the absolute demand for effort were reducing,
one might expect a sense of there being less to do. But the precise
opposite is the case: working hours, both formal and informal, are
expanding; the duties to be performed are also expanding; and we are
even required to undertake personal development, facets of which, such
as empowerment, appraisal, time management, and so on, themselves
both engender more work *and* assume that we are not yet doing enough.
Inescapably, most recent approaches achieve shareholder benefit not

through the excision of unnecessary labour, but by the reallocation of the work of those 'let go' to those retained, irrespective of whether they have the capacity to do it without detriment to themselves and, therefore, to the organization. Thus management knowledge has been charged that it traditionally contributes to, and reinforces, the 'ideal' that those who must be employed should be as productive as they can be made to be, irrespective of consequence (see, for example, Burrell and Morgan, 1979). This is comparable to judging the success of the medical profession in terms of how many treatments are dispensed without regard to the demand for treatments, or that of the legal profession in terms of numbers of lawsuits executed without regard to the incidence of disputes. The production of management knowledge is not informed by a sense of how much work needs to be done and what resources are available to do it, nor by a sense of efficiency as a means to an end, but by the assumption that efficiency is an end in itself.

Gurus at Work

How is it that the one group of people (the beneficiaries of labour intensification) can convince another group (the intensified) to do things against their interest, engaging a part of the latter group (managers) to achieve its routine compliance? This is very much the province of the guru.

The exhortation to work hard, directed at those whose role in society is to work for others, has always been an important function for those who act as agents on behalf of the ones for whom the work is to be done. Thus, for example, the Church has always taken such a role, defining the moral obligation to work hard in terms of it being a passport to Heaven – virtue was associated with hard work. With the advent of work organization in the form recognizable today, such theological considerations gave way to philosophical ones, and representation of the virtue of hard work became the province of moral philosophy and economics (see, for example, Ure (1967) and Smiles (1897)). Such virtue was less religious, more the secular virtues of patriotism, good citizenship and moral well-being. By the end of the nineteenth century, however, work, management and organization all moved into the sphere of science, initially as part of engineering and later as part of the blossoming social sciences. At this stage, the virtue of hard work became a scientific imperative for the diffuse social benefit of the great economic machine. Once work entered the province of science those who can legitimately explain the imperative virtues of hard work must be specialists in that science. Where once the gurus of work were moralists, now they are management gurus.

The word 'guru' means a spiritual teacher, and it derives from the Sanskrit word for venerable. 'Venerable' means worthy of worship, and its Latin origins are connected with Venus, the goddess of love: we should worship our gurus as fountains of love for us. In order to influence, gurus need to have a believable message. To carry authority the message needs to be acceptable to would-be disciples. To be sanctioned by the powerful it needs to say things that do not challenge but reinforce the dominant interests (for an overview, see also Huczynski, 1993). Just as important as the content of the message, however, is the person who delivers it. Kennedy (1991: xiii) comments of the contemporary guru that 'Packaging, indeed, is half the art, or even more.' Later, she adds to this the desirability of 'a gift for self-promotion' (1991: xviii). For the authorized guru, two qualities are necessary for success: the message *and* the messenger. If the messenger is not 'venerable', the message will struggle for acceptance. Kennedy (1991) lists 33 management gurus, 'leading management thinkers', all of whom are associated, directly or indirectly, with attempts to increase the efficiency of labour. As she implies, this is, effectively, a defining characteristic of gurudom in the field: 'the concept of the management guru with his or her [inconveniently, as there is only one "her", Rosabeth Moss Kanter] prescriptives for performance' (1991: ix). (To this extent writers such as Ure and Smiles might feel unjustly omitted, as precursors of this movement.) Both guru and message must be evangelical, literally, bringing the good news, the gospel. And the good news is always about how things can, and are going to, improve. Even the more analytically pessimistic gurus – in the field of management, Charles Handy might be an example – will have a solution to the problem in mind. Gurus are always associated, somehow, with betterment.

One more requirement for success as a guru is a channel of communication, to advertise the good news. Previous gurus brought together those to be enlightened by the good news using the pulpit. Pulpit is linked etymologically with stage, and this reflects the significance of performance as an element of proselytization (see, for example, Clark and Salaman, 1996). The importance of performance in this respect also emphasizes that the good news is profoundly monological and demands the suspension of disbelief. But, while previous gurus might target their audiences in hundreds and thousands, the audience of the management guru runs into millions, and the pulpit or stage is no longer adequate. For the contemporary management guru the channel of communication most frequently used is that which Derrida (1994) calls 'media teletechnology', most particularly television, video, film. Not only must the message be heard, the performer must also be seen.

Derrida on Telly

Foucault has argued that knowledge and power are profoundly interconnected and mutually informing: knowledge constitutes and is constituted by power. There are, according to Foucault, no conditions under which this is not so. Knowledges are formed discursively in terms of who can say what, where, when and how, and a major function of the discourse is to regulate these conditions by rules of inclusion and exclusion. These rules themselves are defined in terms of the operative episteme, the extensive social, political and other conditions that define what can be called knowledge in a particular epoch. Thus, no knowledge discourse can be seen as a value-neutral science, since it is always formed in terms of ideological contents and constraints. Foucault identified the contemporary episteme as 'the capitalist regime of truth' (for example, Foucault, 1980: 132–3), an episteme which represents, contains and advances the interests of capitalism. Capitalism, therefore, cannot merely be seen as a philosophy of money making money, but must be understood as an integral condition of the system of governance, which Foucault defines in terms of 'the disposition of people and things' (1979).

Management knowledge, therefore, is not management knowledge *per se*, but knowledge about management, and organization, which is congruent with this capitalist regime of truth. Thus the description of problems and the prescription of solutions relevant to management and organization are delineated *a priori*, by conditions of acceptability within the episteme. This is the context in which management gurus operate. More than this, as gurus they are the 'spiritual leaders' of management knowledge as a discourse operating within the capitalist regime of truth. Management gurus are the evangelical purveyors of the good news of capitalism. The content of the messages of the gurus is conditioned by this interest. Notwithstanding Clark and Salaman's (1996: 89) observation that the prerequisite of gurudom is to have a set of ideas that can be identified with the individual guru, and thus be different from one to another, the meta-message is always the same – and, usually, in the form of how to increase efficiency in the context of its unexamined and unsubstantiated relationship to profitability. The details may even be directly contradictory from guru to guru, as is the case, for example, with the prescriptions of Herzberg and Kanter on communication and remuneration, without threatening the consistency of the meta-message (see Jackson and Carter, 1995). In this sense, the details of the content are relatively unimportant because the theme is – and must be, to remain consistent with the episteme – the same.

Derrida (1994) argues that the dominant discourse of the capitalist interest is supplemented and sustained by three cultural apparatuses: the political, the mass media and the scholarly/academic, which cooperate to ensure the continuity of capitalist hegemony. The major tool of this activity is what he calls 'techno-mediatic power'. It is the combination of academic discourse, media dissemination and political approval that gives this cooperative effort its 'unheard-of power'. Derrida's contention is that this process cannot begin to be analysed without recognition of what he calls its 'spectral effects' (for example, 1994: 54). It can be suggested that there are several aspects to this. First, the essence of techno-mediatic power is the image. The image is ephemeral and ethereal, transient and insubstantial. It is, none the less, far more influential than the specific content of the message. Thus the content is subject to, and evaluated in terms of, its presentation and the attractiveness of the presenter. (A nice example of this can be found in videos that disseminate the management guru and his or her ideas, which typically mix lecture presentations with cameos of, for example, informal chatting or home life, portraying the individual guru as a real human being.)

Notwithstanding the insubstantiality of techno-mediatic power, it is also ubiquitous: the tele-technology with which the hegemonic message is transmitted is available to, used by, and valued by everyone (who matters). And, although transient, it is also infinitely renewable, to be re-transmitted. Because of these attributes it could be argued that the techno-media typically operate in the realm of the hyper-real, and it is, perhaps, precisely this that makes it so powerful, because it defines its own realm of the 'real'. Management gurus have always made full use of the techno-media.

Lyotard on Victims

Derrida (1994) also points out that the use of techno-mediatic power functions to condition our view of what democracy means and, thereby, constitutes a serious threat to democratic process. Because techno-mediatic power is transmitted and received in a format that effectively precludes inter-communication, it also excludes all those who are not part of the cultural apparatuses, and constitutes them merely as objects of the activities of those who are. At both macro and micro levels the effect of this is that the receivers of the message have no voice in the process. This lack of voice is the defining characteristic of the victim (Lyotard, 1988). Victims, according to Lyotard, are those whose presence in the discourse is only as objects to be talked about. They are 'divested of the means to argue' (1988: 9) because the discourse is conducted in a language or idiom that they do not share and in which their experience cannot be expressed. There are reported cases from colonial administrations where members of the colonized were tried for an offence by the colonizers in a language that they literally did not understand – a foreign language. But the case does not have to be as literal as this. It is worthy of note that Lyotard discusses two particular examples to illustrate his point: the first is the survivor of Auschwitz; the second, more directly from the realm of management, is a labour dispute. In these cases the natural language of the disputants may be the same but the significations of the words themselves as perceived by the different parties are simply incommensurable, and one set of signifieds is dominant, that of the not-victims. A further example can be offered in the language of the management gurus who talk, for example, of downsizing, right-sizing, delayering in the name of efficiency and/or global competitiveness, a language which is meaningless to those who become the victims of this process and who, equally, cannot express their experience of it. To the victim it means, for example, redundancy, loss of livelihood, an uncertain future. The language/experience of the employee is not just unrepresented but also unrepresentable in such a discourse – she or he has no means to speak of her or his experienced reality. The effect of this activity is a definition of democratic organization in which employees have the democratic right to be over-worked, under-paid, made redundant and so on, in the name of some diffuse social benefit which is defined independently of their interests, and which excludes the very possibility of consideration of these interests.

Management gurus contribute to the maintenance of the hegemony of the capitalist regime of truth. They are part of the apparatuses that utilize techno-mediatic power to assure this hegemony, and maintain an ostensibly democratic discourse that, none the less, excludes the ultimate objects/victims of their knowledge claims. These knowledge claims, their educative function and their form of presentation are fundamentally important to the system of governance, in particular and as a whole, because they do not merely speak of the ways in which 'people and things should be disposed', but also, in the phrase of Shaull (1993: 16), 'to facilitate the integration . . . into the logic of the present system and bring about conformity to it'.

Image/Knowledge

Gurus Old

Around 1993 a rather strange book appeared. This undated text was published posthumously by family and friends of the author. It contains a recommendatory foreword by a well-known and respected academic (albeit without institutional affiliation). On the surface, the book is a biography, yet the publisher's blurb says that it has been written in the form of a novel, though this is hardly borne out by the text itself. The same blurb cites, among a wide range of potential readers, a main group in practising managers. The book's attention-grabbing title is *Time Study in Treason*, and an intriguing subtitle poses the question as to whether the subject should be seen as patriot or collaborator. This subject was French by birth but became a naturalized American, had a rags-to-riches life full of event and was the intimate of world leaders – one of his claims to fame was that his house was used for the controversial marriage of the recently abdicated Edward VIII and Mrs Simpson. He was arrested in North Africa, extradited to the US and committed suicide in anticipation of being charged with treason. His name was Charles Eugene Bedaux. Who?

Bedaux was a major contributor to the development of Scientific Management (see Thorpe, 1991). Active in the 1920s and 1930s, and the operator of a world-wide consultancy, he ranks alongside Frederick Winslow Taylor and Frank Bunker Gilbreth in the annals of Scientific Management though, unlike them, he is usually mentioned in passing (see, for example, Townley, 1994). His relative obscurity is undoubtedly a function of alleged nefarious activities, which allegations include trading with the enemy in the Second World War (he committed suicide in 1944). In British industrial relations, the Bedaux system was thought by workers to be so exploitative that, some 30 years or more after its heyday, it was still common to hear work study people disparagingly referred to as 'the Bedaux men'. The system fell into disrepute. It was claimed that it was widely (ab)used as a means to cut rates. In one company, which used the Bedaux system throughout the 1930s, the system went into decline and 'by the end of 1940 the name Bedaux had been erased from the company records' (Hardwick, n.d.: 108). Whether this was a consequence of the failure of the system or of a desire to disassociate from the name of Bedaux is open to debate. Yet some 50 years after Bedaux and his system were buried, both literally and figuratively, a book appears which, while not glossing over the allegations against Bedaux – but equally not judging him on them – counterposes this with terms such as 'brilliant', 'genius', 'misunderstood and much-maligned pioneer', 'an amazing man with a vision' and so on.

The text of *Time Study in Treason* invites the reader to reassess Bedaux's life and work, and clearly implies that such reassessment ought to be positive. It is, *tout court*, an invitation to restore Bedaux to his erstwhile guru status, at least as a historical figure. Some might argue that any potential contribution that the Bedaux system could make is purely a matter of the knowledge Bedaux produced, and, in some ways, that is the message of the book. But it also represents the recognition that the knowledge needs to be dispossessed of the taint of the man. In order to revise our opinion of the knowledge, we have to revise our opinion of the man, first. It is this intimate conjunction of the person and the knowledge that makes this case characteristic of the construction (or, here, reconstruction) of a management guru.

Of the triumvirate of Taylor, Gilbreth and Bedaux, Gilbreth is also of interest here since his 'mediatization' has been markedly different. Gilbreth's major contribution to Scientific Management was the development of Motion–Time Standards. Like Taylor and Bedaux, Gilbreth is susceptible to the description of obsessive. His mission in life was to reduce working methods to their most economic form and, to facilitate this, he developed a classificatory system of movement, named, rather narcissistically, with an anagram of his own name, the Therblig. So keen on work efficiency was Gilbreth that he turned his family life into an exposition of his theory, one example being his routine for bathing his 12 children, based on calculations which enabled each child to be done in 'the time it takes one record to play' (Gilbreth and Carey, 1949: 46) – the records were French and German language lessons. Although Gilbreth is probably not quite so well known as Taylor, it is arguable that his influence in terms of practice has been more enduring. His contribution was the emphasis on standardization and conformity of movement in work processes as a basis for establishing standardized time calculations, latterly known as Predetermined Motion–Time Systems. Despite its durability as a technique, it has also been viewed by some as a particularly dehumanizing aspect of Scientific Management, which robs the worker of all traces of individuality in the performance of work. Gilbreth's contribution is the epitome of the philosophy of the one best way.

As a consequence of a biography of Gilbreth written by two of his children, his life became the subject of a humorous 'bio-pic', *Cheaper by the Dozen* (1950), which constructed him as a harmless and lovable eccentric and consummate family man. The endearing eccentric 'professor' is a classic stereotype of influential knowledge producers, clearly replicated in fictional characters such as Dr Dolittle and Professor Brainstawm. Indeed, *Cheaper by the Dozen* is a classic film of a particular genre, occasionally shown on TV as a heartwarming depiction of family values in the context of the American Dream (the film is prefaced by the caption 'The True Story of an American Family'). While the focus on Gilbreth the lovable family man detaches him from the operation of his methods in an industrial setting, the film, none the less, clearly and deliberately, promotes these methods through associating them with precisely this lovable eccentricity. Gilbreth is portrayed as a tireless evangelist for efficiency, the classic ingredient of the management guru, whose gurudom is established by the very making of the film itself. Yet this type of approach in its industrial setting has been characterized, for example by Rose (1978), in terms of silliness and barbarity. In this light, perhaps Gilbreth's work – if not the man – is less Dr Dolittle than Dr Strangelove.

Gurus New

More recently, management gurus have themselves adopted, and adapted, similar means to promote their message. The management video has become a central feature in the dissemination of management knowledge. The sheer scale of such dissemination is amazing: alongside specialist management video production companies, management school productions and self-marketing productions, respectable long-standing media organizations such as the BBC also produce them. Some would argue that this is as it should be: a 'leading edge' profession using modern technology to disseminate its ideas as widely and as efficiently as possible, at a price. Others would argue that such videos belong less to the diffusion of knowledge industry than to the entertainment industry. In the tradition of knowledge production and diffusion, it was the knowledge itself that was important. However obnoxious, insanitary or ungodly knowledge producers were, this could be ignored, and the focus was on what was actually said or, more likely, written. Now the medium *is* the message.

A good example of this, and of what might be called the 'Gilbreth syndrome', is to be found in a well-known video from the BBC Education and Training stable, *Dr Kanter Plays Atlanta*. (How lucky that Kanter and Atlanta rhyme! How fortunate that she was not invited to play Hamlet, North Carolina, or Truth or Consequences, New Mexico!) We learn about Rosabeth Moss Kanter that she is the most sought-after speaker on management in the world, and that she can charge $17,000 per hour, at 1988 prices.[1] We also learn about Dr Kanter that she lives in New England (nice place), has a husband and son (how sweet), and that 3,000 business men have come from all over the Southern USA 'simply to see her famous performance', a privilege that those watching the video can now share. According to the video's sleeve note, this experience shows us 'How to promote and encourage new ideas, innovation and creativity to bring positive change to your company'. How strange that Dr Kanter's domestic arrangements are so helpful in this respect. Obviously, wholesome American living is to be preferred in creating management gurus, and failure in this department is bad for the image. And, therefore, the knowledge? Perhaps this is why Bedaux fell into obscurity, compared to the, though not exactly lovable, at least well-intentioned all-American Taylor, and the certainly lovable though roguish Scots-American Gilbreth. How could an allegedly Nazi sympathizer think all-American management thoughts?

Touching up Herzberg

An even better, and rather more disturbing, example of this process of image management is furnished by another BBC offering. In the early 1970s, Frederick Herzberg gave a lecture in the UK to a live audience of managers on his Motivation–Hygiene theory. This was subsequently transmitted in 1973 in normal television schedules under the title *Jumping for the Jelly Beans*. In the 1980s this was issued by the BBC as a video, part of a compilation called 'Management Classics', in which 'Three management gurus expound their philosophies on business' (the other two are Dr Lawrence J. Peter on 'The Peter Principle' and Robert Townsend on 'Up the Organization'). However, on comparing the two versions of Herzberg's lecture, it becomes clear that, for issue on video, a passage of about 150 words has been edited from the text, from the section subtitled KITA, Herzberg's acronym for 'Kick in the Arse' as an instigation to movement. Some 150 words do not sound much, but it is, in this case, very significant. In the following extract the edited section appears in italic.

If you're hungry and I offer you food, you'll do something for me. Do you *want* to do something for me? [pause] The answer is no. But if you're hungry enough, *will* you? The answer is yes. [pause] Ha, Ha. In other words, I can get you to *move* [pause] and this is what I call KITA. [music] That's the simplest, easiest way to get anybody to do anything, ha, ha, is to kick 'em in the ass. [laughter] And you can do it either positively or negatively. Er, positive . . . negative KITA is threatening, positive KITA is offering them a reward. One is the carrot, one is the stick. [pause] *Er, and er, the only difference between them is the difference between rape and seduction. [laughter] Ha, ha, negative KITA is rape, ha, ha, that is, threatening a person. Positive KITA is a bonus [pause] er, that's seduction. Er. And it's infinitely worse to be seduced than to be raped. 'Cause if you're raped you might as well accept it as a negative occurrence in life, but to be seduced means you become a party to your own downfall. [laughter] Ha, ha, you know, every woman's been seduced said he really loved me, and I really loved him, you see. And the companies really love you and you really love the companies. Ha, ha, gentlemen, you lost your virginity. You're jumping for the jelly beans. [laughter]* Now, if I kick you in the ass, you'll move. And if I want you to move again, what must I do? I gotta kick you again, right? In other words, I can charge a man's battery but unless he has his own generator he's not motivated. Does he want to do a good job because he wants to do a good job, that's motivation. Does he want to do a good job because he gets a bonus, he wants a house, a car, a Jaguar, that's movement. [pause] So what do you get by treating people well? [pause] You can get some movement. [pause] But it's not motivation. [music]

How might this editing be explained? Obviously, it is not because of the need to save a few seconds of tape time, so it must be to do with the content. Why is this content no longer admissible? (It is notable that the excision also deletes the only time in the video that Herzberg used the phrase 'jumping for the jelly beans', which remained the title of the video, so it was an important decision.) One possible explanation might be the change in cultural values. Perhaps in 1973 it was acceptable to joke about rape in what would appear to be, predominantly if not exclusively, a male locker-room environment, even when transmitted on public television. In the 'politically correct' 1980s, this was no longer 'good form'. There are, however, other striking and dating aspects to Herzberg's performance. He smokes a lot even when talking, his cigarette performing the sort of gyrations more normally seen, these days, in *film noir* detective stories. He lights his cigarettes from a box of matches, not from an American-style book, or from a lighter, although they were known in the 1970s. On one occasion the smoke appears to enter an unauthorized nasal channel, causing the loss of articulation well known to smokers. His teaching aids appear to be only chalk, a rag duster and a dilapidated easel-mounted blackboard which seems to have escaped being cleaned of its chalk residue for many a year, on which Herzberg scribbles rather untidily (and apparently non-consecutively, in both versions) – no BS 5750 here. By the 1980s, no self-respecting management guru would be seen dead in such an amateurish *mise-en-scène*. Times have changed, expectations have moved on. Perhaps the omission of Herzberg's views on rape and seduction are just a bit of harmless cleaning up, to try to make the message more topical in the eyes of a contemporary audience? It would be difficult to do anything about the visual aspects, but a bit of harmless textual editing . . . ?

We would suggest that this is *not* the explanation for the editing, for a number of reasons. As already suggested, the credibility of the messenger is certainly of equal importance to the credibility of the message, if not considerably more so. The video has not been updated solely for 'cultural' reasons, but both Herzberg and his message have been sanitized – and the reasons for this are not just some perception of the value of his ideas, but probably, more importantly, commercial. In the eyes and ears of a modern audience, these potentially offensive remarks substantially detract from the plausibility of Herzberg as a guru, and, therefore, from his credibility: how could someone who can joke about rape, who shows such lack of sensitivity to the experienced world of the weak, come up with an explanation of human motivation? There is something deeply unpleasant about Herzberg's imagery in this passage, and in its warm-humoured reception by the cream of British management in the audience. But if Herzberg loses credibility, so does his theory, and the market for the video disappears. It might even damage the image of the BBC. Yet this bowdlerization misrepresents the content of the ideas in favour of the image.

That the explanation for the editing is not cultural is supported by the retention, elsewhere in the video, of other material which, though less offensive, might still be seen as suspect by some modern audiences. For example, as support for his counsel against telling workers everything – what he calls over-communicating – Herzberg asks 'If you tell your wife everything, do you think she will forgive you?' Compared to suggesting that rape is preferable to seduction, this is just laddishness. Again, giving an illustration of a non-competitive question (which, apparently, the choice between rape and seduction is not), Herzberg asks the audience if they would rather he killed their wife or their daughter – this is more obviously a joke. The profound sexism of Herzberg's presentation generally is not a candidate for sanitization, and, if it might cause offence, can be presented *as if* it is a historical phenomenon. It does not necessarily detract from the credibility, either of him as a guru or of his message. But the rape/seduction passage has profound implications for his credibility in both respects – it had to go. It is not possible to conceive a rape approvingly in culturally relativistic terms: it was as horrible a crime in 1973 as it is now. To joke about this – let alone to say that rape is preferable to seduction – is to cast serious doubt upon Herzberg's judgement. The type of audience at which this video is aimed – managers – could not now let themselves be seen to be condoning such attitudes. Sexual harassment in work organizations is now a big issue. But the ramifications go further than this: if Herzberg's judgement on this matter is flawed, perhaps it is flawed on other matters as well – the Motivation–Hygiene Theory, perhaps? The editing of the material actively encourages us to accept ideas about which there is evidence which might raise doubts in the minds of those otherwise attracted to the ideas. The editing addresses Herzberg's image as a guru, but its impact concerns the knowledge itself. The editing does, and is intended to, deceive.

In the technologically sophisticated world we now inhabit we all know, even if not always consciously, that editing is a ubiquitous feature of tele-technology. But we tend to assume that it is a creative activity, in a positive sense. The two versions of Herzberg's talk show that this is, by no means, necessarily the case. In the case of management gurus, we are considering the wide dissemination of ideas that might be applied, in the work setting, to each and every one of us. It is important, therefore, that we should be able to be confident that this knowledge is as sound as possible and that it has integrity. The process of dissemination itself, however, focuses not on the knowledge but on the image. Management gurus cannot simply be assumed to possess some special insight that they promote for the sake of betterment. What they possess, for many reasons of which few are to do with knowledge itself, is access to techno-mediatic power. Gurudom is not about knowledge, it is about image, money and power.

Management Image Management

Performance has always been an important feature of those who seek to encourage not only compliance with, but also belief in, the essential rightness of the interests of those with power. The modern vogue of management gurus' use of visual media is merely the latest manifestation of this. The problem with the live performance in the pulpit or on the stage is that it cannot be edited, since it occurs in 'real-time'. With the advent of record-and-reuse visual media – film, television, video – the live performance can be improved upon by judicious reconfiguration of the performance, while still retaining the impression of being live. It is even possible to reconfigure to the extent that the received performance is completely different in message from the original performance. Editing is, of course, a ubiquitous process with all media, as any writer knows, but where the message is physically separate from the messenger, judgement is restricted to the knowledge claims. There are, to be sure, linguistic aspects which might influence reception – use of language, imagery, and so on – but this still remains distinct from the author as a person. With the advent of visual media, however, other powerful influences on our reception of the message arise.

While we may be aware instinctively of editing processes, it is also a truism that 'seeing is believing'. Editing trades on this belief, because we have no way of knowing what ends up on the cutting-room floor: we cannot see it so we have to assume that it is not there. In the case of management gurus' use of visual media, it is particularly clear that the dissemination of their knowledge claims is part of the processes of techno-mediatic power in the service of the capitalist regime of truth. Editing in this context is especially important because, by removing inconsistencies of whatever type, the potency of the message is concentrated. As an aspect of the 'spectral' effects of such power, the knowledge shifts from being an end in itself to being just a part of the general process of 'mediatization'; this includes, for example, a shift of focus from the knowledge to its presentation. This shift of focus involves the prioritization of image management, which, paternalistically, denies that the audience is intelligent enough to distinguish between the person and the knowledge, at the same time as blurring this distinction by making them appear to be synchronous.

It must also be remembered that the videos of the management gurus are produced for specific pedagogic purposes. Use of this medium is encouraged as innovative teaching practice – perhaps not coincidentally by one of the triumvirate of cultural apparatuses, the scholarly/academic, identified by Derrida (1994) as being active in supporting capitalist hegemony. In this process, teachers are encouraged to communicate and reinforce the normative values of, and service to, sectional interests which authorized gurudom represents and which, through the process of editing in pursuit of authority, may censor the message, both intended and unintended. A pedagogy that uncritically includes such material becomes hyper-real, because it speaks of a world of people in a language that is not cognate with their experience, but is cognate with the ideology of an interest that seeks to exploit them. This hyper-real language is used to define the reproduction of the democratic process but does so, effectively, by moving us further away from democratic interaction, by removing the possibility of interrogation and of independent exercise of judgement. It could be suggested that this use of techno-mediatic power, rather than reinforcing organizational employees as democratic actors, constitutes them as potential victims of a dominant interest which, by definition, does not include them, however much it implies that, even if now excluded, inclusion is a real possibility. This interest has a normative approach to work where the only fate of organizational employees is to have their work intensified, an objective sanctioned, promoted and reinforced by media-competent management gurus.

Acknowledgement

We are grateful to the BBC for permission to quote from *Jumping for the Jellybeans*.

Note

1 This accolade was given, by 1995, to Tom Peters, attendance at one of whose seminars cost £700 per person for 400 people – £280,000 for a day's work. Clearly, money is a

significant indicator of the importance of the knowledge. Perhaps not totally humorously, Herzberg joked that his views on the importance of money were not taken seriously until he increased his fees!

References

Arendt, H. (1958) *The Origins of Totalitarianism*. London: George, Allen and Unwin.

Burrell, G. and Morgan, G. (1979) *Sociological Paradigms and Organisational Analysis*. London: Heinemann.

Carchedi, G. (1980) 'The proletarianisation of the employees', in T. Nichols (ed.), *Capital and Labour*. London: Fontana.

Clark, T. and Salaman, G. (1996) 'The management guru as organizational witchdoctor', *Organization*, 3 (1): 85–107.

Derrida, J. (1994) *Specters of Marx*, trans. P. Kamuf. London: Routledge.

Foucault, M. (1979) 'Governmentality', *Ideology and Consciousness*, 6: 5–21.

Foucault, M. (1980) 'Truth and power', in C. Gordon (ed.), *Michel Foucault: Power/Knowledge*. London: Harvester. pp. 109–33.

Gilbreth, Jr, F.B. and Carey, E.G. (1949) *Cheaper by the Dozen*, London: Heinemann.

Gorz, A. (1989) *Critique of Economic Reason*, trans. G. Handyside and C. Turner. London: Verso.

Hardwick, C.M. (n.d.) *Time Study in Treason*. Chelmsford: Peter Horsnell.

Huczynski, A.A. (1993) *Management Gurus*. London: Routledge.

Jackson, N. and Carter, P. (1995) 'The "fact" of management', *Scandinavian Journal of Management*, 11 (3): 197–208.

Kennedy, C. (1991) *Guide to the Management Gurus*. London: Century Press.

Lyotard, J.-F. (1988) *The Differend*, trans. G. van den Abbeele. Manchester: Manchester University Press.

Rose, M. (1978) *Industrial Behaviour*. Harmondsworth: Penguin.

Shaull, R. (1993) 'Foreword', in P. Freire, *Pedagogy of the Oppressed*. London: Penguin.

Smiles, S. (1897) *Self-Help*. London: John Murray (orig. published 1859).

Thorpe, R. (1991) 'The history and development of management services', in T.J. Bentley (ed.), *The Management Services Handbook*, 2nd edn. London: Pitman. pp. 3–20.

Townley, B. (1994) *Reframing Human Resource Management*. London: Sage.

Ure, A. (1967) *The Philosophy of Manufactures*. London: Frank Cass (orig. published 1835).

Figure 9.1 Frenetic Bond Dealers, *Jez Coulson/Insight, 1997*

9

Fictional Money (or, Greed Isn't so Good in the 1990s)

Linda McDowell

> Greed is good.
>
> G. Gekko, *Wall Street*

> As stupid as it may sound, none of this is really real money.
>
> Nick Leeson to David Frost in a television interview, Autumn 1995

In this chapter I want to draw some parallels between the fictional representations of the world of high finance in 1980s films and novels and the 'real' world of City bankers in the early 1990s. Although there are similarities in the plots and in the ways in which both sets of actors are represented – whether on celluloid, in fiction or in the pages of the financial press and the broadsheets – the denouements are sadly different. For fictional heroes, the outcome takes one of two forms, both flattering to the protagonist. The first is a combination of getting your girl (or, less often, your man) and continuing affluence, perhaps with its edge blunted by good works or charitable donations. The second, more self-sacrificing, alternative is the rejection of the venality of money and a righteous re-embracing of basic family values. Real men, the factual 'heroes' of the City and Wall Street in the 1990s, are more likely to find themselves banged up for a period than walking off into a warm embrace.

In order to address these comparisons I want to draw on three sources. The first is the analyses by cultural theorists of the 'sexy/greedy' genre of Wall Street/City films in the second half of the 1980s; the second is my own survey in 1992–3 of 50 men and women employed by three investment banks in the City of London;[1] and the third is the press coverage of the downfall of Barings, a 'blue-blooded' and ancient merchant bank in the City of London. The bank was, apparently, brought to its knees by a 'rogue trader', Nick Leeson, through speculation and fraud on the Singapore Stock Exchange in 1995. In all three sources, there is a common narrative construction of the heroic traits and characteristics of the 'wildmen' of the financial world who make and lose fortunes moving huge fictional sums of money around the globe.

I want to address questions about the meaning of money in a contemporary capitalist economy, and examine how particular images of power and masculinity are associated with assumptions about and representations of money and the world of capital. I shall argue that hegemonic representations of the world of merchant banking and merchant bankers affect the social practices and everyday interactions of 'real' actors with specific class and gender, ethnic and personal attributes. All material social practices are deeply imbued with and are undertaken within the context of a set of cultural and symbolic meanings, but the world of merchant banking and the composition of the key social actors in the City are perhaps particularly saturated with symbolic significance. The 'old' world of the City of London, with its distinctive built environment reflecting the nineteenth-century expansion is paralleled by class- and gender-specific images of banking: the white, male and bourgeois world of the public school, élite universities and masculine clubs. In the United States, too, there is a similar (if less venerable) Ivy League/East Coast tradition of bourgeois white masculinity that dominated banking in its initial development and expansion. These images are counterposed to contemporary images of 'fast' money and slick operators in the cut-throat deregulated financial world represented in films such as *Wall Street* (1987) or the UK television serial *Capital City*, and in the actions of a whole range of actors in the UK and the US who made a 'fast buck' by cutting corners and operating close to the edges of legality. Indeed, the 1980s was the decade in which 'greed is good for you' was extended as a motto not only for individual self-gratification but also as an economic mantra for national and international expansion. These media images of fast money exert an influence not only on the popular imagination and representations of the City but also affect material social practices in the financial world, from recruitment to relations with clients. It is this relationship between 'image' and 'reality' that this chapter addresses.

The aim, however, is to deconstruct this binary, the distinction between 'image' and 'reality', drawing on that strand of literary and social theory in which objects and everyday social practices are constituted and may be read as texts or narratives. In holding to a belief that what is important is the connections between representations and material practices, the approach here is closest to what Game (1991) has termed a 'materialist semiotics'; that is, an understanding of meaning as both temporal and embodied, affecting the way social practices are conducted. As Game (1991: x) suggests, 'this approach to meaning breaks with distinctions between representation and the real, text and context, theory and practice', arguing that reality is fictitious or that the fictitious is real. While these arguments are familiar to cultural theorists, they are less common in the disciplines in which money is a central concern – in economics, economic sociology and economic geography. A number of scholars in these disciplines have, however, begun to argue that in contemporary capitalist economies – based on flows of information and symbols rather than material goods – signs and symbols, representation and meaning must enter our analyses (Lash and Urry, 1994; Watts, 1994). As Lash and Urry (1994: 61) have suggested, 'culture has penetrated the economy itself

... symbolic processes, including an important aesthetic component, have permeated both consumption *and* production.' Further, Thrift (1994: 331) has made a plea for the analysis of money markets in general, and the City in particular, 'as socially constructed institutions and dealing in money as a social and cultural affair'.

Thus, the focus here is on images and icons, films, novels and plays, and images of financial sector workers, addressing questions of love and desire, clothes, language and personal style. Fictional images of money and banking constructed in 1980s films, novels and plays continue to find echoes in the 'serious' pages of the 1990s' quality press whose editors, I am sure, would deny that they produce fiction. One of the most interesting aspects of the social construction of the 1980s' images of money and finance was their transformation from seriousness to fun. Images of finance became fashionable, and financial sector work was no longer portrayed as work but as interpenetrated with leisure activities: making serious money was seen as frivolity. In the 1990s, however, the pleasure was lost and the love of money was seen as more likely to damage your health or restrict your liberty than enhance your lifestyle.

Representing Money: Fictional Financial Actors

As Lash and Urry (1994) suggest, popular cultural images of economic acts and actors are important aspects of power in contemporary informational economies, in which the trade of financial instruments and money becomes an ever more important part of a nation's economic calculus. They suggest, therefore, that to understand the operation of global economic forces, an analysis of cultural forms must play a key part. Drawing on Habermas's (1984, 1987) analysis of transmitted communications in the form of speech acts as part of the operation of power, Lash and Urry (1994) argue that a large part of global transmissions are utterances that have a 'poetic' as well as an economic function. 'Narratives and music in popular culture typically operate through such a poetic function. American movies . . . achieve their effect, not so much through the acceptance of utterances, but from communications constituting the very media within which one assents or objects' (Lash and Urry, 1994: 29). Such media representations are thus part of the way in which classificatory categories are constructed. Films and television are thus an essential part of the way in which economic actors are constructed and their behaviour and attitudes are represented. As Lash and Urry (1994: 29) emphasize, 'poetic discourse is constitutive of the rituals through which we operate.'

In that genre of Wall Street/City films and novels that were produced in the 1980s and early 1990s, an interesting set of binaries was established in the portrayal of the main characters and their moral dilemmas. Two versions of humanity, usually but not always male, are constructed to allow a comparison between good and evil. The dimensions of difference that are explored in this genre revolve variously around old financial world/new financial world, insider/outsider, corrupt/redeemable, and senior/junior, to allow old-style morality fables to be played out. In a fine review of Hollywood big business/financial speculation films of the 1980s, Judith Williamson (1991) argued that that decade's business and enterprise culture was characterized by a profound cultural unease. She suggested that the great achievement of Hollywood cinema in the late 1980s and early 1990s was to dramatize both business achievement and the social indignation it engendered within the same moral framework as a single narrative.

Perhaps the classic example of these films in which the financial world is both glamorized and celebrated but also criticized is *Wall Street* (1987). *Wall Street* is a conventional morality play, in which seduction and fall precede a redemption in which old-fashioned virtues triumph (Denzin, 1990). In the film, alternative models of masculinity – presented as contrasted versions of the rule of the father – struggle for the soul of the young protagonist. Conventional patriarchal authority vanquishes the moral ambivalence but desirable lure of easy money. Significantly, a similar struggle between alternative versions of masculinity may be identified in factual (as opposed to fictional) portraits of the key male actors within merchant banking, as I have argued elsewhere (McDowell and Court, 1994b).

Judith Williamson (1991) has also argued that it is significant that several examples of this genre are life-swap stories. For example, in *Trading Places* (1983) a black, fake blind and crippled beggar, played by Eddie Murphy, switches with a privileged WASP to become a financial wizard. The typical US enterprise culture message, therefore, is 'anyone can do it', should they want to, of course. Bud Fox, the young hero of *Wall Street*, played by Charlie Sheen, came from solid blue-collar origins, rather than penury like the protagonist of *Trading Places*, and the simple family-centred values of Bud's true father in the end overcome the seductive lure of the City and the wiles of his false father: his Wall Street boss. In the life-swap versions, however, the protagonists are less likely to relinquish the world of money altogether. The resolution that assuages their unease and the envy of the audience is the use of their new found experience and wealth for the greater social good. Thus, in *Trading Places* the beggar is metamorphosed into a businessman with a heart, maintaining a commitment to social justice in the process. Another example of the same storyline, but with a female protagonist, is *Working Girl* (1988) in which the working-class heroine wins out over her upper-class-bitch boss without abandoning loyalty to the girls in the typing pool and, incidentally, getting her man as well. In both films, the protagonists' ability to make money is portrayed as 'natural' and, interestingly, in both these 'swap' films the key characters are the 'other' of the US financial world (which is not distinguished by its diversity). Indeed, women and people of colour are most noticeable by their absence. But here we have the classic outsiders in morality tales – a black American and a woman – as the winners who lose nothing. These are no mephistophelean pacts with the devil but conventional morality tales, a sanitized US version of all-round gain.

Williamson (1991) also identifies a strong message of performativity and masquerade in these financial morality tales. Particular types of clothes are important as disguises for the masquerades to succeed. This, too, was a particularly important theme in the interviews that I carried out with 'real' actors in the City banks in London (see McDowell, 1997). *The Secret of my Success* (1987) is a particularly clear example, in which Michael J. Fox plays a postboy in a big firm who, by changing into a business suit and putting up wall charts in an empty office, becomes what he is pretending to be. Fox's friend in the postroom refers to the executives as 'suits'. Similarly, Melanie Griffith in *Working Girl* masquerades as her boss by changing into her clothes. But, as Williamson (1991: 155) argues, as well as becoming what they 'do' (or masquerade as), 'in these films what the characters do (business) becomes endowed with what they are (good).'

Williamson (1991: 155) argues that 'the prevalence of life swap and *doppelgänger* themes in these movies suggests an ambivalence towards, and a sense of polarity within, the "ethics" of business; a recognition that there are deep contradictions within the moral framework each film employs.' She draws attention to *Big Business* (1988) as the most baroque combination of this mix of life swaps and *doppelgänger* where two sets of identical twins are mixed up at birth. 'One of the scrambled pairs grows up in a country community whose entire livelihood depends on an industry owned by the city company inherited by the other pair. This allows a separation of values between the financial side of business (City/slick/ruthless) and the production/goods side (Country/quaint/wholesome)' (Williamson, 1991: 156). She also suggests that there is an interesting problem with some of these films: as the US economy turns more and more to financial dealing, to invisible trades or fictional products, the films themselves emphasize physical products and commodities. Even *Wall Street*, despite its moral ambivalence and tendency to glamorize financial wheeling and dealing, nevertheless suggested morally that speculation is bad and 'real work' good. Martin Sheen, who plays Bud's natural father, is a union representative and long-time employee in the aircraft company which the ruthless surrogate father, Gordon Gekko (Michael Douglas), wants to destroy. Here the real patriarch represents the *real* world of goods and transport compared to the endless invisible circuitry of high finance. As Williamson (1991: 159) comments:

> It is intriguing that for vehicles of mass culture in a supposedly postmodern age Hollywood films are remarkably interested in what might be termed the stock market's *referents*, the actual things dealt in by big business. And it is

the 'real' people, who are close to these 'real' things (radio, pork bellies, cornfields, airplanes, apples), who are shown as having the power to succeed in that slippery world.

Williamson argues that the US versions of morality tales on Wall Street and its environs, although easy to criticize politically, are in the end moving as they 'channel and express a real moral and spiritual indignation at capitalist values, [although] ultimately it reclaims them for the status quo' (1991: 160–1). It is noticeable that British equivalents of these films are lacking. Instead, 'fast money' has been captured either by television or on the stage in, for example, the television series *Capital City* and Caryl Churchill's play, *Serious Money* (1987). In these British examples, the moral edge or fable-like message of the US films is absent. The typical British tale is rather one of trickery and facile success than a titanic moral struggle. Thus, in *Serious Money*, dealing is portrayed as a game. 'It's the most fun I've had since playing cops and robbers' suggests the female protagonist, Scilla. Later in the same scene, just to ram home the point, she says she loves her work 'because it's like playing a cross between roulette and space invaders.' This imagery is repeated (as I shall show) in media comment on 'real' financial dealings and scandals. Although the greed, corruption and unscrupulous nature of those tied up in the drama of high finance are emphasized, albeit in a glamorized fashion, moral indignation is underplayed in British financial dramas. The stance is more one of fascinated awe and envy, and the denouement is seldom a reassertion of higher moral values but rather the material success of the hero, and with increasing frequency the heroine, through the same schemes and tricks that suffuse the plots as a whole.

Turning from celluloid to text, the exemplar of the US genre of money/high finance novels is Tom Wolfe's *Bonfire of the Vanities* (1988).[2] Here, as in the films analysed above, Wall Street is portrayed as a battleground between the forces of good and evil. The protagonist, Sherman McCoy, is a bond dealer, a representative of the new 'masters of the universe'. Unlike many of the heroes of the films, however, Sherman is no outsider: rather, he is a WASP, from the right class background – Yale and Wall Street – and so a representative of the values of the 'old' financial world that is under attack from the 'new' fast operators. But McCoy is not all he seems: rather than a solid pillar of the establishment, content in his bourgeois respectability, he is uncomfortable with his life, marriage, work and New York itself (and his suspicion that McCoy was really a 'hick' name). The book is a masterpiece of moral ambiguity, part farce, part tragedy, as Wolfe parodies the values of a class and a system he despises. Unlike the popular films, this book is no homespun folksy tale of brothers under the skin, nor a fable about the supposed openness of US society but instead a satire on the fall of the financier and financial system.

Most of the British 'City novels' generally compare unfavourably with the relative subtleties of *Bonfire*, although the serious British writer,

David Lodge, used the City as a comparator to the serious worlds of industry and the academy in his 1988 morality tale, *Nice Work*. The classic stereotypical 'barrow-boy' image pervades British representations of merchant banking and this is central to Lodge's novel, although in this example the 'boy' is female. Debbie in *Nice Work* is successful, like the protagonists of the US films, because of her 'natural' attributes and background.

> The barrow-boy mentality they call it. Quick wits and an appetite for non-stop dealing . . . I couldn't last for half-an-hour in Debbie's dealing room – fifty people with about six telephones in each hand shouting across the room things like 'Six hundred million yen 9th of January!' All day. It's a madhouse, but Debbie thrives on it. She comes from a family of bookies in Whitechapel. (Lodge, 1988: 89)

And, as we shall see, this image of 'natural' talent fostered by an East London upbringing is a common narrative in the description of real dealers.

In *Nice Work*, Lodge's experience and sympathies clearly are not with investment banking but elsewhere – with the academy or the factory, where 'real work' is done, whether the product is a furnace or a manuscript. The unspoken final part of the common saying in Lodge's title 'nice work if you can get it' applies above all to the 'frivolous' world of banking. Here we see parallels with the nostalgia of the US films – an agricultural past of the frontier years of nineteenth-century North America – but based on manufacturing in the case of Britain's nineteenth-century imperial heyday.

A growing number of more 'popular' City novels have also been published in Britain in the 1980s and 1990s in which the central theme of a grand moral struggle between different values is underplayed. In the representatives of this genre, the struggles are rather between personal moral integrity in relationship and the lure of a love affair with the flash representatives of fast money: an accurate reflection of the individualism of Thatcher's Britain. As an example of this genre I shall examine two novels, chosen solely for the reason that their authors work or have worked in merchant banking and I was able to talk to both of them in the course of my empirical work in the City. The first is *The Highest Bidder* by Janet Cohen (1992) and the second *Nest of Vipers* by Linda Davies (1994). With few pretensions to literary excellence, these two thrillers reflect the detailed first-hand knowledge of their authors and so have the added benefit of being an insider's view of the City and its practices and attitudes at the beginning of the 1990s (albeit re-represented as fiction). What is particularly interesting about them, however, is the fact that the key protagonist in both cases is a woman. Moreover, they are unashamedly rich, aggressive, sexy and successful, key players in their own right in the 'new' world of finance capital.

Cohen's protagonist is a senior partner in a City firm of solicitors, battling on behalf of the management against the unscrupulous owner of a construction company in the north west. In the novel, the blunt, gruff, overweight and rich owner (representing the real world of production/ construction) is not the embodiment of 'decent' values as in the Hollywood films, but instead the villain of the piece who gets his come-uppance through the efforts of Caroline, Oxford educated, well con-nected, poised and from an old City family. Caroline is, in the curious but admiring words of her creator, ' a savage, able creature' (1992: 17). This 'savage' creature, prone to the use of bad language (an indication of her savagery perhaps), had entered the City to partially restore the fading family fortune. Her moral dilemma comes in the shape of a love affair with a married government minister involved in the deal she is working on. His background – father a small businessman (but grand-father a judge) and professional army – contrasts with hers, but the driving force behind their careers is similar. Whereas she needed the money, he had gone into politics to 'restore the family name as well as to do good'. Here we see some of the same themes of naturalness and charity as in the US films. While tough and ambitious in the business world, the protagonist of *The Highest Bidder* lets her man go, unable to compromise in the end, in either love or money. The novel is curiously ambivalent in its celebration both of the 'yuppie' lifestyle – designer food and clothes play a significant part in establishing the ambience – and its defence of the solid middle-class virtues of family life. In one sense this novel, with its strong female protagonist, seems to counter the Holly-wood version of the confused single working woman, who, without a man to give meaning to her life, becomes seriously unhinged. But it reinforces the message of the US films about social mobility, showing that, in the 1980s and 1990s, (British) women, like US men, can have it all. This is a message that I found was not endorsed by the majority of my respondents working in the 'real' world of money. They were conscious of the opportunity costs of serving mammon (McDowell and Court, 1994a, b).

My second example, Linda Davies's *Nest of Vipers*, is a conventional spy story. Davies's protagonist, Sarah Jensen, is also a highly successful woman, a foreign exchange trader in the City who is placed undercover in a merchant bank to investigate corruption. Here the masquerade/ charade identified by Williamson is a literal metaphor, and the struggle is between Sarah's attempts to remain true to herself rather than become the charade she is acting. In this novel there is little moral ambivalence in the portrayal of the world of big money. The City is unambiguously represented as corrupt, peopled by a cast of liars and cheats, involved in international scandals and drug deals. Sarah's ability to make money as a dealer is portrayed in the same way as in Hollywood films – as a 'natural' gift. 'She had an instinctive feel for the markets and a flair for taking risks. She took great delight in her successes, but if she lost money, unlike many other traders she never took it to heart' (1994: 19). In this way, Sarah remains untainted by the City and its tarnished values. The metaphor of naturalness which runs through this text, and the others, plays a key role in the way in which the City employees whom I interviewed also spoke of traders. It was an attribute referred to not only by traders themselves but also by others in talking about this aspect of investment banking.

The counter-world of espionage which Sarah enters in *Nest of Vipers* to uncover the shady goings on in the City is hardly less murky. The novel unfolds as a heroic tale of one woman's attempt to remain true to herself, finally rejecting the monetary and patriotic values of the modern world, as represented by the City and the secret service, for the old verities of the simple life, landscape and friendship. In a re-run of the 1960s hippy dream, Sarah escapes to Kathmandu, eluding the representatives of both the state and finance capital.

I found that an escape to a rural idyll was a consistent theme among my own interviewees, many of whom expressed a desire to move into the country after making their money in the City. Linda Davies, herself, left a lucrative City job for just this dream, not in her case in the country itself but the sylvan surroundings of a London suburb and the lure, perhaps specific to women, of a notebook (nowadays a Mac PowerBook), the kitchen table and a future as a great woman novelist.

Many of the men and women whom I interviewed also expressed ambivalence about their chosen careers – in the strongest expressions a number hoped to remain 'untainted' by the money; in more optimistic versions to be able to 'do some good later on'. Indeed, one of the banks in which I interviewed had a well-developed scheme of practical charitable action work in the City and another a large charitable foundation. Yet others, and especially women, argued that their workplace persona was not 'the real me'. It is clear that the moral ambiguity that is such a pronounced theme in many of these fictional representations of merchant banking and merchant bankers is an aspect of everyday attitudes in the City of London in the early 1990s as well as a textual construction. In the texts considered here, the world of money is represented as a paradox: seductive and pleasurable, yet evil and corrupting. Images of nature and 'naturalness' – whether as female beauty or the natural talents of young male traders who work on gut feelings – are counterposed to a world in which success is achieved through masquerade and disguise, through charade or, more judgementally, by deception. And it is to a literal deception that we shall turn at the end of this chapter. First, though, I want to suggest briefly that a set of dichotomies is as evident in the social construction of financial sector workers as in films and novels.

Real and Fictional Money in the 'New' City

It is commonly suggested that the old world of the City and Wall Street was broken apart in the 1980s, primarily through deregulation of the markets, globalization and internationalization as foreign banks and finance houses penetrated national arenas and volumes of dealing and trading increased enormously (Lewis, 1989, 1991; Budd and Whimster, 1992; Thrift, 1994). In both the journalistic and academic accounts of the effects of the 1980s' transformations, a dualistic narrative that relies on the notion of metamorphosis from a stuffy old City (parodied in images of bowler hats and umbrellas) to the world of fast money and smooth operators is apparent. As I read and re-read the transcripts of interviews that I carried out with a range of City employees in 1992 and 1993, I found myself moving closer and closer to those images of bankers in the films and novels about the City discussed above. It became clear to me that, despite the world of money, money markets and high finance being a serious, material world, it was also a fictional one. The young men and women to whom I talked (and almost all my respondents were under 40) made their living by moving invisible sums around the globe or by advising companies to invest, divest and take over other firms whose products and workers would never be seen. In the 'real' City, the commodities dealt with in the new financial world themselves become increasingly fictional entities: futures trading (in commodities that do not yet exist) and junk bonds, for example. Invisible earnings, something called credit, which, as Grace (1991: 118) points out, is really debt, and the new future – the derivative – are hard to define, let alone make visible, and, as the Barings' débâcle so vividly illustrated, it seems as if those with their hands on the levers of power are themselves unable to comprehend the nature of the products they are trading. Although the City has long dealt with variants of these commodities, the element of fiction seems to have heightened in recent years as extreme losses and gains become public knowledge. In 1993, for example, the British government 'wasted' millions from the reserves trying to prop up the pound, at the same time as the financier/speculator/philanthropist Georg Soros made millions of dollars by astute currency deals. And, in 1995, Nick Leeson brought down Barings apparently single-handed by 'hiding' losses of \$8 million in a fictional 'errors' account known only by the numbers 88888. As Grace (1991: 119) suggests, 'Clearly, then, a world of high fiction is observable, a daily soap opera, full of the most extreme occurrences. Everyday economic life has become a fiction of terrifying realism, a horror scenario with such convincing special effects that, at times, you really feel you too are there, in the middle of it.'

And as I talked to my respondents, I noticed that several of the key themes in the fictional representations of high finance found echoes not only in media images of 'real-life' financiers in the pages of the broadsheet and specialist press, but also in the ways in which my interview respondents spoke of their own lives in the City. An image of the world of high finance as a melodrama or a soap opera was a common one, and many of my informants spoke of their workplace behaviour in terms of performance and parody, as well as unreality.

While I have argued elsewhere that this narrative of a new, fictional financial wold is over-simplified, neglecting as it does significant differences between merchant banks, it has proved to exercise a powerful pull on the imagination. Not only did the bankers whom I interviewed retell a tale of cultural difference between the old and the new financial actors, but the same narrative was crucial in the media reconstruction of the dramatic fall of Barings in 1995. Before examining this melodrama (Tickell, 1996), I shall briefly illustrate the key dimensions of the binary or 'doubled' social world of the City of London through the words of a small number from a sample of City employees whom I interviewed in 1992 and 1993.

The binary world of the new City divides its key actors into an updated version of the older-style élitist and paternalist banker and an extreme (hetero)sexualized version of the slick and fast 'lad'. It became clear to me as I talked to a range of people in merchant banks that there is a cultural divide in British banks based on the recruitment of people with different class backgrounds, educational credentials and cultural capital for particular types of work. A rigid class and status hierarchy divides workers in different parts of the bank. There is a huge difference between the traders and dealers and the corporate bankers. As numerous respondents explained, 'There's a cultural divide between them, between traders and what I might call small 'e' executives.' This respondent, a man in his mid-twenties, himself a product of Eton and Trinity College Cambridge, went on to explain the nature of the divide:

> In corporate finance, the social background of people is quite narrow – Oxbridge, Bristol, Exeter – so that gives a certain social division immediately. By contrast, the trading floor is very different. Much more sort of, as they say these days, yahoo . . . With regard to social group, the trading floor's one end and the rest of the bank the other.

So divided by class and educational background, in the minds of my respondents as well as popular imagination, the staid and still élitist, old-fashioned world of quiet dignified corporate boardrooms and offices is a world away from the exchanges and dealing rooms. In corporate banking, a 37-year-old woman respondent, not herself English, working in a prestigious merchant bank, explained: 'They [my immediate colleagues] are traditional English bourgeois with the habits of a particular, very self-selected, reinforcing group of people. They are quite theatrical to watch.' And a 25-year-old woman professional in the capital markets division of the same bank elaborated:

> It's a job which appeals to and gets done by a certain sort of person. Probably the criteria that go with it almost inevitably means public school, or if not actually public school then that sort of person, if you see what I mean. I suppose it's all to do with the hard work, the team playing, the families, the ethics of what we're doing. There is an implicit code of honour there which all fits the sort of public school training.

Here we have a vivid illustration of the old gentlemanly code of conduct. It was this 'code of honour' that Nick Leeson broke with such spectacular results.

Class background, bodily styles and workplace practices on the other side of the cultural divide are utterly different. Despite the demise of certain aspects of market-based trading and its replacement by screen-based dealing in open-plan offices, the atmosphere and range of tolerated behaviour in dealing rooms continues to reflect floor-trading. Exchanges are sites of spectacle where exotic goods are traded and the body is allowed out of control – shouting and gesticulating are required forms of interaction. Like a medieval fair, the exchange is a dual site: a marketplace, a site of commercial exchange, in which goods from national and international markets are traded, but also a site of pleasure, unconnected to the 'real' world and standards of normal behaviour. The ultimate trader is a heterosexual male. His characteristic site is the floor of the stock exchange, in the midst of chaos. The spectacle of hysterical traders is a familiar media image every time there is a stock market 'adjustment'.

The men recruited to work in these arenas are, in the words of my respondents, 'natural traders', 'natural mathematicians, good with figures', whose 'chief characteristic is basic raw intelligence'. One man, in capital markets, described them as 'barrow boys, natural sellers. If they weren't selling bonds, they'd be selling fruit and vegetables in the East End.' Capturing this common view in a Radio 4 interview (4 March 1995), the commentator Ann Leslie described traders as 'young men with too much testosterone playing a larger version of Sonic the Hedgehog', a view reminiscent of the protagonists of *Capital City*.

These recorded views are themselves partly fictional. They are based on prejudice, on the books, films and plays examined above and perhaps on envy from men who work in less 'exciting' areas of investment banking, as much as on a detailed analysis of the range and variation of class backgrounds and educational credentials of employees in a sample set of dealing rooms. As one of my interviewees, who was actually working as a trader, pointed out somewhat ungrammatically, 'the trading floor's much wider in fact in regard of social group nowadays.' And I found that the majority of the traders and dealers whom I interviewed were not in fact East End barrow-boys but graduates of good solid red-brick universities, although not the Oxbridge colleges of their peers in the corporate divisions.

This doubled construction of a class-specific masculinity was important in distinguishing between men who were outsiders and men who were insiders. In cases of financial disrepute and scandal, it was the former who found themselves to be disposable, whereas the latter fully expected the solid class connections that had linked the key actors in the City together for so long to protect them as the bougeoisie closed ranks to protect its own. As the rapid unfolding of a crisis at Barings was to show, these assumptions proved to be true only in part. I want now to turn to the Leeson affair which provides a vivid illustration of the ways in which these versions of masculinity and media representations of 'real' events interpenetrate to produce a particular interpretation of a financial *cause célèbre*.

Tainted Money: the Construction of an Outsider

In 1995, in a remarkable coincidence of fiction and fact, my arguments about representations of men and money seemed to be amply confirmed. Indeed, I began to feel some of the terror alluded to by Grace (1991) as, while I was writing a book about cultural change and representations of the City of London, the real world began to mirror my text. Nick Leeson, a derivatives trader on the Singapore Stock Exchange (Simex) brought down Barings Bank. Here, all the elements of fictional financial dramas were in place. Leeson himself was constructed by the press as a stereo-typical trader: if not quite the barrow-boy cum financial wizard of folk history, he was at least a council house boy from Leytonstone (an area in the eastern outer suburbs of London). In the newspapers he was variously described as 'a plasterer's son whose education finished at his local comprehensive' (*London Review of Books*, 34 March 1995), and 'a scion of a working class family from a council estate' (*Daily Telegraph*, 28 February 1995: 3). In fact, Leeson had attended a neighbourhood gram-mar school (state-funded but selective), but while there he was an aggressive hustler (at least in retrospect), reported to be 'proud and arrogant' and 'cocksure'. As an adult, according to an *Observer* report, 'around town, he was the typical London trader, drinking too much and behaving badly'. Once on a pub crawl, he 'dropped his pants in front of a group of women and, when asked, refused to apologise . . . In the world of the dealing rooms, such antics were common' (*Observer*, 5 March 1995: 24). The *Guardian* described him in more flattering terms, attributing to him 'a pocket calculator mind, a ruthless gambling instinct, together with an ice-cold ability to handle risk' (*Guardian* 'Outlook', 4 March 1995: 23). But, in perhaps the most satisfactory twist to the tale, it appeared that Leeson, far from being a mathematical genius, had failed his mathematics A level (a British school-leaving certificate). This was the man who, if the story still emerging is to be relied on, had single-handedly brought down the longest-established bank (and one of the most blue-blooded) in the City of London.

Barings had been founded in 1762 by German merchants who, throughout the succeeding centuries, became important figures in the British establishment. Five members of the family received hereditary peerages and have variously been imperial governors and ambassadors, and Governor of the Bank of England, as well as marrying into the aristocracy. In the late 1960s, members of the Barings family further enhanced their reputation by transferring their individual shareholdings to a charitable foundation, although they remained voting directors of the Bank. Despite the appearance of respectability and rock solid security, it has become clear from press coverage and the Bank of England inquiry into Barings' dealings that the head office in London had little knowledge and less control of the Singapore operation. As long as Leeson was turning in huge profits (and Barings Futures Singapore made £8.8 million in 1993), he was given a long rein. In the year ending June 1994, Leeson had been given a Simex award for top volume in customers' trades and a £450,000 bonus had been in prospect for 1995. As one of my respondents told me earlier, 'for us, the bottom line is profit. As long as we keep on making money, few questions are asked.' But, as Leeson was so painfully to find out, when the gravy train stops, it is class connections that matter.

The press coverage of the Barings affair confirmed the stereotypical images and cultural divide in banks outlined above. The image of Barings as an entity conveyed by the media was that of the 'old' City, characterized by a close network between élite actors. Thus a *Sunday Telegraph* leader suggested that 'the fall of a British bank, and particularly an old and distinguished bank, is a cultural event for this country. The fall of Barings is the financial equivalent of the closure of Trinity College, Cambridge, or St Bartholomew's Hospital, or a Guards regiment' ('Sunday Comment', *Sunday Telegraph*, 5 March 1995: 33). The irony of the comparison with St Bartholomew's Hospital (which the Conservative government of John Major had earmarked for closure) apparently escaped the leader writers, but the overall impression is clear. Leeson, on the other hand, was constructed as the classic outsider who had failed to understand the unwritten rules of a club that he should never have been admitted to. His solitary status was emphasized by labelling him ' a rogue trader' (Peter Baring, speaking to bankers on 26 February 1995) or a 'rotten apple' (Governor of the Bank of England, *Channel 4 News*, 27 February). As the *Observer* astutely pointed out, 'The search for a scapegoat is on and nobody better than a single rogue trader from the wrong side of the class divide' (5 March: 24), although in a less individualist vein, the *Observer* writers recognized that the case also represented 'a classic battle between the two sides of Barings – the old merchant bank tradition and the new trading spirit'. Thus, in a comment on the whole affair by a financial commentator in a serious broadsheet, Brummer (1995) argued that 'In the UK there has certainly been a deep public suspicion that Nick Leeson, replete with his working class background and his Estuary English, was being framed by the toffs.'[3]

In an extraordinary illustration of my argument about the significance of representations, it was reported towards the end of 1995 that a film was to be made of the Barings collapse, with Hugh Grant as Nick Leeson. That Grant – the quintessential English upper-class toff of *Four Weddings and a Funeral* – should be named shows the continuing strength of the élitist image of bankers in the popular imagination. Grant's carefully cultivated screen persona more nearly parallels that of the élite actors or young princes of corporate finance.

These views of Leeson are, of course, retrospective and to a large extent constructed to conform to the popular press's image of a trader. Before his fall, Leeson was reported to have owned a yacht, a luxurious home in an élite area and was portrayed drinking with friends or partying with his wife, a glamorous young blonde, who was miraculously transformed into a loyal waif in the press images of her during Leeson's imprisonment in Frankfurt. Later she was portrayed in the British press as standing by her man and, apparently, working in a frilly pinafore in that most English of institutions, the teashop. In fact, the Leesons' hotshot lifestyle was greatly exaggerated. Leeson was neither fabulously well paid – his basic salary in 1994 was £48,000 – nor a star trader. He was rather a middle man who serviced international investors sent to him by the sales group in London. 'To me he was a good floor manager who had a lot of money to throw at the markets. That's it. The star trader image is a myth' (senior American trader working in Singapore, reported in the *Sunday Times* 'Business Focus', 9 July: 4). The profits purportedly made for Barings by Leeson were equally mythical. His paper profits of $50 million now have to be offset against the $80 million deficit in the secret 88888 account used in his deception. And in London, before he moved to Singapore, Leeson had worked in the settlements department or 'back office', an arena of merchant banking akin to, in the words of one of my respondents, 'a sausage factory', lacking the prestige and glamour of trading. His experience there, however, was what enabled him to hide the 88888 account for so long.

As was noted at the time of the Leeson débâcle, it would have been inconceivable for these frauds to have been perpetrated by a woman – in the main because there are so few women dealers and traders, let alone a trader who was also in charge of the back-office functions as Leeson had been, but also because of their 'characters'. The characteristics apparently required for success in dealing, trading and selling (be it honestly or dishonestly) are exactly those attributes conventionally associated with masculinity. As some of my respondents explained, 'you have to be tough and ruthless to succeed' and 'there seems to be an incredible need to bite everybody's head off and knock them out of the way and trample on their heads.' This echoes the unforgettable opinion of John Gutfreund, the former head of Salomon Brothers, that traders have to 'wake up each morning ready to bite the ass of a bear'. It seems unlikely, however, that the full role of City actors in the Barings affair other than Leeson will ever be uncovered despite a British and Singapore enquiry. In this sense, the City connection proved reliable despite the humiliating sale of Barings to a Dutch bank, ING, for £1.

Conclusion

The 1980s and the first half of the 1990s witnessed a remarkable hold of the City on the popular imagination. The combination of elemental sex and greed is now common in press coverage of financial affairs, which themselves seem to have become more unrealistic than their fictional representations. In 1995 the press gleefully commented on the downfall of the then Deputy Governor of that once august institution, the Bank of England, who, in a plot more salacious than the cheapest pot-boiler, was sacked when his mistress, herself a serious financial journalist, revealed that they commonly had sex on the carpeted floor of the Grand Old Lady herself. The days when Levi (1987: 13) argued that financial stories were too dull for general readership because 'pinstriped blood does not show up easily on the walls' seem remote indeed. In 1995, semen on the carpet was judged headline material by the broadsheet and tabloid newspapers alike. Representatives and representations of money continue to thrill us in the scale of their rise and potential fall, and if the plot is now more likely to end with disgrace than noble sacrifice or self-fulfilment, the moral seems even more applicable to the dour *fin de siècle* nineties.

Notes

1 Full details of this survey and its analysis are to be found in McDowell (1997).

2 *Bonfire* was made into an appalling film, released in 1990 ('strained, miscast and missing all its targets', according to *Halliwell's Film Guide*, 1995), with Tom Hanks miscast as Sherman McCoy. It seems that the film's audience was not ready for a more nuanced version of the fall from grace, preferring the familial homilies of Wall Street.

3 In fact, the classic connections of the Barings family let them down this time, when the Bank of England failed in its attempt to organize a rescue package for the bank.

References

Brummer, A. (1995) 'Singapore report points the finger', *Guardian* 18 September, p. 21.
Budd, L. and Whimster, S. (eds) (1992) *Global Finance and Urban Living*. London: Routledge.
Churchill, C. (1987) *Serious Money*. London: Methuen.
Cohen, J. (1992) *The Highest Bidder*. London: Michael Joseph.
Davies, L. (1994) *Nest of Vipers*. London: Orion.
Denzin, N. (1990) 'Reading "Wall Street": postmodern contradictions in the American social structure', in B.S. Turner (ed.), *Theories of Modernity and Postmodernity*. London: Sage. pp. 31–44.
Game, A. (1991) *Undoing the Social: Towards a Deconstructive Sociology*. Milton Keynes: Open University Press.
Grace, H. (1991) 'Business, pleasure, narrative: the folktale in our times', in R. Diprose and R. Ferrell (eds), *Cartographies: Poststructuralism and the Mapping of Bodies and Spaces*. Sydney, Australia: Allen and Unwin. pp. 113–25.
Habermas, J. (1984) *The Theory of Communicative Action*. Cambridge: Polity Press.
Habermas, J. (1987) *The Philosophical Discourse of Modernity*. Cambridge: Polity Press.
Lash, S. and Urry, J. (1994) *Economies of Signs and Space*. London: Sage.

Levi, M. (1987) *Regulating Fraud: White Collar Crime and the Criminal Process*. London: Tavistock.

Lewis, M. (1989) *Liar's Poker: Two Cities, True Greed*. London: Hodder and Stoughton.

Lewis, M. (1991) *The Money Culture*. London: Hodder and Stoughton.

Lodge, D. (1988) *Nice Work*. London: Chatto.

McDowell, L. (1997) *Capital Culture: Money, Sex and Power at Work*. London: Routledge.

McDowell, L. and Court, G. (1994a) 'Missing subjects: gender, power and sexuality in merchant banking', *Economic Geography*, 70: 229–51.

McDowell, L. and Court, G. (1994b) 'Performing work: bodily representations in merchant banks', *Environment and Planning D: Society and Space*, 12: 253–78.

Thrift, N. (1994) 'On the social and cultural determinants of international financial centres: the case of the City of London', in S. Corbridge, R. Martin and N. Thrift (eds), *Money, Space and Power*. Oxford: Blackwell. pp. 327–55.

Tickell, A. (1996) 'Making a melodrama out of a crisis: reinterpreting the collapse of Barings Bank', *Environment and Planning D: Society and Space*, 14: 5–34.

Watts, M. (1994) 'Capitalisms, crises and cultures 1: notes towards a totality of fragments', in A. Pred and M. Watts (eds), *Reworking Modernity*. New Brunswick, NJ: Rutgers University Press.

Williamson, J. (1991) '"Up where you belong": Hollywood images of big business in the 1980s', in J. Corner and S. Harvey (eds), *Enterprise and Heritage: Crosscurrents of National Culture*. London: Routledge. pp. 151–61.

Wolfe, T. (1988) *Bonfire of the Vanities*. London: Jonathan Cape.

Figure 10.1 Kiss of Death, *20th Century Fox, 1995*

10

Masculinity and Madness

Rolland Munro

Opening Titles

Freeways stretch towards us and into the horizon. A slim line of mono-rail snakes alongside speeding streams of automobiles. Images of power and freedom. Intimations of modernity. Icons of progress. Masculinity.

It is a fine, bright day and the camera holds everything in view. The slow pan along concrete supports of the 'raised' freeways might be the opening shots of any film, but, instead of moving on to new terrain, the close-ups linger. Gradually, as the camera holds the same ground, huge rusting heaps of scrapped automobiles come into view, mile after mile, just below the surface of the freeway. Modernity is being placed alongside its 'normal atrocities'.

Barbet Schroeder's evocative opening of *Kiss of Death* (1995) deconstructs the icons of man's progress as a spiritual desert. Dumped in mass graves, and stripped of gloss and hype, this endless waste of abandoned cars reveals skeletons more hollow, more empty, than any skull. There is no space for the soul here, no rest for feeling. So this is where the American enlightenment leads. It is the end of the yellow brick road. It is hope abandoned. More than a paving-up of paradise, it is the 'tip' of reason.

This is a first theme, the proximity of modernity and madness. This huge breaker's yard forms the main setting for a film in which passages to freedom mutate into dunghills of progress. Minutes before, driving to the cinema in the dusk of evening, my friend and I were high on modernity. Snaking round the roundabouts, speeding past other cars. A carnivalesque of automation. A moment of madness. And – eyes peeled to the road – we were 'right in' there. Now, in the opening titles, we have arrived at our destination.

Except we have overshot. We have gone too far. We are still speeding as Little Junior, the mobster played by Nicholas Cage, expresses regret over having splattered a new soundbox with his victim's blood. Not all the perfumes of Arabia will restore his soundbox to its pristine condition. As he carefully wipes the black plastic, still wearing surgical gloves, his remorse is only for the 'waste' of this new purchase, not the waste of a colleague whom he has just punched to a pulp inside the breaker's yard. So this is a second theme, the proximity of reason and madness.

First Take

This chapter discusses images of organization in *Kiss of Death*, Barbet Schroeder's re-make of the 1947 *film noir*. As with its 'original', the Ukrainian director depicts a duality of organization: reason and madness exist side by side, just as do justice and violence. However, his juxta-position of modernity's freedoms alongside 'normal atrocities', announced in the long opening sequence, is also sustained throughout the film in ways that produce a critique of Western society as saturated by masculinity and madness.

A speciality of *film noir* is its play on the 'gaze': there is an emphasis on the closed-off spaces of modernity, with a traditional emphasis on the interiors of rooms. Here two devices come together. First, in the darkened room, shadows are visually enlarged through the camera work and made more menacing through the musical score. Violence and death are made present in the very places where they are normally thought of as absent. So that homes are no longer 'dwelling places', spaces free of angst, but perform instead as sources that amplify fear. Secondly, the camera placings and the soundtrack address spaces that tend to be overlooked. A 'gaze' hides as much as it reveals and an audience is made alert to each potential victim's 'blind spot'. Together, shadows and sounds magnify the dangers of places that lie outside the eye's 'lines of sight'.[1]

In more recent films of its genre, this celebration of shadows has turned towards a restoration of 'forgetting'. Thus, as in Benoit's *Subway* (1985) and the hilarious *Delicatessen* (1991), the location of subways and sewers implies a remembering of modernity's 'blind spot'. The iconography is of dark tunnels, of forgotten places that lurk below the everyday gaze, only waiting to rise up and overpower a 'surface' civilization. These underworlds are revealed to be an indispensable 'supplement' to progress; the madness that accompanies the exercise of reason. But few films do more than invert the hierarchy here. The pillars of masculinity remain untoppled. Instead of a top-down 'gaze', we get the male view, as it were, bottom up.

In developing the theme of reason and madness alongside a theme of modernity and madness, Schroeder's images are three. First, there is an integration of technology with everyday life. Technology such as the automobile is not 'other' to the human, but is often incorporated in ways that make possible those particular representations and performances that identify themselves as masculine. Secondly, in performances of masculinity, there is a magnification of the self that goes on to disparage the very technology that serves its prosthetic extension. This vaulting ambition to come out on top produces a 'forgetting' of the very props that atomize persons as 'individuals' in the first place. Thirdly, there is the way in which organizations spill over into each other, even when they are being held apart as legal and illegal, or 'good' and 'bad'.

These are provisional images, for it must be remembered that we are already 'in' the male gaze – a way of seeing the world that can only temporarily 'forget' that automobiles turn into rust heaps, that self is fluid, never centred, and that organizations have their dark sides. Considered as a critique of modernity, therefore, *Kiss of Death* acts more as a subversion of masculinity, rather than its overthrow. In exploring this later, it is important to consider whether Schroeder's portrayal of the feminine as the pulse of family life, the warmth that defeats the shadows of our dwelling places, offers anything like an alternative vision. It can, of course, be argued that a division of labour along gender lines is too conservative, too romantic; but I think we should be careful here not to invoke an intellectual space that sees itself as aloof from this proximity of masculinity and madness. There is perhaps no exit from madness and, to illustrate this, I will briefly discuss Derrida's essay on Foucault as a 're-make' of Foucault's earlier analysis of Descartes. Madness is the ostensible topic for both pieces of writing; and Descartes, with his stress on logic and method, is the philosopher's icon of reason and modernity.

Flashback

Logos, the vehicle of reason, might be considered as the first kiss of death. In beginning a discussion on reason and madness, we shift now to another re-make. This is Derrida's *essay noir* 'Cogito and the History of Madness'. Here it is freeways of thought that reach into the horizon; and logic is the monorail of reason that snakes its madness around us.

Lurking below the monorail is the scrapheap of defunct philosophers. First on the heap, of course, is the putative 'founder' of modern philosophy, René Descartes. Descartes's equation of knowledge with certainty is based on his claim to be able to distinguish reason from all other forms of thought, especially madness. Indeed, it is in order to adduce the very impossibility of this separation that makes him a favourite target for every would-be patricide. For the philosophers, it's always 'Time to clean up your own backyard.' And here Derrida, for all his talk of difference, is no exception (see also Helmling, 1994). As Husserl and Heidegger have already seen, Descartes requires deletion; Descartes's 'liberation of speech' makes his Cogito ('I think') an obligatory passage, one ripe for (repeated) elimination in any de-centring of the self.

The ethics of deconstruction do not permit argument to take the form of throwing stones at the 'house' of the author from another 'ground' (Derrida, 1982). Nor does Derrida (1982: 135) support Heidegger's method of deconstruction. For Derrida, holding on to the same ground – the technique that Schroeder mimics in his opening sequence – rather than 'moving towards an opening', risks sinking into the 'autism of closure'. Yet, in announcing the Cogito as his ostensible target, Derrida (1978: 31–63) exactly proceeds by way of making a 'close reading'.

Keeping a 'black and hardly natural light' (1978: 61), he enters the interiors of Descartes's construction, lengthening the shadows of the text in ways that makes madness present within its very walls – the same menace that Descartes thought he had so carefully excluded.

In entering the 'shelter' of the Cogito, Derrida wants to show up Descartes's blind spot. In his intricate camera work, holding each 'letter to the letter' (Helmling, 1994), and in his relentless soundtrack – homophony, repetition and an endless 'breaking-up' of words – Derrida shows that Descartes's moment of truth, his isolation of reason, depends on a momentary escape from the *logos*. Reason – made distinct by Descartes *as* reason – depends on a momentary indifference as to whether he is thinking truth, or thinking madness. As Derrida (1978: 58) goes on: 'when reason and madness have not yet been separated, when to take the part of the Cogito is neither to take the part of reason as reasonable order, nor the part of disorder and madness, but is rather to grasp, once more, the source which permits reason *and* madness to be determined and stated.' Thus, Derrida establishes the proximity of reason and madness. These are not opposites, as is usually understood, but margins of the same phenomena to be found 'alongside' each other.[2]

In this way, Derrida reframes the source of Descartes's certainty – his foundation stone for modern philosophy – and, instead, reveals the Cogito to be an example of 'madness': the madness of those 'seeking to *shelter themselves*, to be sure of having protections against madness' (Derrida, 1978: 310n). The madness, Descartes's madness at the very moment of the 'mad audacity' of the Cogito (1978: 56), is to have over-privileged certainty. This accomplished, the motive for Derrida's heap, it turns out, is not Descartes. It is the dumping of Foucault, Derrida's 'master'. For, in his recognizing that madness is never excluded by reason alone – indeed, that reason is accomplished only by 'emprisoning madness' (p. 61) – Foucault's crime, in the eyes of Derrida, is to have already broken up the Cogito. Foucault has been there before. Yet, when Derrida uncovers this, '[w]hich amounts to saying that madness is never excluded except *in fact*, violently' (p. 310n), he goes too far.

Finding himself merely tracing the footsteps of Foucault, Derrida is unhappy just to jump on the corpse of Descartes, the already dead. Thus, the twist in the plot: not all the writings of philosophy can return our soundbox to its pristine, Cartesian condition. 'From its very first breath, speech . . . is able to open the space for discourse only by emprisoning madness' (pp. 60–1) and Derrida cannot make himself exempt. Setting out to 'wipe' philosophy off its soundbox, speech, he discovers his footsteps are taking him elsewhere. In his every move, he finds a 'trace' and the trace is Foucault's. As Derrida notes himself, his reading is: 'despite all appearances to the contrary, profoundly aligned with Foucault's' (p. 59). Instead of enrolling Descartes as part of the project of difference, Derrida finds he is but tracing his own ideas *as* Foucault's.

With nowhere to go – other than to disengage with the 'extremity of the hyperbole, which Foucault seemingly has not done' (p. 60) – Derrida attempts to situate himself 'within the interval of this remorse, Foucault's remorse, Descartes's remorse according to Foucault' (p. 61). But like Little Junior's remorse, mentioned above, there would be something mad in just attempting to 'wipe' the traces. Far from 'wiping' the source of his own speech, he himself traces out his secreting of Foucault's footsteps into the heart of his essay. In asking 'How would Foucault read this text?' (p. 46), he creates a picture of it being Foucault who first casts the stones at Descartes's house. So, in an abortive double bluff, Derrida reports himself to be at the scene of the crime. But, it is the wrong crime we are left looking at. By announcing that 'we shall follow Foucault's reading of the text' (p. 45), Derrida has pulled Foucault into his breaker's yard and, as his footsteps hollow after Foucault's, he knows, like a stalking rapist, just how much Foucault despises thought in the form of mere 'iteration'. So Foucault has to go too.

Derrida's desire, as 'an admiring and grateful disciple', is to out-master the man he calls the 'master' (p. 31). So Derrida will not work, as it were, for another organization, Foucault's emphasis on the proximity of reason and madness. And so he overshoots. Derrida's rape of the master turns into a serial killing. But, no matter. By this time, we are well into the plot of patricide and need hardly worry about Derrida's dismissal of Foucault's book as offering a 'Cartesian gesture for the twentieth century'. His pulping of Foucault as 'totalitarian' (p. 57) and 'violence itself' (p. 57) has become, for philosophy, just one more 'normal atrocity'.

Images of Organization

Why film? Examples of organizations appear in other media, notably the novel (Czarniawska-Joerges and Guillet de Monthoux, 1994). Yet movies seem an obvious medium for portraying 'organization' to a student audience, with its many advantages of a visual engagement over the tedium of the textbook.

Interestingly, there is little evidence of this potential for film being realized. Soldiers, nurses, doctors, lawyers and police appear endlessly in films, but primarily as characters, even stereotypes, and, typically, in movies that make their own genre as war films, soaps, thrillers, or courtroom dramas. Organizations of various forms appear, such as labour unions, but these tend to serve as background, as in *On the Waterfront* (1954), which dwells lovingly on Marlon Brando's 'method' of muttering and strutting, but gives scant attention to the longshoremen. We see much organization *behaviour* – how nasty or kind people can be to each other – but learn little about how organizations themselves actually work.

The record of movie-makers for depicting organizations at work seems conspicuous by its absence. John Hassard, for example, spends many,

many hours viewing to find an occasional snippet of 'factory life' to show students. His findings – the cold steel of the machine shop in the opening sequence of *Saturday Night, Sunday Morning* (1960), Frank Gilbreth's demonstration in *Cheaper by the Dozen* (1950) of how he taught his 12 children to take a one-minute bath, and excerpts from Charlie Chaplin's *Modern Times* (1936) – illustrate occasional moments when 'organization' breaks through *as* a subject. Well, almost breaks through; for the extended shots of factory machinery serve as little more than atmosphere for the real story of the long factory hours that the hero, played by Albert Finney, must endure in order to earn his Saturday night and Sunday morning; and Frank Gilbreth's demonstration of taking a bath to the new headmistress of his children is a comic vehicle to illustrate his psychic obsession with efficiency.

For the most part, cinema seems content to remain 'outside' the world of organizations and celebrate people as people. Centred in a myth of everyone having a core self, plots remain humanist stories of love, greed and revenge. Perhaps this, then, is our first clue to finding 'organization' on screen? That processes of organizing are most effectively portrayed indirectly and in passing.[3] Viewed in this way, we might begin to understand the potential riches that lie in cinema's refusal to reify an 'organization'. Indeed, cinema's contribution to organization theory may lie in its obstinate treatment of organizing as always related to all other forms of organized life.

Filming the 'Organization'

The Mafia is the exception; it is the one organization revered by Hollywood. There is no shortage of films about the Mafia and, appropriately, given Hollywood's own links, it is often referred to on screen as the 'Organization'.

Given cinema's reluctance to abstract organization away from people *as* people, it is easy to appreciate Hollywood's passion for the Mafia. The Mafia is 'family'. So everyone can relate to this. The Organization has its own code, which must be obeyed. So interest is stimulated by offering insight into a secretive and closed order. And the Mafia never forgets. So the audience can feel fear. And so on. In an endless circulation between stories and reality, it is also impossible to separate myth from their actual methods. Nor is it necessary, although movies sometimes have to be viewed as the Mafia's own propaganda machine, propagating a message of fear in the reiteration of phrases like: 'We never forget.'

Indeed, in the cinema adaptation of John Grisham's *The Firm* (1993), it is not the organization of the firm of lawyers, but the Organization that dominates. In the novel, Grisham offers an unusually vibrant depiction of everyday office life – where momentum is sustained by a photocopier, in the basement pumping iron. All this is abandoned in the screen version for a celluloid chase of the lawyer hero by the Mafia. In merely filming a race against time, the movie's conception of organization need be no more sophisticated than that of chronology. One close shave after another – with suspense built up through deferral rather than difference.

More recently, both Martin Scorsese's *Goodfellas* (1990) and his aptly titled *Casino* (1995), considered by many to be a re-hash of the earlier film, portray the 'scams' that form part of the organization of the Organization. Each of these two screenplays, unusually for films, spend time detailing something of the running of the Mafia organization. *Goodfellas* deals with the rough and tumble organization of 'protection' as a prelude to the punks, on whom this depends, all trying to kill each other off; while *Casino* spends much of the first third of the screenplay depicting the smooth creaming-off of cash from The Riviera, a Mafia-run casino, between 1973 and 1983. The latter film ends with the big corporations massively rebuilding Las Vegas, transforming it into a Disneyland of gambling, most suitable for Saga holidays.

Eventually, even in *Casino*, the various scams that build on each other, and make up everyday life in The Riviera, are returned to background and the story once more is 'carried' by people. The remorseless message – that everyone 'is here to take your money' – delivered by means of a talk-over and symbolized by showing more backhanders than hand-shakes cut together with repeated shots of the same mechanized shute of coins, turns firmly into a traditional plot of love, greed and revenge.

Two Versions

In that Barbet Schroeder's film also deals with the Organization, I want now to consider some of the imagery of *Kiss of Death*. The earlier *film noir*, shot in black and white, starred Victor Mature as a basically straight guy, someone who can't quite disentangle himself from the criminal element of his youth. This theme is also intrinsic to the re-make, but there are important differences in the rewriting which extend the notion of organization beyond a sense of people doing things for, or to, other people.

In both versions, the hero gets caught in a bungled job. Whereas in the early version he robs a jewellery store to get Christmas presents for his kids, in the later version, Jimmy (David Caruso) is embroiled into driving a trailer of stolen cars by a 'blood cousin', who begs for help in order to save himself from being killed by a mobster, Little Junior, for failing to 'deliver' on time. The 1990s are, after all, the age of customer care, an era of on-time delivery.

In both versions the hero goes to prison. Rather than 'squeal' to the District Attorney in exchange for a reduced sentence, he relies on a mobster lawyer to get him parole and pay money to support his wife. In the 1947 version, the mobsters are just lying and don't pay up, while in the later version it is the cousin, who also runs the breaker's yard, who intercepts the money, taking most of it. This forces Jimmy's wife to take an office job in the cousin's breaker's yard, where he can force his unwelcome attention upon her, a problem that culminates in her being raped by the cousin after he's got her drunk. Thus the cousin completely dishonours the 'blood' bond on which he has relied. In contrast, the Organization honours its debt. It may rule by fear but, in the re-make: 'We look after our own.' The message is that institutions, or at least this one, make longer and more durable networks than do kith and kin.

In the original and the re-make, the hero's wife dies early in the story. Each has gambled that the hero will go straight, but each finds her relationship and her hopes of making a home, a 'dwelling place', destroyed. In the early version, the first wife commits suicide; while in the second version, significantly, the car she is driving, to get away from the unwanted attentions of Jimmy's cousin, runs into the path of a huge truck. The devastating crash is a final 'break-up' of family that portends the consequences for femininity, especially when it is forced out of its warm extension of the hearth into the lengthening shadows and madness of masculinity.

Both versions of the film depict the hero's revenge. Once he learns of his betrayal, the hero agrees to talk to the District Attorney and adopts the device of naming everyone involved in an earlier heist except one – the one who has betrayed him. In making this erasure, Jimmy is effectively condemning his cousin to death: the mob, by tracing this 'erasure of a trace' (Derrida, 1982: 66), see the cousin as the man who has 'fingered' them. In both versions, the penalty exacted by the Organization is strikingly violent. In the original, it is a hired killer who extracts revenge by pushing the man's mother downstairs in her wheelchair; while in the re-make, in a genre closer to *Reservoir Dogs* (1992), Jimmy's cousin is beaten to a pulp inside the office walls of his own breaker's yard by Little Junior, the son of a Mafia member and stripclub owner, and his associates. However, if the execution in Schroeder's version is more communal, it is also much more clinical. Its ritual nature is symbolized by the rubberized gowns donned as the hoods gather round the victim like surgeons; the application of ultimate sanctions being less for revenge and more one of necessity. As the song Little Junior plays on his soundbox to drown the cousin's screams, says: 'It's time to clean up your own backyard'. In parallel to an ethos of care, currently being promulgated by today's new managerialism, the Mafia also know how an occasional exercise of power is exemplary in its instruction to others.

In both versions, the mobster is drawn to the hero and tries to befriend him, talking openly about his philosophy of living. But the portrayals of the mobster vary. In the earlier black-and-white version, the mobster's talk and his laugh readily reveal him to be close to insanity, taking a perverse pleasure in his own twisted viciousness. In the later colour version, the characterization is more subtle. Little Junior's voice is affected by his asthma, but otherwise he is almost devoid of feeling in matters of killing or hurting others. Yet, in his conflation of ethics with aesthetics, he continuously authors his own morality into the most fastidious of distinctions. Indeed, his faith in his self-inflicted acronym, BAD – balls, attitude, direction – appears as a parody of the new managerialism's entanglement with 'macho' management.[4]

A further twist in the plot is similar. In both films, the District Attorney is not content with the first deal, but ups the stakes. Having promised the hero freedom for talking, he now demands a further round of help – one that, in the re-make, ensnares the red-haired hero in helping to catch the same mobster who has exacted the Organization's revenge on the cousin. This means that Jimmy has to go back on his promises to his new wife, the friend of his first wife and someone who used to look after his children. Unexpectedly, Little Junior is not convicted and, in both films, the stage is set for him to take his revenge on the hero and his new family.

Technology and Organization

As in Schroeder's opening sequence, the automobile is ever-present. Cars feature in the early version, but they enter mainly as icons of modernity. Flash cars, like flash women, are available to whoever has the money to buy and they do little more than stereotype the quick money of the successful gangster. In the re-make, however, the automobile is no mere addition; it penetrates almost every facet of the film as the harbinger of madness.

The car *is* technology. The automobile runs through all the forms of employment we see in the film: the crooks who steal the cars; the wreckers who break them up and cannibalize them in order to make them untraceable; and the mobsters who ship them out to sell in other countries. And then, on the other side, there are the detectives who spend all their time tracing the cars, together with the Feds who are out to break this 'multi-national' racket.

The car is also prominent in many of the scenes, especially in the key transitions. Cars have to be broken into, a facility which Jimmy has to perfection, and cars are broken up. Deals are done in cars, both for and about cars. Dealers are done to death in cars. And gifts are made of cars. For example, after he has blown a hole in the head of the stolen car dealer – having got Jimmy to sit next to the dealer in the passenger seat – Little Junior calmly offers Jimmy a car previously refused by the dealer as payment (because it was 'red' and he was superstitious of red).

Cars, car-ports and the cars of the breaker's yard, these provide much of the interiors for much of the film. Indeed, their pervasiveness registers them as 'interiors', even in the American outdoors. The icons of freedom become full of menace and danger. In this way, Schroeder incorporates the American landscape into *film noir* without losing its integrity.[5]

Prosthetic Extension

In the form that Schroeder portrays them, automobiles are vehicles of masculinity. In the intricate camera work, the car reveals itself to be a highly available, and socially regarded, means of magnifying male 'presence'. As a form of prosthesis (Strathern, 1991), therefore, the car acts as a supplement to the failing project of reason – the modern male. The more powerful, sharper, faster, more expensive the car, the bigger the 'big man'.

The automobile, then, exists as more than modernity's principal means of physical extension. But, indirectly, Schroeder goes further than this. Presence – magnification – also involves organization. Cars, symbols of status as both privately and company owned cars, do not stand alone – much more is required to support their presence. In the face of other men wanting to come and take a car away, much organizing today, in terms of policing, financial and legal infrastructure and car insurance, is required to help ensure someone can treat a car as their individual property.

There is also more than a simple prosthesis of the car in the performances. For example, in the early version, the mobster is a 'big man' through the fear he generates. His eyes, his laugh, his walk, all these say that here is someone who will stop at nothing; someone who knows no borderlines. In contrast, played deadpan by Nicholas Cage, Little Junior is full of borderlines. They just happen to be the borderlines of distinctions of his own making; or rather, as his acronym BAD illustrates, of his own haphazard borrowing.

In some of the funniest moments of the film, the script gives Little Junior many of the lines we associate today with the 'me' culture: the point being that it is this prosthetic move on culture – the incorporation into oneself of what is definitively the prerogative of others – that, for others, induces an uncertainty and unpredictability about crossing over borders that have become unseeable to all but oneself. Indeed, Little Junior is so self-absorbed with his aesthetic niceties of moral conduct as to appear unable to be in a relation to anyone except himself. Yet, because no one dares tell him, he seems unable to realize the impotence of this position. The exception to this is the stripper, who calls him a 'faggot' while he is lifting her up as a set of weights. This is the only occasion that we see Little Junior touching a woman.

Schroeder also balances an interesting relation between male forms of possessions, as signifying the madness of those so 'possessed', and feminine possessions. In contrast, for instance, to Little Junior's very visible artefacts, his asthma equipment, his cars and his hirelings, the women in the film have almost no technology. Or, more strictly speaking, they are associated with a *distributable* technology. For example, early on in Schroeder's film, one of the women is studying to help make a better life. The idea is that, while possessions like cars remain particular to individual persons, books, and hence education, are available to all. Only one person owns a specific car. And so it is male cars, the Rolls, the Mercedes, and the Lexus – cars that require a great deal of money to buy, and mark people out as different, as rich – that are stolen.

Another technology, one that is already distributed, is the body. This is the technology exploited by the 'other' women of Schroeder's film. In the strip club owned by Little Junior's father, the dancers gyrate their bodies. Again the theme is one of availability to all. The women give their bodies on the basis of 'look, but don't touch'. It is a way in which they can be professional and keep an identity at which they can work hard for respect. In this way, his portrayal of (some) women as 'warm' goes past its close proximity to conservative values. If women don't *have*, it's also because they don't *need*. Like Jimmy and the only other family man in the film, a black detective who overcomes his hate for Jimmy for being involved in the shooting that has left his right eye permanently weeping, women are not intrinsically caught up in this madness. Their prosthesis is more contained, more communal.

In brief, Schroeder's vision of organizational logics relates women to forms of technology that are intrinsically distributable or shareable. Schroeder's emphasis, therefore, is in direct contrast to the current Hollywood portrayal of 'strong' women as pushy. As it is typically portrayed, this theme not only maintains the convention of women lacking solidarity with each other, but returns it to a teen magazine portrayal of 'girls' fighting for the males. For instance, Sharon Stone in *Casino* and more especially the lead women of *Showgirls* (1995), also set in Las Vegas, are all professional 'working girls', but are competing to out-do each other. In these bigger budget films, the 'feminist' message is garbled by a 'go for it' culture that lets the heroines, at least temporarily, get sucked into the maelstrom of coming out on top.

Boundaryless Organizations

As already mentioned, Hollywood sees organizations as made up of people. But, to adopt one of Derrida's terms, there is always a 'hinge'. The automobile acts as a 'hinge' between a prosthetic magnification of the male and the unparalleled brutality of the twentieth century. Through such 'hinges', the celluloid of the screen always delivers more than the screenplay intends. The same car passes from the car thief to the breaker's yard, and from the breaker's yard to the mob. The same blood passes to the 'cousins' and passes from the dead man to the soundbox.

Additionally, there is always a contact man who belongs to both organizations. What, then, makes organizations different? And, more poignantly, who keeps them apart?

In *Kiss of Death*, organizations spill over into each other. This is where Schroeder's film is helpfully different. In his vision, all organizations, except the family, are male and they are all the same. It is a view heralded in the early version. Caught in the remorseless requests of the District Attorney, the frustrated hero remarks: 'You're all the same.' For the hapless person caught up between the organizations of the Mob and the law, there can be no difference. Both extract help and both employ violence; each is exacting in its demands and its punishment. As befits an enterprise culture, both also do deals. In Schroeder's version, for example, Little Junior's release from trial is secured by the FBI offering the District Attorney the advancement of being made a judge. And both legal and illegal organizations are endless in their entanglement; for example, it is the Feds who make this deal with the DA rather than reveal to the court the illegality of their attempts to break up the Mafia's car ring. In the permutations of all the various individuals trying to come out on top, there is no escape from madness. Like moving about on an amoebic strip, changing organizations merely shifts the surface.

As mentioned above, the only time Little Junior touches a woman – women are presented in Schroeder's film as if they are outside the laws of organization – is to lift her, as if she was a dumb-bell, in order to demonstrate the fruits of his pumping iron. When a punter at his and his father's strip club touches one of the 'dancers', Little Junior shames him by making the offender dance almost naked in front of everyone. It is the same person who will finally help Jimmy bring about Little Junior's downfall.

So here, side by side, is a traditional reading of organization in the form of a division of labour. Men and women occupy different spaces; and, in a supplement of this, men and women labour a division over what is masculine and what is feminine. Persons, to be persons, conduct a labour of division (see Hetherington and Munro, 1997) in keeping things – themselves and their organizations – apart. And this labour of division includes work for the audience, a labour of division that goes beyond a simple matter of telling apart heroes and villains. In both versions, the hero and villain will both attempt revenge; but, drawing on an audience that always takes sides, one man's 'justice' has to be kept distinct from another man's 'malice'.

Schroeder's networks of relations are complex. At one end of an entanglement of males, caught up in their images of the masculine, are loyalties between petty criminals, based on old ties, the deals that have been calculated and have to be repaid, however impossible the situation. And, at the other, lie fears about who can, and will, draw on the ultimate sanctions that such deals make possible. Of course, killing someone for 'failing to deliver' may seem to be a step too far – a sanction more extreme than most contemporary managers might contemplate. Yet there is an obvious parallel between the tactics of the mob and the repertoires of 'macho management', with its 'normal atrocities' of dismissals, redundancies and factory closures.

Credits

There are many organizations in this chapter. Perhaps too many – but this is the point. Like the film *Kiss of Death*, I have tried to avoid 'confining' organization within the frame of a single and specific definition. Together, Foucault and Derrida help to show us the futility, and eventual terror, that can arise from attempts to enforce 'reasonable order'.

Drawing on Barbet Schroeder's film *Kiss of Death*, and Derrida's ritual execution of Foucault – it is hard not to recall also the grotesque 'car boot' scene in *Goodfellas* where the punks (Joe Pesci and Robert De Niro) lift the lid of the boot momentarily to kill a mummified godfather – I have tried to weave together these stories of 'normal atrocities'. As Schroeder and Derrida portray them, the automobile and philosophy are both vehicles of masculinity and each has its madness.

Schroeder's plot also lets us follow Derrida's, so let me recapitulate the story of the film one last time. The 'hinge' in *Kiss of Death* occurs when the male hero is captured and brought by car – and then literally by a car lift – to the place where the audience expects his execution. This is not only a brilliant moment of liminality (the cinematic photography is unsuccessful on video), it is film-making at its most supreme for it reveals to the audience *their* 'blind spot'. At the very moment when the audience can see no credible way out for Jimmy (or the film-makers), the car lift 'lifts' (Derrida's 'relève') the audience into a moment of 'excess', a moment when mobsters and racketeers are re-levered as the FBI and the police arguing over the killing of the stolen car 'dealer' (who turns out to have been an FBI plant). Thus, the forces of good and the forces of evil are revealed to be no mere duality propping each other up. Both sides are calling themselves 'organizations', and they are, in the way they run things, structural equivalents. These organizations are masculine and mad.

We find a similar moment in Derrida. Derrida's *essay noir* intimates a ritual elimination of Foucault by the new radicals. But as he sinks deeper into the footsteps of Foucault, the audience can see no way for Derrida to come out on top. Until, that is, Derrida lifts Foucault up and reveals him to be no more than a twentieth-century Cartesian. Foucault's poststructuralism is thus revealed, by Derrida, to be merely the new forces for ordering and organizing thinking. But, aggrandized as audience, we need not be convinced. When Derrida goes masculine, goes mad to come out on top, to out-master the master, the madness of his massacre reduces him, at least on this occasion, to being little more than a footnote to Foucault.

Schroeder's depiction of masculinity is helpful as it offers a vision of 'extension' and instructs how this may be acted out in the performance of identity (see also Strathern, 1991; Munro, 1996). In contrast, always decentred, always kept at the margins – and perhaps keeping themselves in deferral – women appear as potential allies for an alternative form of extension, one that keeps being 'deferred' by men. So, although almost always reduced to the artefacts of 'difference', this is the 'interval', the organization space, in which women enter Schroeder's film. When they attach themselves as partners to women, men can be good. Detached, men are deadly.

The limits of this division as a hetero-normalization of society are obvious, but Schroeder's depiction of the masculine and the feminine as *organized* worlds is more interesting and subtle than most. These are not just worlds apart, worlds in which there can be only occasional meeting places. They are worlds in which personhood is enveloped within networks of endless obligations, not merely the strictures of sexual stereotyping. Thus, while others, such as Margaret Atwood in *Bodily Harm* (1995), also capture the madness of masculinity, Schroeder does not follow Atwood in making madness innate to men. We can conceive of masculinity, instead, as an effect of their organizing principles, as an effect of their predilection for, and access to, the props of technology.

In male hands, reason has become the 'kiss' of death. Trading on the dualism of the masculine being different from the feminine, action being different from thought, objects being different from subjects, and so on, reason is always prefigured in ways that 'detach' it, that make it lose touch (Cooper, 1993), and defer intimacy for a logic condemned to (con)testing an 'out there' reality. Riding around in their cars, or in their philosophies, those who would be masculine are entrapped in the endless circuits, and consequences, of an unreasonable representation of the male, of endlessly performing an impossible truth regime.

Notes

1 There are numerous permutations. Of interest, for example, is Hitchcock's *Rear Window* (1954) where the hero, played by Jimmy Stewart, sees a murderer burying his victim's body. In a reversal of the genre's reliance on the victim's blind spot, the murderer realizes that he has been seen and the hero knows exactly when the murderer is coming to get him, but is unable to move out of harm's way.

2 Derrida (1978: 46) attributes the expression 'alongside' to Foucault, but it is also a motif for Heidegger.

3 Somehow, despite the plethora of recent videos, the study of organization is elusive to celluloid. But perhaps not impervious? In a brilliant development of the comic's ability to carry glimpses of organization, Ian Latimer, while at Rank, revolutionized organization training films by his formula of using comedy actors such as Ronnie Barker and Penelope

Keith, a formula made standard following its adoption by John Cleese and his Video Arts group.

4 The parody is based on Little Junior's conviction that people choose their 'own' acronyms. But his unhappy choice of terms reveals instead how much each of us can be caught up in the play of current discourse. Jimmy's riposte of FAB – fucked at birth – suggests, in contrast, a more realist interpretation: for the 'blood' relations who looked after him were criminals and are the people who have ruined his life.

5 An interesting comparison in terms of location and the 'blind spot' comes from Scorsese's *Casino*, discussed earlier. Like *Kalifornia* (1993), *Red Rock West* (1992) and the German/US film *Dead Man* (1995), Casino draws on *film noir* by framing meetings between mobsters in the desert, like the streets of Manhattan in *Taxi Driver*, a definitively American landscape. As with the enlarged shadows of poorly lit rooms, the desert is evocative of danger, amplified by the audience's knowledge that the place is full of buried bodies. As the psychotic mobster, played by the charismatic, under-sized Joe Pesci, remarks in one of his many talk-over sequences: 'It's in the desert where lots of the town's problems are solved. Lots of holes in the desert and a lot of problems are buried in those holes. Except you gotta do it right. I mean, you've gotta have the hole already dug before you show up with the package in the trunk.' The hero, played by Robert De Niro, explains his decision to meet his enraged former buddy in the desert in terms of a would-be killer's inability to drive both cars back. The 50:50 danger of being killed, where no one can see, is removed by the killer's 'blind spot': two cars need two drivers to erase the trace of the killing.

References

Cooper, R. (1993) 'Technologies of representation', in P. Alionen (ed.), *The Semiotic Boundaries of Politics*. Berlin: Mouton de Gruyter. pp. 279–312.

Czarniawska-Joerges, B. and Guillet de Monthoux, P. (eds) (1994) *Good Novels, Better Management: Reading Organizational Realities in Fiction*. Chur, Switzerland: Harwood Academic Press.

Derrida, J. (1978) *Writing and Difference*, trans. A. Bass. London: Routledge and Kegan Paul.

Derrida, J. (1982) *Margins of Philosophy*, trans. A. Bass. Hemel Hempstead: Harvester Press.

Helmling, S. (1994) 'Historicizing Derrida', *Postmodern Culture*, electronic journal at http://mus.jhu.edu/journals/postmodern_culture

Hetherington, K. and Munro, R. (eds) (1997) *Ideas of Difference: Social Spaces and the Labour of Division*. Sociological Review Monograph. Oxford: Blackwell.

Munro, R. (1996) 'A consumption view of self: extension, exchange and identity', in S. Edgell, K. Hetherington and A. Warde (eds), *Consumption Matters: The Production and Experience of Consumption*, Sociological Review Monograph, Oxford: Blackwell. pp. 248–73.

Strathern, M. (1991) *Partial Connections*. Maryland: Rowman and Little.

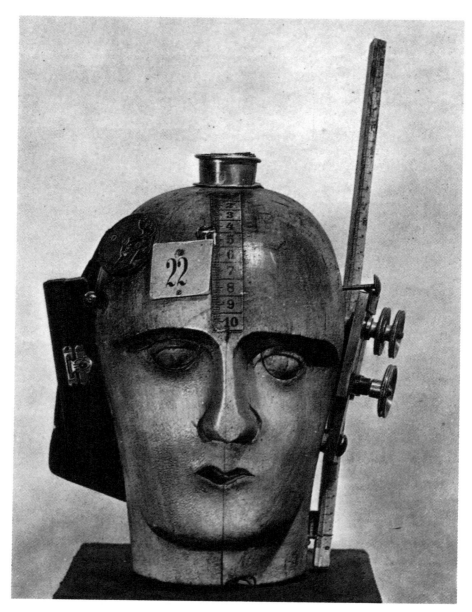

Figure 11.1   Mechanical Head, *Raoul Hausmann, 1919–20, DACS*

PART IV

ORGANIZATIONAL FUTURES

11

Cyborganization: Cinema as Nervous System

Martin Parker and Robert Cooper

> This history is a tale for its own sake. Many, and perhaps most, of the facts presented in these pages will be found to be new or at variance with the generally accepted traditions and writings of the motion picture.
>
> Ramsaye, *A Million and One Nights*, p. v

In the first part of this chapter, Parker spends a lot of time exploring what cyborg films 'mean', and then tries to conclude that they 'mean' 'nothing'. He explores the theme of body horror and the paranoia about the large corporation that is often a sub-text of these films. This textual analysis then gives way to a discussion of what cyborgs are, and how cyborganization takes place. Parker concludes by romanticizing the cyborg and demonizing the capitalist organization at the same time as he doubts his own judgement. In Part II, Cooper explores a range of ideas – cyborg,[1] cybernetics,[2] nervous system,[3] cyborganization[4] and cinema[5] – that help us to understand the intellectual sources of our fascination with filmic-literary science fiction and its real-life expression as science fact-ion. His Contingent Supplement is a series of brief essays on the theme of the human–machine relationship and the increasingly unstable reality produced by contemporary information-communication technologies, including cinema. In effect, Cooper provides a vocabulary of ideas that constitutes a background discourse to the developing techno-scientific–industrial complex of our late-modern world.

PART I

In the Beginning there was Flesh?

> You are about to begin reading Parker and Cooper's chapter, *Cyborganization: Cinema as Nervous System*. Relax. Concentrate. Best to close the door; the TV is

always on in the next room. Find the most comfortable position: seated, stretched out, curled up or lying flat. In an easy chair, on the sofa, in the rocker, the deck chair. Well, what are you waiting for? Stretch your legs, go ahead and put your feet on a cushion, on two cushions, on the arms of the sofa, on the wings of the chair, on the piano, on the globe. Take your shoes off first. Adjust the light so you won't strain your eyes. Make sure the page isn't in shadow. Your hands, the book, your chair, the eyes, your brain, the ink. So here you are now, ready to attack the first lines of the first page. (With apologies to Calvino, 1982)

There are a lot of *cyborgs*[1] around nowadays. The cinema, in particular, is a place where you often meet terminators, unisols, synthetics, robocops, androids and simulants, usually inhabiting ultra-modern dystopias or post-apocalypse nightmares. The popularity of films like *Blade Runner* (1982), *Robocop* (1987), the *Terminator* films (1984, 1991), *Eve of Destruction* (1990) as well as the *Tetsuo* films (1989, 1991), *Cyborg* (1989), *Universal Soldier* (1993) and many others serves to demonstrate something about the importance of the cyborg as a contemporary cultural icon. These are visions of cybernetic techno-golems: entities manufactured through the grafting of hard shiny bits of metal into flesh – or even with flesh that is really a sophisticated form of plastic and memories that are no more than a computer program. These cyborg bodies always require the help of external supports in order to complete and realize themselves and usually have a violently expressed nostalgia or ambivalence towards their own and others' 'humanity'. Of course, this is not just about films. For a while now cyborgs have replaced robots as stock characters in popular science fiction, being featured in television programmes such as *Star Trek* and *Space Precinct*, cartoons, novels, computer games, comic books, play figures and even as cybernetic laser toys to attach to the arms or heads of children (see Gray, 1995, for a much longer list).

But, of course, we are all cyborgs – particularly nowadays. Our bodies are only, were only, ever given realization through their connection with material objects. The hand becomes a hand when it holds a book like this one. The eye becomes an eye when it sees a word like this one. Cyborgs aren't just found in cinemas. You are one now, and always. This approach to the everyday relations between humans and technology lays emphasis on the development and use of 'external' things in the development of supposedly 'internal' processes. The solid world outside and the private spaces of cognition then become intimately connected. Indeed, in practice, there may be no workable distinction between them. The term *cyborganization*[4] (Cooper and Law, 1995) describes the general process by which human organisms always supplement their incompleteness by engineering technologies that combine with their bodies to create new 'cyborganic' spaces populated by 'cyborganisms'. The cinema is one of these spaces and happens to be one in which a great deal of representational work has already been done (first by film-makers and then by academics) to question the idea that flesh is the beginning and end of human being. Curiously, many of these films also contain some rather interesting representations of organizations – but more of that later.

So, much of the argument in this chapter should be read as being about representation – not just about cyborg films. After all, the representations of bodies, machines and organizations that circulate in much contemporary academic work rely on this 'common-sense' distinction between different categories of things. Instead, I wish to suggest that thinking about the cinema itself (and some of the 'science fiction' films shown within it) can provoke a radical challenge to the way in which we think about these divisions. *Cinema*[5] has the capacity to disorient and destabilize our conventional ways of thinking. The order we spend a great deal of time trying to construct can rapidly be disordered while we inhabit that particular cyborganic space. The boundaries between real and imagined blur as our bodies respond to what we see/feel on screen. The linear time we often inhabit is fragmented as stories jump from 'past' to 'future'. Spaces of 'here' and 'there' dissolve. People we have never met do disturbing or beautiful things to us. Machines and animals talk and rationality becomes contingent on patterns of light and sound. Now I am not suggesting that cinema is the only sociotechnical system that makes these things happen. Books, compact discs, computer games, television, cassettes, advertising hoardings, the world wide web, newspapers, video, records and theatres all do this as well, but cinemas do it 'densely', they make it more difficult to escape back into the 'real world'. The exit doors may be marked but it is difficult to get there in the dark.

In recent years (and, as usual, rather later than children or cinemagoers) academics also seem to have been going through a kind of cyborg fetishism, this chapter being another example. Approaches vary, some writers coming in from film and cultural theory (Best, 1989; Poster, 1992), others from technology studies and social theory (Haraway, 1991; Featherstone and Burrows, 1995; Gray, 1995). This chapter will attempt to straddle both of these literatures. I will begin with some comments about the films as texts, treating them as a kind of 'evidence' that allows me to put forward certain suggestions about popular understandings of the relationship between technology, humanity and organizations. A particular focus of this section will be exploring the demonology of the big corporation upon which many cyborg films rely. Then I will turn to the more theoretical issues posed by the notion of *cyborganization*[4] and which are taken up more fully in the Contingent Supplement by Cooper which follows. After all, it is deceptively easy to allow these films to make the cyborg into something strange, something different from ourselves. Instead, I will suggest that patterns of *cybernetic*[2] organization are actually rather mundane and that perhaps paying too much attention to spectacular cyborgs actually disguises that fact. You don't need to have glowing red eyes and a gun for an arm to be constituted by non-human materials. How could you read without this book?

Cybernetic Organisms, Mad Science and Big Corporations

> This unit needs millions of dollars in parts. You can't expect authorization for that kind of cash outlay overnight. Be reasonable.
> OCP executive explaining why they are unable to rebuild Robocop

The most common readings of cyborg films are that they represent a combination of technophobia, or at least technoscepticism, combined with a very gendered form of body horror. First, central to most of the films I mentioned in the introduction is a Frankenstein's monster narrative of scientific arrogance. As Andrew Tudor (1989) notes, mad science is the most dominant theme in horror films. In other words, the threat is most often not a war from another world or a supernatural intervention but is secular and dependent on something that human beings did in the first place. It might be added to this that, from *Metropolis* (1926) onwards, the embodiment of science in science fiction films has often been the robot or cyborg. This monster (usually male) lives because it was created (usually by a man) to fulfil an instrumental purpose but, at some time during the film, we discover the unintended despair and/or anger that this 'object' now feels. The neutrality of science, or the scientist, and the rhetoric about efficiency or progress, are revealed as dangerous arrogance as the creat(e)ure turns out to be both a tragic victim and a violent dysfunctional machine.

These 'don't mess with nature' themes are common enough in science fiction and horror, but in contemporary cyborg films they are given added impact through a visceral focus on bodily destruction or reassembly. Though this was again one of the elements in early Frankenstein films – brains in jars and so on – the contemporary technologies of film allow the exploration and explosion of bodies to be entirely different in its impact. The two Shinya Tsukamoto films *Tetsuo: The Iron Man* (1989) and *Tetsuo II: Body Hammer* (1991) illustrate these themes in graphic detail. Through car crashes, sex, medicine, experimentation and violence the textures of meat and metal, *nervous systems*[3] and machine systems, are continually combined in brutal ways. Nerves become wires, oil is saliva, limbs are tubes, the penis a drill. Respectable and bespectacled Japanese 'salarymen' push metal into their bodies and mutate into violent rusty cyborgs that groan and sigh as they batter each other into submission. These two are extreme examples but in all of these films flesh is penetrated, sliced, crushed, dissolved as the bodies of cyborgs and humans are subjected to extreme violence. In sum, it would seem that cyborg films show us something about our fears of science's impact on our bodies. To be more specific, they show us something about male fears and desires – there are few female cyborgs and most of the male ones have hard (not leaky) bodies (see Featherstone and Burrows, 1995). We may admire their capacity for physical violence or their good looks but, as with the original Frankenstein film, we are supposed to feel both horror and pity towards these mutant creations of science. According to this reading these are morality tales for the twentieth century.

Now I don't want to suggest that this interpretation of cyborg films is wrong, but I do want to add something to it. I want to do this by looking in more detail at where the science comes from because it seems to me that, in these films and others, the real enemy is no longer science in the abstract, or the single Dr Frankenstein, but the big corporation or state that sponsors them. The demonology of big organizations in science fiction is a topic that, to my knowledge, hasn't received a great deal of attention (though see Burke's, 1989, Corbett's 1995, and Jameson's, 1995, comments on Cronenberg films). However, it is a theme that has been central to much recent fantastic fiction. Spy dramas, such as the Bond films and the *Man from UNCLE* had the organizations SPECTRE and THRUSH, respectively, as their most enduring enemies. These were external enemies, thinly disguised versions of the KGB. However, latterly it seems that many of the plots in programmes like the *X Files*, *Babylon 5*, *Deep Space 9* or *Wild Palms* are premised on a high degree of paranoia about the actions of the internal corporate élite or the military–industrial complex. Similarly, films like *THX 1138* (1970), *Soylent Green* (1973), *Rollerball* (1975), David Cronenberg's remake of *The Fly* (1986) and its sequel *The Fly II* (1989), as well as *Total Recall* (1990) contain very clear references to the corporate interests that structure their worlds. In *Rollerball*, for example, the hero Jonathan is lectured by a senior corporate executive when he refuses to be retired from an exceptionally violent gladiatorial game. As with many sequences like this, the representative of the organization argues that something has to be the case because this is the corporate interest. In response, the hero asserts their individualism and stresses the immorality of whatever particular action is being under-taken. A bureaucratic utilitarianism meets an obstinate kind of virtue ethic and the moral usually seems to be that the ends do not justify these particular means.

An excellent illustration of these themes comes from the Alien trilogy: *Alien* (1979), *Aliens* (1986) and *Alien 3* (1992). The company, the Weyland–Yutani Corp. ('Building Better Worlds'), wants an alien back on earth because, as Carter Burke, the company's representative in the second film tells us, it would be 'worth millions to the bio-weapons division'. The company will sacrifice anyone and employ any means to achieve its goal. The films are replete with conflict between the highly individualistic Ripley and the corporation. In the first film, Ash – again a company representative who turns out to be a 'synthetic' – tries to kill her by pushing a pornographic magazine down her throat. The second film contains a boardroom meeting at which Ripley is disciplined for not being aware of the 'dollar value' of the alien-infested spaceship she left to crash. The phrase is repeated later in the film as a justification for not blowing up the L426 installation that is now populated by aliens. Ripley's righteous anger at Burke's attempt to get her and a small girl impregnated by the aliens later in the film leads her to condemn his corporate morality. 'You know Burke – I don't know which species is worse. You don't see them fucking each other over for a goddam percentage.' In the final film she, now carrying the last alien in her stomach, commits suicide rather than allow the creature to fall into the company's grasp. The cold, twisted organization people who work for Weyland–Yutani seem the real monsters in these films. The alien is merely following its nature, while they precipitate the killing through their greed.

Though the Alien trilogy has cyborg characters – Ash a villain, Bishop (from the second film), a hero – the monsters were not constructed by the corporation. The cyborg films are very similar in organizational demon-ology, but the relation between the monster/cyborg and its maker is rather different. In *Robocop*, for example, the cyborg is struggling between asserting an individuality – as Murphy, the policeman whose body was used to make the cyborg – and his status as 'product'. This central dilemma is built into his very programming.

Directive 1: Serve the Public Trust
Directive 2: Protect the Innocent
Directive 3: Uphold the Law
Directive 4: Classified

This last directive was inserted by a corrupt executive at Omni Con-sumer Products (OCP) and prevents 'our product turning against us'. As the film shows, Omnicorp's corporate office towers 95 storeys over the crime-ridden streets of Detroit. The company has traditionally invested in markets regarded as non-profit – hospitals, prisons, and now law enforcement – through the Security Concepts Inc. division because 'shifts in the tax structure have created an ideal atmosphere for corporate growth'. This is a city almost owned by OCP and bearing the imprint of its previous corporate patron; the Henry Ford Memorial Hospital and Lee Iaccocca Elementary School are given passing mentions, while a showdown takes place at the now abandoned River Rouge plant, Ford's showpiece factory in the 1920s.

The narrative takes us into the heart of this vision of a commercial world in which executives do anything to climb the career ladder, observe the washroom status hierarchy and talk a corporate newspeak to conceal the basic immorality of what they are doing. As one of them put it, Murphy 'volunteered' for the cyborg programme by dying. In fact, he was killed by a criminal employed by an OCP executive who had 'placed prime candidates according to risk factor'. In the second *Robocop* film the difference between the criminals and the executives is even slimmer, partly because they talk the same language. The drug godfather 'offer[s] our customers the opportunity to control every aspect of their emotional lives' and celebrates his business for the social good it does: 'do you know how many people we employ?' Even patriotism gets brought in, the drugs are marked 'made in America' because 'we're going to make that mean something again.' The plot of *Robocop 2* hinges on OCP and the drug cartel attempting a hostile takeover of Detroit because it will be better run in the hands of 'responsible private enterprise'. However, corporate justice is such that, even when they are discovered, a few middle-range employees are sacrificed and the top executives manage to get away with no blame.

Yet, despite the best efforts of OCP, in both films Murphy/Robocop manages to overcome his product status and stand up for individual judgement against corporate utilitarianism. He never forgets who he really is. His singular personhood and sense of duty stand out against collective corporate values and he resists violence, psychological manipulation and even disassembly. He refuses to be a 'unit', a 'product' and insists on being Murphy. The guilty here are those organization people who have sold their conscience for a dollar, who refuse to take responsibility for their actions, who try to convince him to believe that he is 'a machine . . . nothing more'. As with the conformist salaryman in the *Tetsuo* films, the obedient military scientists in *Universal Soldier* or Weyland–Yutani employees in the *Alien* films, the condemnation is aimed at the employee who follows the company line. The cyborg themselves cannot really be blamed because, as the drug dealer in *Robocop 2* tells Murphy, 'I don't blame you. They programme you and you do it . . . I forgive you.'

Robocop and the Universal Soldier remember that they are really human but the T101 in *Terminator 2* (1991) becomes more human through contact with 'real' humans. He is a machine through and through – we can see how he was constructed – but his warmth and humour and his 'learning circuits' allow him to become more than just a robot. Importantly, like Ripley, he ends up sacrificing himself in order that Cyberdyne Systems will not be able to produce the technology that causes the machines to wage war on the humans. Yet again, the corporation is the cause of the threat and it takes a humanized robot to ensure that Cyberdyne does not make huge profits by accidentally destroying humanity. 'I know now why you cry' he says, before lowering himself into a vat of molten metal. Jane Connor, the woman both threatened and saved by Terminators, sums up the paradoxical humanism of the film: 'if machines can learn the value of human life then maybe we can too.'

Perhaps the most extreme example of this moral identification can be found in *Blade Runner*.[5] The cyborgs here are 'replicants', engineered by the Tyrell Corporation to do hard and dirty work on other planets. Unfortunately for the corporation, these manufactured proletarians are rebelling and some have escaped to Earth. The Nexus-6 replicants are top-of-the-line models (perfect 'skin jobs') with implanted memories that can only be detected through 'empathy tests'.[5] They are, apart from their capacity for ultraviolence, all but human. Deckard, who may be a replicant himself but thinks he is human, is employed to hunt these cyborgs down and kill them but suffers something of a crisis after falling in love with one of them who also believes that she is a human being. The factual and ethical confusion that the film relies on allows us to blur the boundaries between 'humans' and 'machines' in a way that privileges neither. However, the clearest moral position in the film is that taken by Roy, the leader of the replicants, when he visits the Chief Executive of the Tyrell Corporation to demand an explanation for their existence. As in *Robocop*, the product then kills the corporate executive. Again, however, our sympathies are with the replicants. They did not ask to be made as they are – self-conscious but with a four-year lifespan. Their agony and anger was inflicted by the managers in a big organization. Their violence is a revolutionary revenge, not merely an act of random brutality.

In general, then, it would seem that these films are certainly part of the long tradition of 'mad science' films. However, it is not only science that is the culprit or threat here but the fact that the scientists and their laboratories are owned and controlled by large companies or state bureaucracies. In spatial terms, we have shiny buildings and rusting heaps of industrial waste, guarded corporate enclaves and decaying inner cities. The immoralities of the big corporation have spawned both the techno-monsters and the urban nightmares. Cyborgs are designed to deal with a corporate problem – programmed to work, to fight, to police, to spy on the company's behalf. These are perfect employees, mobile versions of the production robots that employers already use to replace mere flesh. No doubt Frederick Taylor would rather have worked with a cyborg to refine scientific management than have to cajole continually some recent migrants who could barely speak English. However, this employee/product turns out to be rather ungrateful. Its own 'humanity', its memories, its conscience, its individuality motivate it to turn against its makers. In classical mythology, the story of Pygmalion suggests the opposite. The King of Cyprus makes an ivory statue of his ideal woman and, after praying for divine intervention, the god Aphrodite brings her to life for him. On seeing King Pygmalion the statue falls in love with him and they marry. Clearly, the cyborg myth is rather a different one. The cyborg is not grateful to be created because its creators have shallow and callous motives. Marge Piercy's novel *Body of Glass* (1992) expresses this well. Her cyborg is a weapon with a conscience and it is precisely this 'human-ness' that causes it to be destroyed by the inhabitants of one of the corporate fortresses. In the films I have looked at, the villain, the bad creator, is essentially the capitalist organization and the romantic response is a violent form of rebellion. But what happens if we stop treating these films as texts to be decoded? What happens if we start to think a little harder about cyborgs?

Cybernetic Organization

While I am, at one level, quite persuaded by the analysis put forward in the previous pages I can see some ways in which it is positively unhelpful. On the one hand, we have the strangely humanoid and humanist cyborgs – Robocop, T101, Roy and Bishop – the synthetic with behavioural inhibitors from *Aliens*. These characters begin to know themselves, make jokes – 'I may be synthetic but I'm not stupid' – and gain our trust and understanding. On the other hand, we have these big corporations – Tyrell, Omnicorp, Cyberdyne Systems, Weyland–Yutani and so on. These are organizations populated by utilitarian capitalists, power-hungry careerists or selfish researchers. In a sense, there is no humanity here, merely economic imperatives and the language of strategy, accounting and marketing. The problem, it seems to me, is that the divide between people and things is firmly in place here. The representations are of good and bad humans, good and bad machines and good and bad forms of organization as *if these things were somehow different.* So, can the word 'cyborganization'[4] help us here?

Think about organization first. Organizing involves making patterns that endure in some way. When we organize something we give it a shape, a direction, a meaning. This is not to say that this pattern necessarily lasts, that the 'pool of order' coheres for very long (see Law, 1994), but it is to point to the importance of looking at organizing as a process, not as a finished outcome (Cooper and Law, 1995). However, when we make these patterns we almost always make them with human and non-human bits and pieces. An organization is therefore a lattice of people and things that make some kind of sense to a number of people. The things (the non-human things) may be fairly simple – uniforms, coffee machines, desks, paper – or complicated – computer systems, office blocks, articulated lorries and so on. Taken together they make a network, a moving mobile, a temporary state of affairs that we can call an organization. Now this surely means that meat and metal are not that radically different. We couldn't *do* 'manager', 'academic', 'reader' or 'cinema audience' if it wasn't for all the various props and accessories that allow us to perform such roles.

It also suggests that things become things when they are organized by us. Take ink, paper, printing presses, word processors, telephone and a hundred other things and they can enable this lump of material in front of you. The lump of material can then be made into a book by relating to it in particular ways. When you 'use' the material, holding it in your hand, scanning it with your eye, then you become a reader and the lump becomes a book. Another way of putting this is to say that you become a cyborg – a temporary assemblage of person and things. There may not be metal inserted into your flesh but, at the moment, you are constituted through a cyborganized relationship. More obvious examples are easy enough to find: wearing spectacles, riding a bicycle, typing on a word processor, watching a film. All these relationships involve conceptual and material connections that allow certain kinds of activity to take place. In other words, we are all *cyborgs*,[1] always.

It would seem then that *cybernetics*[2] is not only a kind of robot-science but a way of understanding the relationships between various kinds of information and communication, various kinds of patterns. Cyborganization is therefore not just a thing, or even a collection of things like actors, buildings, projectors and celluloid, but a continually shifting set of relationships. The openness and mutability of these relationships is what allows for the production of art/efacts, like *cinemas*[5] and films. After all, if the relationships were fixed, then only one form of production could exist and only one kind of product could be produced. This, in a metaphorical way, is the essence of the endless dichotomy between Fordist, mechanical, modern or bureaucratic representations of organization versus post-Fordist, organic, postmodern or flexible formulations. In other words, all organization is both sides of these impossible divides at once, both stable and flexible, systematic and *nervous*.[3] It has to be that way if both repetition and innovation are to be possible, and they always are because one would make no sense without the other.

Another way of putting all this is to say that organization is the systematic distribution and redistribution of organs, both human body parts and manufactured tools. For my purposes, they are conceptually the same thing since they both embody some notion of intentionality or purpose, a physical or conceptual relationship between the organs of a system. The organs of the cinematic cyborg and the organs of the corporate body are not that dissimilar in terms of a relationship between parts of a 'system', in the loosest sense of that word. This way of thinking about technology and organization clearly moves us away from either a calculative view of systems in which humans are irrelevant – 'a dream of absolute clarity' – or one in which human intentions are sovereign – 'the revenge of sociologists, psychologists, ethnographers, hermeneuticians, management experts, organizational scientists and other "softies"'. Rather, we should be considering the 'impossibility of allocating humanity and non-humanity in the first place' (Latour, 1995: 299–300).[4] The distributions and delegations of cyborganization are all different ways of connecting information, not information as messages transmitted from A to B – from film to eyes and ears to brain – but as mobile patterns of repetition and difference. The organization of flesh and other things that constitute the social is hence predicated on these shifting divisions and unities.

Preface to the Contingent Supplement

> As a technified, schizoid subject, Robocop symbolises the disintegration of the bourgeois humanist ego, its ruination in the postmodern

scene of toxic poisoning, technological deprival, surveillance and body invasion.

Best, 1989: 50

Well, perhaps. In this chapter so far I have tried to confound the expectations of some readers by moving steadily away from the idea that cyborg films 'mirror' some kind of reality 'out there'. Cultural analysts, like Best, would no doubt like to have a monopoly over that project but I doubt its very foundations. I simply don't recognize their rhyme or reason. After all, cyborg films don't tell us anything about the world. Neither does film or the cinema in general. The world of cyborganization simply is; it doesn't ask to be understood, framed or ordered. We might expect or want the world to be like that but there is no intrinsic meaning to events, no position from which academics (like the ones who wrote the book you are holding) can insist on their particular version of the world with any authority other than rhetoric. The supplement usually tell a different story after all. Or the same story in different words.

As should be clear by now, I believe that the danger of a focus on the spectacular cyborg and the demonology of the organization is that it presents a dichotomy where one doesn't really exist. This is particularly true in political or ethical terms. After all, the singular heroism of the revolutionary cyborg is based on a (masculine) romantic individualism that does little to address the constitution of (capitalist) forms of organization. Cyborganization, whether repressive or emancipatory, is constituted through some kind of partial connection or conversation between human and non-human actors. Enduring, and morally driven, social change should therefore not assume the primacy of Murphy-type human(ist) heroes. In a cyborganized world, there is no one place where guilt and redemption can be located. At the same time, however, I am intrigued and seduced by the cyborg's form of resistance, by its refusal to accept the utilitarian 'bottom line' within the corporate body that created it. After all, just because the cyborganized world doesn't ask to be understood or judged I don't think it follows that understanding or judgement doesn't happen (Parker, 1995, 1996). On the contrary, they are a part of the pattern-making, and so too are your, my and the cyborg's judgements about particular forms of organization. At the end of the film, if I have to choose, I'm usually a cyborg on the side of the cyborgs.[1] But, then, my judgement makes me nervous.

M.P.

PART II

Contingent Supplement

1 Cyborg Manfred Clynes (Clynes, 1995; Clynes and Kline, 1995) neologized the term cyborg from 'cybernetic organism' in 1960. Clynes, a neurophysiologist and space scientist, researched the development of 'artefact–organism systems' – cyborgs – in order to free astronauts from routine flight-maintenance, so 'leaving man free to explore, to create, to think, and to feel' (Clynes and Kline, 1995: 31). Clynes saw the cyborg as human prosthesis, as a device for augmenting human powers.

While Clynes's cyborg was a tool devised for humanistic goals, Donna Haraway (1991) portrays the cyborg as 'a *hybrid* of machine and organism' in which the separate terms of machine and organism dissolve into a miscegenation that is 'multiple, without clear boundary, frayed, insubstantial' (1991: 177). Less of a thing and more of a process, Haraway's cyborg realizes itself through the 'plasticity of informational patterns (e.g., databases, electronic money)' which makes 'possible the combinational play of matter and thus the continuous disassembly and reassembly of new forms and patterns' (Cooper and Law, 1995: 268). Haraway's cyborg thus engenders a space of infinite patterning through telecommunications technology, computer design and database construction. Biotechnology is the exemplary science of the cybernetic organism because it translates living organisms into 'problems of genetic coding and read-out . . . In a sense, organisms have ceased to exist as objects of knowledge, giving way to biotic components, that is, special kinds of information processing devices . . . The world is subdivided by boundaries differentially permeable to information' (Haraway, 1991: 164). In contrast to Clynes's anthropomorphic cyborg which perpetuates the traditional subject–object dichotomy, Haraway's cyborg relativizes 'the difference between living and mechanical systems' and radically challenges 'the line of demarcation drawn between the natural and the artificial' (Johnson, 1993: 105).

2 Cybernetics Briefly defined, cybernetics is the science of communication and control in humans, animals and machines. Where communication and control means *organization*. Cybernetics views organization as a measure of structure, pattern. The practice of organization is thus understood as the construction and maintenance of pattern out of chaos, dissipation. It's the *continuous* work of maintaining pattern or order in a continually dissolving world. Or, as Norbert Wiener (1954: 86), the founder of cybernetics, puts it:

> Our tissues change as we live: the food we eat and the air we breathe becomes flesh of our flesh and bone of our bone, and the momentary elements of our flesh and bone pass out of our body every day with our excreta. We are but whirlpools in a river of ever-flowing water. We are not stuff that abides, but patterns that perpetuate themselves.

So, organization is the reproduction of patterns, stability, in a context/ contest of permanent change, instability. But Wiener means more than this. Cybernetic patterns move across different domains; they are acts of ordering which translate food into flesh and bone, flesh and bone into working bodies, bodies into machines, and so on. Cybernetic organization as stabilities-in-movement denies the fixed term, the specific location, the subject–object dichotomy.

> The effect of cybernetic explanation, the modelling of human mental processes on mechanical control systems and vice versa, is to relativize the difference between living and mechanical systems, pointing towards a theory of complex systems in general. The philosophical implication of cybernetic theory would therefore tend to be a certain parenthesis of the anthropological or the anthropomorphic. . . . (Johnson, 1993: 105)

As the cybernetic thinker Gregory Bateson (1973: 454) argues, 'The mental world – the mind – the world of information processing – is not limited by the skin'. Human agents are not simply minds or 'bodies that inhabit the universe' (Virilio, 1994: 27). Instead, according to the cybernetic view, agents 'become *bodies inhabited by the universe, by the being of the universe*' (Virilio, 1994: 27). Thus, human agents do not simply live *in* the world, they do not simply *use* tools, nor do they simply *consume* food and air. To be 'inhabited by the universe', by its 'being', means that the agent is a temporary term or position in an ever-active matrix of order–disorder. So, to summarize: cybernetic organization means three things: (a) ordering, patterning; (b) patterning or organizing *between* apparently different systems, e.g. body–tool–environment; and (c) the continuously active and never-ending process of ordering.

Two further points need to be made about the order–disorder relationship. The first concerns the general bias to think order and disorder as *separate* forces in opposition to each other, as if the act of separation, of thinking biplicitly, were itself a form of reassuring order and control. The second point – and more important to our argument here – concerns the historical privileging, especially in the development of modern science, of order over disorder, as if order were somehow 'naturally' primal and transcendent, as if disorder were the degradation of a pristine and originary state of harmony. In a related discussion, Ilya Prigogine (1989) has noted a similar fate in the history of the concepts of stability and instability. In modern science, says Prigogine, 'The notion of instability has been ideologically suppressed' (1989: 396) and glossed in favour of determinism and control. But recent work in science has supported the cybernetic view that stability/order and instability/disorder are mutually constituting forces: 'order and disorder are created simultaneously' (1989: 398). Such systems are called *strange attractors*, where stability and instability are mixed. Living can only be understood by means of strange attractors – complex systems whose complexity is characterized by a correlative stability–instability. And, as we shall later argue, it is this complexity, this complicity, that describes such man–machine systems as modern cinema.

There's another way of framing the order–disorder relationship – through that branch of cybernetics called 'information theory'. Cybernetic information is defined by the idea of probability: information is what is *least probable.* In other words, information is inversely proportional to its probability. The less likely a message or event, the more information it provides. Novelty and surprise thus constitute information. As Wiener (1954: 105) puts it: 'a piece of information, in order to contribute to the general information of a community, must say something substantially different from the community's previous stock of information.' There's also the implication here that information as novelty or surprise is vital to a community's life; as if the community as an information system would die without the stimulation of the new. From this, an important general principle emerges: all human agents are 'open', they necessarily depend on unpredictability and surprise.

Wiener's (1954) coupling of information with community is further illustrated in Umberto Eco's (1989) essay, 'Openness, information, communication', which discusses information theory in relation to the communal role of art. Eco argues that unpredictability and novelty are vital to the artistic experience and will. The artist, especially the avant-garde artist, is compelled to contravene convention in order to provide artistic power – or informational vitality – both to him/herself and the community. But the community is also pulled in the direction of order and control. Order is necessary and what's necessary comes to be seen as the 'natural order of things'. Yet openness to information and disorder is not merely just as 'natural' as the closure of order but *logically constitutes the order–disorder of things.* Like Prigogine, Eco asserts the *necessity* of novelty and surprise to openness. New life, the possibility of sur-vival, is *necessarily* the creation of new information.

Cybernetic organization/information is thus 'living form in the making' (Goodwin, 1994), where *making* is the continuous mixing of order–disorder. Equally, we might call it 'self-organized criticality', 'an excitable medium', or even the 'edge of chaos' (Goodwin, 1994), all terms that dramatize the transitional *in-betweenness* of the order–disorder nature of organization/information.

3 Nervous System   Michael Taussig (1992) introduced the metaphor of the Nervous System to describe the restless and even restive nature of the modern world: a system of *nervousness*, in fact. Taussig's Nervous System is an extension of the idea of cybernetic organization to the complexities of the social–economic–political world. Like Prigogine (1989), Taussig underlines the *mutuality* of order *and* disorder:

> I am referring to a state of doubleness of social being in which one moves in bursts between somehow accepting the situation as normal, only to be thrown into a panic or shocked into disorientation by an event, a rumour, a sight, something said, or not said – something that even while it requires the normal in order to make its impact, destroys it. (Taussig, 1992: 18)

This mutuality or doubleness of social being is a 'desperate place between the real and the really made-up' (Taussig, 1993: xvii), between fact and fiction, stability and instability. It's a place of biplicit thinking[2] where we have to act as if conventional order were the norm: 'We dissimulate. We act and have to act as if mischief were not afoot in the kingdom of the real and that all around the ground lay firm' (Taussig, 1993: xvii). So, the Nervous System problematizes the normal, makes us see it as a strange attractor,[2] a place of correlative stability–instability where – and this is the significance of Taussig's argument – instability is culturally and cognitively *censored* just like Prigogine's (1989: 396) critical observation on modern science in which 'the notion of instability has been ideologically suppressed.' But Taussig goes further: what we *normally* think of as fact or the real is a state of fictions or 'dream-images' – 'hopelessly hopeful illusions of the intellect searching for peace in a world whose tensed mobility allows of no rest to the nervousness of the Nervous System's system' where 'immense tension lies in strange repose' (Taussig, 1992: 10).

The nervousness and fictionality of the Nervous System is also Gianni Vattimo's (1992) theme in his analysis of the late-modern *society of generalized communication* in which the proliferation of the mass media and information technology stimulates a perpetual condition of 'oscillation' and 'shock'. The society of generalized communication is a society of cybernetic organisms,[1, 2] centrally defined by a range of technologies (including cinema)[5] constructed to transmit information: 'it is primarily and essentially defined by systems collecting and transmitting information' (Vattimo, 1992: 15). And, significantly, information itself is subject to the same dissembling logic that characterizes Taussig's doubleness of 'the real and the really made-up': for 'in-formation' is both that which *informs* or *enfirms* and that which *un-forms* or *in-firms*. Mutual stability–instability. Information thus becomes an 'excitable medium', a process at 'the edge of chaos' (Goodwin, 1994), expressing the nervousness of the Nervous System. We see the emergence of such collapsing and condensing forms in Vattimo's (1992: 16) idea of the 'contemporaneity' of the contemporary world. Contemporaneity doesn't just mean events that happen at the same time. It suggests both compression and interlacing – a co-involvement in space *and* time. For Vattimo, the special nature of late-modern technologies of communication and information transmission is their production of 'contemporaneity'. Vattimo's 'contemporaneity' is a version of Walter Benjamin's (1970: 225) portrayal of modern methods of mechanical reproduction: 'Every day the urge grows stronger to get hold of an object at very close range by way of its likeness, its reproduction.' As Taussig (1993: 36) points out, this is another way of expressing Benjamin's 'insight into mimesis as the art of becoming something else, of becoming Other', mimesis as the 'sensuous connection with things', where the body and its senses blur with their objects of contact. Such continuous merging and dissolution of subject and object is Taussig's way of calling attention to the 'nervousness' of 'contemporaneity' and which, for Vattimo, eventually leads to the 'unfounding' of what Taussig (1993) calls the dissimulated firmness of reality. 'The advent of the media enhances the inconstancy and superficiality of experience . . . it allows a kind of "weakening" of the very notion of reality' (Vattimo, 1992: 59) – the nervousness of the Nervous System.

Benjamin's (1970) characterization of mimesis emphasizes the process of *'becoming* something else'. It's not the 'something else', the other term, that needs to be understood but the very act of mimesis itself. And to show us how this works, Taussig (1993) draws on an early paper by the French sociologist Roger Caillois (1984, but first published 1935) which discusses mimesis in terms of the simulation of space, i.e. Vattimo's 'contemporaneity'. Caillois notes a general tendency for living organisms to simulate aspects of their environment; for example, leaf insects resemble leaves. But it would be better to say that *space simulates* organism and environment. Or, following Virilio (1994), that organisms are 'bodies inhabited by the universe, by the being of the universe' rather than 'bodies that inhabit the universe'.[2] On this view, space is not simply a distance between two points but a *beckoning-becoming void* – a 'temptation by space', as Caillois (1984: 70) calls it. In humanistic terms, there is loss of self: 'Then the body separates itself from thought, the individual breaks the boundary of his skin and occupies the other side of his senses . . . He feels himself becoming space, *dark space where things cannot be put*. He is similar, not similar to something, but just *similar*. And he invents spaces of which he is "the convulsive possession"' (Caillois, 1994: 30). He becomes *nothing*, no thing, in this assimilation to space. Mimesis is the dispossession of identity by similarity. It's when the 'informing' of information becomes 'unforming'. Built into the Nervous System itself, mimesis *compels* the agent to invent 'spaces of which he is the "convulsive possession"'. As though abducted by space. Not just a 'nervous' idea but a 'scary' one, as Taussig (1993: 34) notes. And, what's more, an idea that helps us see Haraway's (1991) *cyborg* in a different light. The miscegenation of machine and organism that characterizes the cyborg now becomes interpretable in terms of Benjamin's 'insight into mimesis as the art of becoming something else, of becoming Other' (Taussig, 1993: 36), as well as expressing Vattimo's (1992) '"weakening" of the very notion of reality'.

Nervous System, society of generalized communication, mimesis, cyborg – all, in their different ways, draw attention to the *medium/media* of technology. Not medium/media in the popular sense of the specific forms of communication media – TV, radio, cinema and so on – but the 'un-form' of what Taylor (1995) calls the *mediatrix* or media matrix: the complex, fleeting, unstable connections and multiplicities that defy conventional logic and analysis. Ostensibly, the mediatrix is 'that which is constituted by the intersection of electronic media and compu-telecommunications technology' (Taylor, 1995: 25). Latently, the mediatrix is beyond formal comprehension, can only be alluded to, precisely because it is literally *medium/media*, literally in the middle, between: 'the mediatrix is nothing but the middle' (Taylor, 1995: 32). And, significantly, the middle is a *muddle,* a confusion: 'The structure of the real is indistinguishable from the structure of the medium. In more familiar terms, the medium is not only the message but is nothing less than reality itself' (Taylor, 1995: 26). Neither beginning nor end (but *both* beginning *and* end), neither here nor there (but *both* here *and* there), neither this nor that (but *both* this *and* that), the medium as middle is the hybridism of the cyborg, the de-definition of form wrought by mimesis, the collapsing forms of 'contemporaneity', and the 'excitable medium' of the Nervous System.

4 Cyborganization Short for cybernetic organization.[2] Where organization is the construction and maintenance of pattern, form, out of chaos, dissipation, the *continuous work* of maintaining pattern in a continually dissolving world.

Cyborganization is the complicity/complexity between human agents and machines that makes continuous pattern-making possible. The historical development of human cognitive systems reflects this cyborganizational complicity/complexity. As the neuropsychologist Merlin Donald (1991) shows, the modern mind is a hybrid of organism and external 'cognitive architectures' such as the alphabet, writing, calendars, clocks, maps, and so on: 'We act in cognitive collectivities, in symbiosis with external memory systems' (Donald, 1991: 382). In this sense, cyborganization is the *externalization* of mind through what Donald (1991) calls External Symbolic Storage devices, which include cinema and computers: 'the individual mind has long since ceased to be definable in a meaningful way within its confining biological membrane' (1991: 359). Moravec (1988) calls this a 'postbiological world': 'Humans evolved from organisms defined almost totally by their organic genes. We now rely additionally on a vast and rapidly growing corpus of cultural information generated and stored outside our genes – in our nervous systems, libraries, and, most recently, computers' (Moravec, 1988: 3–4). Clearly, the culture of External Symbolic Storage and the 'postbiological world' are also versions of Vattimo's (1992) society of generalized communication.[3] In these hybrid systems, what does hybridism mean? What does cyborganization mean by the hybrid? First, we must note that the cyborganizational hybrid is *not* anthropomorphic; it is not an extension of the human agent. We might just as readily say that the agent is an extension of the machine: 'it becomes immaterial whether one says that machines are organs, or organs, machines. The two definitions are exact equivalents' (Deleuze and Guattari, 1983: 285). Equivalence and non-distinction is the first feature of the cyborganizational hybrid. The hybrid is the *middle* of the mediatrix (Taylor, 1995).[3] The hybrid as middle is never a locatable place or term; we can't say it's *in* the middle. It's always *on its way* somewhere, always in movement, always *becoming.* 'To become is never to imitate, nor to "do like", nor to conform to a model . . . There is no terminus from which you ought to arrive at . . . For as someone becomes, what he is becoming changes as much as he does himself'

(Deleuze and Parnet, 1987: 2). This is how we are meant to understand Haraway's (1991) cyborg – not as a thing-like structural 'hybrid of machine and organism' but as a process of becoming in which the cyborg is 'multiple, without clear boundary, frayed, insubstantial' (Haraway, 1991: 177). The cyborg moves at 'the edge of chaos' where it is 'living form in the making' (Goodwin, 1994), sur-viving, living-on, becoming: 'In a sense, organisms have ceased to exist as objects of knowledge, giving way to biotic components, that is, special kinds of information processing devices' (Haraway, 1991: 164). Hence, it's not the objects nor the components but *information as becoming* that marks the cyborganizational world: a 'world subdivided by boundaries differentially permeable to information' (Haraway, 1991: 164). And not *merely* 'permeable *to* information', for information as process, as becoming, is itself constituted by 'subdivision', 'boundary', and 'difference', terms which are not only different ways of saying information but implicitly contain the idea of informational order–disorder as a doubly or mutually composed *interfold*, i.e. the mimetic hybridism of Caillois's notion of the 'similar'. In other words, subdivision, boundary and difference are versions of mimesis and hybridism; spaces where similarity and difference are knotted together, strangely doubled, in an 'unfinished heterogeneity' (Cooper and Law, 1995: 269) of parts and whole. Cyborganization is the re-production of such 'unfinished heterogeneity': 'cybernetic organization/information has one feature that is most interesting: it remains forever "unfinished". *It remains forever unfinished precisely so that it can keep on going*' (Cooper and Law, 1995: 267). Information as *becoming*. Viewed thus, information has no destination; it doesn't go anywhere since it has nowhere to go; it simply keeps on moving, all the time maintaining its differences, its spaces of mimetic division. Division is *always* unfinished. This is the point of Jacques Derrida's (1987) well-known study of the postal system, in which he subjects the 'postcard' and its transmission to an informational-mimetic analysis. The conventional understanding of the postal system is that it transmits information – letters, postcards, and so on – from sender to addressee; it supposes a direct line between the two and thus a perfect system of communication (although admitting that occasionally letters may *accidentally* go astray). The postal system thus occults the significance of the space of division between sender and addressee. For the postal system, the sender and addressee constitute the communication process and division is simply a barrier to be overcome; for Derrida, the space of division constitutes communication, out of which sender and addressee form/firm their identities. Derrida's version of the postal system is a Nervous System, an 'excitable medium', whose space has the same character as Taylor's (1995: 34) *mediatrix*: 'Within the mediatrix, things neither come together nor fall apart. Circuits are not closed but open, constantly changing, and repeatedly shifting. Governed by neither the inclusive logic of both/and nor the exclusive logic of either/or, (the middle) apprehends that which stands between'.[3] Such a space 'resists reflection', says Taylor, precisely because of its unfinished heterogeneity, or, in the cybernetic language of Bateson (1973: 419), 'the cybernetic nature of self and the world tends to be imperceptible to consciousness' because consciousness, like the postal system, works in terms of linear purpose and identity whereas cybernetics recognizes the latent agency of the hybrid, interlacing 'circularities of the self and the external world' (1973: 420). So the postal system is that cultural and cognitive system of censoring noted by Taussig (1993) and Prigogine (1989),[3] a place of dissimulated reality, of 'immense tension . . . in strange repose', where the unfinished heterogeneity of information as division is 'a debased, lateralized, repressed, displaced theme, yet exercising a permanent and obsessive pressure from the place where it remains held in check' (Derrida, 1987: 270). Mutual stability–instability again. All this makes the postal system a site of 'self-organized criticality' on 'the edge of chaos',[3] a site that is permanently divided from itself, in the divisions between the printed and written letters, words and sentences on the postcard between the artist's design and the printer's impress, between the manufacturer's production run and the public's purchase, between the sender and the addressee – a series of points marked by the struggle between order and disorder, stability and instability; where possibilities of deviation, drift, errancy, of things going wrong, *interfold* with the requirements of direction, plan and rectitude. Derrida's reinterpretation of the postal system reveals it as a divided state of being, a collection of discrete elements that *neither fit nor do not fit together*, parts that must remain apart so that they can *suggest* (but not realize) completeness. And where the transmission of information is the repetition and iteration of this divided space, this unfinished heterogeneity.

It's this sense of information – information as division – that Italo Calvino (1987) conveys in an essay, 'Cybernetics and ghosts', in which the late-modern world is seen as a cybernetic space of 'discontinuity, divisibility, and combination' (1987: 9), where discrete elements – letters, words, numbers – can be endlessly permutated and combined. As if to recall Taylor's mediatrix as a space that 'resists reflection' and Bateson's cue that cybernetic processes are 'imperceptible to consciousness', Calvino links the possibilities offered by the infinite (i.e., unfinished) permutability and combinability of elements to the unconscious. The unconscious is the 'unexpected meaning or unforeseen effect' – Taussig's (1992) 'nervousness of the Nervous System' and Vattimo's (1992) 'oscillation' and 'shock'[3] – 'which the conscious mind would not have arrived at deliberately' (Calvino (1987: 21). Here, Calvino puts his finger on the sub-versive character of cyborganization: the repetition and iteration of divisions as discrete parts that differentially combine to create new, unfinished 'wholes'. Again, it's *information as becoming*. Calvino's cybernetic machine is also Haraway's cyborg which realizes itself through the 'plasticity of informational patterns (e.g. databases, electronic money)' which make 'possible the combinational play of matter and thus the

continuous disassembly and reassembly of new forms and patterns'
(Cooper and Law, 1995: 268).[1]

5 Cinema From the Greek *kinema*, movement. Conventional
approaches to cinema distinguish between *film* (the screen and the
moving images projected on to it) and *cinema* itself, which covers the
economic, technological and cultural system of production and reception
that serves to realize film. In its filmic sense, cinema is viewed as a visual
medium or art form which simply serves to represent something –
reality, a story – for someone, and which, like Derrida's postal system,
assumes a model of communication based on identity. But, as we've
already hinted, cinema can also be viewed as a cybernetic technology in
which the human agent and the machine form a hybrid in an
informational complex of stability–instability.[2, 3]

This is how Merlin Donald (1991) understands cinema: as a form of
cyborganization, a hybrid of organism and external 'cognitive architectures', which, along with TV and computers, constitutes the 'machinery'
of 'the hybrid modern mind' (Donald, 1991: 382, 355). And, in the different intellectual context of late-modern ontology, it's also how Gianni
Vattimo (1992) sees cinema in his society of generalized communication:
as a technology of information transmission that *performs* the social and
cultural mind, not just the communication of reality but its expression and
performance: 'The structure of the real is indistinguishable from
the structure of the medium. In more familiar terms, the medium is not
only the message but is nothing less than reality itself' (Taylor, 1995: 26).
This, too, is the philosopher Gilles Deleuze's (1986, 1989) interpretation of
cinema: reality as medium, medium as motion. Cinema, for Deleuze, is
'the machine assemblage of movement images' (Deleuze, 1986: 59). But
it's more than that – it's a technological version of human life and culture:
'it is the universe as cinema itself, a metacinema' (1986: 59). While cinema
represents life, life re-presents itself as cinema, i.e. as movement. Cinema,
body, brain and thought together constitute a cybernetic organism, a
technological nervous system, 'a cinema of the brain' (Deleuze, 1989: 204).
It's not the conventional idea of the film-goer viewing a film for the
purpose of entertainment. For Deleuze, the film-goer wants to *become* part
of the cinematic environment in which cinema, body and brain make up a
cyborganizational experience.

> One way of becoming a machine is to hook yourself up to one: video games,
> media, television, the new nonumbilical telephones (that transmit through
> walls), etc. This technology is described by some as an external nervous system
> connected to us by a variety of devices that radically change our sense of time
> and space. (Jardine, 1987: 155)

The conventional view of cinema is that it is a window on the world; it's
assumed to *represent* some aspect of the world. In Deleuze's view,
cinema is not about representation; it's not *what* we see but that *with*

which, according to which, we see: 'The structure of the real is indistinguishable from the structure of the medium. In more familiar terms, the medium is not only the message but is nothing less than reality itself' (Taylor, 1995: 26). Cinema is thus *medium* in the most literal sense and as such is beyond formal comprehension, can only be alluded to because it is literally in the *middle,* between, and so without intrinsic order or direction.[3]

Deleuze interrogates the representation/medium distinction in cinema through the *audiovisual* character of film: 'There is a distinction between speaking and seeing, between the visible and the articulable: "What we see never lies in what we say", and vice versa . . . the audiovisual is disjunctive . . . it is not surprising that the most complete examples of the disjunction between seeing and speaking are to be found in cinema' (Deleuze, 1988: 64). Speaking articulates the *meaning* of a figure or event; it represents it in a systemic or narrative form. Seeing reveals only the visual form of the figure, without the help of words that name the structure. A hidden tension lies here: can we read the words *and* look at the letters that constitute them *at the same time*? Can we see a film as representation *and* as medium *at the same time*? Deleuze's answer is no: representation and medium, the articulable and the visible, are in necessary conflict: 'the audiovisual battle, the double capture, the noise of words that conquered the visible, the fury of things that conquered the articulable' (Deleuze, 1988: 112). This is cinema as Nervous System, or Taussig's (1993) doubleness of social being and its dissimulated firmness of reality. Taylor's (1995) contrast between the specific forms of media – TV, radio, cinema – and media as mediatrix also helps us to understand Deleuze's antagonism of the articulable and the visible. The *specific* media *represent*; the mediatrix simply *mediates* without any necessary order or direction.

Cinema as representation-articulation works according to a hierarchy of original and copy where the original has both a temporal and a 'truth' value over the copy, so that the original is thought of as cause, and copy, effect. But the argument from the medium-visible perspective denies such cause-effect direction:

> There can never be an original until there is a copy, which retrospectively creates the 'originalness' of the original. There can never be an original until there is a copy of it. In a sense, then, the original can be said to be constituted by the copy, just as cause and effect . . . can be reversed, from a temporal perspective, once we realize that it is always the effect that comes first, causing us to look for its cause. (Brunette and Wills, 1989: 74)

Nor does this mean that the copy creates the original, since that would be just another form of representation-articulation and the positing of yet another hierarchy: 'Rather, the relation between reality and, say, a documentary on it, would be displaced and redefined such that the two terms came to be seen as mutually constituting each other. The relation between them would thus be an intertextual one' (1989: 75). It's the

equivalent of Deleuze's (1986) idea of meta-cinema: while cinema represents life, life re-presents itself as cinema. And this, of course, is also
Taylor's (1995) mediatrix whose *middle* is a *muddle* since it has no one
direction, no hierarchy.[3]

The dissolution of direction, order, is a definitive feature of cyborganization. As we've said, equivalence and non-distinction comprise the first
feature of the cyborganizational hybrid. It's what Vattimo (1992: 59) calls
'oscillation' and 'disorientation' in the society of generalized communication where the proliferation of media technologies creates 'a kind of
"weakening" of the very notion of reality' which now 'presents itself as
softer and more fluid'. Vattimo cites Walter Benjamin's diagnosis of
cinema as the technical reproduction of an increasingly inconstant and
superficial reality. What's more, says Vattimo, modern cinema draws
attention to its own deconstructive role in the production of such
cyborganizational 'nervousness'. He cites Ridley Scott's *Blade Runner* as a
film that foregrounds the sense of 'contemporaneity'[3] and representational necrosis created by the new cyborg technologies. For Vattimo,
Blade Runner is not so much a science-fiction *story* but more a disclosing
of Deleuze's (1988) antagonism of the articulable and the visible in which
the 'combinational play of matter and thus the continuous disassembly
and reassembly of new forms and patterns' dominates (Cooper and Law,
1995: 268).

The cultural historian Mark Poster (1990) captures Vattimo's sense of
representational necrosis in his analysis of human–computer interaction:
'Computer science . . . is a discourse at the border of words and things' –
hence it illustrates Deleuze's articulable-visible conflict:

> a dangerous discipline because it is founded on the confusion between the
> scientist and his or her object. The identity of the scientist and the computer
> are so close that a mirror effect may very easily come into play: the scientist
> projects intelligent subjectivity onto the computer and the computer then
> becomes the criterion by which to define intelligence, judge the scientist,
> outline the essence of humanity. (Poster, 1990: 148)

And Poster reports the anxiety of one computer scientist that 'we run
the immense risk of being unable to recognize when we are becoming the
subjects of the instruments we created to be our subjects' with the comment that: 'Artificial intelligence and human intelligence are *doppelgängers*,
each imitating the other so closely that one scarcely can distinguish them'
(Poster, 1990: 148–9). Here again we meet Benjamin's (1979) idea of
mimesis, the process of '*becoming* something else', where it is not the
'something else' that needs to be understood but the very act of mimesis
itself as 'a science of mediations – neither Self nor Other but their mutual
co-implicatedness' (Taussig, 1992: 45), mimesis as mediatrix.[3] Neither the
scientist nor the computer, neither the film-goer nor the film, but their
mediation. When Haraway (1991) defines the *cyborg* as 'a hybrid of
machine and organism', it's not the machine or the organism that specially

interests her but their *hybrid* mediation.[1] This is a different space from the ordered representations of the articulable where every image or copy has a meaningful referent or original. It's space without order or direction, in which terms constitute each other as equals; it's the space of the visible that refuses articulation, where figure cannot precede ground nor subject dominate object. Together, the two spaces – the articulable and the visible – add up to Deleuze's (1988) 'audiovisual battle'.

The space of hybrid mediation, of the visible, of the cyborg, differs in another significant way. Unlike the space of the articulable, ordered by the speaking subject, the space of mediation is preconscious, primitive. This is what Calvino (1987) and Bateson (1973) mean when they say that the cybernetic organism/machine works at the level of the unconscious and when Taylor (1995) describes the mediatrix as a space that 'resists reflection'.[4] It's also Benjamin's (1970) way of understanding the mimetic nature of modern methods of mechanical reproduction (including cinema) which rely upon the synthesis of vision and touch – the 'optical unconscious', as Benjamin calls it, where the eye (as bodily organ) merges mimetically with the cinematic images: 'not merely our sensous blending with filmic imagery, the eye acting as a conduit for our very bodies being absorbed by the filmic, but . . . the eye grasping . . . at what the hand cannot reach' (Taussig, 1992: 146). Hence tactile vision, which is unconsciously compulsive as in Caillois's (1984) exposition of mimesis as the loss of the self through 'temptation by space'.[3] Both hand and eye are seemingly incomplete and so compelled to make connections beyond themselves – another version of the idea that the transmission of information is the repetition and iteration of divided space.[4] Unfinished heterogeneity again but with a difference, for Benjamin's optical unconscious portrays the body as part of a more general process of the transgression of boundaries, distinctions. The eye does not merely *see* the film image – it merges with it (and takes the body with it). It's when *vision* becomes *fusion*, where vision–fusion is the space of the visible that refuses articulation. And it's this that prompts Vattimo to cite Benjamin's analysis of cinema as the technical reproduction of an increasingly inconstant and superficial reality. At the level of the visible, Benjamin's reproduction technologies con-fuse the real and its representation-articulation. For precisely this reason, cybernetic organization has to be understood as the reproduction of pattern, stability, in a context/contest of permanent change, instability. As we've seen, cybernetic organization denies the fixed term, the specific location, the subject–object dichotomy and insists that the human agent is a temporary-tentative term or position in an ever-active matrix of order–disorder.[2] Deleuze (1988) expressed the same idea in his image of the 'audiovisual battle' where representation-articulation is a *contesting* of the real.

Poster's (1990) computer scientists are also caught up in a *contest* to preserve their sovereign human agency from 'contamination' by the machine (just as realist cinema insists that the film-goer 'sees' film as the conventional representation of a real event or story). At stake here is perhaps the ultimate *test*: are machines human (and, inversely, are humans no more than machines)? In one sense, Haraway has already answered this question: 'The machine is not an it to be animated, worshipped and dominated. The machine is us, our processes, an aspect of our embodiment' (1991: 164). But the question will never be answered that simply, not least because it contains a necessary and intrinsic contest between the unitary identity claimed by representation-articulation and the unfinished heterogeneity of the medium-visible. The contestatory aspect of this incompatibility is raised in the computer scientist Alan Turing's (1950) famous question: Can machines think? For Turing, the answer lies in the act of *imitation* (we would say mimesis, or even becoming) and not in trying to understand the intrinsic properties of 'machine' and 'thinking'. In other words, the test of whether a machine can think like a human being lies not in the specific nature of human intelligence (whatever that is) but in the extent to which the machine can imitate human behaviours. This is why Turing is careful to devise a way of operationalizing the question so as to reveal the work of imitation *per se* rather than the subject and object of the imitation. Like Deleuze (1988), Turing wants to escape from the space of representation-articulation so that the space of the medium-visible can emerge.

Turing's test consists of what he calls the 'imitation' game, which is played with three people: a man, a woman, and an interrogator (of either sex). The interrogator's task is to identify, through strategic questioning, who is the woman; the man's task is to confuse the interrogator by imitating the behaviour of a woman. The interrogator's only contact with the other players is through their typewritten responses to the questions. The Turing test then substitutes a computer simulation (imitation) for the man. If the computer can successfully simulate the man's task by completely confusing the interrogator, then the computer can be said to think like a human being. In effect, the Turing simulation tests (and con-tests) the representational-articulation view of the world, which assumes the existence of more-or-less stable identities, by subverting conventional categories (of intelligence and human-ness), by denying the distinction between practice and thought (theory), and by 'pushing the boundaries of the known and familiar almost to destruction' (Wood, 1988: 221). Thus Turing enables us to see cyborganization in a different light: that of *test* and *con-test*. Haraway's (1991) cyborg is not simply 'multiple, without clear boundary, frayed, insubstantial', it also actively contests the unitary categories and hierarchical divisions of conventional form. Prigogine's (1989) mutual stability–instability becomes mutual contestation.[2] Taussig's (1992) Nervous System and its 'doubleness of social being' is also a site of contest between the norm and the ab-norm. Derrida's (1987) postal system contests the unfinished heterogeneity of *division* as 'a debased, lateralized, repressed, displaced theme' which exercises 'a permanent and obsessive pressure from the place where it remains held in check' (Derrida, 1987: 270).[4] Cybernetic organization/information, which earlier we called 'self-organized criticality' on the 'edge of chaos',[2] can now be more clearly seen as *test/con-test*.

The test/con-test of Turing's simulation is repeated in Vattimo's (1992) contention that modern cinema is the technical reproduction of an increasingly inconstant and superficial reality. And, as we've noted, Vattimo cites the film *Blade Runner* as an example of contest between the representation of stable identity and the intertextual doubling of mimetic instability. At the level of representation, *Blade Runner* tells the story of a small group of android replicants in a Los Angeles of the twenty-first century, who, having illegally returned to Earth from Mars, are targeted for elimination by a hired bounty hunter. The androids represent a genetically advanced type, endowed with abilities and capacities equal, and even superior, to those of human beings. The critical problem for the bounty hunter is to distinguish the androids from the real humans before destroying them. In effect, the film repeats the essential features of the Turing simulation. At every step, the decidability of what's human/natural and what's unhuman/artificial is in question. To help make (and thus *confirm*) these distinctions, the bounty hunter applies an empathy test, designed to elicit differences in empathic capacity between androids and humans in response to a series of set questions. Here, let's note that the empathy test literally *makes* the desired distinctions and does not simply record what is *already* there. In other words, it's a test that con-tests or attempts to force a decision in a situation that seems intrinsically undecidable. In contrast, the Turing test con-tests or attempts to force an 'indecision' in a situation that seems so obviously decidable.

The test/con-test of Turing and *Blade Runner* repeats Deleuze's (1989) discussion around Kant's famous ontological question, 'What are we?' The con-test in the film is between those who think they know the answer to this question (the humans like the bounty hunter who 'know' they're 'human') and those non-human, technological forces (symbolized in the androids) which deny such absolute divisions and thereby suggest that the question is fundamentally inappropriate. Deleuze himself replies to the question by also denying that it's answerable in terms of the simple binary opposition: we're human, you're machines. He goes on to argue (here following Michel Foucault) for the thesis that 'Man is dead' and that the '*surhomme*' (the 'more-than-Man') has begun to make its appearance with the impact of cybernetics and information technology by which 'the forces within man enter into a relation with forces from the outside, those of silicon which supersedes carbon, or genetic components which supersede the organism' (Deleuze, 1989: 131–2). This creates a cyborganizational field of forces and forms which Deleuze calls an 'unlimited finity' (we might also call it a field of unfinished heterogeneity) in which 'a finite number of components yields a practically unlimited diversity of combinations' (1989: 131). Clearly, Deleuze's 'more-than-Man' is Haraway's (1991) cyborg which, as we've seen, realizes itself through the 'plasticity of informational patterns' which 'make possible the combinational play of matter and thus the continuous disassembly and reassembly of new forms and patterns' (Cooper and Law, 1995: 268).

Deleuze's unlimited finity appears in *Blade Runner* in many guises. The inhabitants of its cityscape speak a hybrid language of English, Japanese, Spanish, German, and so on. The viewer is thus reminded that language itself is a variable combination of letters that in this case burst through the order imposed on them by word and sentence. *Blade Runner*'s polyglot dramatizes our earlier question: can we read the words *and* see them as media *at the same time*? In other words, it's Deleuze's con-test of the audiovisual again. Unlimited finity appears also in the form of the genetically engineered androids which are products – like the humans from whom they're copied – of combinations of genetic components, the chains of the genetic code, which 'supersede the organism'. In *Blade Runner*, in Deleuze, in Haraway, our attention is constantly drawn to the cybernetic information out of which things are made, and the conflict between speaking and seeing which this engenders for the human agent.

These insights help us to see *Blade Runner* as an example of Deleuze's view that cinema is not just a window on the world, is not simply about conventional representation, is not *what* we see but that *with which, according to which,* we see. No longer an opening onto a transparent visual field, cinema/film is a surface on which moving data are inscribed, on which information can be received, recorded, and transmitted onwards. And, borrowing from the art theorist Leo Steinberg's comments on the painter Robert Rauschenberg, Deleuze (1989) compares cinema/film to a surface that stands 'for the mind itself – dump, reservoir, switching centre, abundant with concrete references freely associated as in an internal monologue – the outward symbol of the mind as a running transformer of the external world, constantly ingesting incoming unprocessed data to be mapped in an overcharged field' (Steinberg, 1972: 88). In short, cinema as *kinema*, nervous system, nervousness.

R.C.

References

Bateson, G. (1973) *Steps towards an Ecology of Mind*. London: Paladin.

Benjamin, W. (1970) *Illuminations*. London: Jonathan Cape.

Benjamin, W. (1979) 'Doctrine of the similar (1933)', *New German Critique*, 17: 65–9.

Best, S. (1989) 'Robocop: the recuperation of the subject', *Canadian Journal of Political and Social Theory*, 8: 44–55.

Brunette, P. and Wills, D. (1989) *Screen/Play: Derrida and Film Theory*. Princeton, NJ: Princeton University Press.

Burke, F. (1989) '"How'd you like to disappear?" Theorizing the subject in film', *Canadian Journal of Political and Social Theory*, 8: 25–43.

Caillois, R. (1984) 'Mimicry and legendary psychaesthenia', *October*, 13: 17–32.

Calvino, I. (1982) *If on a Winter's Night a Traveller*. London: Picador.

Calvino, I. (1987) *The Literature Machine*. London: Picador.

Clynes, M. (1995) 'Cyborg II: sentic space travel', in C.H. Gray (ed.), *The Cyborg Handbook*. London: Routledge. pp. 35–42.

Clynes, M. and Kline, N. (1995) 'Cyborgs and space', in C.H. Gray (ed.), *The Cyborg Handbook*. London: Routledge. pp. 29–33.

Cooper, R. and Law, J. (1995) 'Organisation: distal and proximal views', *Research in the Sociology of Organisations*, 13: 237–74.

Corbett, J.M. (1995) 'Celluloid projections: images of technology and organizational futures in contemporary science fiction film', *Organization*, 2: 467–88.

Deleuze, G. (1986) *Cinema 1: The Movement Image*. London: Athlone.

Deleuze, G. (1988) *Foucault*. Minneapolis, MN: University of Minnesota Press.

Deleuze, G. (1989) *Cinema 2: The Time Image*. London: Athlone.

Deleuze, G. and Guattari, F. (1983) *Anti-Oedipus: Capitalism and Schizophrenia*. Minneapolis, MN: University of Minnesota Press.

Deleuze, G. and Parnet, C. (1987) *Dialogues*. London: Athlone.

Derrida, J. (1987) *The Post Card: From Socrates to Freud and Beyond*. Chicago: Chicago University Press.

Donald, M. (1991) *Origins of the Modern Mind*. Cambridge: Cambridge University Press.

Eco, U. (1989) *The Open Work*. London: Hutchinson.

Featherstone, M. and Burrows, R. (eds) (1995) *Cyberspace, Cyberbodies, Cyberpunk*. London: Sage.

Goodwin, B. (1994) *How the Leopard Changed its Spots*. London: Weidenfeld and Nicolson.

Gray, C.H. (ed.) (1995) *The Cyborg Handbook*. London: Routledge.

Haraway, D. (1991) *Simians, Cyborgs and Women: The Re-invention of Nature*. London: Free Association Books.

Jameson, F. (1995) *The Geopolitical Aesthetic: Cinema and Space in the World System*. Bloomington, IN: Indiana University Press.

Jardine, A. (1987) 'Of bodies and technologies', in H. Foster (ed.), *Discussions in Contemporary Culture*. Seattle: Bay Press. pp. 151–8.

Johnson, C. (1993) *System and Writing in the Philosophy of Jacques Derrida*. Cambridge: Cambridge University Press.

Latour, B. (1995) 'Social theory and the study of computerised work sites', in W. Orlikowski, G. Walsham, M. Jones and J. DeGross (eds), *Information Technology and Changes in Organisational Work*. London: Chapman and Hall.

Law, J. (1994) *Organizing Modernity*. Oxford: Blackwell.

Moravec, H. (1988) *Mind Children: The Future of Robot and Human Intelligence*. Cambridge, MA: Harvard University Press.

Parker, M. (1995) 'Critique in the name of what? Postmodernism and critical approaches to organization', *Organization Studies*, 16 (4): 553–64.

Parker, M. (1996) 'Shopping for principles: writing about Stoke-on-Trent's Festival Park', *Transgressions: A Journal of Urban Exploration*, 2 (3): 38–54.

Piercy, M. (1992) *Body of Glass*. London: Penguin.

Poster, M. (1990) *The Mode of Information: Poststructuralism and Social Context*. Cambridge: Polity Press.

Poster, M. (1992) 'Robocop', in J. Crary and S. Kwinter (eds), *Incorporations*. Cambridge, MA: MIT Press. pp. 436–40.

Prigogine, I. (1989) 'The philosophy of instability', *Futures*, 21: 396–400.

Ramsaye, H. (1926) *A Million and One Nights: A History of the Motion Picture*. London: Frank Cass.

Steinberg, L. (1972) *Other Criteria: Confrontations with Twentieth Century Art*. New York: Oxford University Press.

Taussig, M. (1992) *The Nervous System*. New York: Routledge.

Taussig, M. (1993) *Mimesis and Alterity: A Particular History of the Senses*. New York: Routledge.

Taylor, M. (1995) 'Rhizomic folds of interstanding', *Tekhnema*, 2: 24–36.

Tudor, A. (1989) *Monsters and Mad Scientists: A Cultural History of the Horror Movie*. Oxford: Blackwell.

Turing, A. (1950) 'Computing machinery and intelligence', *Mind*, 59: 433–60.

Vattimo, G. (1992) *The Transparent Society*. Cambridge: Polity Press.

Virilio, P. (1994) *The Vision Machine*. London: British Film Institute.

Wiener, N. (1954) *The Human Use of Human Beings: Cybernetics and Society*. New York: Houghton and Mifflin.

Wood, M. (1988) 'Signification and simulation: Barthes's response to Turing', *Paragraph*, 11: 211–26.

12

Computers and Representation: Organization in the Virtual World

Warren Smith

Virtual reality. Cyberspace. Gibson's (1984) 'consensual hallucination' has proved a compelling and influential image. Indeed, its power to generate considerable enthusiasm is matched only by an equal proclivity to produce cynicism and profound boredom. This chapter examines the cultural treatment of the computerized representation of alternative environments by virtual reality systems. We find this a fertile ground for speculation. A popular interpretation emphasizing the transcendental possibilities offered by artificial worlds is contrasted with an analysis of their conceptual underpinnings. We find that, far from transcendence, virtual reality offers a pure form of 'organization' in which every decision and action is completely, and literally, accountable.

However, casting ourselves as enthusiasts for a moment, reaching for hyperbole, we may choose to treat virtual reality as a fundamental leap forward, the creation of a new medium offering the promise of a simulated reality more convincing, more beguiling, than conventional representations. Through this technology we are offered the promise of producing artificial environments able to convince us that we are inhabiting another place. One day we might traverse computer generated landscapes, awash with the sights and sounds of our favourite places. Alternatively, we are offered arenas within which prototype buildings may be designed and tested, computer-generated doll's houses with limitless furnishings. Cyberspace offers a realm with a multiplicity of uses, a shared space through which we can transcend geographical separation: indeed, a 'virtual organization' in which we can go about our daily business. Our enthusiasm will know no bounds. We are drawn completely into the simulated world. We have attained, through virtual reality, the final phase of McLuhan's (1964) extension of man, the technological representation of consciousness.

Faced with such boundless eagerness it is easy to be cynical. Put on a virtual reality helmet today and the response is likely to be akin to being trapped in a rather poor cartoon. It may well be difficult to reconcile the hype with the experience of cumbersome three-pound headsets and rather slow computer graphics. Surfing the internet certainly tries the

Figure 12.1 The Coroner's Dream from the VR Installation Archeology Mother Tongue by Toni Dove and Michael Mackenzie sponsored by the Banff Centre for the Arts

patience: a painfully slow trawl through what seems like pages of irrelevant trivia. Are we forced to conclude that these are merely futuristic novelties, destined to go the way of all fads? Or that interest is merely the product of a 'rhetoric of corporate hype coupled with a romanticism filtered through popular science fiction' (Markley, 1994a: 435)? Alternatively may we be the impatient witnesses of the embryonic stages of a technology of fundamental importance?

Pioneers continue to make optimistic noises, insistent that virtual reality does not suffer from the same basic technical difficulties that have plagued similarly ambitious, overpublicized programmes of the past. Artificial intelligence is a prime example. In contrast, the basic technology is available, and has been since the early 1960s. Progress is restricted, not by conceptual inadequacy, but by a lack of computing power that is easily remedied (Pimentel and Teixeira, 1993). Indeed, Milton Krueger, an early innovator, maintains that the prophesying of intellectuals has only followed the production of working systems (Krueger, 1991: xvi). Thus our conjectures enjoy a degree of technological foundation.

However, the extent of these speculations has led to a proliferation of definition. Markley (1994a: 433) notes that 'virtual reality' is increasingly used as a catch-all term covering everything from e-mail to video-game cartridges. In its most restricted sense, it can refer to that configuration of hardware in which a helmet containing video monitors is worn by a user. Images are transmitted through the monitors so that the user is entirely surrounded by a three-dimensional virtual world. Furthermore, as the user moves his or her head, a computer translates the movement and updates the image to take account of these positional changes. As a result, the system does not allow the user to shake the illusion by turning his or her head away (Benedikt, 1991). Other senses are also liable to be appropriated by the hardware. Data gloves are under development in order to allow the movement of our hands to be recognized, and through force feedback systems, to give virtual objects a tactile sense. The goal of virtual reality is therefore to simulate, through technology, the 'full ensemble of sense data' that make up experience (Woolley, 1992: 5). A technological vision of this ultimate goal is a system based on direct neural input. Computers would attempt to bypass the sense organs and send information directly to the brain. For example, retinal imaging envisages the use of a computer-guided laser beam with the capability of activating the rods and cones in the eye in order to 'paint' an image (Aukstakalnis and Blatner, 1992: 302). The ultimate replacement for head-mounted units is optimistically forecast to be a pair of spectacles in which a laser scanning device is positioned (Krueger, 1992: 77). This persuades O'Sullivan (1994: 298) to suggest that, in virtual reality, 'there is no media between the viewer and the illusory world; illusion is maintained into the nervous system.'

Yet we may shy from definitions tied to a particular configuration of technology. For example, Steuer (1992: 76) seeks a definition of virtual reality by considering the notion of 'presence'; that is, the sense of being in an environment. While many forms of representation have this quality – books may in some sense transport us to other worlds – virtual reality creates a form of *tele*presence in which computers are the means of our transportation, either by being the communication medium or by actually generating an environment. Biocca (1992: 6) produces a similar definition, suggesting that virtual reality refers to any computer-simulated environment in which the user feels present. In this, it is used as a psychological variable, a measure of the conviction of the simulation. In this approach, e-mail and the proposed full sensory simulation would both be examples of virtual reality, but of different magnitudes.

Therefore, we find that there are a number of concepts associated with the term. Given this confusion, Heim (1993) sets himself the objective of identifying the essential dimensions of virtual reality by examining a number of central ideas. First, he notes the frequent emphasis on 'simulation' since the increase in definitional capability of computer graphics makes it possible to produce representation with a high degree of realism. Perhaps in time this will be indistinguishable from reality. Yet this hardly presents a radically new form of representation for this is merely cine-realism, albeit generated by a different medium. We can envisage computer actors able to be programmed to perform unperformable feats, but is this 'virtual reality'? It seems that another dimension must be added to our definition. Heim (1993) maintains that virtual reality insists on the existence of a degree of 'interaction'; therefore, it embraces any electronic representation with which a user can interact. Thus there has to be a movement away from one-way causality: the user must be able to influence proceedings. However, this remains rather general. We do not necessarily believe that we are entering virtual reality when we copy a file, yet this manoeuvre meets the criteria of our current definition. Heim offers a means of improvement by suggesting the importance of 'immersion'. Virtual reality, therefore, should have the capability to appropriate sensory perception and control what is perceived. This leads to the previously expressed notion of 'telepresence', that the commandeering of our senses allows us to be placed in an electronic environment. We may be physically located in our offices and living rooms, but our senses are fed with information from another place. Immersion is achieved when we are persuaded, to a greater or lesser degree, that we are occupying a non-physical environment.

For the present, we may restrict the term 'virtual reality' to refer to a computer system in which devices, like headsets and data gloves, are used with the objective of providing a 'complete' sensory experience. 'Cyberspace' we may take to be a more general term referring to the arena created by computer media. To enter virtual reality is also to enter cyberspace. However, cyberspace may also refer to less encompassing digital experiences – for instance, interacting through e-mail or navigating the internet.

Nevertheless, we might still wonder why futuristic visions of computer-simulated worlds have attracted so much attention. Is it because they offer a vision of what our future will be like? Is our interest stimulated by the feeling that soon our everyday lives will be infused by another, virtual, world? We might not be restrained by technical infeasibility for it seems that immersion in high-definition, computer-generated worlds is a realistic prospect. Thus we cannot summarily dismiss virtual reality on the grounds of technological infeasibility. We are told that 'everything informational and important to the life of individuals and organizations will be found for sale, or for the taking, in cyberspace' (Benedikt, 1991: 2). Furthermore, current prototype systems have been found to engender strong emotional responses associated with their real-world equivalents, even though their performance is marred by poor graphics and inadequate response times. For instance, a virtual racquet ball game produced responses similar to those displayed in the real world. Tension, the competitive urge and tantrums are all on show (Aukstakalnis and Blatner, 1992).

Possibly, our interest is partly stimulated by the general attraction of technology. Computers, it seems, offer a particular allure. Heim (1993: 85) suggests that we are captivated by the clear-cut, linearity of their processing. Their capacity for reducing complexity, capturing and controlling knowledge, offers a world without the confusion of our everyday lives. There is something clinical, clean and simple that makes the virtual world attractive. Yet, for these reasons, we also fear technology. The familiar fears of being overwhelmed with information, of losing our identity through the triumph of logic are magnified in cyberspace. In a nightmare scenario, virtual reality will lead us into losing our sense of reality, submerging us within a purely artificial world (Schroeder, 1993: 8). The dystopic visions of William Gibson and *Blade Runner* become real.

However, it seems that the cultural response to virtual reality has tended to ignore this pessimistic scenario. Typically, Biocca (1992: 6) suggests that there is something about its perceived potential that has particular resonance, that somehow it connects with a desire for freedom from physical restraint, indeed from reality itself. As Heim (1993: 86) puts it, 'a desire to extend our finite being'. Consequently, this chapter contends that virtual reality is more usually viewed as part of a re-enchantment of science and is presented with something approaching emancipatory zeal. Virtual reality is seen as a means of achieving, through science, new forms of expression and mystic experience. In Heim's terms (1993: 124) it 'promises the Holy Grail', while for Schroeder (1994: 524) it is a form of technology offering no less than transcendence. Let us investigate this idealism.

Embracing the Virtual

> On the other side of our data gloves. We've become creatures of coloured light in motion, pulsing with golden particles. Forget about Andy Warhol's petty promise of fame for fifteen minutes. We will all become angels, and for eternity! Highly unstable, hermaphrodite angels, unforgettable in terms of computer memory. In his cubic fortress of pixels that is cyberspace, we will be as in dreams . . . Just press the key ENTER. (Stenger, 1991: 52)

An enthusiastic statement. It embodies a tendency to view virtual reality as offering transcendental possibilities: lying beyond the computer interface is a world of freedom and opportunity. Somehow it proposes a 'free space' in which participants can exercise self-expression and self-discovery (Laurel, 1991). Porush (1994: 553), admittedly with a degree of reservation, recounts some of these prospects: cyberspace promises to unite art and technology; it will bypass the body, thereby empowering the disabled and eliminating discrimination; in capturing the world's data, it will facilitate universal education and through universal access will reinvigorate democracy by offering non-hierarchical freedom of expression and personal contact. As a result, virtual reality is treated as something more than a piece of technology with mundane improving consequences. It is not merely a better computer interface, nor an improved means of communication, it is something that can actually transform our lives.

Consequently, it seems almost taken for granted in the literature that virtual reality has the capacity to pose fundamental questions: that it presents 'a metaphysical laboratory, a tool for examining our very sense of reality' (Heim, 1993: 83). It is portrayed as offering the opportunity to transcend normal visions of reality: a heavenly city made real, affording escape from the bounds of everyday existence and allowing the achievement of free will (Benedikt, 1991). It will also inevitably challenge our notions of our own world and its simulation. Entering the virtual realm compels us to embrace issues of perception and representation, as we are forced to reconcile our body and mind (Elkins, 1994: 250).

It is perhaps in the relationship between the mind and body in cyberspace that we find the origins of this mysticism, for in the virtual world we are supposed to escape the restrictions imposed by our earthly bodies. Indeed, Gibson (1984) contributes a graphic depiction of the future redundancy of the physical body: without the enhancement of cyberspace we are merely 'meat'. If, as Tomas (1991: 32) suggests, cyberspace 'overthrows the organic architecture of the human body' then we may be released from our earthly form. Accordingly, Stenger (1991: 56) speaks of the possibility of 'resourcing yourself', for virtual reality offers the beguiling prospect of a fountain of youth from which we may drink when we strap on our headsets. In this world, we can assume abilities beyond our earthly capacity; indeed, we are no longer confined to our everyday identity. We can be who we want to be. Stone (1991:

109) suggests that to 'enter cyberspace is to physically put on cyber-space'. Thus, if we are male, then we can become female.

Unshackled from our physical bodies, we therefore become tran-scendent; we take a new digital form with the freedom and power of angels. In fact, we are offered the supreme power of creating worlds, for virtual reality offers the potential to design our own convincing realities. Dreams can be realized, since our representations will be limited only by our imagination. For Lanier, a virtual reality pioneer, it is 'an experience when you are dreaming of all possibility . . . that anything can happen' (quoted in Woolley, 1992: 14). And creation itself is freer, representation of thought is offered numerous new possibilities. We may indulge our individuality completely, giving it expression through the production of personalized computer-generated environments. As Novak (1991: 229) dreamily suggests, 'my thought is my arrow. I combine words and occupy places that are the consequences of those words.' It represents a place where 'it-can-be-so' triumphs over 'it-should-be-so.' For in these worlds we are no longer bound by the laws of nature. Even if we accept that there are consistent laws governing our own reality, in the virtual world we may ignore them and create our own. There is no reason why virtual worlds have to follow the ordinary rules of physical reality. We can shape an interaction that is controlled by our own laws of action and reaction. Thus, 'empowered by the personal computer, liberated by VR, the individual becomes God of his or her own universe' (Woolley, 1992: 9). We are offered the chance to be gods, able to change our shape and form at will. Worlds can be created and afterwards we can decide the manner in which they are to be inhabited. Given this, it is appropriate that the original use of 'virtual' was as the adjectival form of 'virtue', where virtue meant to have the power of God (Woolley, 1992: 60) – the power to create worlds.

Furthermore, this power is without cost. In wandering the world without leaving the room, we are able to have experiences without the fear of danger. As Fricke 1994: 277) desires, 'we can reach the sun without melting our wings.' Without our earthly bodies we may take risks without having to bear their costs. While we may create worlds, we can live without fear. We may enjoy an omnipotent infancy.

In these writings we see virtual reality portrayed as an arena in which we can throw off the burdens of our material existence. Freed from the laws of physics and an earthbound existence, we can become tran-scendent. For Benedikt (1991: 5), it offers no less than an opportunity to re-enter God's grace and to sample an experience embracing enlightened human interaction. Of course, this has nothing to do with the virtual reality of today, but it does attempt to connect with a technology that could be. Porush (1994: 538) sees an association with early treatments of space flight, which he identifies as the supreme myth of early science fiction. Clearly resonating with the preceding sentiments, we find a portrayal of a desire for liberation from our earthbound bodies and an elimination of the physical restraints on our experience. Although space flight is now considered somewhat mundane, virtual reality offers a new mythology.

However, it is a mythology in which virtual reality appears to have assumed a rather unlikely rosy hue. Markley (1994a: 435) concisely summarizes this tendency, 'The rhetoric of cyberspace characteristically invokes the pleasure and power of an imaginative world made whole . . . [with] emphasis on fullness, plenitude, and mystical unity. The crucial metaphors used to evoke cyberspace are self-consciously holistic, transcendent, sublime.' However, this rhetoric is rather curious. Even if we allow for its futuristic zeal, it is strange that a diametrically opposed view of virtual reality also readily suggests itself. Nor is it one that merely points to the primitive capacity of present-day technology in order to add a note of realism to the fevered speculation. Instead, we may also look towards a future technology to suggest that virtual reality exemplifies the achievement of a supremely organized form of representation. Consequently, entering a virtual world is to enter a controlled world, a world in which every detail is a planned decision; to join a 'virtual organization' is to be supremely organized. Accordingly, we must acknowledge that the assumptions at the heart of virtual reality rest on a belief in the fundamental mathematical structure of nature, hence, 'nothing exists in the synthetic world that is not literally numbered and counted' (Heim, 1993: 105). Far from re-enchantment, virtual reality assumes that science and technology can gain access to areas of perception and experience previously neglected.

Virtual 'Organization'

Conversely, we may actually be inclined to view virtual reality as a particularly 'lawful' experience. Novak (1991: 242) conceptualizes these 'laws' as being layered. First, the computer hardware running the virtual world is subject to the laws of physics. Secondly, there are the laws produced by the hardware itself; that is, the computer's protocol and its operating system. Then there are the laws governing the conceptual structure of the virtual world being represented; that is, the rules governing their creation. Finally, there are the rules concerned with the operation of the experience and those regulating interaction within the simulated environment. Only then may we consider the preconceptions and desires of those entering cyberspace. They are, of course, all subject to these 'higher' laws.

Furthermore, in the virtual domain these desires are also treated, necessarily so, as subject to consideration through law. As Porush (1994: 547) suggests, the production of convincing virtual realities will depend on the construction of a model of cognition in order to strengthen the power of the simulation. A key task of virtual reality systems will be to understand and predict as much as possible about participant behaviour so that the most appropriate responses can be produced. Indeed, Woolley (1992: 21) goes as far as to suggest that psychology is the physics of virtual reality. Hence, 'just as physics is about revealing the laws that govern the physical realm, so psychology is about revealing the laws that govern the mental or imaginary realm. Virtual reality, then, is about discovering this world as it is determined by these laws.'

Consequently, a virtual world rests on a data-oriented view of perception, in which perception is seen as a matter of data input to the mind from the environment. Therefore, in order to achieve a greater sense of reality, we require greater quantities of data. This results in the body being viewed mechanically as an input device. Consider this description by Rheingold, 'Our eyes are stereo input devices; our eyeballs and necks are sophisticated, multiple degrees of freedom gimbals for moving our stereo sensors' (quoted in Coyne, 1994: 66).

In essence, the conception of perception and representation held by virtual reality is a correspondence view in which a belief exists that the real world can be represented through the application of laws. Accordingly, its feasibility depends on the supposed existence of a numerical basis to human thought (Coyne, 1994: 66–7). While Stenger (1991: 51) suggests that Descartes's world has become brittle, and that 'Cyberspace will shatter it like a mirror', this is clearly contentious. As Markley (1994b: 487) outlines, many speculations have failed to acknowledge the conceptual foundations of virtual reality in twentieth-century mathematics. For instance, with the mechanization of differential equations came the possibility of modelling phenomena; for example, the flight of an aeroplane. Furthermore, by treating flying numerically through recording the degrees on a compass, the knots on an airspeed indicator and the feet on the altimeter and varying these with respect to the pilot's manipulation of the controls, the first flight simulators could be produced (Woolley, 1992: 47). These, of course, are embryonic virtual reality engines. In time, a link was made with graphical representations. Turning the simulator's controls could be coupled with the manipulation of a image. We might be stationary but the ground can be made to move.

Again, we are compelled to acknowledge the centrality of mathematics to cyberspace. Virtual reality can be conceived as being primarily concerned with the mathematization of spatial entities. The generation of computer graphics is dependent on Cartesian geometry. Hence virtual worlds are predicated on the basis of the mathematization of space and the reliance on the rules of perspective. Images are generated by pure mathematical systems of coordinates, while movement is simulated by adding or subtracting from these coordinates (Woolley, 1992: 53–4; Elkins, 1994: 254). Consequently, Coyne (1994: 71) suggests that if virtual reality works then it must be seen as a vindication of one aspect of Cartesian geometry, that space can be reduced to numbers. Indeed, our immersion within computer environments can only be achieved if we, ourselves, are similarly reduced to 'bits' (Novak, 1991: 225). We cannot exist in virtual reality without being transformed in the language of the computer. In cyberspace, 'all reality becomes patterns of information. When reality becomes indistinguishable from information, then even Eros fits the schemes of binary communication' (Heim, 1993: 90). In an artificial world, we will find that even emotions are subject to mathematical interpretation.

Furthermore, the mathematics utilized by virtual reality rests on traditional assumptions. Its logic and metaphysical assumptions seek to reduce complex expression to simple statements. In resolutely following the Platonist tradition, mathematicians believe 'that numbers represent instrumentally simplified or model situations and that they are capable of revealing an underlying order and harmony to the universe' (Markley, 1994b: 496). It is perhaps ironic that such methods are seen as a route to transcendence, for the developers of virtual reality systems are likely to remain unconvinced, or blissfully ignorant, of the philosophical ruminations of cultural theorists. These are the people producing the software, and they remain wedded to contrary notions. They remain deeply suspicious of the cultural 'colonization' of cyberspace (Markley, 1994b: 487). Indeed, Ivan Sutherland, often identified as the progenitor of virtual reality systems, described virtual reality as a 'looking glass into a mathematical wonderland' (quoted in Biocca, 1992: 18). Accordingly, attitudes to the natural world are revealed by the manner of attempts to simulate it. As Schroeder (1993: 10) points out, 'the problem of how we understand reality is linked to the way we recreate reality by means of computer simulation.' For instance, the virtual reality entrepreneur Milton Krueger (1991: 265) suggests that successful simulation may persuade us to believe that we are beginning to understand the laws of nature. Therefore, we are now afforded the opportunity to move from analysis to synthesis: we may create. Thus 'once we have apprehended these laws, we see that they can be used in new ways.' As Markley (1994b: 496) points out, for its proponents 'cyberspace is . . . an instantiation of true forms, real "laws"'. They reason that if we can use mathematics and rules of perspective to represent reality in virtual reality engines, if we can use psychology to 'predict', and organize responses to, participant behaviour, and if we are persuaded, in practice, that these rules and laws may be used eventually to produce representations indistinguishable from reality, then we must have discovered something critical about the physical world itself. Their conclusion is that it must also be underpinned by the same rules.

This then, is, the foundational conviction of virtual reality. Ivan Sutherland again clearly reveals this thinking when he expresses his belief that the 'ultimate display' would be a room in which the computer could control the existence of matter (Biocca, 1992: 18). His intuition is that if geometrical laws can be used to reproduce size and shape then it must be possible to conceive of using mathematical physical laws to reproduce qualities like mass (Woolley, 1992: 21). We are entering the Starship *Enterprise*'s Holodeck, in which, as Heim (1993: 89) suggests, *forms* become the product of *information*.

Of course, this logic may also result in the opposite conclusion. Our continuing failure to produce convincing virtual realities may lead us to the belief that we must also know nothing about reality itself (Aukstakalnis and Blatner, 1992: 283). We may decide that, as the potential amount of input and output data is so large, the complexity required by a persuasive artificial environment is unbounded. Accordingly, simulation might always be beyond the computation power of any computer. Indeed, we may go further and be persuaded to reverse our earlier conclusions about the nature of reality. Maybe cyberspace necessarily involves the production of a technology fundamentally different from those currently conceivable, an 'irrational' technology. Thus, any attempt to represent the many 'irrational' effects of the human mind through existing science will result in failure. It is not possible to describe the brain mechanically (Porush, 1994: 540).

Nevertheless, the base assumption of virtual reality, as it is currently conceived, is a belief in the mathematical structure of the universe. For if we accept that there is a mathematical structure to the universe then we are encouraged to believe that it might be simulated by a computer. A virtual world is an attempt to provide such a computation. Developments in chaos theory and fractal mathematics seem to encourage these sentiments. For example, fractal geometry may be used to provide a more accurate approximation of the forms and structure of natural objects. Thus, 'it can be used to make precise models of physical structures from ferns to galaxies. You can describe the shape of a cloud as precisely as an architect can describe a house' (Barnsley, quoted in Coyne, 1994: 66). Landscapes in computer-generated landscapes are frequently generated with fractal structures. Chaos theory suggests that, although the universe is shown to be complex, new techniques may be outlined that hold the promise of more accurate description and perhaps even offering the possibility of computation (Woolley, 1992: 96; Porush, 1994: 547). Consequently, we see presented the prospect that a better understanding of complex mathematics might enable improved prediction and simulation. It is suggested that calculation of previously intractable phenomena is conceivable. We may not go as far as to draw the implication that 'the entire universe could be simulated and our destiny calculated' (Woolley, 1992: 74). However, this is precisely what is offered in a virtual world, a world constructed entirely through mathematics.

Therefore, we should not ignore the question of control in cyberspace. After all 'cyber' is derived from the Greek word *kyberman* meaning to steer or control (Benedikt, 1991: 129). Far from offering freedom and release, virtual reality may involve a particularly pervasive form of control. This may be examined with reference to Spring's (1991: 7–8) use of control in order to conceptualize the history of the human–computer interface. Our earliest interaction involved little more than the human manipulation of an inanimate object. Here, the computer was merely a machine that carried out repetitive operations, mimicking limited human activity but at a much greater speed. Interaction is limited to the provision, by the user, of an explicit instruction containing no room for deviation. At this point, control clearly rests with the user. The second era is associated with the development of expert systems in which a dialogue between the user and the system is enabled; control is therefore shared. In the third era, the constructed system simulates an environment based on rules and knowledge about that environment. In this case, control resides outside the realm of the computer–human dialogue. The user is only one of many sources of data and is therefore no longer the dominant force in the interaction. Virtual realities clearly fit into this third category: they are a form of interface characterized by an environmental simulation where control largely resides away from the user's influence.

We have seen that an opportunity to assume God-like power has been associated with virtual reality, that a possibility of creating worlds and constructing their laws has been presented. As Heim (1993: 95) suggests, 'What better way, then, to emulate God's knowledge than to generate a virtual world constituted by bits of information? To such a Cyberworld a human being could enjoy a God-like instant access.' But we may ask who is to hold this power? Who is to create and control this world? Are users really free to float as angels? Heim seems to suggest that the real opportunity for God-like power lies securely with the creator of a virtual world. Remember, in a virtual world there is nothing that has 'not been literally numbered and counted' (Heim, 1993: 105). The designer has predicted every move, and is forced to disallow those he or she cannot predict. Therefore, although the participant cannot assume the role of God, he or she knows that someone has. Laplace's demon has found a place in cyberspace.

Again, transcendental romanticism seems inappropriate. A world that is entirely known cannot be romantic, for where is the desire to search and discover when everything is potentially predictable? Thus, 'set up synthetic reality, place yourself in a computer-simulated environment, and you undermine the human craving to penetrate what radically eludes you, what is novel and unpredictable. The computer God's eye robs you of your freedom to be fully human. Knowing that the computer God already knows every nook and cranny deprives you of your freedom to search and discover' (Heim, 1993: 106). There is a sense of being consumed, isolated and controlled in an electronic dream.

Under these circumstances, far from being a source of re-enchantment, virtual reality actually results in disenchantment. In its attempt to control human perception and experience, it seeks to extend the influence of science. In this case technology 'would not only have come to dominate the external world, but could be able directly to manipulate the aware-ness that human beings have of the world, albeit an artificial one' (Schroeder, 1994: 526). Perhaps our interpretations should have remained true to the oppressive vistas of the technology's progenitors, for Gibson (1984) referred to cyberspace as 'an infinite cage'.

In essence, the central issue coalesces around the question of design. We may pursue the possibility of freedom and suggest, as does Stone (1991: 107), that the user is more than just a participant – he or she is also the creator of the simulation. We may conceive of virtual reality as Laurel's (1991: 95) 'empty space'. Or we may more readily accept Krueger's (1991: 7) belief that virtual realities require the designer to accept reduced control, 'to think in terms of a structure of possibilities that leaves the final realization of the piece in the hands of each participant'. However, this is clearly an over-simplification. Information has to be transmitted through some interface, which has its rules, and it is the designer who knows these rules. The designer decides which details are relevant and how they should be presented; user autonomy exists only with respect to elaborate logic trees in which all possible 'choices' are anticipated. Virtual reality can be seen initially, through its emphasis on interaction, as a challenge to the essentially linear tradition of storytelling and the structured methods used in conventional media. However, its plots are still essentially linear, albeit a complex path, but one which has been completely preconceived and entirely mapped. For the designer has 'to take account of all the options a participant might want to avail himself of in a given world' (Pimentel and Teixeira, 1993: 159).

Furthermore, the interface may have a particularly disruptive effect on the experience. Dove (1994: 282) points out that any medium forces us to accept its conventions and structures, but we attempt to ignore them in order to enhance the experience. However, she points out that, ironically, in computer media the fact of interaction may actually lessen the experience. The activity of choice becomes a constant interruption that brings the reader back to the material fact of the text. Similarly, in his discussion of the importance of the 'prompt', or cursor, in computer representation, Truck (1991) makes an associated observation. Thus, the prompt acts not only as a signifier of the presence of the virtual world, but it also lays down a marker identifying a crossroads. It makes a demand for choice but can only accept decisions that it can understand and provide a response; it must assume that the user knows certain things. The prompt is therefore a request for standard knowledge. In many ways there is a contradiction here, for while the interface needs to be as transparent as possible in order to heighten the experience, it is also required to operate, visibly, in a fashion that allows the participant to understand his or her relationship to the process and, indeed, its rules of interaction.

Though we may assume that there will be nothing as obtrusive as a prompt, in virtual reality we will find plenty of signs that our experience is purely artificial. Inevitably, there will be other consequences of the interface that will disrupt our experience. The interface will frequently cause our digitized mind to be reacquainted with our physical body. Thus, 'that chafing is the remainder of the various quotients of the organic and inorganic, the irrational surd that is left over when the digitized, abstracted, mechanized, morphed, desexed body is recalled to its original fallen "meat"' (Elkins, 1994: 252). In other words, often we will probably feel quite sick.

However, it is the very existence of interaction, albeit interaction that is completely organized, that allows virtual reality to be treated as offering the potential for becoming a radical form of representation. Although we have been forced to concede that this interaction is largely controlled, it still exists and this may separate it from other media. As Biocca (1992: 11) points out, the 'viewers are now in the TV set'. Indeed, virtual reality is frequently examined with reference to this comparison, portrayed as a medium with the potential to be more powerful than television. It has been estimated that if we use virtual reality for the same amount of time that we currently watch television then we will spend almost 20 years of our life in an artificial world (Biocca, 1992: 14).

Therefore, the necessity of granting the user a degree of choice might represent a challenge to our usual notions of authorship. We may suggest that traditional ideas of composition are threatened in an inter-active medium. However, it is preferable here to draw a distinction between cyberspace and virtual reality. In cyberspace we may be more confident in reducing the emphasis on authorial intent. We can imagine, and indeed see, electronic writings circulating without any identifiable author. For instance, a document might travel endlessly, constantly being updated by those who read it. Inevitably, there are then persuasive links to be drawn between electronic writing and the theoretical assertions of poststructuralist thinkers (Grusin, 1994). However, as we have seen, in virtual reality we may be less clear about the potential for participants to create their own experiences.

Alternatively, we might seek to characterize virtual reality as a more overwhelming representational form. Virtual reality, through the use of headsets and similar devices, tackles representation by enclosing the observer within it. The effect is to minimize the distance between the observer and the observed. Does this mean that representation itself has been altered, that it has become more encompassing (Elkins, 1994: 252)? A film may transform us temporarily to another world; even a simple tool like a hearing aid has the potential to change our perception of reality. Indeed, Spring (1991: 3) suggests that even the most primitive applications of computer technology have the effect of creating alternative realities: merely by pressing a button an effect is created elsewhere. However, virtual reality systems might be treated as excep-tional, for in attempting to inform all of the senses they may have the potential to influence the whole mind (Pimentel and Teixeira, 1993: 146).

In virtual reality, we are not merely looking at data, we are actually immersed within it. We have the possibility of investigating three-dimensional representations of that data (Aukstakalnis and Blatner, 1992: 9). Here form is governed by representation, for the objects that we perceive are given shape by a virtual reality engine. Hence 'the mathematical machine uses a digital mould to reconstitute the mass of empirical material so that human consciousness can enjoy an integrity in the empirical data that would never have been possible before computers' (Heim, 1993: 89). Thus, cyberspace permits us to 'redirect data streams into different representations . . . The boundaries between subject and object are conventional and utilitarian; at any given time the data representing a user may be combined with the data' (Novak, 1991: 234). The experience might not be transcendental, but it will be different from a visit to the cinema.

Furthermore, even if virtual reality is, or is forced to be, a designed experience, this allows it to be treated, like any other medium, with respect to issues of form, aesthetics and art (Laurel, 1991: 97). Indeed, virtual reality may combine and integrate the techniques of painting, film, sculpture and literature with those of music and theatre. It can encompass different art styles (Stone, 1991: 107). Again, it may not offer transcendence but it may propose a new form of representation, or even a unifying one, for Lanham (in Grusin, 1994: 481) notes that the digitization required by computers produces desubstantiation, in that the whole of the visual arts has to be reduced to a 'common digital denominator'. Perhaps in virtual worlds we shall find the arts removed to a kind of common ground, forced to conform to a mathematical equivalency.

Conclusion: Return to Reality

Thus we may wonder, as does Porush (1994: 553), how culture has managed to move from cyberspace as a postmodern vision of hell to a futuristic, breathlessly idealistic, celebration of an imagined technology. Although the rhetoric of cyberspace may be one of liberation and imagination, I have suggested that the experience is of a world under control, a world totally organized; hence, 'no matter what is represented, the interface supplies a shape and a form' (Heim, 1993: 80). In this, far from freedom, we have entered a world in which our every move has been anticipated and calculated. We are vulnerable to surveillance from the all-knowing 'central system monad' responsible for total organization (Heim, 1993: 106). Furthermore, it seems that 'cyberspace is the return of the Cartesian repressed in the age of semiotics: a celebration of the universe as ultimately computable, an effort to render "reality" as an effect of the "virtual" world of mathematics' (Markley, 1994a: 438). Its genesis lies in a view of the world as consisting of a fundamentally lawful, mathematical structure. How else can we be persuaded of the viability of constructing a convincing simulation? Nevertheless, many treatments have been found to neglect this reliance of virtual reality on a fundamentally mathematical view of the world. We may therefore finally rest on an alternative definition, 'cyberspace is the idealized projection of the values and assumptions, the seemingly foundational principles, of the mathematics of advanced number crunching on which virtual technologies depend' (Markley, 1994b: 549). Consequently, it seems paradoxical that a technology developed from methods aimed at modelling and manipulating human nature through mathematical techniques has been portrayed as offering a futuristic utopia. It still might prove to be a compelling experience, but it will also be a taste of absolute organization.

References

Aukstakalnis, Steve and Blatner, David (1992) *Silicon Mirage: The Art and Science of Virtual Reality*. Berkeley, CA: Peachpit Press.

Benedikt, Michael (1991) 'Introduction', in Michael Benedikt (ed.), *Cyberspace: First Steps*. Cambridge, MA: MIT Press.

Biocca, Frank (1992) 'Communication within virtual reality: creating a space for research', *Journal of Communication*, 42 (4): 5–22.

Coyne, Richard (1994) 'Heidegger and virtual reality: the implications of Heidegger's thinking for computer representations', *Leonardo*, 27 (1): 65–73.

Dove, Toni (1994) 'Theatre without actors: immersion and response in installation', *Leonardo*, 27 (4): 281–7.

Elkins, James (1994) 'There are no philosophic problems raised by virtual reality', *Computer Graphics*, 28 (4): 250–4.

Fricke, Krista (1994) 'Introduction: virtual reality: venus return or vanishing point' *Leonardo*, 27 (4): 277–8.

Gibson, William (1984) *Neuromancer*. New York: Acebooks.

Grusin, Richard (1994) 'What is an electronic author? Theory and the technological fallacy', *Configurations*, 3: 469–83.

Heim, Michael (1993) *The Metaphysics of Virtual Reality*. Oxford: Oxford University Press.

Krueger, Milton W. (1991) *Artificial Reality 2*. Reading, MA: Addison-Wesley.

Laurel, Brenda (1991) 'Virtual reality design: a personal view', in Sandra K. Helsel and Judith Paris Roth (eds), *Virtual Reality: Theory, Practice and Promise*. Westport, CT: Meckler. pp. 87–102.

McLuhan, Marshall (1964) *Understanding Media: The Extensions of Man*. London: Routledge.

Markley, Robert (1994a) 'Introduction. Shreds and patches: the morphogenesis of cyberspace', *Configurations*, 3: 433–9.

Markley, Robert (1994b) 'Boundaries: mathematics, alienation, and the metaphysics of cyberspace', *Configurations*, 3: 485–507.

Novak, Marcos (1991) 'Liquid architectures in cyberspace', in Michael Benedikt (ed.), *Cyberspace: First Steps*. Cambridge, MA: MIT Press.

O'Sullivan, Dan (1994) 'Choosing tools for virtual environments', *Leonardo*, 27 (4): 297–302.

Pimentel, Ken and Teixeira, Kevin (1993) *Virtual Reality: Through the New Looking Glass*. New York: Windcrest.

Porush, David (1994) 'Hacking the brainstem: postmodern metaphysics and Stephenson's "Snow Crash"', *Configurations*, 3: 537–71.

Schroeder, Ralph (1993) *Virtual Reality: Social Impacts and Cultural Dimensions*. Westport, CT: Meckler.

Schroeder, Ralph (1994) 'Cyberculture, cyborg post-modernism and the sociology of virtual reality technologies: surfing the soul in the information age', *Futures*, 263 (51): 519–28.

Spring, Michael B. (1991) 'Informatting with virtual reality', in Sandra K. Helsel and Judith Paris Roth (eds), *Virtual Reality: Theory, Practice and Promise*. Westport, CT: Meckler. pp. 2–17.

Stenger, Nicole (1991) 'Mind is a leaking rainbow', in Michael Benedikt (ed.), *Cyberspace: First Steps*. Cambridge, MA: MIT Press.

Steuer, Jonathan (1992) 'Defining virtual reality: Dimensions determining telepresence', *Journal of Communication*, 42 (4): 73–93.

Stone, Allucquere Rosanne (1991) 'Will the real body please stand up? Boundary stories about virtual cultures', in Michael Benedikt (ed.), *Cyberspace: First Steps*. Cambridge, MA: MIT Press.

Tomas, David (1991) 'Old rituals for new space: *rites de passage* and William Gibson's cultural model of cyberspace', in Michael Benedikt (ed.), *Cyberspace: First Steps*. Cambridge, MA: MIT Press.

Truck, Fred (1991) 'The prompt and virtual reality', *Leonardo*, 24 (2): 171–3.

Woolley, Benjamin (1992) *Virtual Worlds*. London: Penguin.

Figure 13.1 Close Encounters of the Third Kind, *Columbia Pictures, 1977*

13

Sublime Technologies and Future Organization in Science Fiction Film, 1970–95

J. Martin Corbett

Science fiction has been defined as a narrative treating of 'a situation that could not arise in the world we know, but which is hypothesised on the basis of some innovation in science or technology, or pseudo-science or pseudo-technology, whether human or extraterrestrial in origin' (Amis, 1960: 18).

Cinematic story-telling hinges crucially on the very visibility of the film image – 'reading' a film involves looking at it. In contemporary science fiction (SF) film, codes of visibility often appear to exceed narrative requirements. The narrative is frequently interrupted by spectacular special effects which invite the audience to contemplate, with awe and wonder, the technological miracles of future worlds represented on the cinema screen. Kuhn (1992) argues that the cinematic codes specific to science fiction are seen at work through the emphasis on special effects and this makes SF the most cinematic of all film genres:

> This is not only because, for the best effect, science fiction films must be seen in cinema auditoria; but also because the technology of cinematic illusion displays the state of its own art in science fiction films. Since the films themselves are often about new or imagined future technologies, this must be a perfect example of the medium fitting, if not exactly being, the message. (Kuhn, 1992: 7)

This chapter explores the images of future organization presented in SF film with particular emphasis on how these representations are shaped by both real and imagined technologies. It is argued that both the use of existing technologies in SF film production and the portrayal of future technologies in SF film narrative reflect an ideological propensity on the part of film-makers to glorify the awesome power and sublimity of things technological. The chapter concludes with a consideration of how current mainstream organizational thinking about the nature of the relation between technology and organization has been influenced by a similar fascination with, and aesthetic elevation of, the technological sublime.

Towards the Technological Sublime: Today's Technology and Tomorrow's World

For many fans of SF films, 'special effects' are the *raison d'être* of the genre. But what makes a cinematic effect 'special'? After all, everything in a film is an effect – something created or manufactured. Stern (1980) argues that the special effects of SF film serve to foreground the 'specialness' of spectacular and powerful new technologies, such as interstellar vehicles, all-powerful sentient computers and androids. Yet it is important to the film-maker that the SF film audience knows that an effect is special. This is achieved by a variety of cinematic techniques. The camera may focus in on the awed faces of actors witnessing the spectacular technical wizardry of the effect. This is clearly seen in the film *Terminator* (1981) when, towards the end of a gruelling and dramatic chase scene, the eponymous Terminator (a cyborg played by Arnold Schwarzenegger) is seemingly destroyed by an explosive ball of ignited fuel, only to reappear slowly through the flames as a chromium-plated endo-skeleton still intent on completing its mission to seek and destroy humanity. The marvellous sublimation of Arnold Schwarzenegger into a terrifying metallic android transfixes the two hunted humans, who are so incapable of averting their gaze that one of them stumbles away backwards still staring at the transfigured character. To heighten the impact of the android's appearance, the analytical gaze of the camera lingers on the horrified yet disbelieving expressions on the faces of the Terminator's quarry before revealing the specially effected transfiguration to the audience.

Another cinematic technique employed to denote an effect as special is to accompany the effect with loud, often electronically synthesized, sound effects. More rarely, film-makers may indulge in 'violent self-consciousness' (Brophy, 1986) and reveal to the audience that they are equally in awe of the technical effects they have created. A good example of this self-consciousness is offered in John Carpenter's 1982 remake of *The Thing*. At one point in this special effects-laden film, a parasitic shape-shifting alien life form absorbs the severed head of an earlier victim. The head slowly turns face upward and eight spider-like legs rip through it, grotesquely lifting it off the floor. Using the head as a body, the creature then scurries past a shocked male colleague of the deceased who manages to utter one sentence before he dies: 'You've got to be fucking kidding!' Thus, special effects are special by virtue of their ability to inspire in the audience a sense of awe and wonder at the technical prowess of the film-maker. They are also the main medium for making visible the invisible, for making the fantastic or supernatural natural to the viewing public (see La Valley, 1985). As Metz (1977: 37) notes:

> In films of the fantastic, the impression of unreality is convincing only if the public has the feeling of partaking, not of some plausible illustration of a process obeying a nonhuman logic, but of a series of disquieting or

'impossible' events which nevertheless unfold before him [*sic*] in the guise of eventlike appearances. The spectator is not the victim of the machination to the point of being unaware that it exists, but he is not sufficiently conscious of it for it to lose its impact.

Just as the technology of special effects represents a key medium for the glorification of cinematic technology and technique, many SF films contain the message that technology is so powerful that it represents the main motor of social and economic development both today and in the future. Thurber (1983) argues that the sublime had become a key concept in the development of SF literature since it is an example of the mingling of the human and the inhuman, or the familiar and the unfamiliar. He traces the idea of the technological sublime to the first SF novel, Mary Shelley's *Frankenstein*, and shows how SF narratives have developed the idea of the sublime through the attachment of science and technology to some of the oldest and deepest human emotions and concerns. Through SF we have become accustomed to seeing in science, and particularly machine technology, some of our greatest and most powerful aspirations and fears. Thurber (1983: 215) notes: 'In its preoccupation with insurrection, freedom versus responsibility, moral and ethical relativity, and proud, independent flight toward some unspecified unknown, the sublime is the archetype of much modern science fiction.'

It is this very elevation of technology to sublimity in SF narrative that prompted Lewis Mumford to allude to 'the essentially archaic and regressive nature of the science-fiction mind' (1970: 134). Indeed, many commentators see a technological determinism at the heart of much SF and argue that this renders SF incapable of progressive social criticism (for example, Bloch, 1959; Kornbluth, 1959; Warrick, 1980). When one examines contemporary SF film this regressive and uncritical portrayal of things technological is demonstrated in a self-consciously spectacular manner.

Technology and Organization in Futurist SF Film

What then is the posited role of technology in our organizational futures as portrayed in SF film? The sources for this exploration consist of Brosnan (1991), surveys by *Starburst* magazine and the CD-ROM databases of the British Film Institute on Anglo-American films in the period 1970–95. These reveal 118 Anglo-American SF films set wholly or in part in some distinctly future time. I have not included SF films set in a past time even if their surface is futuristic (e.g. the *Star Wars* trilogy), nor films set in the present where extraordinary events occur (e.g. *ET* and *The Thing*). Selecting one's own examples makes it easy to defend generalizations, so I have concentrated on 40 of these films where technology plays a significant role in the narrative. The films that are discussed in more detail in this section have not been chosen arbitrarily, but are the ones that have received the most attention from media and cultural theorists (see Corbett, 1995).

Of these 118 futurist SF films, only a small number show anything remotely resembling the utopian vision of technological modernity projected in early SF films such as *Things to Come* (1938). Interestingly enough, in these films (which include the seven *Star Trek* movies) this optimism is achieved by constructing a virtual socioeconomic universe within the confines of a spaceship. In such films, the astronauts' adventures have no relevance whatsoever to the economic and social life of the rest of humankind. The remaining films display future society ruled by some form of conspiracy, monopoly or totalitarian apparatus. It would appear that the only future that seems unimaginable to most SF filmmakers is a better one. In 40 of these films futurist technologies play an important role in creating and maintaining such dystopias.

At first sight, then, futurist SF films do not appear to glorify technology but to offer a social critique. However, Weiskel (1976) argues that such dystopian and disturbing representations of technology serve to foreground technology as the 'negative sublime'. Such is the awesome power of futurist technologies that they are able to determine the shape and culture of future social organizations. As the philosopher Edmund Burke (1757) argued, the sublime does not have to be ethically positive. Thus, in films such as *THX1138* (1970), *Zero Population Growth* (1971), *Soylent Green* (1973), *Westworld* (1974), *Stepford Wives* (1975), *Logan's Run* (1976), *Sleeper* (1976), *Zardoz*, (1976), the *Alien* trilogy (1979, 1985, 1992), *Terminator* (1981), *Star Trek II: The Wrath of Khan* (1982), *1984* (1984), *Runaway* (1984), *Back to the Future II* (1985), *Robot Holocaust* (1987), *The Handmaid's Tale* (1990), *Hardware* (1990), *Demolition Man* (1993), *Judge Dredd* (1995), and *Time Cop* (1995), future social organization is represented as a living hell with totalitarian technology holding humankind in its thrall.

A double effacement is at work in such films, as the film-maker's technology which makes these negative sublime technologies visible (through the use of special effects) is itself invisible. All the other effects which make up the film (such as editing, lap dissolves, costume, sets and make-up), and occasionally even the narrative itself, are transformed from cultural artefacts to mundane, natural objects. It is therefore legitimate to consider what is backgrounded and taken for granted in contemporary futurist SF films by this foregrounding of technology.

To deconstruct SF film it is important to consider the ideological role played by technology in the narrative. Kuhn (1992) argues that SF films speak, enact, even produce certain ideologies that cannot always be read directly off their surface content. Technology plays a powerful ideological role in contemporary futurist SF film, usually representing anything that threatens the 'natural social order'. The antidotes most commonly mobilized to deal with this threat are representations of conservative values associated with nature. This is the romanticism that lies at the heart of traditional SF: the confrontation between good and evil, nature and technology, the known and the unknown, the spontaneous individual and the mindless mass. From this perspective, technology is feared because it is a metaphor for the possibility of reconstruction that puts the stability of conservative institutions in question (Ryan and Kellner, 1988). Technology thus has ambivalent potentialities: it can be good or evil but what matters is its power. The wonder of present-day technology makes the future, however dystopian, believable; and it is ever more wondrous future technology, however malevolent, that makes this future possible.

Behind the negative sublimity of technologies of the future lurk representations of future organizations that are clearly resonant with the present. SF films tend to play on the audience's concerns about technology-out-of-control (see Dean, 1978; Biskind, 1983), but when one looks beneath this surface technophobia, one sees patriarchy portrayed as the 'natural' social order under threat from technology. Note for example, in the film *Star Trek II: the Wrath of Khan*, 'the traditional values, and in particular the repressed and withholding interpersonal style, of the white male bourgeoisie' (Byers, 1987: 39). This film is silent on the economics of future society, although much of the action takes place abroad the *Enterprise* and the crew's behaviour and hierarchy reflect traditional middle-class values. This suggests little economic difference between now and the future. As with most of the episodes in the original *Star Trek* television series, the underlying theme of the movie is the difficulty of maintaining human values in a technologically advanced culture. The answer lies, according to *Star Trek* creator Gene Roddenberry, in personal moderation, self-control, obedience to authority and objectivity (see Takings, 1983). This is made clear in *Star Trek II* by the portrayal of the villain – the genetically engineered 'superman' Khan – as egotistical, intellectual, non-conformist and driven blindly by a passion for vengeance. It is Khan, a child of technology, who threatens the stability of the human race through his attempt to appropriate the most powerful technology ever created by humans – the Genesis Project. In 'good' hands, Genesis is capable of creating life on dead planets; in 'bad' hands it can be used to create death on living planets.

On the surface, the vision of the future in the film, represented within the microcosm of the starship *Enterprise*, suggests a future without any systematic racial, national, class or gender conflict (there is a black captain, a Russian, an Asian, a woman, even an alien on the bridge). The only hierarchy is a meritocracy based on military rank and experience. However, a deeper examination reveals that loyalty to bourgeois patriarchal structures of power and values is of paramount importance in the film. Khan signifies the 'bad' father as he leads his band of young space-hippie terrorists to their death. Khan represents a malevolent and unnatural authority figure. Captain Kirk, on the other hand, is the 'good' father who leads a young crew of obedient, loyal and clean-cut uni-formed trainees on their first mission.

A more malevolent patriarchy is evident in *THX1138, Zardoz, Logan's Run, 1984, Sleeper, Demolition Man, The Handmaid's Tale,* and *Soylent Green*. These films share a vision of a future where sexual procreation is under state control and is either strictly prescribed or (more usually) proscribed by a technocratic regime. Here we have 'unnatural' social organization sustained by technocrats (with the aid of supercomputers) intent on stamping out all vestiges of individual expression, and especially female sexuality. In all of these films, a male-dominated state technocracy controls the human body, thereby achieving the mechanization or 'mechanomorphism' (Szasz, 1970) of the citizen.

The mechanization of sex suggests the development of a science of reproduction and hedonics that attempts to divest sex of its mystery and uncertainty and to render it as something that can be efficiently regulated by a ruling technocratic élite. Technology no longer simply controls production but extends its power to the control of reproduction. For Easlea (1983), Broege (1986) and others, machines are sexual extensions of men and, in these SF films, machines are powerful enough to enable a male élite to play out the ultimate technological fantasy of human creation without the mother – the appropriation of maternity by patriarchy through the creation of truly 'docile bodies' (Foucault, 1979). This process reaches its zenith in *Stepford Wives* and *Westworld* where men replace women with robot replicas eager to submit to the former's sexual demands.

The ideological character of these films stands in greater relief when they are compared to one of very few progressive futurist SF films, *Alien*. As in *Star Trek II*, most of the action in *Alien* takes place inside a spaceship – in this case a vast towing vessel bringing 20 million tonnes of mineral ore to Earth. But while *Star Trek II* reaffirms the values of traditional patriarchal conservatism, *Alien* offers a terrifying vision of a technocratic capitalist future gone wrong. The film disrupts and even reverses the romantic rhetorical strategy of establishing a strong opposition between technology and nature, equality and liberty, and unknown and known employed in the vast majority of SF films. From the very start of the film, when the crew of the spaceship *Nostromo* are released from suspended animation by the omnipresent ship's computer (called Mother), it is clear that they are all children of technology. Indeed, the early scenes in the film reveal every crew member to be an impersonal and rather abrasive technocrat.

The crew of the *Nostromo* work for a giant interstellar corporation whose stated (initially secret) policy is that all other considerations are secondary to the return to Earth of a living alien. The crew become victims of corporate greed and the vengeance of a terrifying alien life form which they disturb once Mother (pre-programmed by corporation technologists) takes the *Nostromo* to the location of the alien's crashed spacecraft.

At first, no patriarchy is evident on board the *Nostromo*, although a class-based hierarchy is. Indeed, Parker (the black male worker) insists that he wants nothing to do with an attempt to rescue anyone or thing from the crashed spaceship unless he is paid for it. Here humanism is constructed as a class luxury – altruism has a price. It is only when it becomes clear that the mission will not jeopardize their salary bonuses, that the crew agree to undertake it. A little later in the film, one female crew member (Ripley) refuses to open the airlock through which a stricken friend and two other colleagues might pass to safety (including a man to whom she seems to be attracted). Ripley cites company quarantine rules and procedures to justify her apparently anti-humanist actions. It is the science officer, Ash, who makes the seemingly human and spontaneous gesture of opening the airlock. The audience feels rather sorry for him as he is hounded and chastized by Ripley for his altruistic actions.

However, as the film progresses it becomes clear that Ash is not the hero. Following the horrific 'birth' of a razor-toothed phallic monster which gnaws its way through the stomach of the stricken male crew member, and the subsequent deaths of two more colleagues, Ripley finally discovers the awful truth about the crew's predicament from Mother. Ash suddenly appears at Ripley's side. She is angry and hits out at him. At first he accepts her trivial violence, but then he loses control. He forces Ripley on to a counter under a wall plastered with pictures of nude women, and begins to shove a rolled up pornographic magazine down her throat. She is saved by Parker and we discover that Ash is not human but a robot sent by the Company to bring back the alien for their 'weapons research', all other considerations being secondary to this mission. A human life is less profitable than that of an alien. The unholy trinity of the monstrous phallic alien, Mother and Ash come to represent the imperialist company – patriarchal high-technology capitalism at its most malevolent and rapacious.

The negative sublimity of futurist technology reaches even loftier heights in films such as *The Final Programme* (1974), *Videodrome* (1983), *Blade Runner* (1987), *Robocop* (1987), *Total Recall* (1990) and *The Body Hammer* (1991). Although all the organizations portrayed in these films are run by a male élite (and all the technical experts are also male), technology only enables patriarchy to be made more durable at the price of total human submission to its power. In these films the power of technology is demonstrated through its ability to confuse illusion and reality to the extent that humans find it difficult to differentiate themselves from machines or to differentiate reality from technological simulation. For example, *Blade Runner* has as its theme the existential question: how do you know if you are human or a manufactured replica? The film tells the story of Nexus-6 replicants genetically engineered by the interstellar Tyrell Corporation to work 'offworld'. They are perfect 'skin jobs' that look and talk like humans. Unfortunately, they have the capacity, over an extended period of time, to develop human emotions and when they do they become uncontrollable.

The Nexus-6 models have a fail-safe four-year 'lifespan' and have also been fitted with in-built memories of a fictitious childhood as a cushion against emotional instability. Despite these controls, replicants have begun rebelling offworld and special police/executioner (blade runner) squads have had to be established on Earth to 'retire' (kill) them on sight. This job is made all the more difficult as the only way in which replicants differ from humans is in their lack of altruism and empathy – a lack detectable only by the use of the Voight–Kampff empathy test. Humans are caught in a technological double bind as this test itself cannot be conducted without the aid of advanced technology. Confirmation that one is not a machine can only be granted by a machine. Thus, the film represents technology as both the cause of ontological uncertainty and the only means to resolve it. In *Blade Runner*, technology has humanity totally in its thrall.

Many of the futurist SF films discussed above offer a more or less happy ending. A typical narrative scenario is as follows: human technologists or scientists create an awesome new technology (cyborgs, computers, nuclear power, or genetic engineering), which then goes out of control and poses a serious threat to humanity (either because it has become sentient and decides to enslave or destroy humanity, or because it falls into the 'wrong' human hands). In these films, this threat is neutralized in one of two ways:

1   The technology is destroyed or neutralized by a heroic human (usually a male) with superior technical expertise and/or control over another powerful technology (*Terminator, Blade Runner, Alien, Aliens, Hardware, Runaway, Back to the Future II, Time Cop, Total Recall* and *Demolition Man*).
2   The heroic humans escape from a technological urban hell and 'return to nature' (*Logan's Run, Zero Population Growth, The Running Man, Zardoz, THX1138* and *Soylent Green*). It is significant that nature is most commonly represented as an idyllic and technologically primitive rural patriarchy in such films.

Futurist SF film-makers offer a simple choice: humanity must either accept the ambivalent potentialities of technological 'progress' and develop new technologies to deal with problems created by other new technologies, or escape from the domination of technology by walking out into the wilderness, to return to the kind of lifestyle associated with times before the industrial revolution. Either way, technology remains and humans must either accept their transformation into cyborgs or become noble savages.

In conclusion, then, we see how contemporary SF films and technological state-of-the-art special effects are almost inseparable, and the viewer surrenders to the spectacle in which humans and manufactured replicas, reality and image, become indistinguishable. In both the production and consumption of futurist SF film we see the glorification of the sublime power of technologies present and future. The production and consumption of celluloid images of future organization are equally enframed by an ideology of technological sublimity. In SF film, not only is the future rendered knowable in the present through the medium of new technology, but that future is itself only possible because of the power of new (imagined) technology. The message, then, is that the future is neither knowable nor possible without technology (see Haywood and Wollen, 1993). As we shall see in the final part of this chapter, such a message is also evident in the contemporary world of business management.

A Look at the Present with an Eye to the Future

Thus far we have looked at the relationship between technology and organization as represented in fictional worlds of the future. We have seen how the production and consumption of SF film is dominated by an ideology extolling the sublimity of technology. But what of the present day? At first glance the double effacement of technology evident in SF film would seem inapplicable to contemporary business organizations. Academic research on the relationship between technology and organization tends to support the notion that technology itself is politically neutral and hence its impact on organizational practice is largely a matter of 'strategic choice' (for example, Braverman, 1974; Buchanan and Boddy, 1985; Child, 1985). Yet, beneath the surface of organizational decisions and technological choices there lurk ideologies that propagate principles and maxims of conduct that serve to validate certain types of knowledge and expertise, and invalidate others (see Corbett, 1996).

When one analyses the ideological context of technology design and implementation it becomes evident that an ideology glorifying the technological sublime plays a key influential role in these processes. Research on the ways in which business organizations 'choose' new technology reveals the dominance of technological and scientific rationality throughout the decision-making process (see Scarborough and Corbett, 1992). This research indicates that the deployment of technology tends to reproduce machine-like notions of rationality, control, efficiency and predictability in organizational discourse. In not lending themselves to simple measurement, human employees invariably figure as an 'inefficient' variable in management equations. By this logic, employee efficiency increases the more it is machine-like (i.e. predictable, routinized and/or controlled by technology). Efficient management thus becomes one of sustaining employee behaviour that more nearly resembles the functioning of a machine than skilled human action.

This process of dehumanization is not as extreme or as dramatic in contemporary business organizations as it is portrayed in futurist SF film. Yet apologists for new organizational technologies, such as business process re-engineering (BPR), more nearly resemble Terminators than humans in their relentless drive to harness the power of new technology to remove organizational 'inefficiencies'. 'Don't automate, obliterate!' extols Hammer, the BPR guru (Hammer, 1990: 104). BPR, like other technology-based change activities in organizations, concentrates on improving information flows and processes and marginalizes human and social issues (Walsham, 1993). Significantly, what emerges from the BPR literature is the frequency with which the high rate of BPR failures is attributed to the failure to obliterate all vestiges of 'inefficient' human and social processes (see Moad, 1993; Thackray, 1993) – a classic futurist SF film scenario. Unlike SF film-makers, however, it rarely occurs to such writers to enquire into the provenance of new technologies or to assess the potential harm they may cause.

So here is the insidious double effacement of technology within contemporary organizations. The foregrounding of technology renders technological rationality and the mechanomorphosis of organizational behaviour more visible, while simultaneously making patriarchal control systems in organizations less visible and thus more durable. Such a view is seldom articulated in a mainstream management literature in which excellent work on the social construction of technology (Bijker et al., 1989) and on actor network theory (Law, 1991, 1994) is rarely cited. Similarly, research on the issues raised by an ideological analysis of futurist SF films (namely, the embeddedness of patriarchy in technology [Cockburn, 1983; Rothschild, 1983; Wajcman, 1991], the eroticization of domination [Easlea, 1983; Hacker, 1989] and the suppression of sexuality as a means of social control in organizations [Foucault, 1979; Hearn and Parkin, 1987]) is almost entirely absent from this literature. Indeed, Mills (1989) argues that the vast majority of management and organizational behaviour texts, far from addressing sexist organizational practices or critiquing the gendered nature of technology and organizational realities, have tended to reflect and hence legitimize them. Gutek (1989) suggests that this serves the interests of men in organizational élites as it preserves the myth that they are analytical, unemotional and rational (i.e. more like machines). It also facilitates the transfer of blame for sexual encounters to women, who must carefully manage their sexuality in organizations.

The lack of visibility of patriarchy in organizations is enabled by technology precisely because the latter is the medium through which those in powerful positions within business organizations are encouraged to know and evaluate the behaviour of themselves and their subordinates. The encouragement to foreground technological rationality is everywhere. SF film-makers, designers and producers of new technology, business school researchers and management consultants all seem to share the same uncritical accommodation to sublime technology. As in so many SF film narratives, the problems associated with new technology must be solved by technical experts and the application of increasingly complex systems technologies. In contemporary main-stream management discourse, if business organizations fail to invest in new technologies they are condemning themselves to the wilderness and, ultimately, to economic ruin and death ('automate or liquidate'). Yet the lesson from our brief analysis of the dystopian images in futurist SF film would seem to suggest quite the reverse. Only time will tell if we have the wit and the will actively to participate in the design and development of new technology, rather than gazing in awe at the future being offered by today's technologists and technocrats. Perhaps, as Franklin (1983) opines, futurist SF films are best seen as warnings – whether intended or not – not to follow the ideological leaders of a technological society that either doesn't know where it's going or sees its own future as hopeless.

References

Amis, K. (1960) *New Maps of Hell: A Survey of Science Fiction*. New York: Harcourt, Brace.

Bijker, W.E., Hughes, T.P. and Pinch, T. (eds) (1989) *The Social Construction of Technological Systems*. Cambridge, MA: MIT Press.

Biskind, P. (1983) *Seeing is Believing: How Hollywood Taught Us to Stop Worrying and Love the Fifties*. New York: Pantheon Books.

Bloch, R. (1959) 'Imagination and social criticism', in B. Davenport (ed.), *The Science Fiction Novel: Imagination and Social Criticism*. New York: Advent Books. pp. 37–56.

Braverman, H.N. (1974) *Labor and Monopoly Capitalism*. New York: Monthly Review Press.

Broege, V. (1986) 'Technology and sexuality in science fiction: creating new erotic interfaces', in D. Palumbo (ed.), *Erotic Universe: Sexuality and Fantastic Literature*. New York: Greenwood Press. pp. 103–29.

Brophy, P. (1986) 'Horrality – the textuality of contemporary horror films', *Screen*, 27 (1): 17–32.

Brosnan, J. (1991) *The Primal Screen: A History of Science Fiction Film*. London: Orbit.

Buchanan, D.A. and Boddy, D. (1985) *Organisations in the Computer Age*. Aldershot: Gower.

Burke, E. (1757) *A Philosophical Enquiry into the Idea of the Sublime and the Beautiful*. 1958 edn. London: Routledge and Kegan Paul.

Byers, T.B. (1987) 'Commodity futures: corporate state and personal styles in three science fiction movies', *Science Fiction Studies*, 7: 29–48.

Child, J. (1985) 'Managerial strategies, new technology and the labour process', in D. Knights, H. Willmott and D. Collinson (eds), *Job Redesign: Critical Perspectives on the Labour Process*. Aldershot: Gower. pp. 107–41.

Cockburn, C. (1983) *Brothers: Male Dominance and Technological Change*. London: Pluto Press.

Corbett, J.M. (1995) 'Celluloid projections: images of technology and organizational futures in contemporary science fiction film', *Organization*, 2 (3/4): 467–88.

Corbett, J.M. (1996) 'Designing jobs with advanced manufacturing technology: the negotiation of expertise', in H. Scarbrough (ed.), *The Management of Expertise*. London: Macmillan. pp. 95–122.

Dean, J.F. (1978) 'Between 2001 and Star Wars', *Journal of Popular Film and Television*, 7 (1): 24–36.

Easlea, B. (1983) *Fathering the Unthinkable: Masculinity, Scientists and the Nuclear Arms Race*. London: Pluto Press.

Foucault, M. (1979) *The History of Sexuality, Volume 1*. New York: Vintage Books.

Franklin, H.B. (1983) 'Don't look where we're going: visions of the future in science fiction films, 1970–82', *Science Fiction Studies*, 10 (1): 19–32.

Gutek, B.A. (1989) 'Sexuality in the workplace', in J. Hearn, D.L. Sheppard, P. Tancred-Sheriff and G. Burrell (eds), *The Sexuality of Organization*. London: Sage. pp. 56–70.

Hacker, S. (1989) *Pleasure, Power and Technology*. Boston, MA: Unwin Hyman.

Hammer, M. (1990) 'Don't automate – obliterate', *Harvard Business Review*, July/August: 104–12.

Haywood, P. and Wollen, T. (1993) *Future Visions*. London: British Film Institute.

Hearn, J. and Parkin, P.W. (1987) *'Sex' at 'Work': The Power and Paradox of Organizational Sexuality*. Brighton: Wheatsheaf.

Kornbluth, C.M. (1959) 'The failure of the science fiction novel as social criticism', in B. Davenport (ed.), *The Science Fiction Novel: Imagination and Social Criticism*. New York: Advent Books. pp. 43–72.

Kuhn, A. (ed.) (1992) *Alien Zone: Cultural Theory and Contemporary Science Fiction Cinema*. London: Verso Press.

La Valley, A.J. (1985) 'Traditions and trickery: the role of special effects in the science fiction film', in G.E. Slusser and E.S. Rabkin (eds), *Shadows of the Magic Lamp: Fantasy and Science Fiction Film*. Carbondale, IL: Illinois University Press. pp. 31–54.

Law, J. (ed.) (1991) *A Sociology of Monsters: Essays on Power, Technology and Domination*. London: Routledge.

Law, J. (1994) *Organizing Modernity*. Oxford: Blackwell.

Metz, C. (1977) 'Trucage and the film', *Critical Inquiry*, 3 (2): 166–85.

Mills, A.J. (1989) 'Gender, sexuality and organization theory', in J. Hearn, D.L. Sheppard, P. Tancred-Sheriff and G. Burrell (eds), *The Sexuality of Organization*, London: Sage. pp. 29–44.

Moad, J. (1993) 'Does re-engineering really work?', *Datamation*, 1 August: 22–8.

Mumford, L. (1970) *The Pentagon of Power*. New York: Harcourt Brace Jovanovich.

Rothschild, J. (ed.) (1983) *Machina ex Dea: Feminist Perspectives on Technology*. New York: Pergamon.

Ryan, M. and Kellner, D. (1988) *Camera Politica: Politics and Ideology of the Contemporary Hollywood Film*. New York: Indiana University Press.

Scarbrough, H. and Corbett, J.M. (1992) *Technology and Organization: Power, Meaning and Design*. London: Routledge.

Stern, M. (1980) 'Making culture into nature: or who put the "special" into "special effects"?', *Science Fiction Studies*, 7 (2): 133–64.

Szasz, T. (1970) *Ideology and Insanity: Essays on the Psychiatric Dehumanization of Man*. New York: Anchor Books.

Takings, D. (1983) 'Star Trek: a philosophical interpretation', in R.L. Myers (ed.), *The Intersection of Science Fiction and Philosophy*. London: Greenwood Press. pp. 93–108.

Thackray, J. (1993) 'Fads, fixes and fictions', *Management Today*, June: 41–3.

Thurber, B. (1983) 'Towards a technological sublime', in R.E. Myers (ed.), *The Intersection of Science Fiction and Philosophy*. London: Greenwood Press. pp. 211–24.

Wajcman, J. (1991) *Feminism Confronts Technology*. Cambridge: Polity Press.

Walsham, G. (1993) *Interpreting Information Systems in Organizations*. Chichester: Wiley.

Warrick, P.S. (1980) *The Cybernetic Imagination in Science Fiction*. Cambridge, MA: MIT Press.

Weiskel, T. (1976) *The Romantic Sublime: Studies in the Structure and Psychology of Transcendence*. Baltimore, MD: Johns Hopkins University Press.

Index

DATE DUE

MAY 21 · FAC			
JUN 2 0 REC'D			
AUG 0 2 REC'D			
JUL 0 9 REC'D			
AUG 1 9 2002			
UG 1 9 2002			
NOV 1 9 2002			
NOV 1 9 REC'D			
MAY 1 9 2003			
APR 2 3 REC'D			
NOV 0 1 2003			
DEC 0 1 2003			
GAYLORD			PRINTED IN U.S.A.